LONDON RECORD SOCIETY PUBLICATIONS

VOLUME XXVIII
FOR THE YEAR 1991

JUSTICE IN EIGHTEENTH-CENTURY HACKNEY: THE JUSTICING NOTEBOOK OF HENRY NORRIS AND THE HACKNEY PETTY SESSIONS BOOK

EDITED BY
RUTH PALEY

LONDON RECORD SOCIETY
1991

SBN 90095228 8

The Hackney Petty Sessions Book is printed with the permission of the rector of St. John at Hackney.

Phototypeset by
Wyvern Typesetting Ltd., Bristol
Printed and bound in Great Britain
at Bookcraft Ltd., Midsomer Norton

CONTENTS

ABBREVIATIONS

Affdt.	Affidavit
B.L.	British Library
D.N.B.	*Dictionary of National Biography*
G.L.R.O.	Greater London Record Office
H.A.D.	London Borough of Hackney Archives Department
Indt.	Indictment
Mich.	Michaelmas
O.B. Proc.	*Proceedings at the Sessions of Peace, and Oyer and Terminer, for the City of London and County of Middlesex*
O.E.D.	*Oxford English Dictionary*
P.R.O.	Public Record Office, London
Recog.	Recognizance
V.C.H.	*Victoria County History*

CONTEMPORARY TERMS/ ABBREVIATIONS USED IN THE TEXT

dd	delivered
jur[at]	sworn
coram me/nobis	before me/before us [as justices]
Arm[iger]	Esquire
ex	excused
pd	paid
cert	certificate [of settlement]
sine die	indefinitely

INTRODUCTION

Hackney in the early eighteenth century

Until a wave of speculative building transformed it during the course of the nineteenth century, Hackney was something of a minor London pleasure resort, one that managed to be consistently popular without ever becoming fashionable. It was a pleasant and attractive stretch of open countryside, easily accessible from the metropolis, ideal for day trips and to which City merchants regularly came to retire or to acquire a second home. Fine views, clean air, pleasure gardens, victualling houses, sporting events, fishing – Hackney had something to offer to rich and poor alike.

The economy of the area naturally reflected the constraints thus imposed upon it. Agricultural and horticultural pursuits predominated but even these were affected by the demands of the leisure market: Hackney was noted for its farms and market gardens and later in the century for its many nursery grounds supplying a wide variety of plants and flowers to the leisured classes. It was famous, from the mid-seventeenth century, for its private schools. Additionally, of course, there were numerous opportunities for employment in the mansions of the rich, in the pleasure industry or any of the ancillary trades that were needed to service so prosperous a community. Hackney was also noted for its brickfields and there was a certain amount of industrial activity. The result, as might be expected, was that there was a buoyant demand for labour resulting in a steady inflow of migrant workers, mostly from surrounding parishes but also from East Anglia, the Midlands, the West Country and Yorkshire. Some of the newcomers were skilled workers but large numbers seem to have been unskilled men seeking to take advantage of the variety of opportunities for economic advancement that were on offer.[1]

Even at this early date, Hackney was already something of a multicultural community. Hackney had long been known for its thriving communities of dissenters, but there was also a large Jewish community,[2] as well as a number of persons of Irish origin.[3] Although there

1. Over half of the settlement examinations taken during the period covered by these documents (1730–1753) reveal that the individuals concerned were settled by service. Most of those who appear in the following pages are described as labourers, gardeners or victuallers.
2. The largest group (Portuguese Jews) had been settled in Hackney as early as the 1670s, and were largely concentrated near the Triangle area of Mare Street. I am indebted for this information to David Mander.
3. With the notable exception of Stephen Ram, it is likely that the majority of the Hackney Irish were extremely poor.

was a substantial black population in London at this time, it is clear from the circumstances surrounding the arrest of George Scipio (**218**), that there were few if any blacks in Hackney.

All these groups were likely to attract considerable hostility. The documents presented here suggest a high level of toleration for only one of them: dissenters. When Robert Royston refused to swear to his settlement, for example, he was immediately offered the option of affirming in case 'he was one of the people called Quakers' (**1051**). The Irish do not figure prominently in these documents, though there is certainly a world of prejudice implicit in the brief notes of the examination of Patrick Larkin (**1036**), revealing both that he was Irish (which was relevant to the application of the settlement laws) and that he was Roman Catholic (which was not). To be Irish (and even worse to be an Irish catholic) at this time was to be subjected to stereotypes of irresponsibility, lawlessness and criminality of the kind that are now directed at Britons of West Indian descent.

Jews, superficially, seem to have fared reasonably well. On one occasion Norris acted extremely leniently to a group of young (and very rich) Jewish men, reducing the charge against them from riot to a breach of the peace (**283**). It is also clear that there was no reluctance to nominate Jews to parochial office. Yet one wonders how far this toleration rested on principle or whether it was not heavily influenced by the extreme wealth of the individuals concerned. The eighteenth century was a period of virulent anti-semitism and there are certainly indications that this was as common in Hackney as elsewhere. One notes in particular an appeal against a rating assessment in 1733 alleging, in effect, that houses kept by Jews had been deliberately over-rated (**692**). Even the willingness to nominate Jews to parish office could (and probably should) be interpreted as exploitation rather than toleration. It is noteworthy that on one occasion, nine of the thirty-five nominees for office were Jewish, a figure that would seem to be out of all proportion to the size of the Jewish community.[4] Many of the Jews rated in Hackney were really resident elsewhere, and therefore far more likely to fine rather than take on the duties of office. Such fines provided a lucrative source of extra revenue for the parish.[5]

Crime in Hackney

As the entries in this volume demonstrate all too well, the apparently idyllic and prosperous rural setting that seemed so attractive to contemporaries screened a world that was just as brutal as that of any city rookery. Major crimes such as burglary and highway robbery were by no means unusual and were regularly reported in the contemporary

4. For this (and for the Jewish community in Hackney in general) see Malcolm Brown, 'The Jews of Hackney before 1840' in *Transactions of the Jewish Historical Society of England*, 30 (1987–8), pp. 71–87.
5. In 1741, the standard fines were: surveyor of the highways £5; overseer of the poor £10; churchwarden £15. A discount rate of £25 was allowed to those who fined for all three offices at once. It had previously been £20. G.L.R.O., P79/JN1/142/38.

press.[6] Such crimes were more likely to be reported there than in justices' notebooks or petty session minutes, simply because the perpetrators stood a good chance of escape. The few that are entered here appear either because the victim had the good fortune to meet with assistance, or because of an application for a warrant to search a suspect's premises.

Yet if direct references to such crimes are infrequent, there are certainly a number of rather more oblique ones. Local legend has always associated Hackney with the highwayman Dick Turpin. Turpin himself does not appear within these pages, but many of his associates (John Jones, Abraham Downham, the Gregory brothers, William Rogers) do. Some of those responsible for convicting his accomplices also appear here.[7]

Of the events chronicled here, some, such as the arrest of the robber John Jones (**164**), add minor but intriguing details to those already given in the only reliable account of Turpin's life.[8] Others may offer additional insights. It seems probable for example that the Jasper Gregory who complained in 1733 of his employer's refusal to pay his wages was one of the three brothers who made up the core of the notorious Gregory Gang (**74**). John Wheeler, who turned King's Evidence against the Gregory Gang in 1735, also had Hackney links and was almost certainly the eldest child of the John Wheeler whose propensity to violence is so fully chronicled in these pages.[9] The evidence that Turpin and other notorious criminals of the day had some sort of regular rendezvous in Hackney, although circumstantial, is nevertheless persuasive.

Turpin and the Gregory Gang aside, the vast majority of crimes noted in these pages are petty offences, albeit often violent ones. Henry Norris's notebook makes it abundantly clear that life in early eighteenth-century England, even in so prosperous a corner as Hackney, was both squalid and brutal. The tale of the toddler stripped and abandoned in the 'necessary house' in order to finance a young woman's need for gin-soaked oblivion makes even so forceful a piece of propaganda as Hogarth's Gin Lane seem understated (**45**). Casual violence was endemic and there are indications of persistent local feuds suggesting high levels of tension and conflict in everyday life. Perhaps the most obvious of these feuds is that relating to the building of the turnpike, an issue which split the vestry on class lines (the 'gentlemen of the vestry' were for the turnpike; the 'townsmen', led by brewer Thomas Rudge, against it) for almost two years.[10] The number of assaults on toll-keepers (**275**, **320**, **321**, **328**, **348**, **1132**) suggests that even after the vestrymen

6. See particularly the collection of press cuttings relating to serious crimes in and around Hackney in the Tyssen collection. H.A.D., H/LD/7/2.
7. Notably John Maslin or Masling (landlord of the Rising Sun in Church Street), Mary Theed (wife of the Hackney pauper Lionel Theed), Dyson Green, Francis Francis and Nicholas Graves (see index).
8. Derek Barlow, *Dick Turpin and the Gregory Gang* (Chichester, 1973).
9. John and Thomasin Wheeler were married in June 1712. Their son John was baptised the following April. G.L.R.O., P79/JN1/24.
10. H.A.D., D/F/TYS/12/1.

had buried their differences, popular resentment remained high.[11]

Justice Henry Norris and his colleagues

Very little is known about the lives and careers of the justices who appear in this volume. They were not descendants of great landed families whose pedigrees can be traced with some confidence; rather, they were drawn from families who were moving up the social scale, and took pains, for that very reason, to conceal (or at the very least gloss over) the origins of their wealth. Samuel Tyssen (d. 1748), who owned lands in Huntingdonshire as well as a plantation in Antigua, was a descendant of a family of Dutch merchants who had settled in Hackney in the late seventeenth century; his nephew was the lord of the manor.[12] William Caslon (1692–1766) was a self-made man. He had made his fame and fortune (of all the justices mentioned here, he is the only one to have merited an entry in *D.N.B.*) as a typefounder. Somewhere in between these two extremes came the others: John Dekewer or De Kewer (d. 1762), a merchant of Flemish descent; Alexander Garrett (d. 1748) and his brother George, members of a prominent Spitalfields weaving family; the silk throwster John Oakey of Bethnal Green (d. 1732); Robert Paul (d. 1762), whose principal residence was in Hatton Garden rather than Hackney, and who owned estates in Northumberland and Surrey as well as in the London area; the banker Stephen Ram (d. 1746), who was wealthy enough to indulge his religious fervour by building a proprietary chapel in Homerton (reputedly in his own garden); and Ebenezer Mussell (d. 1764), of whom we know little beyond the fact that he had antiquarian tastes and the money with which to gratify them.[13] Mussell may in reality have been the most interesting of them all, for only a somewhat quixotic character would have stepped in at the demolition of Aldgate to buy the remains and re-erect them as a residence, Aldgate House, on Bethnal Green.[14]

But the figure who emerges most clearly from these manuscripts is of course Henry Norris himself. The Norris family was established in Hackney in the middle of the seventeenth century by Henry's grandfather, Hugh I (d. 1661), a prosperous London merchant who became an alderman and treasurer of the Levant Company. It then passed to his son Hugh II, also a Turkey Merchant. At his death in 1693 the property

11. It has not been possible to trace a contemporary account of the arguments involved, but it is likely that the townsmen blamed the poor state of the roads on the increase of wheeled traffic (of and for the wealthier sections of the community) and on the failure of the gentlemen of the parish (in their capacity as magistrates) to enforce existing laws concerning road repair. They may also have seen the tolls as a sort of new tax, one which would fall disproportionately on the middling and lower orders. Robert W. Malcolmson, 'A set of ungovernable people': the Kingswood colliers in the eighteenth century' in John Brewer and John Styles (eds), *An ungovernable people. The English and their law in the seventeenth and eighteenth centuries* (1980), pp. 95–96.
12. Francis John Tyssen (1717–1781), who was, incidentally, one of the few gentlemen of the parish who supported the opposition to the turnpike.
13. See the various catalogues of his *Curious and valuable library*, *Curious coins, medals and medallions*, and *Roman and Egyptian Antiquities* in the British Library.
14. The venture was shortlived. His widow remarried and her new husband cleared the site for redevelopment. Tower Hamlets local history library, 460, 587, 890, 3190.

passed to his children Hugh III, Henry and Hester, but by 1715 it had been reunited in the hands of the younger son, Henry (born *c.* 1676).[15]

Henry Norris also became a merchant; in addition to his Hackney property, he also held lands in Southwark and the City. We know little of his character and personal life, although his justicing activities certainly suggest a man of somewhat harsh and authoritarian views.[16] He was a fervent supporter of the Whig government of the day: so much so that in 1731 he (along with Samuel Tyssen) was chosen to sit as a member of the notoriously packed jury that convicted Richard Francklin, publisher of the opposition journal, the *Craftsman*.[17] Over the years he had prospered remarkably well, managing to establish his older son, Hugh IV, as a landed gentleman, and leaving himself free to bequeath his Hackney property to his younger son, Henry II.

By the mid 1720s Henry Norris had, in his own mind at least, arrived. William Stukeley's drawing of his house in Grove Street reveals what to modern eyes is a splendid timbered mansion, one that probably dated back to the first half of the sixteenth century.[18] To early-eighteenth century eyes however it must have looked hopelessly old fashioned, and it was almost certainly in need of considerable repair.[19] In the spring of 1729, Norris (who had been living elsewhere in Grove Street whilst his own house was let to Robert Ainsworth)[20] arranged for its demolition and for the construction on the same site of a splendid classical residence, complete with four privies (two, presumably for family use, wainscotted in mahogany, and two, for less august personages, merely

15. I am indebted to David Mander for assistance with this section and also to Tim Baker for the opportunity of seeing the as yet unpublished entry in the *V.C.H.* from which much of this information is drawn.
16. It is perhaps unfair to draw too many conclusions about his personal life from his will. One cannot always expect so formal a document to reveal the kind of pain and distress at family estrangements that is so poignantly portrayed in the will of Ebenezer Mussell, and hinted at in that of Robert Paul. It is nevertheless striking that Norris's will contains no religious sentiments and no personal bequests, other than mourning money to his immediate relatives. Nor are there any charitable ones. The wills of his colleagues at the petty sessions abound with expressions of piety, and with directions for the disposal of personal keepsakes (like Samuel Tyssen's 'largest and best diamond ring' to his son William), for bequests to a wide circle of relatives and even to servants (Alexander Garrett, Stephen Ram). Stephen Ram, Alexander Garrett and John Dekewer also made a number of bequests to charity. P.R.O., PROB 11/878 (Henry Norris); PROB 11/767 (Samuel Tyssen); PROB 11/751 (Stephen Ram); PROB 11/766 (Alexander Garrett); PROB 11/654 (John Oakey); PROB 11/881 (John Dekewer); PROB 11/903 (Ebenezer Mussell); PROB 11/877 (Robert Paul); PROB 11/915 (William Caslon).
17. L. Hanson, *Government and the Press 1695–1763* (1936), p. 68; *Gentlemen's Magazine* 1, p. 538.
18. The drawing is reproduced in *Transactions of the London and Middlesex Archaeological Society* 22 (1968), p. 28, and also in Isobel Watson, *Hackney and Stoke Newington Past* (1990), p. 28.
19. The terms of Ainsworth's lease strongly suggest that the house was unsound. H.A.D., D/F/NOR/4/4. I am indebted to David Mander and Isobel Watson for drawing my attention to this document.
20. I am indebted to Isobel Watson for this information. For Robert Ainsworth (1660–1743), see *D.N.B.*

lined in pine).[21] The building contract, which survives in the Hackney Archives, is a remarkably detailed document, telling us not only about the new house, but also about Norris's determination to secure value for money.[22]

In 1723, Norris became a member of Hackney's select vestry. It is difficult to believe that a man of such wealth and respectability could possibly have found his social status still in question. Yet in the eyes of his contemporaries, Henry Norris continued to occupy a somewhat ambivalent social position. He may have been rich, he may have lived like a gentleman, but it was not clear that he actually was a gentleman. In the list of new members of the vestry, he is described merely as 'Mr Henry Norris'. Only in April 1726, was he at last accorded the coveted title of 'Esquire'.[23]

In a sense therefore one suspects that his decision to become an active magistrate, following his appointment to the Bench in November 1727, was in its own way just as ostentatious a badge of social status as his new house (completed in the summer of 1730) was self-evidently intended to be. Indeed to contemporaries, it was probably the more important social indicator of the two, which is precisely why levels of activity of Middlesex justices act as something of a reverse index of social status: the lower a justice's social status, the more likely he was to wish to be seen to be one.[24] Becoming an active justice clearly gave Norris much power in the community (and it must have been extremely satisfying to have reached a position from which one could confer a similar honour on one's neighbours)[25] but it also resolved all doubts about his social status. His conduct as a justice (which was, by contemporary standards, impeccable) enhanced his claim to gentry status still further, and one suspects that his reputation for integrity was just as important a part of his legacy to his descendants as his house and fortune. When in 1739 a list of 'Chief Gentlemen of the Parish' was drawn up, Henry Norris's name topped the list.[26] By the time of his death in 1762, there was no longer any doubt that the Norris family had made the precarious transition from trade to gentry.

Process and Procedures

It is perhaps appropriate at this point to remind readers that Middlesex was an anomalous jurisdiction, and that the structure of the courts in the county was therefore unique. Elsewhere in England, the judges of the

21. A sketch of the house, which was demolished in the 1860s to make way for development, is reproduced in Isobel Watson, *Gentlemen in the building line* (1989), p. 21.
22. H.A.D., D/F/NOR/3/1. Isobel Watson describes it as 'A very early example of a highly developed form of building contract', *Gentlemen*, p. 116.
23. G.L.R.O., P79/JN1/141.
24. Cf. Landau's study of Kent justices which shows that in urban/urbanizing areas, it was the justices with least status who were most likely to act. Norma Landau, *The justices of the peace, 1679–1760* (Berkeley, 1984), pp. 324–6.
25. Thus it was Norris himself who was responsible for nominating John Dekewer to the Commission. B.L., Hardwicke Papers, Add. MS. 35603, ff. 229–232 (undated but *c.* 1751).
26. H.A.D., D/F/TYS/12/1.

royal courts came into each county on circuit twice a year to deal with serious offences at the county assizes. Lesser offences were tried by justices of the peace in quarter sessions.[27] But as Middlesex was the seat of the royal courts of justice, it was technically unable to have assize courts. Commissions of oyer and terminer (to enquire into and try treasons and felonies, etc.) and of gaol delivery (to deliver and try prisoners in the county gaol), which were in other counties directed to the judges on circuit, were in Middlesex directed to the judges of King's Bench and Common Pleas and to some justices of the peace. In practice the judges did not attend the sessions of oyer and terminer and only occasionally attended the sessions of gaol delivery. The volume of business in Middlesex was such that the sessions met eight times a year instead of quarterly as was customary elsewhere.

Matters were further complicated by the fact that Newgate, the county gaol of Middlesex, was shared with the City of London and was effectively under the City's control. Indictments for the sessions of the peace or for the sessions of oyer and terminer were heard at the Middlesex Sessions House, Hicks Hall in Clerkenwell. Indictments for the Middlesex gaol delivery were also initially heard before the grand jury at Hicks Hall as they had to be processed via the commission of oyer and terminer, but the actual trials took place at the Old Bailey before the Aldermen of the City of London, with (until 1754) some Middlesex justices of oyer and terminer in attendance.

It is important to note that the gaol delivery was precisely what its name indicates and that it heard only cases involving prisoners in Newgate, or those who had been bailed from it. When committing a suspect to prison therefore a justice of the peace was making certain assumptions about the nature of the case and the appropriate venue for trial. Persons committed to New Prison or to the House of Correction (also known as Bridewell) were likely to be tried (if tried at all) at Hicks Hall, although it was always possible for them to be transferred to the custody of the keeper of Newgate shortly before the opening of the sessions, if trial at the Old Bailey was thought to be more appropriate or more convenient. Just such a transfer occurred in the cases of Joseph Hall, William Tilly and Edward Marshall (**7**, **8**, **278**, **281**). Those committed directly to Newgate would be tried at the Old Bailey and were probably facing serious, possibly capital, charges.

The justices met regularly outside of the general/quarter sessions to transact other business. Petty sessions were held for each Middlesex division and in addition to these divisional sessions there were also parochial petty sessions. The precise structure of these sessions varied from time to time (as did the business they transacted), depending on the availability of local justices. The deterioration in the Hackney petty sessions book in the early 1740s and subsequent cessation of entries until 1751 may reflect a temporary failure in record-keeping, but it is likely that it also indicates the collapse of the petty sessions. Middlesex in

27. For a more detailed picture of the work of these courts in this period, see J. M. Beattie, *Crime and the Courts in England 1660–1800* (Oxford, 1986).

general was certainly suffering a shortage of justices in the 1740s and a list of candidates for the magistracy drawn up *c.* 1751 refers quite specifically to the lack of magistrates in Hackney: 'there being only Mr Norris . . . now a justice'.[28]

Not every parish possessed its own petty sessions and those that did exist were likely to collapse from time to time. Parishes that did not have their own petty sessions had to take their business to one in a neighbouring parish,[29] or wait for a meeting of the divisional sessions. The division of work between a parochial and a divisional petty sessions was therefore always fairly fluid, and the balance that was achieved in Hackney may not reflect what happened in other parishes or in other divisions.

A final point to be borne in mind is that the initiative in laying charges lay with the prosecutor, who could bypass the local justices completely and present a case directly to the grand jury at the general/quarter sessions (often without any prior notice to the defendant) or even directly to the King's Bench itself.[30] If the grand jury found that there was a case to answer, a bench warrant would then be issued to take up the alleged offender (**276**, **279**).

The documents presented here may well be unique. Petty sessions books survive for a number of areas, often because, as in Hackney, the minute books came to form part of a collection of parish records. Justices' notebooks are rather more ephemeral: only twenty-four items falling into this broad category (some of them fragmentary) survive for the whole of the century.[31] It is extremely rare for a justice's notebook to survive together with a contemporaneous petty sessions minute book.[32] Each document is interesting in itself, providing useful insights into everyday life as well as the administration of the parish. Taken together, however, they provide a fascinating account of the work that an ordinary justice of the peace was expected to undertake outside of sessions.

The justicing notebook

The cases recorded by Norris in his justicing notebook were probably all heard in his home at Grove Street. Although the entries or recognizances occasionally reveal the presence of another justice (**30**, **38**, **48**, **228**, **333**, **341**), it is not usually possible to tell whether anyone

28. B.L., Hardwicke Papers, Add. MS. 35603, ff. 229–232.
29. Thus the Hackney petty sessions book occasionally minutes business relating to Bethnal Green (**936**), Bromley St. Leonard (**919**), Mile End (**176**, **885**, **886**, **890**, **897**, **937**) and Stratford Bow (**670**, **702**, **749**, **811**, **812**, **859**, **874**, **899**, **900**, **907**, **929**).
30. Thus in the autumn of 1740, Edward Batty (see index) commenced a prosecution in the King's Bench against John David Barbutt and William Crispe for an assault committed in Clapton. P.R.O., KB 10/25/1, Michaelmas 14 Geo. II, indt. 38.
31. I am indebted for this information to John Styles.
32. In the only other example known to the writer, that of the Kent justice Paul D'Aranda, the documents cover a single year; the Norris notebook and Hackney petty sessions minutes cover twelve. Two other Kent justices, Sir Wyndham Knatchbull and William Brockman, have also left justicing diaries together with brief notes of other sessions that they attended, but these notes do not amount to a full record of business transacted. Kent Archives Office, U442/045, U951/03, U951/04; B.L., Add. MSS. 42598, 42599. I am indebted to Norma Landau for these references.

else was present. It is thus particularly interesting to discover (from the account of the committal of Faxton and Smith in the *Old Bailey Proceedings*) that on that occasion at least, Norris's court room was crowded with people, most of whom were probably curious bystanders rather than witnesses (**35**). The capture of highwaymen (and the high reward that would ensue) was however a somewhat unusual and exciting event; it is unlikely that Norris's court customarily provided the kind of entertainment that attracted sightseers to the courts of more active metropolitan justices, but it is nevertheless important to stress both the informality of the proceedings and the possible presence of a number of extraneous persons.

It is perhaps important to realise that the notebook was only part of a series of documents, such as recognizances, entries in gaol calendars, affidavits, confessions and informations, that could be generated by criminal cases. The *Old Bailey Proceedings* reveal, for example, that the reference in entry 35 to a confession is not to an oral one but to a sworn document taken before Norris and returned to the sessions for use at the trial. Since the survival of sessions papers in Middlesex is very poor, and since proceedings at quarter/general sessions were rarely reported in the press, Norris's notebook often supplies the only details of a case beyond that which can be gleaned from the formal record. It also gives information about cases that were dismissed which it would be impossible to reconstruct from any other source. It is an added bonus that Norris included so much detail about the evidence given, with the result that his notebook is far more informative than justicing notebooks (notably that of William Hunt of Wiltshire and Richard Wyatt of Surrey)[33] that have been published hitherto.

Norris was probably the most active justice in Hackney, but except for a brief period during the later 1740s he was not the only one: recognizances and committals relating to Hackney residents were also made by his colleagues at the petty sessions. To read through the entries in his notebook, in the knowledge that what appears there represents no more than a sizeable fraction of the totality of petty crime in Hackney, is to be left in no doubt of the unrelenting tedium of a justice's criminal business, made up as it was of an apparently interminable succession of assaults, occasionally enlivened by a few broken windows, the theft of the washerwoman's laundry or the arrival of an unlicensed pedlar.

Over two-thirds of the offences brought before Norris involved some form of assault, ranging from simple threats to an alleged homicide (**318**). Most of these assaults appear to have taken place outside the family, though a number of incidents of domestic violence are also recorded. In over eighty per cent of these cases no further process is recorded, the possession of a justice's warrant probably being enough to force some sort of settlement. The remainder were mostly settled, sometimes even before the parties had come to Norris's house, and

33. Elizabeth Crittall (ed), *The justicing notebook of William Hunt 1744–1749* (Wiltshire Record Society, 1982). Elizabeth Silverthorne (ed), *Deposition book of Richard Wyatt, JP, 1767–1776* (Surrey Record Society, 1978).

sometimes during the hearing itself, a process that could be somewhat time-consuming (**26**, **267**). Only a handful of cases (not necessarily the most serious) went any further, with the offenders bound over to appear at the general/quarter sessions, gaoled for lack of sureties, or indicted. With only two exceptions (**110**, **279**), all those who were indicted at the general/quarter sessions confessed and were fined 1s. Such a verdict usually indicates that the parties concerned had reached some prior agreement (probably involving monetary compensation).

Allegations of theft or damage to property form the second largest category of offences. Most were comparatively trivial and amenable therefore either to mediation (**22**, **86**, **287**), or to a short term of imprisonment under that useful early eighteenth-century formula of being 'idle and disorderly and of dishonest conversation' (**29**, **56**, **130**, **337**). Many of these cases demonstrate clearly the essential characteristics of summary jurisdiction. Justice was swift, but it was also rough. Defendants, denied legal representation and the right to present their case to a jury, were at an obvious disadvantage. In effect they were at the mercy of the justice, who might or might not be sympathetic to their plight.

Much of the material presented here suggests that Norris had little sympathy with the plight of the poor. In this, his administration of summary justice offers a striking contrast to that of the Wiltshire justice William Hunt, whose virtually contemporaneous notebook shows that persons taken before him accused of pilfering from orchards or gardens (offences likely to be associated with high-spirited youth or with poverty and hunger) were likely to be treated with leniency. Where statute law gave an alternative to imprisonment, Hunt ensured that damages and fines were adjusted to the means of the offender so that the punishment for failure to pay (whipping) was rarely administered.[34] Norris's treatment of those brought before him was very different. He may well have believed that proximity to London made Hackney's farms and market gardens too vulnerable a target for the poor and/or criminally inclined. He was undoubtedly also aware of the peculiar difficulty involved in deterring such crimes, since at common law the theft of growing crops could not be larceny no matter how valuable the produce stolen.[35] His determination to protect local growers led him to impose high fines (amounting to the equivalent of at least two weeks' average wages)[36] which the offenders were unlikely to be able to pay, and he appears to have had no hesitation at all in ordering them to be whipped instead (**353**, **354**). He readily imprisoned those found pilfering crops (**338**, **339**, **346**), even when they were obviously poor and in want (**338**, **346**). The

34. *The justicing notebook of William Hunt*, p. 14.
35. At common law, the theft of things annexed to the freehold (such as growing crops) was merely trespass. Only when the crop had been picked or harvested did the theft become larceny, the gravity of the offence then deriving, as in all larcenies, from the value of the goods stolen.
36. A male labourer might earn between 9s. and 12s. a week at this time; even a skilled worker would only get between 10s. and 15s. a week. Women's wages, of course, would be even lower. George Rudé, *Hanoverian London: 1714–1808* (1971), p. 88.

one case in which he and the prosecutor appear to have shown some degree of leniency, was one in which the prosecution case was unsound: it being doubtful whether taking windfalls was an offence at all (**336**).[37]

A very small number of offences brought to Norris involved major felonies: highway robbery, theft in a dwelling house, grand larceny. Such cases are particularly informative. They reveal a great deal about the wealth (in terms of both money and goods) of comparatively ordinary people: the case of Mary South, for example, establishes that the victualler, Edward Batty, had over £50 in money (a small fortune by the standards of the day) simply lying around the house, while Francis Trumble's apparently humble victim nevertheless owned a watch worth 30s. (at least two weeks' average wages even for a skilled artisan) (**60**, **606**, **302**).

They also demonstrate what contemporary critics termed 'pious perjury' in action. Thus Mary South, accused of stealing 33 gold guineas and a further £25 2s. 0d. in other coins, was found guilty of stealing to the value of 39s. only (**60**, **606**), and Jane Grew accused of stealing clothing worth 2s. 9d. was convicted of stealing goods to the value of 10d. (**45**). The difference in both cases was literally one of life or death. Theft from a dwelling house of 40s. or more, or theft from the person of 12d. or more were both capital offences. By downvaluing the goods stolen, the jury ensured that neither woman would hang, but would instead be transported to the American colonies. Male juries committed 'pious perjury' on behalf of their own sex too, but they were rather more likely to do so for women, presumably for the simple reason that even the most hardened of proponents of capital punishment were likely to be revolted by the thought of a woman on the gallows.[38] In other cases, the jury returned what was known as 'a partial verdict' and so reduced the gravity of the charge. James Darlington, for example, was saved from the gallows when he was found guilty of theft but not of breaking and entering (**298**). 'Pious perjury' and partial verdicts formed a central element of the administration of the contemporary criminal justice system, saving thousands from execution for relatively trivial offences.[39]

These cases show just how quickly the contemporary criminal justice system worked. Isaac Dennis had to wait six weeks for his trial (**143**) but this was unusual: Faxton and Smith, Jane Grew and Francis Trumble were all tried within a month (**35**, **45**, **302**). Others were processed even more quickly: John Seagrave and Mary South and Esther Hewson were tried within a week of their alleged offences (**111**, **60**, **606**).

They also reveal a great deal about the factors that affected an individual's progress through the courts. The eighteenth-century legal

37. It is difficult to believe that any charge for the theft of windfalls would have been sustainable, windfalls by definition being of little or no value. Some contemporaries may even have seen the taking of windfalls (like gleaning) as one of the legitimate perquisites of the poor.
38. On the leniency commonly shown to female offenders both before and after conviction, see Beattie, *Crime and the Courts*, pp. 436–9.
39. Ibid., pp. 424–8.

system was built on a system of private prosecution, so that any failure on the part of the prosecutor was fatal to the success of his or her case. The account of William Tilly's case in the *Old Bailey Proceedings*, indicates that he was acquitted because of the failure of his prosecutor to turn up at the trial (**8**). This was by no means impossible, although the accuracy of this particular report may be questionable. Poor persons may in general, however, have been reluctant to prosecute simply because of the expense. It was not until 1752 that any statutory provision was made for assistance towards costs.[40] The difficulties facing poor persons who might not fully understand the legal process or who might lack the financial resources necessary to prosecute were recognized by the vestry which would on occasion permit prosecutions to be carried on at parish expense (**8**, **241**).[41]

The state attempted to encourage certain types of prosecution by providing rewards, which in the case of highway robbery and burglary amounted to £40 per conviction. At times of particular concern about the level of violent crime in the London area, an additional £100 was provided by royal proclamation. Just such a proclamation was in force in 1732, so that those responsible for the capture and conviction of Thomas Smith and Thomas Faxton received a total of £280 for their night's work. It was alleged at their trial that Faxton's confession had been obtained by holding out the hope that he would be admitted as an evidence for the crown (thus enabling him not only to escape the gallows but also to entitle himself to part of the reward). Norris denied that any incentive had been offered, but such an offer could easily have been made whilst the men had been imprisoned overnight or even in the room in which they were examined, which was so crowded that Norris may not have heard or seen everything that went on. Such tactics were commonplace, and the amount of money involved certainly arouses some suspicion. If nothing else, the prospect of a share in £280 might well have been enough to turn an uncertain eyewitness identification into a very positive one.[42]

A rather kinder side of the contemporary judicial process is shown in the case of Francis Trumble (**302**). Captured after what now seems like an almost classic Hollywood chase across the lanes and fields of Hackney, Trumble was clearly a desperate and potentially very violent man. His defence consisted entirely of a parade of witnesses testifying to a family history of mental instability and to his own 'melancholic' and suicidal tendencies. Although convicted Trumble did not hang. Like almost fifty per cent of those condemned to death under the contemporary 'bloody code', Trumble received a royal pardon.

Legal technicalities could also protect an accused person. One notes

40. Ibid., pp. 42–48.
41. A number of other prosecutions (including one for murder) carried out at parish expense are also noted in the vestry minutes. The attorney used was Samuel Sadleir. P79/JN1/142, pp. 65, 122.
42. On thieftaking conspiracies generally see Ruth Paley, 'Thieftakers in London in the age of the McDaniel gang' in Douglas Hay and Francis Snyder (eds) *Policing and prosecution in Britain 1750–1850* (Oxford, 1989), pp. 301–341.

in these entries for example the attempt by Isaac Dennis to defend himself (unsuccessfully) on a charge of highway robbery by claiming that he had merely asked for charity (**143**) and the acquittal of Esther Hewson (**60**, **606**) because the jury were not convinced that she knew that Mary South had stolen the coins in question, although it is difficult to envisage quite how else a servant girl could have come into possession of such a large sum of money. Details of a rather more interesting legal debate are preserved in the Hackney Archives. In January 1751, the brothers John and Miles Nutbrown[43] were accused of burgling the house of Joseph Faikney (a capital offence). The house was Faikney's summer residence; at the time of the crime it was empty and Faikney had not decided whether to renew his lease. The judge directed the jury that since Faikney had no settled intention to return to the house, it could not be held to be a dwelling house within the meaning of the statute and that consequently the crime did not amount to burglary. The Nutbrowns were found guilty on a lesser charge, and sentenced to transportation.[44]

On a number of occasions, the notebook records that search warrants were issued following complaints of theft (**17**, **169**, **174**, **202**, **236**, **248**, **322**, **347**, **351**). Contemporary legal textbooks contain much information about the ways in which search warrants could be executed but very little about the circumstances in which it was proper to issue one, beyond a broad statement to the effect that general search warrants were improper. The Norris notebook suggests that there were few safeguards. It records a return to the warrant or further process in only three cases (**174**, **248**, **347**), only one of which resulted in sufficient evidence to continue the prosecution. Although it is always possible that the others were processed via another justice, a search of indictment and recognizance files strongly suggests that no further action was taken in any of these cases. It seems likely therefore that these search warrants were issued on very little evidence. Indeed one notes that on three occasions warrants were issued to search a number of houses (**17**, **169**, **236**). In practice, the difference between this sort of indiscriminate 'fishing expedition' and one authorized by a general warrant seems minimal.

A less dramatic part of the justices' business related to burials in woollen. Under 30 Car. II c3 an affidavit to the effect that a corpse had been buried in woollen (unless the cause of death was plague), taken before a justice of the peace, had to be delivered to the minister of the parish within 8 days of the burial. The penalty for default was £5, of which half went to the poor of the parish and half to the informer. To be buried in anything other than a woollen shroud at this time was as

43. Probably a generation younger than the Miles Nutbrown who appears in this volume on charges of assault and failing to maintain his family (**127**, **343**, **996**).

44. The case is interesting, not just for the legal argument concerning the definition of a dwelling house, but because it illustrates some of the deficiencies of the *Old Bailey Proceedings*, which appears to give a full account of the evidence before recording the verdict but which gives no indication whatsoever that such a technicality was ever considered. H.A.D., H/LD/7/1, f. 35; *O. B. Proc.*, January 1751, R *v* Nutbrown.

ostentatious a mark of conspicuous consumption as could be imagined. Those who did not wish to be buried in woollen (at least one Hackney resident was buried in velvet instead)[45] may well have arranged to pay an amount equivalent to a moiety of the fine directly to the churchwardens.

By the later eighteenth century this act had largely (but not entirely) fallen into disuse, but it is clear from these documents that it was being enforced in early eighteenth century Hackney, to the extent that the vicar was prepared to lay an information for non-compliance (**837**).[46] One parish searcher (Ann Fisher) who was foolish enough to believe that no-one would notice if she collected the appropriate fees without actually bothering to swear the affidavits, was dismissed from office in 1736.[47] Occasionally, the affidavits were sworn at the petty sessions, but it was not necessary to do so, and it was more usual for them to be taken before a single justice. Checklists containing extremely brief notes of such affidavits appear at intervals throughout the Norris notebook and have been removed for the convenience of the reader to the end of the notebook entries (**356–60**).

The petty sessions minute book

The Hackney petty sessions met roughly once a fortnight. For most of the period covered here it met at the Mermaid Tavern (later the Old Mermaid) on the east side of Church Street (now Mare Street).[48] In the 1750s it met at the Blue Posts Tavern, formerly Templars House, a more substantial establishment, which had been used occasionally for vestry meetings.[49]

A recurrent theme of applications to the Lord Lieutenant by and on behalf of those wishing to be selected as justices of the peace was the need to have sufficient local magistrates to transact parochial business.[50] To have what was, as in Hackney, virtually a parochial petty sessions was certainly convenient, but it was also important in other ways. Almost all aspects of parochial administration involved extremely sensitive issues (the fairness or otherwise of rating assessments, the vigour with which the settlement laws were applied, the criteria adopted in granting or refusing alehouse licences, even the appointment of parochial officials) which depended to a large extent on the justices' sympathetic use of their discretionary powers. A justice who was involved in the local community, and even better, one who was involved

45. G.L.R.O., P79/JN1/218.
46. The vicar's memorandum book (which relates to a slightly earlier period), shows that he kept careful records of such affidavits. H.A.D., D/F/TYS/18.
47. She was replaced by Mary Wasley (**199**). G.L.R.O., P79/JN1/141/180.
48. Not to be confused with the more substantial Mermaid Tavern, with its own assembly rooms, bowling greens and extensive gardens, which was established on the opposite side of the road at some stage in the mid-eighteenth century. I am indebted to Isobel Watson for this information.
49. William Robinson, *The history and antiquities of the parish of Hackney*, 2 vols. (London, 1842), vol. 1, pp. 78, 149; Benjamin Clarke, *Glimpses of Ancient Hackney and Stoke Newington* (London, 1894, reprinted 1986), p. 111.
50. Alnwick Castle, Northumberland, MS. Y/IV/6/a.

in the vestry, was more likely to ensure the smooth running of parochial affairs and, perhaps more importantly, to protect the parish, than one who was not.

The justices out of sessions were responsible for swearing in a number of local officials. In January, they had to meet to appoint surveyors of the highways, selected from a shortlist of names submitted by the vestries. In Middlesex this appears to have been one of the functions of the divisional sessions rather than of a parochial petty sessions (Hackney was in the Tower division, which had a court house in Whitechapel). The petty sessions was more concerned with the appointment of overseers of the poor, constables, headboroughs and ale-conners. Overseers of the poor had to be appointed within a month of Easter, from a shortlist of candidates submitted by the vestry. The offices of constable, headborough, and ale-conner were technically manorial offices and it was only when the Court Leet failed to appoint or to swear such officers or when a serving officer died or left the parish that the justices were empowered to step in.[51] A number of those sworn into office by the justices were substitutes, and it is important to note that although such men were likely to be of lower social status than the person they replaced, they nevertheless still had to fulfil all the normal criteria for appointment to office.

Settlement examinations, taken for the purpose of assigning individuals to the parishes which would relieve them if they became indigent, comprised a very large part of the business of justices out of sessions. Historians have usually assumed that such examinations were intricately bound up with applications for poor relief. More recently it has been argued that a substantial proportion of examinations taken during this period stemmed from attempts to regulate migration.[52] It is clearly inappropriate to enter fully into the Hackney evidence here, but it should be noted that bringing in a list of new inhabitants was one of the duties of the beadle (**361**) and that individuals were regularly summoned *en masse*, sometimes more than twenty at a time (**990**, **994**, **1048**), to be examined as to settlement, usually in the autumn. Preliminary analysis confirms that more than one pattern was in operation. Some of those examined were in need of relief (**425**, **456**, **701**, **727**), but most were neither indigent nor in imminent danger of becoming so. Some, on the contrary, seem to have been quite comfortably established.[53] Many of

51. Hackney was something of an exception in the metropolitan area in that its court leet continued to meet. In practice, most constables and headboroughs elsewhere in urban Middlesex were appointed by the vestry and sworn in at petty sessions.
52. Norma Landau, 'The laws of settlement and the surveillance of immigration in eighteenth-century Kent' in *Continuity and Change*, 3 (1988), pp. 391–420, and 'Regulation of immigration, economic structures, and definitions of the poor' in *Historical Journal*, 33, 3 (1990), pp. 541–572.
53. Some were rated to the highways (payment of which did not confer rights of settlement). George Fox, summoned in 1731, is known to have had an apprentice (**188**, **233**, **400**, **464**, **480**, **731**). Two of those nominated to the office of overseer of the poor in 1736 (a position only open to 'substantial householders') were certificated men (**873**). One of them, William Stokes, later rented lands to the value of £80 a year, and had served as surveyor of the highways (**920**, **684**). I intend to write more fully about the use of the settlement laws in Hackney elsewhere.

them were given time to obtain a certificate: that is a sworn document granted by the officers of the parish of settlement, certifying their rights of settlement. Once an individual had been made to obtain such a document neither (s)he nor his/her dependants were likely ever to obtain rights of settlement elsewhere. Significantly, the petty sessions was largely concerned with examining individuals not settled in Hackney. Very few came for the purpose of obtaining a certificate from Hackney to another parish (**546**, **626**, **722**, **734**, **745**, **1005**), suggesting that there was high net inflow of migrant workers.

In Hackney, it was customary for examinations to be taken at the petty sessions rather than before a single justice. The notebook contains only two examinations before a single justice. Margaret Baldry and James Bishop (**6**, **53**) were both indigent. It is likely that they were taken before Norris as a mere formality to the granting of relief and that the parish officers were satisfied that they were settled in Hackney. The case of James Bishop, however, demonstrates just why parish officers usually preferred to wait for a petty sessions meeting. For in the course of his examination, Norris decided (incorrectly) that Bishop was settled elsewhere. It was therefore necessary for Bishop to be re-examined, since an order to remove him to his parish of settlement required the signature of two justices.

The overseers of the poor could give emergency relief as and when necessary but longer-term assistance was given only to those whose names were enrolled on the list of parish poor.[54] Only the justices could authorise medium or long-term relief to those not on the list, or could overrule the overseers' refusal of emergency relief. Instructions to the overseers to relieve necessitous individuals (some of whom are known to have had no settlement in Hackney) are regularly minuted here.

Those who were deemed to be in need of assistance because of their own failure to work or refusal to maintain their families ran the risk of summary imprisonment. As in any form of summary process, the individuals concerned were at a considerable disadvantage. The petty sessions minutes refer to three individuals who were committed to gaol for refusing to maintain their families: Richard Evans, Grace Chandler and Lionel Theed (**2**, **363**, **615**); another, John Curtis, appears in the notebook (**211**). Theed seems to have had a long history of illness (**411**), but the parochial officials were perhaps distracted by the fact that his incapacity failed to prevent his wife's regular pregnancies. In the cases of Evans and Chandler, the subsequent pattern of relief suggests that both overseers and justices had, in their zeal to protect the parish purse, confused fecklessness with the onset of some chronic illness. Able-bodied individuals who wished to abandon their families did not usually stay around long enough to be arrested (**582**, **740**, **805**, **942**, **996**, **1087**).

A similar desire to protect the ratepayer lies behind the treatment accorded to unmarried mothers. Single, pregnant women were called

54. Such individuals were required to identify themselves by means of a pauper's badge, and since the churchwardens' accounts for this period include disbursements for the purchase of such badges, it is clear that they were worn in Hackney.

before the justices and asked to identify the father. Customarily, he would be made to enter into a recognizance for good behaviour which would be returned to the Middlesex sessions and continued until after the birth of the child. Steps would then be taken to ensure that the parish was reimbursed for any expenses attendant on the actual delivery and to secure some sort of maintenance agreement (usually by means of a bond of indemnity to the parish). Whether women did identify the true fathers or, as contemporary legend suggests, falsely accused the man they thought most able to shoulder the financial burden, remains an open question but Elizabeth Brace (who claimed to be unable to identify the father of her child) and Phoebe Hams (who told the justices it was none of their business) seem to have been unusually independent (**1063**, **1137**). Single mothers almost always named someone. Putative fathers who refused to maintain their illegitimate children were liable to imprisonment on summary process, even if they were too poor, or, as in the case of Samuel Bayly, too ill to do otherwise (**566**).

Another regular feature of petty sessions work was the binding out of pauper children as apprentices. With very few exceptions, such children were bound to masters (or mistresses) in other parishes. Since Hackney never paid more than 40s. as a premium for the apprenticeships,[55] one can be fairly certain that these children were not going to be taught particularly marketable skills and that they would always exist perilously close to the margin between poverty and indigence. Apprenticeship was unlikely therefore to secure the children's future, and may on the contrary have exposed them to exploitation and danger; it did however confer rights of settlement, thus freeing Hackney from any subsequent demand for poor relief. The desire to be rid of paupers probably underlies the treatment afforded to former pauper apprentice, Sarah Crew, and her family.[56] Having once foisted her onto another parish, there was no point in allowing her to give birth to her illegitimate child in Hackney (**623**, **641**). The whole purpose of binding out apprentices to another parish was that Hackney rid itself not just of one generation of paupers but of future generations as well.

From 1729, alehouse licences were renewable annually in September at a special (Brewster) sessions held for that purpose. In later years, it became usual for the Brewster sessions to be adjourned rather than closed so that applications could be made throughout the year. In the the early eighteenth century, however, local magistrates continued the pre-1729 custom of granting permissive licences under the signature of two justices at any time during the year to run until the annual renewal date. When, as in Hackney, the petty sessions was closely tied into the local government structure, it became possible for the justices to exercise a tight control over licensing. The criteria by which licences were granted or withheld in Hackney were fairly standard ones: the wish to restrict the number of alehouses in order to discourage excessive

55. It is perhaps instructive to compare this sum to the £500 left by Alexander Garrett for the apprenticeship of his own son. P.R.O., PROB 11/766.
56. Her settlement examination reveals that she had been apprenticed by the parish to a hog butcher, and had subsequently worked as a servant. H.A.D., P/J/P/68.

consumption of alcohol,[57] coupled with the need to ensure that landlords were persons of good character.

From the point of view of the élite such criteria were both acceptable and desirable. In practice, however, the justices' decisions often seem to be somewhat arbitrary. One notes in these entries for example the way in which a licence was initially granted to Stephen Carr and then withdrawn a mere two weeks later on grounds of misbehaviour, although no such punishment was given to his opponent John Price, who seems to have been equally guilty (**488**, **489**, **498**). Some applications were refused 'there not being any vacancy', (**420**, **661**, **768**, **927**), others were granted seemingly with no reference to the number of vacancies at all (**812**, **824**, **987**, **988**, **1086**), and with just a hint of suspicion that influential connections could be useful (**953**). Part of the explanation lies in the way in which additional factors were taken into account. One notes in particular the refusal of licences to those who were not settled in the parish (**488**, **489**, **697**), and the decision to grant a licence to Thomas Hilliard on the grounds that he was unable to earn his living in any other way, although the terms of this successful application were little different from those of the application which had been refused a year earlier (**661**, **743**).

From the point of view of the justices, one can understand why these decisions were made, but for the ordinary individual who found his livelihood under threat or the value of his property suddenly altered by a decision outside his control, many of the justices' decisions must have seemed both arbitrary and capricious. Little wonder that Morgan Bynon carefully cleared the matter of the licence before disposing of his property (**784**). Strict control of licensing could, however, confer a certain amount of power on the licensees. For the licence appertained to the individual rather than to the property and this fact could be used to good effect in any dispute with the property owner. Thus Nathaniel Roberts, thrown out of his ale-house on Stamford Hill, was able (albeit briefly) to make trouble for his successor who had no licence (**1080**, **1086**), whilst a Mr Hannand, whose tenant simply moved next door, found that he was unable to obtain a licence for his new tenant (**768**), and Markham Spearing discovered too late that his licensee had arranged a transfer without his knowledge (**921**, **927**).

Lesser offences dealt with at the petty sessions included sabbath breaking and swearing. Neither figure very prominently, although prosecutions for sabbath breaking are more common in the section dealing with the early 1750s, perhaps because that was a period when heightened awareness about crime rates fuelled a demand for moral reform. Although some of those summoned for sabbath breaking were described as being in 'indifferent' or 'bad' circumstances and excused (**1103**, **1105**), it seems likely that most of those prosecuted were relatively prosperous individuals and that the justices chose to make an

57. Thomas Hilliard's petition to the general/quarter sessions in 1733 makes it clear that the Hackney justices were imposing an arbitrary upper limit on the number of ale-house licenses to be granted. G.L.R.O., MSP/1733/0ct/78.

example of them as a warning to others. The Greyhound in Homerton (kept by Joseph Sowter) is, for example, identified by William Robinson as a tavern and tea gardens which 'was the resort of most of the Newmarket and sporting men of the time: there was a cock pit and regular cock fights' (**1093**, **1102**, **1108**).[58] Likewise the Shoulder of Mutton and Cat (sometimes Cat and Shoulder of Mutton and sometimes merely the Shoulder of Mutton) was a substantial establishment adjoining London Fields (**1091**, **1103**). Similar considerations may also apply to convictions for swearing or cursing: certainly for the justices to convict their own coachmen (men of high standing in contemporary domestic establishments) was to serve notice about the limits of tolerable behaviour in an ostentatious, and perhaps humiliating, manner (**209**, **819**).

Vexatious and malicious prosecutions

Its dependence on private prosecution meant that vexatious actions were endemic to the eighteenth-century legal system. These entries demonstrate clearly that this was true even at the lowest levels of the criminal justice system, for many of these comparatively minor cases appear to have been brought for purely vexatious reasons. On 18 August 1736, Ann Folliot was accused of assaulting Mary Kingsland; the very next day her husband accused Mary Kingsland's husband of the same offence (**193**, **194**). John Price and Stephen Carr both accused each other of assault (**37**, **38**). It is surely more than coincidence that William Hewson's accusations against Edward Batty were virtually contemporaneous with Batty's unsuccessful prosecution of Hewson's wife (**60**, **606**, **63**). Such examples could be multiplied virtually *ad infinitum*.

The notebook even contains one case of a prosecution that was malicious in the strict legal sense of the word.[59] It includes two accounts of accusations of theft involving Matthew Walter or Walters. In 1731, Walters accused Jacob Hales of stealing fruit; the affair was compromised (**22**). A year later Hales accused Walters of stealing several pots of myrtles, whose value meant that the offence amounted to grand larceny (**52**). Norris threw the charge out. The prosecutors then arrested Walters on a warrant from justice Thomas Robe and he was again taken before Norris. Hales failed to attend, no doubt because he thought (correctly) that Norris would dismiss the charge. Undeterred, Hales then had Walters arrested yet again and took him before Sir William Billers, possibly altering his evidence to make the case more convincing.[60] Walters was subsequently acquitted at the Old Bailey and was allowed a copy of his indictment, a form of process, rarely granted by the judges, that was the essential preliminary to commencing an action

58. William Robinson, *The history and antiquities of the parish of Hackney* (1842), p. 226.
59. A prosecution brought for reasons of spite is, in the strict legal sense, merely vexatious. Only if the prosecution is pursued for reasons of spite in the full knowledge that the accusations are without foundation, does it become malicious.
60. Note that Norris's account of the case draws attention to discrepancies in the prosecution evidence as given to him and as stated at the Old Bailey trial.

for malicious prosecution.[61]

The burden of judicial duties

It is perhaps necessary to stress what a considerable commitment these justices were making. One doubts that any of them had received a high standard of education. If they had, it would have been, at best, a narrowly classical one; they were certainly not trained as lawyers. Yet the notebook volume, kept as it is almost entirely in Norris's own hand,[62] suggests very strongly that single justices customarily acted without benefit of legal advice. This would not be surprising, as there is evidence to suggest that even the most active of metropolitan justices sometimes had to call in local attornies as and when they were needed.[63]

Norris and his colleagues probably relied on a justices' manual to guide them through the complexities of the legal process.[64] And one should not underestimate just how complex the legal process could be. Many apparently straightforward entries actually raised quite difficult legal issues. The most obvious one was the classification of an offence. It was the justices' duty to effect reconciliation wherever possible, except in cases of felony, for compounding a felony was, in itself, a serious crime. Unfortunately, the difference between a felony and a misdemeanour was not always obvious. In at least two cases, Norris was uncertain enough note to that an alleged theft could be compounded 'it not appearing to be a felony' (**22**, **135**).[65]

There are at least three felony cases (four, if one counts his dismissal, against the wishes of the prosecutor, of the accusations against Walters) in which Norris's actions may have been technically incorrect. In 1731, he discharged three men accused of horse-stealing (a capital felony) 'finding no cause upon ye whole to commit them'; it is not clear whether the prosecutor wished to pursue the charge further (**14**). In 1738, Norris judged the case against Sarah Thompson, also accused of a capital felony, to be weak and was clearly instrumental in persuading the prosecutor to drop charges (**274**). To modern eyes, accustomed to a system of prosecution in which the state plays a major role and to the idea that

61. On malicious prosecution, in general, and the obstacles to redress (particularly the refusal of a copy of indictment), see Douglas Hay, 'Prosecution and power, Malicious prosecution in the English courts, 1750–1850' in Hay and Snyder, *Policing and prosecution*, pp. 343–395.
62. Occasional entries are in other hands (possibly two). One appears to be that of Samuel Sadleir, clerk of the petty sessions.
63. Thus in 1748, John Poulson described how depositions were sometimes taken by himself, sometimes by his clerk and sometimes by attornies summoned for the purpose. It is not clear whether his clerk was an attorney or the clerk that he used in the course of his normal business transactions. P.R.O., KB1/9/2, Mich. 22 Geo. II, R *v*. Poulson and others, affdt. John Poulson 27 June 1748, re-sworn 24 October 1748.
64. Perhaps W. Nelson, *The office and authority of a justice of peace*, which had reached its eleventh edition by 1736, or that by their colleague on the Middlesex bench, Nathaniel Blackerby, *The justice of peace his companion*, first published 1723.
65. In neither case does the entry contain enough information from which to judge the correctness of his decision. The theft of fruit (**22**) would have been a felony if it had been stolen on an occasion subsequent to the picking; the value of the stolen tools (**135**), which was crucial to the distinction between felony and misdemeanour, is not given.

pre-trial committal proceedings take place before a magistrate, this may seem unexceptional. But as has been pointed out, the eighteenth century legal system was based on private prosecution. Once a sworn allegation of felony had been made, it was up to the grand jury to decide whether the evidence was sufficient to support an indictment. It was not the function of a justice to sift out bad cases. It is significant that Norris's note of the Thompson case refers to the prosecutor's willingness to drop the charge, but it also records that the prosecutor had sworn to the truth of the allegations. Technically, Norris had no option but to process the case further, that he did not illustrates the very wide discretion customarily exercised by justices and prosecutors alike.

A far more serious case was that arising from the arrest of George Scipio (**218**). Scipio, described in the notebook entry as a chapman of Shoreditch, was accused by Anne Godfrey of having been involved in stealing her washing. The offence concerned is clearly stated to have been felonious. Scipio had been arrested because a black man had been seen in the vicinity of the crime and he was self-evidently the only black known to the complainant. The evidence against him was poor and it seems unlikely that a grand jury would have been willing to process an indictment against him. Nevertheless, Anne Godfrey swore to an information against him and Scipio was made to enter into a recognizance to answer the accusation. But the charge was subsequently withdrawn, and it must have been withdrawn with Norris's full knowledge and consent because the recognizance was not certified to the general/quarter sessions. Again, the only correct course of action was to proceed. Indeed it is possible that in dropping the case, both Norris and the prosecutor laid themselves open to a charge of compounding a felony. Equally, in saving the court the bother of dealing with a possibly frivolous allegation, Norris was exercising his discretion in a manner that would almost certainly be applauded rather than condemned by his colleagues on the bench.

Legal technicalities were even more important in the conduct of non-criminal cases, although it is probable that in these at least the justices were able to call on the expertise and advice of their clerk who was almost certainly an attorney.[66] There were occasionally difficulties even in apparently straightforward matters such as compelling payment of the rates (**1096**, **1100**). The major area of difficulty however was probably that created by the application of the settlement laws. The law established very simple categories of entitlement to settlement: birth, servitude, apprenticeship, and payment of parochial taxes. The lives of individuals however were not always ordered quite so neatly, with the result that a vast body of case law had been built up. The majority of Hackney settlement examinations (which survive in a separate volume)[67] reveal complex histories of movement and employment, from which it is often extremely difficult to attribute the correct parish of settlement.

66. For the greater part of the petty sessions book, this was Samuel Sadleir. The later entries (that is, all those from 1751) are by Richard Dann.
67. H.A.D., P/J/P/68.

Any mistake on the part of the justice might lead to further legal action, either in the form of an appeal or in the form of a civil or criminal prosecution. In reality, such actions were extremely rare, but it seems likely that conscientious justices took the possibility extremely seriously. Certainly, the fear of litigation was cited by Sir Thomas de Veil as one of the reasons why it was so difficult to persuade men to become active magistrates.[68] One of the defences he suggested was that justices should keep a detailed account of the business they transacted so that a court could see that they had acted without any malicious or evil intent. As can be seen from these pages, this was advice that Norris had clearly taken to heart.

The work of a justice also required a considerable commitment in terms of time. None of the justices who appear regularly within these pages could be said to have been exceptionally active, especially in terms of criminal business. During the period considered here some half dozen justices shouldered the burden of criminal cases in urban Middlesex. In 1732, over 2000 recognizances were returned to the general/quarter sessions by 78 justices: just under half of them by six exceptionally active justices (Gifford, Hilder, Manley, Mercer, Philips and Robe). Over seventy per cent of the justices returned less than twenty-five recognizances each; twenty-one justices (just over a quarter) returned only one. Henry Norris returned three, Samuel Tyssen none, Alexander Garrett 15, John Oakey 11; Norris, Tyssen and Garrett also co-signed one. In the period covered by these entries, Henry Norris regularly returned between two and six recognizances a year; when he returned more (in 1738 and 1739 there were eight) the figures are distorted by a single case producing multiple recognizances.[69] Yet his notebook shows that even apparently inactive justices might be dealing with complainants at least once a fortnight (and sometimes twice a day), and that he had to reserve one day a week simply for dealing with the parish searcher's affidavits about burials in woollen.[70]

The Hackney petty sessions met at least once a fortnight. It dealt mainly with Hackney business but also occasionally with business arising from neighbouring parishes such as Mile End and Bethnal Green. Although Norris, Ram, Tyssen and Dekewer all lived in Hackney, Robert Paul's principal residence was in Hatton Garden, Mussell lived in Bethnal Green, Alexander and George Garrett in Spitalfields. It is not unreasonable to suppose that just as they were prepared to travel to Hackney, so some of the Hackney justices may also have regularly attended petty sessions elsewhere.

It is likely that Norris and his colleagues were also heavily involved in

68. Sir Thomas de Veil, *Observations on the practice of a justice of the peace intended for such gentlemen as design to act for Middlesex and Westminster* (London, 1747). Norris may well have been familiar with the content of the pamphlet, since it had apparently been circulating in manuscript form for many years before publication.

69. On both occasions a single case produced five recognizances (**279**, **284**).

70. Landau's study of Kent justices similarly shows that documents resulting from returns to the sessions or assizes provide an imprecise and potentially extremely misleading picture of judicial activity. Landau, *Justices*, pp. 177–9, 183.

the work of the divisional sessions: the few surviving records of the local Brewster Sessions suggest that they were indeed extremely active there. They would also attend the quarter/general sessions of the peace, and Alexander Garrett was assiduous in his attendance at the commission of oyer and terminer. All in all, it would not be unreasonable to suggest that these men would have been spending between one and a half and three full days a week purely on justicing business. Nor would this have been the only call on their services: Norris, for example, was also a vestryman, treasurer of the 'unappropriated monies' of the parish, one of the trustees of Dr. Spurstowe's bequest, and a commissioner of the Tower Hamlets Court of Requests. Like his colleagues John Dekewer and George Garrett, he was also a Governor of the London Hospital, a position that was undemanding in terms of committees and meetings but which probably ensured a constant stream of applicants for patronage.

Corruption and partiality

The justices of urban Middlesex and Westminster were renowned for their corruption, but the justices whose activities are chronicled here appear to have been the epitome of magisterial rectitude: indeed, when George Garrett applied to join the Middlesex commission, the chairman of the Bench specifically stated that 'his father and brother (now dead) always behaved well'.[71] Norris's notebook makes it clear that he accepted fees for justicing work: it would have been unusual if he did not. But his level of involvement in criminal business was so low that the amounts involved would have been far too small to arouse suspicion of his motives.[72]

Cross checks to other records confirm that Norris (and, by implication, his colleagues at petty sessions) were scrupulous about the transaction of justicing business. With the one exception of the Scipio case, recognizances were properly certified to the sessions, unless the matter had been agreed, when, in accordance with contemporary practice, they were cancelled. Fines levied for the use of the poor were promptly paid over to the parish.[73]

The way in which Norris processed complaints would also have helped to convince contemporaries of his integrity. His main concern, as has already been pointed out, was to persuade the parties concerned to make up their quarrel or to compound the offence. Discouraging litigation in this way was one of the hallmarks of correct magisterial conduct: one of the reasons that the eighteenth century was one of historically low rates of recorded crime was that justices saw it as their duty to divert

71. B.L., Hardwicke papers, Add. MS. 35603, ff. 229–232.
72. In 1732 they would have amounted to something in the region of 40s. for the work detailed in the notebook. A further £6-£7 would have been paid for all the petty sessions activities. These sums, of course, were technically payable to the clerk rather than to the justice.
73. Some justices (including William Hunt) distributed such sums personally, or permitted the complainant to do so, but Norris ensured that the penalties were paid over to the churchwardens. Crittall (ed), *The justicing notebook of William Hunt*, entries 514, 516, 518, 519, 521, 523–9, 531–2, 534, 537, 540–2, 550, 567, 569; G.L.R.O., P79/JN1/218.

minor cases from the courts rather than to facilitate their progress through the legal system.

Yet to suggest that Norris and his colleagues were not corrupt in the eyes of their contemporaries is not to excuse them from all accusations of partiality. For whatever else they did, these men most certainly did not administer justice impartially. We can learn a great deal about the prejudices and social values they shared simply from the wording of some of the entries. Ordinary people were summoned to appear, whilst those of higher social status were treated rather more politely (**640**). The resolution of an alleged case of horsestealing (a capital felony) depended entirely upon the parish clerk's judgment of the respective characters of plaintiff and defendant (**14**).[74]

Perhaps too we should attempt to see Norris through the eyes of those ordinary individuals who sought to use him to gain access to the legal system. For it must be recognised that Norris's attempts to reconcile disputes often amounted to a denial of such access. And it was a denial with a clear class bias. Norris regularly committed poor men and women to gaol on the flimsiest of evidence, yet when poor people came to him for the protection of the law, he did his best to discourage them, offering them a form of dispute arbitration in its place and forcing those who did wish to take their cases further to enter into extremely high recognizances.[75] What these entries show us more clearly than anything else, is that for Norris, and probably also for most of his colleagues on the bench, there really was one law for the rich and another for the poor.

Note on editorial method

The originals of both documents are held in the Greater London Record Office. The notebook (M79/X/1) formed part of a deposit of Hackney manorial records made in 1961 by Lawrence, Messer and Co., solicitors, on behalf of the then Lord Amherst; it is a stray, and has no connection with the manorial records. The petty sessions book (P79/JN1/214) forms part of a collection of parish records deposited in 1955 by the rector of St. John at Hackney. It includes a number of loose documents, mostly draft settlement examinations and draft minutes. Notebook entries were made in chronological order but Norris left himself sufficient space to fill in details of any subsequent action taken. Occasionally he doubled back to fill large blank spaces, and these entries although out of order have been left in their original positions.

The notebook and petty sessions book have been transcribed in full, except that in the petty sessions entries the signature of the clerk has

74. No one seems to have thought it relevant to ask why the defendant should have been doing business with a man of known bad character in the first place.

75. In most cases, including those destined for the Old Bailey, principals were usually bound in £20 with two additional sureties of £10. It will be noted that although Norris occasionally bound individuals for a lesser sum (**1**, **84**, **193**, **203**, **315**), his standard recognizance was £40 rather than £20 (**30**, **41**, **43**, **48**, **63**, **100**, **110**, **123**, **143**, **218**, **228**, **235**, **241**, **250**, **256**, **273**, **279**, **281**, **305**, **316**, **333**, **348**) and in serious cases rose to £50 (**35**, **76**), £80 (**606**), or even £100 (**45**, **302**).

been removed and the opening rubric has been replaced by a shorter format of place, date and attendance. Additional information has been inserted, where appropriate, from the draft minutes. For the sake of clarity and to save space, all entries (including lists in tabular form) have been rearranged into paragraphs; sub-headings in long lists have been italicized. For the convenience of the reader entries have been numbered.

Surnames and place-names have been left in their original form in the text but for the index place-names have been modernized and surnames are entered in their most frequently used form with variations in parentheses. The names of acting justices have been indexed only where they are mentioned in the body of the text; that is, attendance lists and signatures on informations and recognizances are not indexed. Punctuation, capitalization and abbreviations have been preserved except where adjustments were necessary to facilitate rearrangement.

Dates have been altered to accord with the modern convention of beginning a new year on 1 January; they have also been extended to indicate the day of the week. Repetitions of the date have been uniformly rendered as 'same day'. Unless otherwise indicated, words enclosed in square brackets indicate supplied words or probable readings where the original text is difficult to interpret. Editorial interpolations are additionally indicated by the use of italics. An asterisk represents a marginal tick in the original manuscript.

Both the petty sessions and the notebook volumes appear to have been entered virtually contemporaneously with the events described. They therefore include a large number of alterations and deletions which sometimes indicate an attempt to correct obvious errors, sometimes reflect a more felicitous choice of words, but which also show the development of attitudes and changes of mind on the part of the presiding justices. In order to preserve something of the flavour of the original, such deletions and alterations have been noted in the text. Unless otherwise stated, all manuscript references are to documents in the Greater London Record Office.

The editor would like to thank all those who have helped her in the course of preparing the text for publication. A particular debt of gratitude is owed to the British Academy who financed the project, to Douglas Hay, and to Norma Landau for her generous assistance and advice. The task of working on Hackney is not helped by the somewhat arbitrary division of records between the London Borough of Hackney Archives Department and the Greater London Record Office, and the editor would like to thank the staff of both, particularly Richard Samways and David Mander, for their help in overcoming these problems. She would also like to thank Tim Baker, Norma Landau, David Mander, John Styles and Isobel Watson for their kindness in reading and commenting on the draft introduction. Thanks are also due to Derek Barlow and Malcolm Brown. Last, but most certainly not least, she would like to thank her husband and her mother-in-law, Mary Thompson, for the endless hours of babysitting that freed her to complete the project.

THE JUSTICING NOTEBOOK OF HENRY NORRIS

1. *Monday, 2 February 1730* Midd^{x}:ss. Thomas Martin of ye Parish of S^{t}: Giles in the Fields Joyner bound in £10:- Upon Condition that ye above bound Tho: Martin personally appeareth at the next generall Session of the peace to be held for the County of Middlesex at Hicks hall in St: John Street then & there to answer the complaint of Mnason Cornish, his Apprentice, for misusing his Said Apprentice & in the meantime to be of the good behaviour & not to depart the Court without licence. Then this Recognisance to be void otherwise remain in full force & Virtue. Captat & recog: 2do die Februarij 1730.[1]

1. Martin was discharged at the February sessions. Cornish petitioned for a release from his apprenticeship on grounds of ill treatment but appears to have been unsuccessful. MJ/SBB/880, recog. 176; MJ/SP/1730/FEB/20.

2. *Friday, 28 April 1730* Sent to ye Clerkenwell Bridewell to be put to hard labour Richard Evans, convicted on ye oath of M^{r} [*blank*] Grier Churchwarden, of being a loose disorderly fellow of ill fame & refusing or neglecting to work & making himself burdensome to ye Parish. *Friday, 8 May 1730* Ordered ye Keeper of Clerkenwell Bridewell to discharge Richd Evans if detained for no other cause than my warrant of 28 Ap: last.[1] [*See* **380**].

1. Evans was in receipt of relief from April 1730 to May 1731. P79/JN1/227.

3. *Monday, 25 May 1730* Admitted & Sworn in John Rook Head borough for the precinct of Grovestreet in ye Parish of Hackney.

4. *Saturday, 30 May 1730* Admitted & Sworn in Jno: Wetherhead Constable for ye Parish of Hackney at ye desire of Mr Ryder who was returned for y^{t} office.

5. *Saturday, 20 June 1730* Dan: Baker & Marg: Sly bro^{t}: before me by Warr^{t} of [*blank*] Manly on complaint of Eliz^{a}: Sly ye Wife for keeping comp^{a}: in a vicious manner – & discharged y^{m} both on ye matter being agreed between all ptyes & at ye desire of ye Complainant.

6. *Monday, 31 August 1730* Marget Baldery widow of Tho: Baldery late a weekly Servt: to Mr Malyn a Brewer at St Margarets hill in Southwark maketh oath that her late husband T Baldery did obtain a Legal Settlement in this Parish of Hackney by living wth Mr Emmott as a yearly Servt: upwards of the Space of one year, about 20 years ago, & that her said husband did since acquire no Settlement in any other parish whatsoever, also that her Said husband has been dead about 2 years & that Since her sd husbands death She hath not acquired any Settlement, that She hath by her said husband 3 Children yet living but they are not in any great degree chargeable to her being all out in Service. Marget Baldery [*mark*]. Jurat 31 Aug: Coram Hen: Norris.[1]

1. Baldery began to receive poor relief from the week beginning 24 August 1730. P79/JN1/227, f. 40.

7. *Saturday, 9 January 1731* Joseph Hall brot: before me for Stealing divers Iron instruments & tools ye property's of Wm Stoakes & other persons unknown ye goods being taken upon him by James Huggett Junr: & himself having nothing to alledge in his own behalf nor denying it & it was farther proved by ye oaths of Ja: Huggett Jr: & Wm Stokes. Committed him to Newprison (to be prosecuted by ye Complainants at ye ensuing Quarter Sessions) by Warrt: dd to James Wootton.[1]

1. Hall was acquitted at the January Old Bailey sessions. MJ/SR/2548, Indt. 65.

8. *Saturday, 9 January 1731* Wm Tilly brot. before me by James Wotton & charged on ye Oaths of Mary Stretton & Catherine Stretton on Suspicion of Stealing in ye house of Sd Mary Stretton, a pr: Sheets 13 Pewter plates 4 dishes & other goods abt: 15 months ago the properties of Sd Mary Stretton. Committed him to Newprison to be prosecuted at ye ensuing Sessions by Mary Stretton by Warrant dd to James Wootton & bound over [ye *deleted*] Mary Stretton to prosecute in £20 & Cath: Stretton to be a witness in £10 penalty to [*sic*].[1]

1. Tilly was indicted (as William Tillett) for felony at the January Old Bailey sessions but was acquitted. The *Old Bailey Proceedings* indicate that the acquittal arose from the prosecutor's failure to appear against him, but this is not confirmed by the original records and there appears to have been no attempt to estreat the recognizance. Samuel Sadleir, clerk to the vestry and to the petty sessions, acted on behalf of Mary Stretton, a widow. The cost of the prosecution, amounting to £1 12s. 6d., was borne by the parish, 'she being too poor and unable to prosecute'. MJ/SR/2548, indt. 34; *O.B. Proc.*, January 1731, R *v* William Tilling; P79/JN1/141/109.

9. *Monday, 8 February 1731* Thomasin Wheeler maketh complaint agt: her husband John Wheeler for beating & abusing her being Sick & for denying to assist in the maintenance of her & her Children & threatning her Saying were no more pity to kill her then to kill a dog. Given her a Warrant for her Husband. [*See* **48**, **89**, **119**, **129**, **553**, **560**, **581**, **582**, **680**].

10. *Saturday, 13 March 1731* Edward Beall and Dyson Green brot before me by Jno: Wethered by Warrt: of Tho: Talboy Esq dated 9 March 1731 charged on the Oath of Jno Wethered & James Wootton Viz: Jno Wethered maketh Oath yt Ed. Beall did forcibly rescue Ed. Baker then in Custody of J Wethered for a breach of ye peace & yt Dyson Green did also refuse to assist him ye Officer wn charged & did on ye contrary assist Baker to escape. James Wootton maketh oath that Ed: Beall did assist ye Sd Baker to escape, also yt Dyson Green was by him charged to assist in Securing Ed. Baker but did refuse or neglect to assist in it. Referred

ye matter wth ye consent of ye Officer Roger Rutherford & ye Plaintiffs to be bro^{t} before us next Monday at the Mermaid at Petty Sessions.
Monday, 15 March 1731 The Complain^{ts}: having agreed ye matter wth ye 2 above pties & Jno: Maslin now bro^{t} before me, discharged y^{m} all on promise of good behaviour in future.

11. *Sunday, 21 March 1731* Joseph Stretton bro^{t}: before me by Mary Preston charged by her on Suspicion of Stealing 4 Tablecloths She lost yesterday out of her own backside in Homerton. Mary Preston Says on her Oath y^{t} She lost yesterday between ye hours of 10 & 12, 3 Table Cloths 1 Damask & 2 Diaper from her backside but knows not who took y^{m} but has a Suspicion of Jos: Stretton. Jno: Preston Says he Saw Jos: Stretton in ye adjoining field lying on his face between 11 & 12 but he did not at y^{t} time See ye Cloths [nor a *deleted*] hanging in their place nor can give any reason for charging Stretton wth taking y^{m}. Dismissed Jos: Stretton not finding Sufficient ground to Charge him.

12. *Saturday, 27 [altered from 28] March 1731* Complaint made by Mary Shaves wife of Wm Shaves living at ye Rose in Stratford ag^{t}: Eliz^{a}: Owers for Seducing Wm Shaves her husband & keeping lewd Comp^{a}: wth him in an unlawfull manner & inticing him to consume that Substance wch Should maintain his family upon her to their impoverishm^{t}: wch She the Sd Mary Shaves maketh oath to & thereupon granted her a Warr^{t}: to take her up & bring her before a Magistrate. N.B. Eliz^{a}: Owers is Said to Harbour at Thomas Collies in Well Street.
Same day Eliz^{a}: Owers bro^{t}: before me upon the above warrant Says her name is Eliz^{a}: Owers, y^{t} She is ye wife of Thomas Owers a Labourer to ye bricklayers near Woodford but has not Seen him Since 5 Ap: last acknowledges her Self wth Child & y^{t} by Wm Shaves. Anne Collie maketh Oath y^{t} Eliz^{a}: Owers has lodged in her house near 2/mo: took the Lodging as a Single person by ye name of Eliz^{a}: Dell & lodged there 3 or 4 nights afterwards went to Bow & staid away near 14 d^{s}: & then came back to her lodging & had wth her Edward Watts whom She called her husband who has lived wth her as Such for ab^{t}: 6 weeks. Mary Shaves maketh Oath y^{t} ye S^{d} Eliz^{a}: Owers has Seduced her husband & kept Comp^{a}: wth him in a Lewd manner & Spent his Substance [and] impoverish^{t} his family in Spending his mo: upon ye Sd E: Owers.
Same day Committed ye S^{d} Eliz^{a}: Owers to Clerkenwell Bridewell to be kept to hard Labour till discharged by due course of law.
Wednesday, 21 April 1731 Sent an ord^{r} to ye Keeper of Clerkenwell house of Correction for discharge of the before mentioned Elis^{a}: Owers unless detained for other cause then by virtue of my Commitm^{t}:

13. *Monday, 26 April 1731* Martha Geers complains ag^{t}: her Husband, Rich^{d}: Geers for beating & bruising her last night in a very grievous manner & threatning her life whereof She made oath. Granted her a Warr^{t} to take up ye Sd Richd Geers to answer ye Complaint. Being bro^{t}: before me Same day by [*blank*], Eliz^{a}: Sowter [and] Martha Geers, Sworn. Eliz^{a}: Sowter maketh oath y^{t} Mrs Geers having Shewed her

husband her bruises he Said he had given her too little. Martha Geers on oath confirms her former complaint. Committed Richd Geers to New-prison for want of Sureties.
Tuesday, 27 April 1731 Admitted Sd Geers to Bail and bound Richd Geers £20, Sam: Sadler £10, Jno: Hankin £10, to appear at next Generall Session of the Peace to answer ye complaint of Martha Geers his wife.[1]

1. The recognizance was returned late. Geers, a gardener, appeared 12 July 1731, when the recognizance was respited indefinitely. MJ/SBB/893, recog. 185.

14. *Friday, 7 May 1731* Wm Corn, Tho Fouch, Hen: Rod bro^{t}: pr Warr^{t} Hen: Trent Junr: charged wth taking a Horse bridle Pilch & Pannell[1] fr^{m}: Ja: Mackdonnelld. Ja. Macdonnald makes oath y^{t} he bo^{t}: a horse of Wm Corn 5 May inst: wch was dd him on paying 2:6 earnest & to pay after £2:15 more & y^{t} after ye 3 defend^{ts}: met him wth ye Horse & took him away by force. The Def^{t}: Corn Says y^{t} he did not deliver ye Horse but was to do it only on receiving ye whole mo: Wm Hewson called Says on oath y^{t} ye bargain was treating in his hearing but not concluded only he heard Ja: Mackdonald Say if he agreed for ye Horse he would pay ye mo: down. Tho: Harris on oath Says y^{t} he saw Corn take ye horse by one ear & deliver him into Macdonalds hands. Humphry Wood Swears y^{t} Mr Corn is a man of a very good Character & Ja: Mackdonald a man of a bad Character. Sam: Sadler confirms ye same of each.
Same day Discharged ye 3 Prisoners finding no cause upon ye whole to commit ym.

1. Pilch: a rug for a saddle or a light saddle. Panel: a cloth under a saddle, a crude form of saddle. *O.E.D.*

15. *Thursday, 13 May 1731* Jos: Parsons bro^{t}: before me by Warr^{t}: of H Ashton & Self charged by Mary Main for an assault on Saterday last by Wm Gibbons. Mary wife of Wm Mayne Swears She was assaulted by Jos: Parsons Sat: last Struck wth a Saddle tree & thrown down on ye ground and her Arm very much hurt. Robt: Wild deposes that he Saw not Mr Parsons Strike her but did see him push her down.
Saturday, 15 May 1731 Bound over Jos: Parsons to answer the complaint at next Gen^{ll}: Sessions, himself in £10, Allen Parsons £5 [and] Nath^{a}: Potts £5, Surety's.[1] [*See* **31**].

1. Parsons, a collarmaker, was discharged at the June sessions. MJ/SBB/893, recog. 186.

16. *Tuesday, 6 July 1731* Sarah Crew complains ag^{t} Jno Annable for abusing & assaulting her last week twice & last Sunday, & in a grievous manner throwing dirt at her & drink in her face. Granted a Warr^{t}: for him.

17. *Saturday, 24 July 1731* Complaint made by Sibella Hunt of Hummerton y^{t} was Stoln fr^{m}: her yesterday out of her house a Cop^{r}: Coffee pot & A box Iron wch She Suspects may be concealed in ye lodging of Widow Parsons or Mr Loyd or Mr Bennett. Granted her a Search warr^{t}:

18. *Friday, 6 August 1731* Complaint made by [Benj^{a}: *deleted*] Wm Brown ag^{t}: Job Everton for assaulting him 31 July last & threatned his life. On oath made granted him a Warr^{t}: to take up Job Everton.
Saturday, 7 August 1731 Discharged ye Warr^{t}: ye matter being agreed between them.

19. *Thursday, 12 August 1731* Complaint made by Jane Ross ag^{t}: Eleanor [*blank*] Servt: maid to Francis Crette for asssaulting her & throwing a Pewter pot & bruising her in breach of ye peace – &c on ye 9 Aug: Granted a warr^{t}: for her.

20. *Monday, 23 August 1731* Complaint made by Jane Ramsey Widow ag^{t}: Joseph Butterfeild for assaulting her throwing her on ye ground & throwing water upon her in breach of ye peace – this morning near her own house – granted her a warr^{t} for him.

21. *Monday, 23 August 1731* Bro^{t}: before me Jos: Brett charged by Jno Coules for running away fr^{m}: Rumford & leaving wth y^{m} a Child to maintain. Discharged him on his promise in future to take care of his child & wth consent of Jno Coules one of the Overseers in behalf of ye Parish of Rumford.

22. *Saturday, 28 August 1731* Complaint made by Math. Walter & Sam. Leader ag^{t}: Jacob Hales gardner to Mr Lamb for taking unlawfully the fruit growing in Mr Lambs Garden wch fruit they bo^{t}: of the Said Jacob Hales. They charge him wth taking Peaches & Nectarines & pduce Roger Rutherford as witness, who wth ye others being Sworn, Rutherford says y^{t} Jacob Hales in his Sight has Severall times taken peaches & Nectarines & encouraged him Rutherford to do ye like. Granted y^{m} a Warr^{t} ag^{t}: Jac: Hales.
Same day On hearing ye Cause advised Hales to make them Satisfaction (it not appearing a felony) wch was done, & ye Def^{t}: discharged. [*See* **52**].

23. *Saturday, 28 August 1731* Ed: Bullock bro^{t}: before me in Cust^{o}: of Hen: Batt, charged by Jno: Collins on oath with profane Swearing twice this day between 3 & 6 a Clock by the name of God – in Marestreet, not denied by Bullock & is convicted of the same.
Same day Issued a Warr^{t}: to the Constables of Bethnal green Hamlet to levy on him 2^{s} for use of ye poor of Hackney or Sett him in ye Stocks 2 hours.

24. *Tuesday, 14 September 1731* Complaint made by Hamilton Smith ag^{t}: Thomas Batmaker, Nicholas Batmaker & John Batmaker for assaulting him last night ab^{t}: 6 at ye Kings Arms in Kingsland in ye Yard beating kicking him & bruising him in [peac *deleted*] breach of ye peace. Granted him a Warr^{t}. for all 3. [*See* **26**].

25. *Tuesday, 14 September 1731* Complaint made by Nicholas Brown ag^{t}: Thomas Holt for Striking him wth a Cartwhip & wth his hand & abusing him [*and*] ag^{t}: George Howe for beating him & dragging him by ye Leg into ye Road in breach &c. last night ab^{t}: 8 or 9 in Kingsland near ye door of his Father Ludlow Brown. Granted a Warr^{t} for [all 3 *deleted*] y^{m} both.
Saturday, 18 [altered from 19] September 1731 On hearing of Tho: Holt, Nich^{o}: Brown confirms by Oath ye abuses from Tho: Holt – but Holt Says Brown [struck *deleted*] flung dirt 1st. Dan. Welmoth says on his Oath y^{t} Brown flung dirt or gravell at Holt before he Struck him. Mary Lodge Swears y^{t} Brown flung dirt 1st but contradicts her Self. Sus: Batmaker Says likewise but it appeared y^{t} She did not See ye beginning. Upon ye whole it Seemed to me y^{t} Holt was ye aggressor but reccommended y^{m} to make it up wch they did & N Brown acknowledged to have recd Satisfaction from G Howe So I discharged both ye Def^{ts}:

26. *Saturday, 18 September 1731* Complaint made by Hamilton Smith ag^{t}: Tho: Batmaker, Nich^{o} Batmaker & John Batmaker for assaulting him on Monday 13:7ber in ye yard of ye Kings Arms in Kingsland, & beating him in a Severe manner. Granted a Warr^{t}: for y^{m}.
Thursday, 23 September 1731 (1) Hamilton Smith, Jno Ellitt, Nic^{o} Brown, Ludlow Brown, Susan Ellitt. (1) swears y^{t} on 13:7ber he was assaulted by Tho: Batmaker J^{r}: & y^{t} Nich & Jno Batmaker assisted him confirmed by the other witnesses. Rich^{d}. Chapman & others called in behalf of ye Def^{ts}: but after a long hearing they agreed the matter & ye Warr^{t}: was discharged. [*See* **24**].

27. *Sunday, 17 October 1731* Mary Mayne bro^{t}: by [*blank*] Collins on complaint of Tho: Blemeney charged by him for abusing him & his wife in words & Striking him Severall blows confirmed by his Oath & likewise by the Oath of Richd Marsland.

28. *Sunday, 17 October 1731* Jos: Butterfield bro^{t}: in by D^{o} & charged by Jos: Cooper on Suspicion of Stealing a Saddle last night but nothing appeared Sufficient to charge him So dismissed him.

29. *Monday, 1 November 1731* Tho: Griffis bro^{t}: before me 1:9ber 1731 in Custody of Hen: Batt charged on oath by Tho: Wood wth having been found last night on ye footpath wth 3 p^{cs}: of wood in a bag upon him between 6 & 7 a clock wch p^{cs}: are Sworn to be ye property of Jno: Townsend by himself, & a 4th p^{ce}: wood was found at his Lodgings in Sam. Fenners house wch is proved to be J Townsends & beleived to be bro^{t}: thither before. Upon full hearing committed him to Bridewell to hard Labour.
Monday, 8 November 1731 Sent by his wife a Warr^{t} for his discharge.

30. *Tuesday, 2 November 1731* Tho: Cooke bro^{t}: before M^{r} S: Tyssen me by Warr^{t}: of our Selves 29:8ber, the Peace being Sworn ag^{t}: him by James Bolton. Tho: Cooke of ye Parish of Hackney bound in his own recognisance in £40 to appear at next Gen^{ll} Sessions of ye Peace to answer complaint of James Bolton for threatning his Life &c mean time to keep ye Peace &c & be of ye good behaviour &c. N.B. was bound in his own recognisance alone wth consent of ye Plaintiff.[1] [*See* **365**].

1. Cooke, a labourer, failed to appear to his recognizance at the December sessions and it was estreated. MJ/SBB/897, recog. 212.

31. *Tuesday, 2 November 1731* Complaint made by Jos^{ph}: Parsons ag^{t}: Wm Mayne for threatning to kill him 30:8ber & thereupon desire Warr^{t}: ag^{t}: to take Surety for ye peace. Granted a Warr^{t}: on his taking ye usuall Oath.[1] [*See* **15**].

1. Mayne, a labourer, was indicted 6 November 1731 and entered into a recognizance before Samuel Tyssen two days later. He was convicted and fined 1s. in January 1732. MJ/SR/2564, recog. 213 and indt. 21.

32. *Thursday, 18 November 1731* Geo: Hobb bro^{t}: in Custody of Ludlow Brown chgd by Sarah Arnold for assaulting her on ye high road & throwing her into a Ditch. She acknowledging her Self to have recd Satisfaction ordered him to be discharged.

33. *Monday, 6 December 1731* Jno: Parmer & Henry Chandler bro^{t} in Custody of Wm Davis Constable each on a charge of breach of the peace also Jno Maslin on a like charge by ye other 2. It appearing that they had agreed ye matter between themselves ordered them to be discharged.

34. *Monday, 13 December 1731* Complaint made by Hannah Preston ag^{t}: her husband Edward Preston for Spending his mo: Idly & neglecting to maintain his family, being a wife & 2 Children & threatning his wife. Made out a Warr^{t}: for him on ye wifes oath & ordered to bring him next monday to the Mermaid. [*See* **87**].

35. *Tuesday, 1 February 1732* Thomas Faxton, & Thomas Smith bro^{t}: before me by Geo: Fowler, [Constable *deleted*] Headborough & charged by Wm Davis on Oath That last night Soon after nine [coming *deleted*] going on ye Hackney road from [Lon *deleted*] Hackney to Lond^{o}: [he w *deleted*] between ye Shoulder of mutton & y^{e} Watch house he was met by Said Faxton & Smith who with great threats demanded his money, & thereupon he dd to Smith w^{t} mo: he had in his pocket wch was 4^{D} in a Silver peece & about 5^{D} or $5\frac{1}{2}^{D}$ halfpence. That Faxton had a drawn knife in his hand. That Smith took his hat from him & returned him his own in place of it. That after parting from them & going forward to London he met wth Mr Rich^{d}: Wingfeild & Mr John Oswald the Master of the Shoulder of mutton wth 2 dogs 2 Mastifs w was [aft ab^{t}: $\frac{1}{2}$ an hour *deleted*] 3 or 4 minutes after he was robbed & gave them an acco^{t}: of his being robbed & wth them returned towards y^{e} mutton to look for y^{e}

thieves but did not find them. In answer to this Faxton Says that he is a Seaman & he was at Newington at the 3 Crowns & came at $\frac{1}{2}$ an hour past 8 & Staid there 2$\frac{1}{2}$ hours or 3 & drank there in Comp^{a}: wth Smith alone & came from thence ab^{t}: 11 a Clock & past over Severall fields & called at a house & drank again & then were going on their road to London & were met by 2 men who took them up on Suspicion of a Robbery & farther He says he went from London [to *deleted*] abt: 7 a clock Strait to the 3 Crowns at Newington & went into no other house before he came thither. He Says y^{t} he & Smith met in Hollywell Lane at a private house ab^{t}: $\frac{1}{2}$ an hour past 6 at night & had not been together yesterday before. T: Smith ex^{a}: apart Says y^{t} he is a Stocking weaver & he was wth Faxton at 3 Crowns at Newington that they went from Lond^{o} between 7 & 8 to y^{e} 3 Crowns at Newington & Staid there ab^{t}: 1$\frac{1}{2}$ hour, & thence came to Hackney to a house wch he does not know & went in & drank & Staid about 1$\frac{1}{2}$ hour or 2 hours & thence were going to Lond^{o}: & were met by 2 men who took them up on Suspicion. He says that he & Faxton were together all day yesterday that they met at 7 a Clock in y^{e} morning & kept together y^{e} whole day till they were taken up that they first met together at the black Dog in Shoreditch. Brian Oram & Richard Wingfield, Sworn. B Oram Says that coming from London about 11 a Clock & being informed of the robbery & having a description of ye persons, being in Comp^{a}: wth Wingfeild & a large Mastiff wth them near the mutton they met 2 men whom they challenged & Siezed Suspecting them to be the persons who had done ye Robbery. They took ye hat of Smiths head & told him they beleived it was ye Same Hat wch was taken from ye pson robbed, that it was however returned to Smith again & that in Mutton lane, Smith threw ye hat on ye ground & [did *deleted*] would leave it there, but he B Oram took it up again. All wch was confirmed by Rich. Wingfeild. Wm Davis on oath Says that the Hat produced & now taken by force from Th^{o}: Smith is as he verily beleives the Same Hat taken from him last night on ye Road. Upon ye whole Committed them by Warr^{t}: to Newga: for Robbery. Tho: Faxton after mittimus made did acknowledge that they together committed ye Robbery & y^{t} he was instigated thereto by Tho: Smith. Tho: Smith on hearing him confess was in great Rage & Said he knew himself Should be hanged for it but y^{t} Faxton Should dye wth. him or to yt effect. He had Said in relation to ye Hat y^{t} it was his own & cost him lately 10^{s}: 6^{D}. whereas Davis Said it cost him w^{n} bo^{t}: but about 5^{s}:6^{D} wch on ex^{a}: ye Hat Seemed most likely.

Same day Wm Davis of Virginia Row in Bethnall green Hamlet Weaver Bound in £50 Penalty. Brian Oram of the Parish of Hackney Gent: [and] Richard Wingfeild Servt: to Randall Beck Victualler at ye Kings head Virginia Row in Bethnall green Hamlet bound each in £20, Geo: Fowler Headborough of Hackney bound in £20, John Dennis Servt: to Mr Shaw [ye Smith *deleted*] of the Parish of Hackney Smith in £20, all by Recogn: To Appear at Hicks hall next Gen^{ll}: Sessions, Old baily &c the first as Prosecutor the other as witnesses ag^{t}: Tho: Faxton & Tho: [Davis *deleted*] Smith & put the Hat into Custody of Geo: Fowler ye Headborough.[1] [*See* **453**, **469**].

1. Faxton and Smith were found guilty at the Old Bailey later that month and sentenced to death. Apart from Faxton's confession, the prosecution case rested solely on identification evidence (both of the highwaymen and of the hat). A number of prosecution witnesses testified that Faxton had been advised to confess in the hope of being admitted an evidence for the crown, but Norris stated that to the best of his knowledge Faxton had made his confession voluntarily and without inducement. Because a proclamation was in force (see introduction) an additional £200 was added to the statutory reward of £80 and distributed as follows: William Davis £16; Brian Oram £70; Richard Wingfeild £70; William Clarke £8; John Dennis £8; George Fowler £8; John Davis £8; Moses Morris £6; John Boustrell £6. There is a particularly full account of the trial in the *Old Bailey Proceedings*, but it casts no light on the reason for rewards to Morris and Boustrell (unless they had been involved in imprisoning the two men overnight). MJ/GBB/312, 140, 145; *O.B. Proc.*, February 1732, R *v* Faxton and Smith.

36. *Saturday, 5 February 1732* John Burch living in Bishopsgate Street in the City of London Driver of a Wheel Barrow with Fruit & Wm Benson of the Parish of Lambeth in the County of Surry Waterman bro^t^: by Jno. Collins headborough and charged by Thomas Vintry of S. Giles without Cripplegate Middx Painter for assisting two Persons unknown in assaulting beating & bruising him in breach of his peace. They not appearing to be the persons that Committed the assault were discharged from that Compl^t^. Nehemiah Ring of the Parish of St Mary Aldermary in the City of London Baker sayes on his Oath as he was coming from London to Hackney on Saturday last between twelve & one of the clock at noon of the same day several others persons with the Prisoners Jno Burch & W^m^. Benson were at an Orange Barrow and Induced him to lay several sumes of money & by false and subtle Arts by playing or using of Dice defrauded him of Eleven Guineas & some Silver and upon his threatening to cause them to be sent to Newgate he got his money again. W^m^. Edwards on his Oath declared that a few dayes ago he saw the two Prisoners gameing at a Wheel Barrow in the foot way leading from London to Hackney. Adjudged Vagrants & Committed to the house of Correction till severally discharged by due course of Law.[1]

1. There was insufficient evidence to convict Burch and Benson of unlawful gaming. Under 1 George I c28 a conviction required the sworn testimony of two or more credible witnesses for each offence.

37. *Monday, 20 March 1732* Complaint made on Oath by Rebecca Carr ag^t^: John Price, M^r^ of ye Dolphin Alehouse at Kingsland for assaulting & beating & wounding Stephen Carr Labourer [last night *deleted*] [*blank*] & Thomas Usher,[1] whose name She does not know. Granted her a Warrant for Jno Price.

Same day Before [me *deleted*] Sam: Tyssen Esq & me, Rebecca Carr & Thomas Usher make oath that John Price assaulted beat & wounded Sd Thomas Usher last night in Kingsland Road without any provocation. Remanded Jno: Price in Custody of ye Officer Ludlow Brown promising to bring Sureties in ye morning for his appearance at ye Sessions. [*See* **38**, **39**, **530**].

1. Usher's name has probably been inserted later.

38. *Tuesday, 21 March 1732* Before Sam: Tyssen Esq & me. Stephen Carr brot: before us by Edwd Cooper on Mr Tyssens warrt for assaulting Jno: Price in his own house & Striking him on Sunday last. Which was proved by ye Oath of Jno: Price.[1] [*See* **37**, **39**].

1. Carr and his wife Elizabeth were convicted at the April sessions of assaulting John Price and fined 1s. Usher was indicted on the same charge but not tried – probably because he was too ill (see **530**). James Martin was listed amongst the witnesses against them (see **46**). MJ/SR/2572, indt. 19.

39. *Tuesday, 21 March 1732* Wm Pugh at ye Wt Horse in little Britain in ye Parish of St: Botolph Aldersgate [and] Thomas Jones of ye Parish of St: Bride's Tobacconist Sureties for John Price. Jno: Price bound in £100 of Kingsland in Parish Hackney Victualler. Wm Pugh [and] Tho: Jones each 50 to appear at ye next Genll: Quarter Sessions to answer the Complaint of Tho: Usher for assaulting beating & wounding him in a grievous manner.[1] [*See* **37**, **38**, **489**, **498**, **530**].

1. Price was convicted and fined 1s. on 23 May 1732. MJ/SR/2572, indt. 84.

40. *Monday, 27 March 1732* Complaint made by Anne Foster upon Oath agt Joseph Scholar for Insulting her at divers times & assaulting her this day in ye house of her Mistress, Mrs Holworthy & also at other times. Granted her a Warrt: for him.

41. *Sunday, 23 April 1732* John Davis of Limehouse Caulker complaineth agt: Jno: Jervase, & Joseph Hill wth 3 others Strangers for attacking him in ye Road of Clapton, assaulting beating & bruising him & tearing his Cloths without any provocation given. Upon his oath thereof made, granted him a warrt: for ye 2 persons.
Monday, 24 April 1732 & on his bringing Joseph Hill on ye 24 Aprill bound over [Jos *deleted*] Joseph Hill of Hackney Victualler in £40, Ralph Meridith of Do Gardner 20, John Sandford of Do Do 20. To appear at the next Generall Sessions of ye Peace to be held at Hicks hall to answer ye complaint of John Davis for assaulting & beating him in breach of his Majesties peace & in ye mean time to be of the good behaviour &c.[1]

1. Hill was discharged at the May sessions. MJ/SBB/901, recog. 156.

42. *Thursday, 4 May 1732* Wm Stanley brot: before me by Rob: Loyd Constable by Warrt: of Rd: Manly Esq for assaulting Mary Stern beating & taking away by force Some Cloths wch it Seems he had bot: for her as his Servt. Upon his allegation yt ye matter was agreed between him & Mary Stern & ye Same confirmed by ye Oath of Rob: Loyd who was present at ye agreemt: made, discharged him out of Custody.

43. *Tuesday, 9 May 1732* Jane Whitehead brot: by ye Beadle [*blank*] Harrill a child of 10 years of age complained of Marget Thomson at ye Cock ale house in Church Street for assaulting her last night wth a Quart pewter pot & wounding her in ye head in a grievous manner whereby She came to be much bruised & lost a great deal of blood. It appeared by ye testimony on Oath of Eleanor Sherrard who together wth Sarah Fletcher neighbours came wth the child that the child was last night after receiving the hurt bro^{t}: into [her *deleted*] E Sherrards house by Mrs Bennett in that wounded condition Stunned & Senseless & the Said Mrs Bennett declared She bro^{t}: the child thither for Shelter lest She Sh^{d} be knocked on ye head by Marget Thomson who at other times has used the child very ill as She declares & last Sunday burned her in a cruell manner in the neck & the marks yet remaining. Granted a warrant ag^{t}: Marg: Thomson & put it into the hand of [*blank*] Harrill to execute. *Friday, 12 May 1732* Baile for the above named Margaret Thompson: James Thompson of Hackney Vict^{r} in £40, Charles Gosdin of the same Vict^{r} £20, John Everratt of Norton Falgate Distiller 20. Upon Condition That Margaret the wife of James Thompson personally appeareth at the next General Sessions of the Peace to be held for the County of Middlesex at Hicks-hall in S^{t}. John Street, to answer Jane Whitchead an Infant for Assaulting beating & wounding her and in the mean time to be of the good behaviour &c.[1]

1. Margaret Thompson failed to appear at the May sessions, and her recognizance was ordered to be estreated. The order was rescinded when she later excused herself by reason of illness. She was finally discharged 9 October 1732. MJ/SBB/901, recog. 157.

44. *Tuesday, 16 May 1732* Mary Uppington & Laetitia Beeston of Cambridge heath Complain ag^{t}: a bad house kept in Cambridge heath by Thomas Baxter at ye Tobacco Roll & Sugar loaf where they Sell Spirits & as is Supposed without a Licence. [*See* **536**].

45. *Saturday, 3 June 1732* Jane Grew bro^{t}: before me by Lewis Nouzille charged by Catherine Brown for Stripping off the Cloths of her child John Brown an infant of 22 months old. She Cath: Brown Says on Oath y^{t} last Thursday afternoon She left her infant Jno Brown wth Anne Grew mother of Jane Grew ab^{t}: 1 a Clock & at 7 a clock She came to look for her child again in y^{e} [house *deleted*] room of Anne Grew who lives in Same h^{o}: wth Cath: Brown but did not find her child but was informed by Anne Grew y^{t} her Daughter Jane had carryed the child away, & she could hear nothing of her child till next morning between 7 & 8 when She was informed it was found in a house of office by Marget Paine & upon Seing [*sic*] it She found ye Child very ill & Stripped of a Poplin Skirt of a Coat a linnen frock & a yard of new dimity being a Cloth pinned before it wch She Suspects were taken away by Jane Grew who in her hearing acknowledged to have taken them away from y^{e} person of y^{e} Child & acquainted her that She had pawned y^{e} Skirt at a Chandlers Shop in Ram Alley Spitall fields for $\frac{3}{4}^{D}$ for a half Q^{r} Ginn wch She drank there, & sold y^{e} frock in rag fair for 6^{D}. & pawn'd y^{e} dimity for 1^{D}. That She desired Jane Grew to go wth her to the S^{d} Shop & there She actually found the Skirt wch was produced to me wch I committed to the Custody of y^{e} Officer. NB was found in ye Shop of Mr Alexander was dd them by the wife who recd it fr^{m}: ye prisoner. Jane Grew replyed that She was in drink when She was out with the child on ye sd Thursday & it then had on the Cloths charged by ye Mother. She Says She lay her Self in the necessary house where the child was found, She denyes She knows how the child lost its cloths. Sarah Pantling of Wheeler Str^{t}: Spitall fields her husband a porter, Mathew Baker, New Geo: Str^{t}: weaver Bethnall green [and] Samuel Michon Church Strt: D^{o} Do Sworn. Sarah Pantling says y^{t} being desired by Cath. Brown to look out for Jane Grew She did go wth her & they found her in a brandy Shop & charged her wth taking the Cloths fr^{m}: ye Child & She acknowledged the taking them & Said She would help y^{m} to y^{m} again & accordingly carryed y^{m} to a Chandlers Shop in Ram alley where [it *deleted*] ye skirt was found. Math: Baker confirms her owning ye taking ye goods from ye Child & pawning ye Skirt as above & y^{t} it was there found. Sam: Michon Says y^{t} ye prisoner owned to him the taking ye dimity apron from ye Child and y^{t} She had [pawned *deleted*] left it at a Chandlers Shop in Hare Street but could not tell him their name. In hearing ye whole matter committed the prisoner to Newgate. Bound over Catherine Brown of Bethnall green Silkwinder in new Geo: Street bound in £100 to prosecute, Sarah Pantling 50 to give evidence, Math: Baker 50 to D^{o} [and] Samuell Michon 50 to D^{o}.[1]

1. Jane Grew, alias Le Grew, was accused of stealing clothing worth 2s. 9d. at the Old Bailey sessions in July. She was convicted of stealing to the value of 10d. and sentenced to transportation. MJ/GBB/313, 8.

46. *Sunday, 4 June 1732* Stephen Carr bro^{t}: before me by James Martin Headborough charged by Ludlow Brown on Oath for assaulting him in his own house & Striking him on ye breast. James Martin on Oath Says y^{t} he was called to Mr Ludlow Browns house to keep the peace that on his entrance he produced his Staff & meeting Carr he Pricked him in the hand wth a Pitchfork & gave him a grievous wound. Referred him to come tomorrow to ye Mermaid to us to bring Security mean time to rem^{a}: in Custody. [*See* **543**, **552**].

47. *Monday, 12 June 1732* Middx.ss Joseph Read of the Parish of S^{t}. John at Hackney in the County of Middlesex Gentleman maketh Oath that on Monday the 5th of this Instant June one Samuel Fenner was Drunk in the said parish. [*signed*] Joseph Read. Jurat 12° die Junij 1732, Coram me, [*signed*] Henry Norris.[1]
[blank] June 1732 Issued a warr^{t}: to the Officers of ye Parish to levy a fine of 5^{s} on ye goods of ye sd S Fenner for his offence of being drunk, according to act of Parliam^{t}.

1. Apart from the signature, the preceding part of this entry is not in Norris's hand.

48. *Monday, 12 June 1732* Thomasin Wheeler of Cambridge Heath complains ag^{t}: her husband John Wheeler for assaulting her & beating her in an unmercifull manner & threatning her life & neglecting to provide for the Support of his wife & [fam *deleted*] 2 Children. Granted a Warrant for him.
Same day On hearing ye cause, committed him to New prison by Warr^{t} from Mr S. Tyssen & me for want of Sureties for his appearance at ye next Q^{r} Sessions to answer ye assault.

Sunday, 25 June 1732 Ordered him J Wheeler to be discharged out of Custody – [the *deleted*] at desire of his wife in her hope of his amendm^{t}.[1] [*See* **9**, **89**, **119**, **129**, **553**, **560**, **581**, **582**, **680**].

1. For the difficulties arising out of Wheeler's commitment see **553**, **560**.

49. *Monday, 21 August 1732* James Thompson of Church Str^{t}: complains ag^{t}: Miles Preston for assaulting him & his wife Margaret Thompson last Thursday 17th Aug: ab^{t}: 7 in ye evening at or near his own door in the footway. Granted him a warr^{t}: on his Oath made.

50. *Saturday, 26 August 1732* Thomas Harrison of Aldersgate Street Gent: complains ag^{t}: Wm Bailis at ye Red lion in Marestreet for assaulting him in ye House of ye Red Lyon beating him & bruising him wth his fist last night ye 25th Aug: Granted a warr^{t}: [there *deleted*] upon Oath thereof made to arrest W Bailis.

51. *Saturday, 9 September 1732* Complaint made by Protheesar Palmer ag^{t}: her Husband John Palmer for threatning her life & turning her out of doors & refusing & neglecting to Provide any Support or maintenance for her tho he is able to do. Granted her a Warr^{t}: for him.

52. *Friday, 15 September 1732* Complaint made by Jacob Hayes, Gardner to James Lamb Esq y^{t} there has lately been Stoln from ye out Houses of Sd Lamb a parcell of Lead about 1 [*illegible*] also out of his garden Two pots of Mirtle Plants Vall: about 4^{s} & y^{t} he Suspects [ye some *deleted*] ye goods or p^{t}: thereof are in ye House or gardens belonging to Matthew Waters in London field in ye pish of S^{t}: Jno at Hackney in ye Co: of Midd^{x}. Granted a Search Warr^{t}: to Search Waters house & Garden. *Same day* Math: Waters being bro^{t}: by [*blank*] Harrill Headb^{o}: [Jac. *deleted*] & a Pot of Mirtles wth y^{m} Jac. Hayes affirmed [they were *deleted*] y^{t} it was one of ye Pots Stolen away as above. Thomas Shepperdson [and] Andrew Grindley make oath that they each of them have Seen the Same Pot in Mr Waters garden for a month past whereas ye Pots were not lost above 2 or 3 d^{s} at most. Upon ye whole discharged the Warrant not finding cause to charge Waters. NB it was acknowledged by both Sides y^{t} Waters had bo^{t}: a Pot of Mirtles of Hayes 2 or 3 months before & Waters alledge this is ye Same Pot wch on ye whole seems very likely. *Tuesday, 19 September 1732* Matthew Waters bro^{t}: by Wm Griffis Headb^{o}: taken up by Warr^{t} of Th^{o}: Robe Esqr on Suspicion of Stealing a Pot mirtles from Jacob Hays ye pperty of Ja. Lamb Esqr but no prosecutor appearing & ye Headborough making Oath that he had given notice to Jacob Hays but he refused to attend, discharged ye Prisoner, & the rather in regard it appeared to be on the matter beforementioned.
NB on a tryall at ye Old Bailey 12th 8ber 1732 of Math. Waters for ye Supposed theft of ye Pot of Mirtles it was Sworn by Jac. Hayes Servt: that there had been 6 Pots only of Mirtles whereof one only was Stolen & 5 remained wch is contrary to w^{t} was Sworn before me of 15:7ber by Jacob Hayes who then Swore to the loss of 2 Pots.[1] [*See* **22**].

1. After his discharge by Norris, Waters was taken before Sir William Billers and entered into a recognizance to answer the same charge. He was acquitted at the Old Bailey in October and the jury granted him a copy of his indictment (see introduction). No attempt by Waters to bring an action for malicious prosecution has been traced in the records of the King's Bench (Crown Side). MJ/SBB/904, recog. 98; MJ/GBB/313, 40; *O.B. Proc.*, October 1732, R *v* Waters.

53. *Monday, 2 October 1732* James Bishop bro^{t}: by ye Beadle Mr Harrill to give an acco^{t}: of his Settlem^{t}: aged near 17 declares on Oath y^{t} he has been informed & beleives y^{t} he was born in ye Parish of S^{t}: Margaret Westminster y^{t} his Fathers name was James Bishop his Mothers name Mary Bishop, that his father & Mother both lived in ye S^{d} Parish that they both lived in a House of £10 pr ann: as he has heard his Mother Say y^{t} his Father died when he was ab^{t} a year old, & his Mother ab^{t}: 6 years, Thatt when his Mother was Sick & unable to provide for them She received Alms from ye Sd Parish & afterwards She put her Sd Son into ye Workh^{o}: in the Sd Parish where he remained near a year & then went out to a Chimney Sweeper upon liking but was not bound, he Staid wth him only ab^{t} 6 wks & then run away, & Since has gained no Legall Settlem^{t}: [1]

1. James Bishop was indigent. He was removed later that day by order of Henry Norris and Samuel Tyssen to the parish of St. Margaret, Westminster. The order was overturned on appeal to the sessions later that month. MJ/SP/1732/OCT, f. 59, 60; MJ/SBB/904, p. 45.

54. *Saturday, 14 October 1732* James Mackgill bro^{t}: before me by Wm Davis Headb^{o}: charged by Edwd: Twist (Surveyor of Hawkers & Pedlars) of S^{t}: Andrews Holborn Gent., for trading without Licence as a Hawker & Pedlar on Wednesday ye 11th: 8ber between ye hours of 10 & 4 afternoon & exposing to Sale a parcell of Linnen Cloth in ye Parish of S^{t}: John at Hackney. Upon my demand he produced a Licence dated 23 June last, but ye Officers alledged it was taken out only this morning, & he did not offer any proof that he had it on the 11th but I adjourned ye determination till next Monday.
Monday, 16 October 1732 On a farther hearing ordered a Warr^{t}: of distress to be dr^{n}: to Levy £12 on ye goods of ye Sd James Macgill for trading as a Hawker &c & not having a Licence at ye time of his So trading & to put ye Same Warr^{t} into ye hands of Wm Davis Headb^{o}: to be applyed as ye Act of Parlaim^{t} [*sic*] directs.
Saturday, 14 October 1732 Midd^{x}:ss: The information of Edward Twist Surveyor of Hawkers & Pedlars &c made before me Henry Norris Esqr one of his Majesties Justices of the Peace for the Sd County who [upon oath *deleted*] Saith that James Macgill was on Wednesday ye 11th October 1732 between the hours of ten & four of the Said day in the Parish of S^{t}: John at Hackney in the Said County, found going from house to house & trading as a Hawker Pedlar or petty Chapman & that he the Said James Macgill did then & there carry to Sell & expose to Sale a parcell of linnen Cloth & that he the Said James Macgill did not although required so to do produce any Licence as the law (in that case

made & provided) directs to qualifye him for his so trading. [*signed*] Edwd Twist.
Edward Barnett one other of the Surveyors as aforesaid maketh oath that the above mentioned information is true & that he was then there present & did see the Sd James Mackgill trading as in the information is mentioned & that he the Sd James Macgill did not produce any License although demanded as aforesaid. [*signed*] Edward Barnett. Jurat 14° die Octobris 1732 Coram me Henry Norris.[1]

1. Under 3 & 4 Anne c4 refusal to show a licence on demand was tantamount to trading without one, and punishable as such.

55. *Friday, 10 November 1732* Mary Bouncer complains ag^{t}: W^{m}Platt a Headborough for assaulting her last Tuesday in the house of Anne Gilman beating & bruising her without any provocation given of wch She made Oath. Granted a Warr^{t}: for him.

56. *Monday, 13 November 1732* Henry Tewson bro^{t}: by Robt: Loyd Headb^{o}: chgd by Wm Cattlin for taking Some p^{cs}: of Iron work out of his Stable near London field this day at noon of Small Vallue under 1^{s} wch he Tewson acknowledged to be true. Sent him to Clerkenwell Bridewell to be put to hard labour.[1]

1. The value of the stolen goods was crucial to that charge, which in this instance amounted to misdemeanour only. Stealing goods to the value of 5s. or more in a stable was a capital felony.

57. *Monday, 4 December 1732* Frances Low complains ag^{t}: Tho: Clark Gardner to Mr Wildey for assaulting kicking beating & bruising her in a barbarous manner on ye 16 9ber last whereby She is now unable to do her business done in Mr Wildeys house in Clopton as She makes oath. Granted a warr^{t}: for him.
Tuesday, 5 December 1732 Thomas Clark bro^{t}: in Custody of Wm Davis & charged on Oath by Frances Low wth assaulting her 16:9ber last being thursday Striking her twice & Kicking her 4 times on ye Hips & ye belly & She has yet 2 bruises yet to be Seen & a pain in her belly wch She apprehends to arise from one of ye Kicks. Tho: Clark in his defence alledges y^{t} She Struck at him first wth a fireshovell but he defended ye blow wth his arm & then did Strike & Kick her. Alex^{a}: McClean called by ye def^{t}: Says he was present & y^{t} Fr: Low did offer to Strike ye def^{t}: 1st but it does not appear to me y^{t} She did Strike him. On y^{e} whole they agreed y^{e} matter & She acknowledged to have recd Satisfaction for y^{e} Injury & I discharged the warrant.

58. *Tuesday, 5 December 1732* Wm Heath bro^{t}: by Wm Griffiths, Head: chgd by Martha Plummer on Oath wth robbing her of $3\frac{1}{4}^{D}$ in Copper mo: & a bundle of Child bed linnen & other things, in [y^{e} deleted] a field behind Brook house upon y^{e} footpath. that he also drew a knife threatning to Stick her & also Struck her down on wch She cryed out murder & assistance came & he was taken. Henry Hurst makes oath y^{t} on [*deletion*] hearing Murder cryed he run to ye place & found ye Prisoner a few

yds from ye woman yt he had a bundle in his hand wch he then flung away, yt it was between 3 & 4 this day. Jno Bracey makes Oath yt he heard an Outcry & made for ye place where he Saw ye woman there & ye prisoner running off. Jno Wells makes oath yt on hearing an outcry he run to ye place but ye man was gone off however he joined in ye pursuit & assisted in taking him. Jeremiah Curtis makes oath yt on hearing ye Outcry he went wth last witness & confirms his testimony. Committed the prisoner to Newgate.
Same day Martha Plummer of Tottenham bound in £100, Henry Hurst Gardner in Clopton £40; Jno Bracey Labourer Do 40, Jno Wells Gardner Do to Mr Meridith 40, Jeremiah Curtis Do Do to Do 40. Bound over as above Martha Plummer to prosecute & ye other 4 to attend as witnesses [next *deleted*] this Sessions.[1]

1. William Heath, a cobbler, was convicted and sentenced to death at the December Old Bailey sessions. MJ/GBB/313, 56; *O. B. Proc.*, December 1732, R *v* Heath.

59. *Wednesday, 6 December 1732* Wm Street complains agt: Geo: Stretton for assaulting & beating him in Well Street being an old man unable to defend himself, done this day. On Oath made granted a Warrt: for Stretton.

60. *Thursday, 11 January 1733* Wm Hewson brot: by Geo: Fowler & charged by Edwd Batty for being concerned in a felony of Some mo: abt: £4 or £50 taken from him by his Servt maid Mary South. Phoebe Fesan at the Bush tavern, Mare street maketh Oath yt: last night at New-prison She heard Mrs Esther Hewson own having recd from Mary South 25 Gs more then was found upon the Said E. Hewson & wch at ye Mermaid on Monday She absolutely denyed. Sarah Peters of Church Strt: on [ye *deleted*] her Oath Saith yt She heard Esther Hewson confess yt She did receive Some Guineas, a parcell in her naked hand without telling, from Ma: South more then had been restored & agreable wth ye above witness, that She went down on Saterday in her Shift and left [ye *deleted*] all ye mo: in her pocket, & when She came up again part was wanting & She knew not wt came of it unless her husband had got it away. Ordered to Search his person & granted a Warrt to Search his house but the mo: not being found ordered his person to be discharged.[1] [*See* **63**, **606**].

1. Mary South and Esther Hewson were tried at the January Old Bailey sessions. South was convicted of stealing to the value of 39s. and was sentenced to transportation. Hewson, who was accused of receiving the coins, was acquitted 'it not appearing that Hewson knew that the money had been stolen'. MJ/GBB/313, 66; *O.B.Proc.*, January 1733, R *v* South and Hewson.

61. *Friday, 12 January 1733* Catherine Fells complains agt: George Fox for assaulting her & Spitting in her face abt 2/m ago & insulting her frequently Since. Granted her a Warrt: on Oath made.
Same day Geo: Fox being brot: by Henry Harrill Headbo: but ye Prosecutor not appearing & Oath being made by Harrill yt She had notice but refused to come I discharged Fox.

62. *Tuesday, 16 January 1733* Anne Trott brot: in by Henry Harrill Headbo: charged by John Davis Churchwarden for being drunk yesterday, Sworn to by him. Convicted her thereof.

63. *Thursday, 25 January 1733* Wm Hewson complains agt Ed: Batty, Tho: Archer, Tho: Hudson, Thos: Smith & Samuell Eadie for assaulting him Striking & dragging him & throwing him into ye river yesterday near Smiths ferry on his Oath made granted a warrt: for them 5.
Tuesday, 30 January 1733 [All 5 *deleted*] The first 4 being brot: by Rob: Loyd W Hewson makes Oath yt on Wednesday 24 Jan: he was going towards ye Marsh Ed. Batty assaulted him puncht him on ye back & afterwards on ye breast &c that yt then ye others came in & Tho: Archer assisted in dragging him along ye field, that Tho: Hudson encouraged ym to misuse him, that Tho: Smith did ye like. Hen. Page [and] Jno Flaxman called by ye Defdts & Sworn. Agreed by Mr Hewson to discharge Thomas Hudson & Thomas Smith – Sam. Eadie did not appear having made his escape at my house.
Tho: Hudson of Clopton gent [and] Sam. Woolmer of Clopton Gardner bound each in £20 for appearance of Edwd. Batty of Clopton Vict [& Tho Archer of Clopton Butcher *deleted*] at next Generall Sessions of ye Peace at Hicks hall & the Principall [*altered from* Principalls] bound [each *deleted*] in £40. Thomas Archer bound in £40, Ed. Batty 20, [and] Sam. Woolmer 20 bound for appearance of Tho: Archer. Afterwards Wm Hewson came back wth Batty & Archer & declared they had agreed the matter & he consented to their finall discharge & likewise of Sam. Eadie who did not appear.[1] [*See* **60**, **606**].

1. Although Archer's recognizance was not returned to the sessions, Batty's was. He was discharged at the February sessions. MJ/SR/2589, recog. 95.

64. *Monday, 19 February 1733* Eliza. North on Oath complains agt. Wm Austen for assaulting her divers times & Striking her a blow on ye head last Saterday in particular. Granted a Warrt: for him.
Same day At Mermaid made up ye matter between being both something in fault.[1] [*See* **619**].

1. Norris has clearly dated this entry 17 February (Saturday), but cross-reference to the petty sessions entry (**619**), makes it clear that 19 February is more likely to be correct.

65. *Monday, 2 April 1733* Elizabeth Crew complains agt: George Mackgain Wm Layton Tho: Baxter Martha Carter Helen Baxter Eliza: Fisher for assaulting & beating her & her Brother Robt: Crew yesterday at 5 in ye evening in ye house of ye Wt Hart at Cambridge Heath ye 2 first Struck Eliza: Crew & ye other abetted them whereof She made Oath. Granted a Warrt: for ym.[1]

1. Baxter, a chandler, and Layton, a labourer, entered into recognizances before Tyssen the following day. They were discharged at the April sessions. MJ/SR/2592, recogs. 144, 145.

66. *Friday, 13 April 1733* Complaint made by Job Hall yt he had lent a black Gelding for hire on ye 20 March last to Thomas Edwards for one day who ran away wth ye horse & can not Since be found, but he has now found ye Sd Horse in ye Possession of Sam^{ll}: Woodfield wch being made oath to granted him a Warr^{t}: to bring y^{e}: Horse and Sam: Woodfield. The Gelding was ye pperty of his father Robert Hall of Cravens Stables in Drury lane where ye horse was let to above Edw^{ds}. The Same was confirmed by ye Oath of Rob: Hall & y^{t} ye pperty of ye horse is in him. On hearing Sam. Woodfield it was agreed he Should restore ye horse to ye right owner.

67. *Monday, 16 April 1733* George North complains ag^{t} Charles Gosdin for assaulting & beating him yesterday in ye afternoon in his own house in Well Street in breach of his Majesties peace.[1]

1. Gosdin subsequently entered into a recognizance before Tyssen which was returned to the May sessions. It was respited indefinitely 8 October 1733. MJ/SBB/909, recog. 53.

68. *Monday, 16 April 1733* Complaint made by Robert Sandy's ag^{t}: Henry Vaughan for feloniously taking away Severall Battens Deals & other goods ye pperty of George Wildey. Robert Southern maketh Oath that the Same is true to his knowledge & y^{t} he saw them taken away by him & y^{t} they were applyed to his own use. Granted a Warr^{t}: to apprehend him.

69. *Friday, 27 April 1733* Eleanor Kingsland bro^{t} in Custody of Hen: Batt by Warr^{t}: of Ja. Brain charged for assaulting Mary Kingsland. Hen: Batt made Oath y^{t} he had ye Def^{t}: in Custody ever since 7 last night & had endeavoured to give notice to Mary Kingsland to appear but [it is tho *deleted*] She not appearing I dischargd ye Def^{t}: [*See* **73**].

70. *Saturday, 28 April 1733* Thomas Johnson bro^{t}: before me by Henry Bat by warr^{t}. of Ralph Harwood 28 Ap: for assaulting Eliz^{a}: Stewart but he was So drunk he could not Stand nor answer So ordered him to ye Cage to be kept & bro^{t}: in ye morning.
Sunday, 29 April 1733 Eliza: Stewart on Oath charges him wth assaulting & beating her last friday & running after her wth a naked knife & threatning her life to wch he made no Sufficient defence. [*See* **71**].

71. *Sunday, 29 April 1733* Sd Thomas Johnson charged by his wife Anne Johnson for assaulting & beating her in a grievous manner on friday last & threatning her life he not being able to give Surety's to appear at next Sessions, committed him to Newprison in Clerkenwell &c. [*See* **70**].

72. *Monday, 7 May 1733* Edwd Martin complains ag^{t}: Mary [Ingram *deleted*] Wingwood for assaulting him & abetting others to beat him Severely this morning at ye Green Man in Church Street. Granted a Warr^{t} for her & She was bro^{t}: upon ye 8 May 1733.
Tuesday, 8 May 1733 On hearing both pties Ed: Martin Swore to ye assault & Mary Winggood acknowledged it. Ch^{a}: Gosdin Sworn but

knew nothing to y[e] purpose. Upon y[e] whole they agreed the matter & discharged her.

73. *Saturday, 19 May 1733* Mary Kingsland bro[t]: in Custody of [*blank*] Brown on Warr[t] of M[r] S Tyssen & complaint of Eleonor Kingsland. Both having agreed y[e] matter discharged y[e] Warr[t]. [*See* **69**].

74. *Monday, 21 May 1733* Jasper Gregory complains ag[t] Jeremiah Woodley his Master for [refusing *deleted*] beating him without cause with an Iron & a broomstick & refusing to pay him his wages being hired at Waltham Statute for a year. On oath made granted a warr[t]: for him.

75. *Monday, 4 June 1733* Sam. Mason complains of Eliz[a]: Wickes for robbing him of mo: 6[s] taken, 2[s] out of a drawer, 2[s] more another time out of a drawer, 1[s] more out another time out of a drawer, 1[s] out of a pocket apron. On his Oath made granted a Warr[t]: to apprehend her.

76. *Monday, 18 June 1733* [John Bowen *deleted*] Thomas Dotchell complains ag[t]: Thomas Williams for beating Anne Dotchell his wife in a barbarous manner made out by y[e] Oath of Mary Mattison done last Saterday in [y[e] *deleted*] Hackney Marsh, Stamped upon her Stomach & beat her about most grievously. Granted a warr[t] for him.
Same day On his being bro[t]: by [*blank*] Griffith Headb[o]: y[e] matter was heard & Mary Mattison made Oath y[t] Tho: Williams did assault her Anne Dotchell and Stamped on her Stomach without her having Stricken him. Tho: Dotchell Swears y[t] She is now extream ill & as he is told inwardly bruised being big wth Child & cannot attend. Sibilla Hunt, Mary Miller, Roger Biston [and] Richard Giglis, Witnesses for y[e] Prisoner but did not invalidate y[e] Evidence given. Thomas Williams of Hackney Labourer in £50, Thomas Pyle of S[t]: Stephen Coleman Str[t]: Bookkeeper £25 [and] W[m] Grudee of Hackney fanpainter £25 bound for appearance of Tho: Williams at next Genll: Q[r] Sessions at Hicks hall to answer the complaint of Anne Dotchell &c.[1] [*See* **78**].

1. The recognizance was returned to the June sessions and Williams was discharged 27 August 1733. MJ/SBB/910, recog 48.

77. *Friday, 22 June 1733* James Coo Complains ag[t]: Simon Rugs [*recte* Nigs] & W[m] Stretton for assaulting & beating him Severall times both at London & Hackney y[e] last time was to day at London in Bishopsgate Street. On Oath made by him granted a warr[t]: to Apprehend them.
Tuesday, 26 June 1733 Simon Nigs bro[t]: by James Bowden. Coo maketh oath to Nigs assaulting him last friday 7night in Hackney near y[e] Church pushing him ag[t] a Post & treading on his toes.
Bound over to y[e] next Genll: Sessions at Hicks hall, Simon Nigs of Hackney Labourer in £20, William Thurston of Hackney Coachman in 10, Edward Poole of Hackney Brewer in 10, for y[e] appearance of Simon Nigs to answer &c.[1] [*See* **91**].

1. Nigs was discharged at the August sessions. MJ/SBB/911, recog. 31.

78. *Sunday, 24 June 1733* Thomas Dotchell [and] Elisabeth Fletcher Sworn. Both say y^{t} they apprehend Anne Dotchell is in great danger of her life lying now extreamly ill by the hurts She received as they are informed in her quarrel wth Thomas Williams. [*See* **76**].

79. *Monday, 25 June 1733* Elis^{a}: Price complains ag^{t}: Richard Wilkinson for beating her wth a Cane & wth his fist & [Stamping upon her *deleted*] kicked her at Severall times ye last time was last night w^{n} he beat her wth a Cane. On oath made by her Granted a warr^{t}:
Thursday, 12 July 1733 On a new Oath made by her granted a new Warr^{t}.
Monday, 30 July 1733 R Wilkinson bro^{t}: by Hen: Harrill in Custody. I heard both Sides & ye assault appeared but the parties did voluntarily agree the matter & he gave her 2 G^{s} for dam^{a}: & wth her consent I discharged him.

80. *Monday, 9 July 1733* Geo: Fowler complains ag^{t}: Tho: Blemmenee for assaulting him & throwing Scalding water on him. On oath made thereof granted a Warr^{t}:
Same day On hearing ye matter it was agreed & discharged the Warr^{t}:

81. *Friday, 13 July 1733* Mary Kingsland complains ag^{t}: Jno: Jones for assaulting her last night & throwing her violently on ye ground & kicking her whereby She was very much bruised & hurt at ye W^{tt} Hart on Camb: heath. On hearing ye matter Mary Kingsland Swore to the assault as above & Abigail Johnson as witness on oath confirmed the Same.

82. *Tuesday, 17 July 1733* Henry Hudson complains ag^{t}: Joseph Good bro^{t} by James Martin in Custody for oversetting his Chaise wth a Cart & breaking it down. Being Sworn he charges J: Good as accessary in the oversetting him in his chaise & breaking it down. Jos: Good alledges y^{t} he did not drive ye Cart y^{t} the name of the Man who drave ye Cart is [Nicholas *deleted*] [*blank*] Nichols, that the name of his M^{r} is Atkinson y^{t} he is called Doctor Atkinson a Surgeon & a Woodmonger at Hermitage dock. Jos: Good Says he lives in Lamb Street near the Market in Spitallfields at Mrs Paynes a Sweating house.[1] Jos: Good Sworn, says y^{t} [*blank*] Nichols as above did drive the Cart. Ed. Farmer Servt to Mr Keeling of Islington says y^{t} he saw Nichols whip his horse. Henry Hudson of Wodstreet Perrukem^{a}: bound in £20 to prosecute [Jos *deleted*] the said Nichols. Joseph Good of Spitallfields Labourer in £10 to appear as evidence at next Gen^{ll}: Sessions.[2]

1. A house in which people were sweated as a form of curative treatment. *O.E.D.*
2. An attempt to indict Edward Nicholls failed at the August sessions. MJ/SBP/13/649.

83. *Sunday, 22 July 1733* George Weaver & Thomas Weaver bro^{t}: in Custody of Hen: Harrill & charged by him for an assault. Hen: Harrill [and] Isaac Balcher Sworn, charge y^{m} both wth an Assault. [Jere: Stacy *deleted*] The matter was agreed between them & ordered them to be discharged.

84. *Friday, 31 August 1733* James Johnson complains ag^{t} Geo: Sulley for assaulting him at Bethnall green last Tuesday. Ja: Johnson [and] Ed. Moyse Sworn both agree to ye fact & granted a Warr^{t}:
Same day Bro^{t}: by Jno Holmes Headb^{o}: on hearing ye matter Geo: Sully bound in £10 of Bethnall Green Hamlet in Stebonheath Victualler, Charles Norris of St: Martins Outwich Joyner in £5, Henry Jonquier of Bishopshall weaver in £5, for appearance of Geo: Sully at y^{e} [Appea *deleted*] adjournm^{t} of the present Sessions at Hicks hall &c.[1]

1. The recognizance was returned to the August sessions and respited indefinitely 8 October 1733. MJ/SBB/911, recog. 534.

85. *Thursday, 6 September 1733* W^{m}. Griffith complains ag^{t} James Dykin for assaulting him yesterday evening in Church Str^{t}: & violently pushing ag^{t} him on his breast wth his head. Granted a Warr^{t}: for him.
Saturday, 8 September 1733 On hearing ye matter it was agreed between themselves & discharged ye Warr^{t}.

86. *Tuesday, 18 September 1733* Jno: Morse complains ag^{t}: Tho: Godwin bro^{t}: in Cust^{o}: of Wm Griffith for breaking his windows & threatning his life. Tho: Godwin acknowledges breaking ye windows 3 Squares but alledges it was his own house in part. Mary Hales Sworn but being ex^{a}: as to ye threat did not make it out. So dismissed Godwin on his promising to amend ye wind^{o}: wch Morse took his word for.

87. *Saturday, 29 September 1733* Hannah Preston complains ag^{t}: her husband Edward Preston for beating her last Wednesday & especially for neglecting to make any provision for his family She having 3 children by him to keep ye eldest 9 years, ye 2^{d} 3y: y^{e} [other *deleted*] 3^{d} under 1 year – to wch She made oath. [*See* **34**].

88. *Saturday, 29 September 1733* Mary Cornish complains ag^{t}: Elis^{a}: Smith for assaulting her & beating her wth a Stick last night on Cambridge heath and bruising her in a grievous manner & tearing her Cap, to wch She made oath & granted a warr^{t}: for Smith.
Monday, 1 October 1733 On hearing ye Cause She acknowledged ye assault but was agreed between ye pties & dischargd ye Warrt.

89. *Tuesday, 2 October 1733* Thomasin Wheeler complains ag^{t}: her Husband John Wheeler for beating & abusing her last night & threatning her life last night. On oath made granted a warr^{t}: ag^{t} him.[1] [*See* **9**, **48**, **119**, **129**, **553**, **560**, **581**, **582**, **680**].

1. John Wheeler's name appears on the New Prison calendar for October, although the date and reason for his detention are unknown. The sessions papers record that he was to be bailed or discharged only by Norris or Tyssen and that he was to pay 2s. on discharge. MJ/SP/1733/OCT/139.

90. [*Tuesday, 11 December 1733* Daniel Brumwell complains ag^{t}: *entry incomplete and deleted*].

91. *Friday, 14 December 1733* James Coo complains ag^{t} Simon Niggs for assaulting him & others in his Coach last night & threatning him in London. On oath made granted a Warr^{t}. NB if find ye Cause made out to bind ye pty in Recognisance to appear at Next Sessions at Guildhall holden for ye City of London & Certifye his recognisance thither. [*See* **77**].

92. *Monday, 24 December 1733* Sam^{ll}: Saunders of Kingsland complains ag^{t}: James Neal for assaulting him & threatning his life last night. On oath made granted a Warr^{t}: for him.

93. *Thursday, 27 December 1733* Martha Nichols complains ag^{t}: Thomas Fouch for assaulting her & beating her last night at ye Blackmores head in Clopton. On oath made granted a Warr^{t}:

94. *Saturday, 29 December 1733* Rob: Knight complains ag^{t}: Edward Life for feloniously taking from him a metall Pot Vall: 5^{s}. On oath made granted a Warr^{t}: to apprehend Ed: Life.[1]

1. There was no attempt to indict Life at either the Oyer and Terminer or the Gaol Delivery sessions held the following month.

95. *Saturday, 26 January 1734* Thomas Hide complains ag^{t}: John Maslin for assaulting & Striking him today in breach &c. On oath made granted a Warr^{t}: for him. On Hearing ye cause Tho: Hide, Jno Preston [and] Geo: Huggins, Sworn. Tho: Hide Says y^{t} Jno: Maslin 1st assaulted him. Jno Preston confirms Maslin 1st laying hold of his Collar. Geo: Huggins does not very certainly know wch began ye assault but by his testimony it Seemed to be Maslin. On hearing ye matter was agreed.

96. *Friday, 1 February 1734* Hen: Batt complains ag^{t}: Robt Wright of Well Street Smith for being drunk & assaulting him in his own house wch being drunk he acknowledged & was convicted.
Thursday, 7 February 1734 Issued a Warr^{t}: to Levy 5^{s} on him or in default thereof to Set him in ye Stocks for 6 hours.

97. *Monday, 11 February 1734* Matth: Walter complains y^{t} his garden has been robbed Severall times of Glasses & plants & y^{t} last night there was a person took out of his garden a glass light & y^{t} he being upon the watch fired at him & he [dropt *deleted*] left ye glass behind & ran away between 12 & 1. Math: Walter made oath to ye above. James Woolcot made oath y^{t} last night near 1 a person run by him being in Mare Street watch h^{o}: & told him he had been Shot at by rogues, & y^{t} being asked his name said his name was Bladwell or Brattell & lived in Dolston & Math: Walter Suspects from this & other circumstances y^{t} ye person he Shot at was Jno Brattle of Dorleston. Granted a Search Warr^{t}. [*See* **100**].

98. *Monday, 11 February 1734* Joshua Bridgman [*deletion*] lives in Hummerton in Adam and Eve yard complains [ag^{t}: y^{t} *deleted*] & Ursula Bridgman his wife Sworn. Y^{e} latter says y^{t} about 3 wks or 4/wks Since

She was forced &c by Rob: Flemming in his own house but y^{t} on ye relation did not appear to be a force. Joshua Briddgman Sworn complains y^{t} on 23 Jan: last Tho: Woodward, M^{r} of the Ad^{m} & Eve wth 2 others on his going into ye house blacked him in ye face y^{t} after Rob: Fleming Shot twice wth a powder at him & wounded him wth powder in ye face & y^{t} afterw^{ds} Rob: Fleming in comp^{a}: wth another Since absconded broke open the door of Sd Josh: Bridgman in breach of the Peace wch last article was Sworn to by his wife. Made out a warr^{t}: for Rob: Fleming & Tho: Woodward to answer the complaint & on hearing it bound y^{m} over to ye next Gen^{ll} Sessions wth Suretys y^{m} Selves in £20: each, [*blank*] in 10: for each.[1]

1. Both were discharged at the February sessions. MJ/SBB/916, recogs. 38, 39.

99. *Monday, 11 February 1734* George Taylor complains y^{t} [last night *deleted*] this morning his house in Well Street was broke open. Geo: Taylor, Ruth Taylor [and] Thomas Prior Sworn. Ruth Taylor found her house entred in her absence & found Severall things packt up to be carryed off Viz a linnen Apron a Silver Spoon a p^{r}: Silver buckles & Some other things. Geo: Taylor confirms ye same. Tho: Prior says y^{t} coming in ye time he found Elis^{a}: Robinson in G: Taylors garden hidden & believed She was ye person y^{t} had been in ye house. Made out a Warr^{t}: to take up Elis^{a}: Robinson.

100. *Monday, 11 February 1734* Matthew Walter maketh Oath that this day he charged William Griffith one of the Headboroughs of the Parish of S^{t}. John at Hackney [to take *deleted*] with one John Brattle whom he suspected to have robbed him and that he [*deletion*] Wilfully suffered him to make his Escape [*signed*] Matt: Walter. Sworn before me the day and year above written [*signed*] Henry Norris.[1]
Tuesday, 12 February 1734 Made out a Warr^{t}: ag^{t}: him. Wm Griffith bound in £40 Gardner, Morgan Bynon 20 Brewer & Victualler [and] Thomas Marsling 20 Barber & Perrukem^{a}: [both] of Hackney.
Same day Taken the above recognisance for Griffiths appearance at Gen^{ll} Sessions. Richd Brattle.
Saturday, 16 February 1734 Math: Walter claims 3 Glasses, Richd Atkins 2 Lights, Tho: Clark 3 D^{o}, Geo: Robinson 4 Seed Cabages, Jno: Wright 3 Lights. All Sworn claim ye goods above mentioned found in R Brattles ground & Stolen from y^{m} Suppose by his Son & ordered them to be dd to y^{m} respectively.[2] [*See* **97**].

1. The preceding part of this entry is not in Norris's hand.
2. Griffith's recognizance was respited at the February sessions and discharged the following April. MJ/SBB/916, recog. 37; MJ/SBB/917, recog. e.

101. *Tuesday, 19 March 1734* Granted a warr^{t}: to Mary Cornish ag^{t} Mary Dudley for assaulting her and forcibly taking away a Milk yoke.

102. *Saturday, 18 May 1734* John Hague complains ag^{t}: Henry Vaughan for assaulting him & farther threatning him ye 15th ins^{t}: in ye house of Luke Townsend. On Oath made granted a Warr^{t}: for him. [*See* **113**].

103. *Monday, 3 June 1734* Jane Chambers complains ag^{t}: Jacob Crew for assaulting & kicking her yesterday at her own house. On oath made granted her a Warr^{t}.
Tuesday, 4 June 1734 On hearing ye cause got ye partyes to agree & he made her Satisfaction.

104. *Saturday, 15 June 1734* Stephen Patmore bro^{t}: by James Martin on Warr^{t}: of R Newton for assaulting his wife Lydia. Lydia Sworn proves ye assault wthout just cause. Geo: Offer Sworn in behalf of ye Def^{t} but was agreed between ye partyes.

105. *Tuesday, 18 June 1734* Wm Burrell of the parish of Hackney Breeches maker bound in the sum of forty pounds. John Starps of the same Butcher bound in the sum of forty pounds. Upon Condition that the s^{d} Wm Burrell personally appeareth at the next General Sessions or Quarter Sessions of the Peace for the County of Middx at Hicks Hall in St John Street after Eliz^{a} Robinson Singlewoman shall be delivered of the Base Child or Children wth. which she is now pregnant then and there to abide the Order shall be made for the Indemnification of the s^{d} parish touching the s^{d} Base Child or Children of which she upon oath hath charged him to be the father and not depart the Court without License.[1] [*See* **728**, **757**, **786**].

1. Burrell's recognizance was respited until the sessions after the birth. No further process has been traced. The note of the recognizance in the sessions book is marked with a cancelled order of estreat, suggesting that Burrell failed to appear but was able to offer an adequate excuse (probably that he had satisfied the parish). MJ/SBB/919, recog. 238.

106. *Monday, 24 June 1734* Sarah Eades of Cambridge Heath complains ag^{t}: John Goodman for assaulting Frances Eades her child a girl of 3 or 4 years old yesterday. On oath of ye Mother made out a Warr^{t}:

107. *Tuesday, 25 June 1734* Joseph Scooling complains ag^{t}: Tho: Baxter & Rob: Crew for assaulting him & beating him [also beating *deleted*] his wife Anne Scooling last night at Cambridge heath. On Oath made by each of them granted a Warr^{t}: for Baxter & Crew.

108. *Friday, 28 June 1734* Anne Booth of Cambridge Heath complains ag^{t}: Joseph Hall for assaulting her ye 24th June in ye Street near her house throwing her down & kicking her. On Oath made granted a Warr^{t}: On their appearance ye affair was made up.

109. *Friday, 12 July 1734* Granted a warr^{t}: to Jno Wix ag^{t}: Tho: Smith for an assault on Oath made by him.

110. *Friday, 19 July 1734* Thomas Scott complains ag^{t}: Nath^{a}: Jones for assaulting him & Striking him Severall blows in ye face. NB warr^{t}: not p^{d}.
Saturday, 20 July 1734 On appearance of Nath^{a}: Jones heard ye Cause & bound over Nath^{a}: Jones of Middle Temple Esqr £40, Math: Hall of Furnevalls Inn Gent 20 [and] Anth^{o}: Peck of S^{t}: Mich^{a}: Crooked lane 20

for appear[a]: of Nath[a]: Jones Esq[r] at next Gen[ll]: Sessions of y[e] Peace to answer y[e] compl[t]: of Tho: Scott.[1]

1. Nathaniel Jones was indicted for assault in August. In October, he in turn preferred a similar indictment against Thomas Scott. It was ordered that the two indictments be heard together. Jones was tried in October 1735; he was convicted and sentenced to be pilloried twice, to be imprisoned in Newgate for a year and subsequently to find sureties for good behaviour for another two years. Scott was not tried and and was granted a stay of proceedings in October 1737. MJ/SBB/920, recog. 44; MJ/SBB/922, recog c.; MJ/SBB/930, p. 52; MJ/SR/2623, indt. 52.

111. *Thursday, 5 September 1734* Samuell Holdsworth of the George at Clapton charges John Seagrave wth Stealing a pewter pot from him this day pperty of Sam: Holdsworth. Thomas Folliott also charges J: Seagrave on Suspicion for Stealing another pewter pot y[e] pperty of Anne Philips. Joseph Hall & Tho: Folliott Say they took ye 2 Pots out of J Seagraves breeches. Sam: Holdsworth bound in £20 to psecute of Hack. Victualler, Tho: Folliott 10 of Beth. green Weaver [and] Jos: Hall 10 of D[o] Brasier, as Witnesses. W[m] Catton Butcher Marestreet officer – placed both y[e] Potts in his hands. NB to bind over y[e] officer to appear & Anne Philips to psecute.[1]

1. Seagrove was acquitted on both charges at the September Old Bailey sessions. MJ/GBB/314, 38.

112. *Monday, 23 September 1734* James Edward Bettell made Oath that Thomas Graves of Hackney Gardener hath used such threatening Words to him that he apprehends he will do or cause to be done unto him some bodily [*deletion*] harm and therefore desired a Warrant for the Peace[1] w[ch] was granted but afterwards y[e] difference was agreed between themselves at their appearance & T Graves was discharged.

1. The preceding part of this entry is not in Norris's hand.

113. *Sunday, 15 October 1734* Luke Townsend complains ag[t]: Henry Vaughan for assaulting his wife Sarah Townsend this evening. On Oath made granted a Warr[t]: [*See* **102**].

114. [*no date* Middlesex. The Information of Elisabeth Thorn Single Woman taken upon Oath before me and the Said Deponent voluntarily maketh Oath that about the beginning of Aprill last She being then a Servant to William Underhill a Writing Master in Church Street in Hackney, the said William Underhill *entry incomplete and deleted*].

115. *Monday, 16 December 1734* Mary Kingsland complains ag[t]: Robert Crew for assaulting her. On Oath made granted a Warr[t]. On Hearing the Cause y[e] pson bro[t]: in Cust[o]: of W[m] Strutton, Mary Kingsland Swore to his assaulting her & y[t] he assaulted his own wife beat & kickt her. Eliz[a]: Fisher Swore to his assaulting his wife. The matter was made up & the pty discharged.

116. *Friday, 20 December 1734* Tho: Cook complains ag[t]: Hen: Vaughan for assaulting him last night in Homerton at the Coach & Horses. On Oath made granted a Warr^{t}.

117. *Saturday, 28 December 1734* John Hall complains ag^{t}: John Gifford & Jno: Hale for assaulting him last Thursday. On oath made granted a Warr^{t}: for y^{m}.

118. *Saturday, 15 February 1735* Middlesex. Robert Hatley Servt to Stephen Ram Esqr of the parish of St John at Hackney in the County of Middlesex maketh Oath that on Monday the tenth day of this Instant February William Gibbons and Thomas Fletcher Gardeners were Drunk in the parish aforesaid. Robert Hatley [*mark*]. Sworn before me the 15th day of February in the year of our Lord 1735, [*signed*] Henry Norris.[1] Signed a Warr^{t}: to Levy ye Penalty on each & put it in Mr Sadlers hands to be given to ye Parish Officers.

1. The foregoing part of this entry is not in Norris's hand.

119. *Saturday, 15 February 1735* Thomasin Wheeler complains on Oath ag^{t}: her husband John Wheeler for assaulting & beating her. Granted a Warr^{t}: for him. [*See* **9**, **48**, **89**, **129**, **553**, **560**, **581**, **582**, **680**].

120. *Monday, 24 March 1735* Compl^{t}: made by Pet. Crop of Old Ford y^{t} were taken out of an outh^{o}: belonging to his dwelling H^{o}: 1 duck, 1 drake, 1 Cock, 6 hens. On oath made grant^{d}: a Warr^{t}: to Search h^{o}: of Edwd: Hudgin Tho: Marshall [and] Edwd Cullimer in pish of S^{t}: M: Strat: Bow.

121. *Tuesday, 1 April 1735* Complaint made by Mary Kingsland ag^{t} Tho: Follard Anne Follard & Jno: Goodman & Eliz^{a}: Goodman for assaulting her last Thursday morn: & kicking her. On Oath made granted a Warr^{t}: [*See* **193**, **194**].

122. *Friday, 4 April 1735* Complaint made by Mary Stretton y^{t} Tho: Cook assaulted her child Wm Stretton by throwing dirt on him & Sworn to by Sam: Hunter. Granted a Warr^{t}: for him. On hearing ye matter it was made up.

123. *Monday, 14 April 1735* Henry Vaughan upon his oath says that in the Evening of the day above written as he was comeing to Hackney near the Red Lyon ale House in Mare Street one John Williams Rode up against him and Struck the Boy who was behind him on Horse back and then Struck him on the side of his head with the handle of his Horse Whip which very much broke his head without his assaulting him. Thomas Warren upon his Oath says that what the said Vaughan has said is true. John Williams of the parish of S^{t}. Ann in the County of Middx Literman £40, Richard Hare of the same Brewer £20, Griffith Carr of the same Distiller £20, For the appearance of John Williams at the next General Sessions of the Peace to be held for the County of Middx at Hicks hall to answer Henry Vaughan for assaulting Beateing & bruising him in breach of his Majesties Peace & not to Depart the Court without License.[1]

1. This entry is not in Norris's hand. The recognizance was returned to the May sessions and respited indefinitely 30 June 1735. MJ/SBB/927, recog. 100.

124. *Wednesday, 30 April 1735* Wm Robinson complains ag^{t}: Francis Francis for an assault & throwing upon him a pot full of Urine upon him, on Oath made granted a Warr^{t}: for him. Afterw^{ds}: was made up.

125. *Monday, 5 May 1735* Sarah Gifford complains ag^{t}: Wm French for assaulting her & cutting her wth a knife of wch She made Oath & made out a warr^{t}: for him.

126. *Monday, 5 May [altered from April] 1735* Elisabeth Dunn complains ag^{t} Mary Griffith & Jno: Griffith for assaulting her to day in Mrs Strettons house. On her Oath granted a Warr^{t}.

127. *Saturday, 10 May 1735* Helen Nutbrown complains ag^{t}: Miles Nutbrown her husband for assaulting her & Stamping upon her & abusing her in a most excessive manner. On Oath made granted a warr^{t}: for him. [*See* **343**, **996**].

128. *Saturday, 10 May 1735* Henry Bridge complains ag^{t}: Mrs Whiffin wife of Jos: Whiffin for assaulting him & cutting his head wth a pewter pot – on Oath. Granted a warr^{t}: for her.

129. *Tuesday, 13 May 1735* Thomasin Wheeler complains on Oath ag^{t}: her husband John Wheeler for beating her very barbarously. Granted a Warr^{t}.
Saturday, 17 May 1735 On hearing ye cause committed him to Clerkenwell Bridewell for Custody in want of Sureties.
Tuesday, 8 July 1735 Ordered his Discharge at his wifes desire. [*See* **9**, **48**, **89**, **119**, **553**, **560**, **581**, **582**, **680**].

130. *Thursday, 15 May 1735* Wm Cullimore bro^{t}: in Custody of Hen: Batt charged by [y^{e} *deleted*] Rich^{d}. Ross Servt: of Tho: Rudge for being found in his Masters Stable pilfering Chainharness & Severall Implements for thievery found in his pocket. Sworn by him & confirmed by Adam Bennett. Committed W Cullimore to Bridewell for Labour.
Sunday, 15 June 1735 Ordered him to be discharged.

131. *Tuesday, 20 May 1735* Sam: Keep complains on Oath y^{t} Severall pewter dishes plates linnen & other goods were Stollen last night out of his dwelling house. Granted a Search warr^{t}.

132. *Tuesday, 27 May 1735* Isaac Belcher compl^{ll}: ag^{t}: Luke Townsend for an Ass^{t}: Sworn. Made a warr^{t}: for him.

133. *Wednesday, 28 May 1735* Lambert Lance of Shacklewell complains ag[t] John Lee Glasier at Mile end [and] Rich[d] Griffith of Mile end Carpenter bro[t]: in Custody of [*blank*] Fussel Headb[o]: both for carrying Guns viz: Fowling p[cs]: & Jn[o]: Lee for threatning to Shoot y[e] sd Lambert Lance & Rich[d] Griffith for assaulting & Striking Andrew Ellis. Jn[o]: Lee acknowledged y[e] carrying a Gun & Shooting a Rook wth it – also that he had threatned Lance. Upon R Griffiths Submission discharged him.

134. *Wednesday, 28 May 1735* Benj[a]: Fowles complains ag[t] Thomas Blemmenee for assaulting & beating him this evening in his own house. On Oath made granted a Warr[t].
Friday, 30 May 1735 He acknowledged himself Satisfyed & y[e] matter made up So discharged y[e] Warr[t]:

135. *Friday, 30 May 1735* Francis Adams bro[t]: by Jn[o]: Saunders Headb[o]: chgd wth running away wth a dung fork & Spade y[e] goods of W[m] Hazard but y[e] matter not appearing to be a felony discharged him.

136. *Thursday, 26 June 1735* W[m] Burrell complains ag[t] Cath. Frost for assaulting & Striking him in her house to day. On oath made a warr[t]: for her.

137. *Tuesday, 1 July 1735* W[m] Smith complains ag[t]: Elis[a]: Middleton for assaulting & Striking him divers times in his own house at Oldford. On Oath made granted a Warr[t]: for her.
Wednesday, 2 July 1735 Upon hearing y[e] cause y[e] 2 July Sent y[e] def[t]: to new Prison for want of Sureties upon y[e] Plaintifs oath to y[e] Assault.[1]

1. Elizabeth Barratt, also known as Elizabeth wife of William Middleton, was found guilty on 25 August and fined 1s. MJ/SR/2638, indt. 24.

138. *Monday, 7 July 1735* Sarah Wheeler makes Oath ag[t]: Mary Kingsland for [breaking her windows & *deleted*] threatning her life & fully beleives She broke her windows. Made a Warr[t]: for her.

139. [*no date* Middlesex. Fisher Jackson Esq[r] of the Parish of S[t] John at Hackney in the County of Middlesex maketh Oath that John Flaxmore of the said Parish *entry incomplete and deleted.*]

140. *Monday, 14 July 1735* Mary Woodward complains ag[t]: Elis[a]: Bare for assaulting her in her Fathers house (being the Serv[t]: to her father) & tearing her headdress & bruising her. Granted a warr[t]: for her. [*See* **141**].

141. *Monday, 14 July 1735* Eliz[a]: Bare complains ag[t]: Mary Woodw[d] for an assault on her. On hearing the cause reccommended them to agree their difference w[ch]. was done. [*See* **140**].

142. *Monday, 28 July 1735* Richard Savage of Bow in Middlesex Farmer complained against Elizabeth Bull of the same Parish Wid[o]: for unlawfully taking out of his yard adjoy[g] to his dwelling house there a parcell of

Faggot Wood which complaint was confirmed by the Oath of Eliz[a]. Clarke his servant. Granted a Warrant to apprehend her.[1]

1. This entry is not in Norris's hand.

143. *Monday, 4 August 1735* Isaac Dennis bro[t]: before me by Charles Blackmore Headb[o]: at the Bear in Hare Street & charged wth robbing of Eliz[a]: Gibbons last Thursday on y[e] Kings highway between Bishops hall & Shore house of 6½[D] & likewise wth robbing of Judith Smith – of 1[s] 1 & three half pence in y[e] field between Bishops hall & Grove Street. The matter of J Smith was by her Sworn but y[e] other was doubtfull. On ex[a]: Is: Dennis confessed he did y[e] robbery on Judith Smith but Said y[t] Rich[d] Noble of Old bedlam & Rob: Glynn in Kate Street were concerned wth him. NB he Says this was y[e] 1st robbery he ever committed. Sent him to Newgate. Eliz[a]: Gibbons Sworn & said She was robbed last Thursday but was so frighted She did not know y[e] person at all. Judith Smith bound in £40 to psecute. Ch[a]: Blackmore of Hare street Carpenter, Francis Pittway of Garden Court Pett: lane brickl[a], W[m] Wilcock Irish Court W[tt]Chappell Labourer, Hen: Northop Betts Str[t]: RatClif highway Lab, W[m] Garland at M[r] Rogers brickl[a]: bl[k]: horse yard near Aldgate [all] in £20 to give evidence. James Barnes Shoreditch Scrivener, Thomas Cordell Tubman & Porter S[t]: Jn[o] Street Bednall green Hamlet Labourer [both] in £20 for Do· The 7 latter bound to appear at &c & give evidence.[1]

1. Isaac Dennis was convicted of highway robbery at the September Old Bailey sessions. His defence amounted to a claim that he had merely asked Smith for 'something out of charity' (the essence of the crime of highway robbery was that the victim was put 'in fear') but the jury were clearly rather more impressed by his confession (which was produced in court) and by evidence that at the time of his crime he had had a knife in his pocket and had threatened to use it (although whether the threat was made in pursuance of the crime or as part of an attempt to evade capture is not clear). He was sentenced to death. MJ/GBB/314/148; *O.B.Proc.*, September 1735, R *v* Dennis.

144. *Tuesday, 5 August 1735* Anne Follet complains ag[t]: Martha Disney for an assault & Spitting in her face. On oath made granted a warr[t]:

145. *Wednesday, 13 August 1735* Dorothy Clavey, firk wom:[1] ag[t]: M[r] Loyds brewh[o]: Beaucock James her Serv[t]: ag[t]: Walkington Kilbington in S[t]: Geo: in y[e] East in Ratclif highway Butcher wholesale. Chgd him wth an assault but on hearing it discharged all ptyes.

1. Perhaps meaning firkin-woman, one who trades with a brewer for small beer to furnish her own customers. *O.E.D.*

146. *Monday, 18 August 1735* Geo: Roswell complains ag[t]: Sam. Keep for beating & misusing him dragging him by ye Hair & beating his head ag[t]: y[e] wall. Granted a warr[t]: on Oath made.

147. *Tuesday, 19 August 1735* Geo: Gravett complains ag[t]: Jn[o]: Curtis for an assault on him in Jos: Whiffins grounds & on oath made granted a warr[t]:

148. *Friday, 29 August 1735* Mary Cornish complains ag^{t}: Henry Bedford for assaulting & throwing her down & bruising her very much at ye door of Tho: Pawlet on Cambridge heath. On oath made granted a warr^{t}: for him. NB was not pd for. Upon hearing ye Cause it was agreed & ye ptyes discharged. [Thomas Follet of Bednall green hamlet Weaver, Jno: Bowler of D^{o} at Nags head Victualler, Henry Bedford of Bednall green *deleted*]

149. *Friday, 19 September 1735* Margaret Jones complains ag^{t}: Mary Kingsland for assaulting her yesterday & Striking her Severall blows in ye house of Ann Philips. On her oath of it made granted a warr^{t}: for Kingsland.

150. *Friday, 19 September 1735* Middlesex. William Platt of the Parish of Saint John at Hackney maketh Oath that James Boughton [?*recte* Bolton] did yesterday in the hearing of the Said Deponent & at the house in the Marsh of John Townsend in the aforesaid Parish profanely Swear two Severall times saying By God each time. [*signed*] W^{m}: Platt. Sworn before me the 19 September 1735 Henry Norris, & Granted a Warrant of this date to demand ye Penalty being 2^{s} for use of ye Poor of this Parish & in case of refusall to Levy ye Same by distress or if no distress can be had then to Set him in ye Stocks for 2 hours & dd ye Warr^{t}: to [*blank*]. [*See* **163**].

151. *Wednesday, 24 September 1735* Elis^{a}: Stewart complains ag^{t}: Hannah Yean for assaulting her last Monday. On oath made granted a warr^{t}: for her.

152. *Wednesday, 1 October 1735* Edward Bullock complains ag^{t}: Mary Blith. On his Oath granted a Warr^{t}: for her &c. On hearing ye Cause was made up between y^{m}.

153. *Saturday, 11 October 1735* James Free complains ag^{t}: his M^{r}. Philip Hickman of Shackelwell for assaulting him & Striking him 2 blows wth a long horsewhip wth out any provocation yesterday of wch he made Oath & made out a Warr^{t}. but ordered J Free to attend me at ye Mermaid next Monday at 11 & Sent Mr Hickman word to be there too.[1]

1. No further process is recorded in the petty sessions minutes.

154. *Monday, 13 October 1735* Tho: Hunt bro^{t}: by my Warr^{t}: of this date charged by his wife Sibilla Hunt for threatning her & y^{t} She goes in danger of her life &c from him. Gave him time to find Sureties till next day.

Tuesday, 14 October 1735 Edward Poole of Hummerton Victualler in £20, James Bolton of D^{o} Cordwainer 20, Tho: Hunt of D^{o} Gardner 40, bound for appearance of Tho: Hunt at the next Gen^{ll} Sessions of ye Peace at Hicks hall &c & in meantime to keep ye peace towards all men & especially tow^{ds}: Sibilla Hunt his wife.[1] [*See* **833**].

1. Hunt was discharged at the December sessions. MJ/SBB/931, recog. 79.

155. *Wednesday, 15 October 1735* [Antonia Rock *deleted*] Sarah Nash complains ag[t]: Thomas Enkell for an assault on her & threatning her & her husband & very reproachfull words. On Oath made granted a warr[t] for him.

156. *Monday, 3 November 1735* Jonathan Grainge at y[e] blue Anchor Bethnall green informs ag[t]: Thomas Curtis Barber in Grocers Alley in the Poultry London for unlawfully killing a Hare wth his Gun this day in or near y[e] lane from Grovestreet common to M[rs]. Johnsons house.[1]

1. Hunting and shooting game were privileges reserved to the very wealthy. Only a lord of a manor or an individual in receipt of a substantial income from landed property was entitled to kill a hare, even on his own property. The penalty for shooting a hare was 20s. or three months' imprisonment.

157. *Friday, 14 November 1735* Henry Hollis complains ag[t]: Tho: Smith for Stealing a brass candlestick Vallue 1[s] from him yesterday in his dwelling house. On Oath made granted a warr[t].

A list of names and dates (relating to burials in woollen) which appeared at this point in the manuscript, has been removed to the end, entry **356**.

158. *Monday, 17 November 1735* Sarah [*deletion*] Hatfield & Elis[a]: North complain ag[t]: Anne Soden for threatning Sarah Hatfields life & to Set on fire their houses. Sworn to by y[m] & Anne Hall & made a Warr[t] for her. On hearing it they agreed & dismist her.

159. *Thursday, 20 November 1735* Randall Dobie complains ag[t]: Rob: Powell for assaulting him knocking him down & Striking him Severall blows last night in y[e] field beyond y[e] Nags head. On Oath made granted a Warr[t]: for her.
Saturday, 21 November 1735 Was agreed & pty dischgd at desire of Plaintiff.

160. *Saturday, 22 November 1735* W[m] Cooke complains ag[t]: Tho: Dent for an assault & beating him, on Oath made granted a Warr[t]: for him.

161. *Tuesday, 2 December 1735* Rich[d] Spurling chgd by W[m] Hen: Halford for assaulting him & striking him yesterday in Church Street on Oath. Made a warr[t]: for him.

162. *Wednesday, 3 December 1735* Jn[o]: Ball complains ag[t]: Joseph Cock for an assault & beating him yesterday in Kingsland. On oath made granted a warr[t]:

163. *Wednesday, 19 November 1735* Middlesex. James Bolton of the Parish of Saint John at Hackney Constable maketh Oath that William Platt of the same Parish Cooper did last Saterday the fifteenth day of this instant November in the hearing of this Deponent and in the house of Edward Poole in Homerton profanely Swear three Severall times Saying each time by God and farther that the said William Platt did at the Same time and place profanely curse three Severall times Saying to Mr Edward Poole God Damn your blood. [*signed*] James Bolton. Sworn before me the 19 November 1735, Henry Norris. [*See* **150**].

164. *Monday, 15 December 1735* Middlesex. Information of Francis Francis & Dissen Green who on their Oaths do Severally voluntarily Say that John Jones late of Homerton is publickly reputed to have been an accomplice in Several notorious late Robberies in this and other Counties & that they do believe the Same to be true. [*signed*] Francis Francis [and] Dison Green. Sworn before me this 15th day of December 1735 Henry Norris. Made a Warr^{t}: ag^{t}: him.
Same day On his being apprehended & bro^{t}: before me Franc: Francis & Dison Green made Oath again to their Information but Jones denyed his having been concerned in any ill deed & alledged y^{t} he readily & freely wthout resistance Surrendred to ye officer on demand wch appeared to be true however on considering all Circumstances I Sent him to Newgate on Suspicion of felony & bound over ye 2 Informers to psecute &c each in £40 penalty.[1]

1. In March 1736, Jones was taken under heavy guard to Chelmsford in order to stand trial for burglary. Dison Green testified that Jones, a carpenter, had been captured only after a severe struggle. Jones was convicted and sentenced to death, but was later reprieved on condition of transportation. For a fuller account of the events surrounding this arrest see Derek Barlow, *Dick Turpin and the Gregory Gang* (Chichester, 1973), pp. 230–1, 242, 252–3.

165. *Thursday, 25 December 1735* Middlesex Information of William Carter & William Jagger both of Oldford in the Parish of Saint Mary Stratford Bow who do Severally depose as followeth that is to Say the Said William Carter deposeth that last night near 12 a clock [five fowls *deleted*] four hens [& a cock *deleted*] of Dunghill Poultry his property were feloniously taken out an outhouse in his yard at his Dwelling house at Oldford and William Jagger deposeth that at the Same time & place he took Edward [*recte* George] Fairclough in the fact of committing the Said felony. [*signed*] Wm Carter [and] William Jagger. Sworn before me this 25 December 1735 Henry Norris. Wm Carter & Wm Jagger bound in £20 each ye former to appear at next Gen^{ll}: Quarter Sessions to psecute & ye other to give evidence on an Indictm^{t} & Sent Edward Fairclough to Newgate.[1]

1. George Fairclough was charged at the January Old Bailey sessions with stealing to the value of 4s., but was convicted of stealing to the value of 10d. only. He was sentenced to transportation. MJ/GBB/314, 188.

166. *Monday, 12 January 1736* Mary Cornish complains ag^{t}: Jno. Wheeler for breaking open her door in ye night assaulting & threatning her friday night last. On oath made granted a warr^{t}: for him.

167. *Monday, 16 February 1736* Jno: White complains ag^{t}: Mary Kingsland for assaulting & Striking him Severall blows wth a Stick last [Wednesday *deleted*] Tuesday evening in ye house of Mr Brown at Camb: heath. On oath made granted a warr^{t}: for her.

168. *Wednesday, 18 February 1736* Marget [Heath *deleted*] Ather complains ag^{t}: John Townsend for abusing Striking & kicking her this morning in ye house of ye Yorkshire grey in Homerton wch She made Oath to & I granted a warr^{t}: for him.
Tuesday, 24 February 1736 Y^{e} Def^{t}: appearing in Cust^{o}: of ye Const^{a}: Bolton who made Oath y^{t} ye Plaint: promised to appear but did not discharged him.

169. *Tuesday, 24 February 1736* Complaint made by Wm Davis of Church Street y^{t} last night his house was broke open & a great pcell of wet linnen was Stoln from him ye pperty of Sundry psons & he Suspects ye houses of M^{rs} [*blank*] Bridge M^{r} [*blank*] Bodicoat in Homerton & M^{r} [*blank*] Pescod in Marestreet to have ye goods concealed. Granted a warr^{t}: for y^{m} houses to be Searched.

170. *Tuesday, 16 March 1736* Catherine Carter complains ag^{t}: her Servt: George Maghey for leaving her Service being under coven^{t}: to Serve her a year from 16 Feb: last. Catherine Carter [*mark*]. Sworn before me the day & year first above written, [*signed*] Henry Norris.[1]

1. The final sentence of this entry is not in Norris's hand.

171. *Tuesday, 27 April 1736* John Jones complains ag^{t}: Peter Dureau for an assault on him last night at Bethnallgreen. On Oath made granted a Warr^{t}: for him.

172. *Wednesday, 28 April 1736* Anne Follet complains ag^{t}: Eliz^{a}: Ryland for assaulting her last Monday in her own house & Scratching her. On oath made granted a warr^{t}: for her.

173. *Monday, 17 May 1736* Tho: Williamson complains ag^{t}: Wm Rogers, [*deletion*] for breaking ye peace & assaulting him & Striking him.

174. *Tuesday, 18 May 1736* Jno Thorn complains of having a water tub wth Iron hoops Stolen from him & desires a Search warr^{t} for it on Oath made granted him one to Search ye House &c of Hen: Wheatly in Bethnall green. On hearing ye matter dismisst it.

175. *Tuesday, 25 May 1736* Rebecca Middleton ag^{t}: Joseph Marwell for assaulting her & Striking her Several blows in ye field near Clopton. On Oath made granted a warr^{t}: for him.

176. *Wednesday, 26 May 1736* Jno: Everton complains ag^{t}: Geo: Fowler for assaulting & beating him at ye Red Cow at Dorleston. On oath made granted a Warr^{t}: for him. On hearing ye Cause & ye ptyes agreed discharged the warr^{t}.

177. *Sunday, 30 May 1736* Eliz[a]: Steward complains ag[t]: James Bull for assaulting & beating her. On Oath made granted a Warr[t]: for him.

178. *Friday, 18 June 1736* James Coo complains ag[t]: John Moslin for assaulting him yesterday in Bishopsgate Str[t]: & divers times here at Hackney. On Oath made granted a warr[t]: for him. NB If there be cause to bind him over to appear at Guildhall & Certifye thither. On hearing the cause & Oath made by Coo of the assault it was agreed.

179. *Thursday, 24 June 1736* Elisabeth Goodman [*altered from* Woodman] complains ag[t]: Jn[o] Wheeler for assaulting her 22 June at Cambridge heath. On Oath made granted a warr[t]: for him.

180. *Saturday, 26 June 1736* Mary Fly complains agt: Prudence Sutton for an assault on her & throwing water on her. On oath made granted a warr[t]: for her.

181. *Tuesday, 29 June 1736* Mary Whitaker complains ag[t]: John Woollard for an assault & rudely putting his hand up her Coats.[1] On her Oath granted a Warr[t]: for him.

1. That is, her skirt or petticoats.

182. *Sunday, 6 June 1736*[1] James Edward Bettell complains ag[t]: Hannah Yane for Striking & assaulting him & threatning him w[ch] being Sworn to granted a warr[t]: for her.[2]

1. This entry is perhaps misdated. It was not customary to transact judicial business on a Sunday, and the position of the entry in the notebook suggests it was more likely to have taken place on Tuesday, 6 July 1736.
2. Yane was already bound in a recognizance (taken before Tyssen, 26 May 1736) to answer for an assault on Mary Pugh. She failed to appear and the recognizance was estreated. MJ/SR/2656, recog. 82, MJ/SBB/935, recog 82.

183. *Thursday, 8 July 1736* Eleanor Atchison complains ag[t]: Mary Kingsland for violently assaulting her & by force taking away from her 2 Aprons & other things being goods pawned by y[e] Def[t]: to y[e] Pl[f]: for 6[s]:6[D] ag[t] y[e] will of the Pl[f]. & offered to return her only 2[s]: 6[D] w[ch] being Sworn to granted a warr[t]: for y[e] Assault.

184. *Thursday, 8 July 1736* Martha White complains against Thomas Harris for Assaulting and beating her. On oath made granted a warr[t]: for him.

185. *Friday, 9 July 1736* Rich[d] Alexander complains ag[t]: Tho: Fouch for an assault on him last night in house of M[r] Wright at Homerton. On oath made granted a warr[t]: for him.

186. *Friday, 9 July 1736* Mary Austen complains ag[t] W[m] Coopman for assaulting & beating her Grand Son W[m] Austen a child of 8 years. On her Oath made a warr[t] for him.

187. *Thursday, 15 July 1736* W^{m} [*blank*] Brown complains ag^{t}: Jno: Wheeler for an assault on him & knocking him down. On his oath made a warr^{t}: for him.

188. *Friday, 16 July 1736* Geo: Fox complains ag^{t}: his Servt: Apprentice Wm Cumberland for assaulting him & tearing his Shirt. On his Oath made a Warr^{t}: for him. [*See* **233**, **731**].

189. *Tuesday, 3 August 1736* Mary Wormlayton complains ag^{t}: Mary Mouse wife of William Mouse for an assault on her ye 31 July at Newington. On her Oath made a warr^{t}: for her.

190. *Saturday, 7 August 1736* Mary Cooper complains ag^{t}: James Ashley for assaulting & grievously wounding Rich^{d}: Davis on ye 5 Aug: in Church Str^{t}: On her Oath made a warr^{t}: for him.

191. *Tuesday, 10 August 1736* Anne Cooper complains ag^{t}: her husband Thomas Cooper for taking away all their goods & going away leaving her & her family to perish Sworn to. 3 Small Children – Tho: Cooper has lodged ye goods at Mr Grays a broker near ye Coach & horses in Aldersgate Str^{t}: near the George Inn. On Complaint of ye Churchwarden Mr Weston made out a Warr^{t}: for him.

192. *Monday, 16 August 1736* Sarah Crew complains ag^{t}: James Hart & Anne Hart his wife for assaulting & beating her & kicking her. On Oath made granted a warr^{t}: for both.

193. *Wednesday, 18 August 1736* Mary Kingsland complains ag^{t}: Anne Follyatt for assaulting & beating her. On her Oath granted a warr^{t}: for her.
Friday, 20 August 1736 On hearing ye cause Mary Kingsland made oath to the assault & bound over for her appearance at next Gen^{ll} Sessions John Carter of Marestreet [lab *deleted*] Farmer, Andrew Guy of D^{o} Labourer [both] in £10 each. [Mary Kingsland *deleted*] Anne Folliot of D^{o} [D^{o} *deleted*] in £10 in penalty of Imprisonm^{t} Recog: not pd.[1] [*See* **121**, **194**].

1. The recognizance was discharged at the September sessions. MJ/SR/2661, recog. 4.

194. *Thursday, 19 August 1736* Thomas Folliot complains ag^{t}: Wm Kingsland for assaulting him in his own house. On his Oath taken made a warr^{t}: for him. [*See* **121**, **193**].

195. *Thursday, 19 August 1736* Eliz^{a}. Heath complains ag^{t}: Wm Pescod for an assault & beating her. On her Oath granted a warr^{t}: for him.

196. *Friday, 27 August 1736* Thomas Watson Servt: to Rachell Gould bro^{t}: a person in custody of Hen: Harrill whose name was Sus: Newcome & charged her wth Stealing fruit out of the garden of Mrs Gould. Hen: Clein Confirms the Same. Both sworn to it. On hearing ye matter

& examination of ye woman who did acknowledge ye fact sent her to Bridewell for 1/mo: for labour as a Vagrant &c.

197. *Monday, 30 August 1736* Mary Austen complains ag^{t}: Joshua Bridgman for assaulting & beating her yesterday. On her oath made a warr^{t}: for him.
Tuesday, 31 August 1736 Discharged ye warr^{t}: & pty at ye desire of ye Plaintiff on her having rec^{d} Satisfaction.

198. *Thursday, 2 September 1736* Silvester Briggs complains ag^{t}: Geo: Ruddle for assaulting & beating him this morning at Temple Mills. On his Oath made a warr^{t}: for him.

199. *Monday, 6 September 1736* Swore in Mary Wasley for Searcher of Hackney.

200. *Thursday, 30 September 1736* Wm Osborn complains ag^{t}: Matthew Penn for an assault and beating him. On his Oath made granted a warr^{t}:

201. *Tuesday, 5 October 1736* Kath: Carter complains ag^{t}: Jno: Whittell [& *deleted*] for unlawfully digging up & carrying away her Turneps out of her field back of Bethnall green. On oath made granted a warr^{t}: for him.

202. *Friday, 22 October 1736* James Coo complains y^{t} he lost lately out of his Coach at Lond^{o}: a bundle of goods being ye pperty of Simon Lambeth trusted to his care to bring in his Stage Coach to Hackney wch goods were feloniously Stolen out of his Coach & he violently Suspects they were taken by Thomas Cook & therefore desires a warr^{t}: to search his house. On his Oath taken granted a Search warr^{t}: to Search Tho: Cooks h^{o}: &c.

203. *Saturday, 30 October 1736* Mary Woodyeard complains ag^{t}: Richd Smith for an assault on her yesterday & upon her Oath made a Warr^{t}: for him.
Same day On hearing ye matter bound over by recognisance Richard Smith of Homerton Coachdriver in £10, Joseph Wright of D^{o} Victualler [and] Edward Poole of D^{o} D^{o}, each £5, for appearance of Rich^{d}: Smith at next Gen^{ll}: Sessions at Hicks hall to answer complaint of Mary Woodyeard &c &c.[1] [*See* **206**].

1. Smith was discharged at the December sessions. MJ/SBB/940, recog. 47.

204. *Monday, 1 November 1736* Rebeccah Crofts complains ag^{t}: Ralph Middleton for assaulting & beating her at Old Ford in her own yard last Saterday. On her Oath made granted a warr^{t}: for him.

205. *Monday, 8 November 1736* Joseph LittleJohn complains ag^{t} Matthew Skigg ye elder & [Anne *deleted*] Mary Skigg his wife of Bethnall green for an assault & wounding him yesterday. On his Oath made a warr[t] for them.

206. *Saturday, 30 October 1736* Middlesex. Mary Woodyard wife of Samuel Woodyard of the Parish of S[t]. John at Hackney in the county of Middlesex maketh Oath that on the 29th day of October [last past *deleted*] Instant one Richard Smith a Coachman did prophanely Curse twice in the parish aforesaid saying each time Damn you when Speaking to this Deponent. [*signed*] Mayry Wodyard. Sworn before me the 30th day of October 1736 [signed] Henry Norris.[1] [*See* **203**].

1. This information has been inserted into the volume; it was originally taken on a loose sheet of paper. Apart from the alteration to the wording noted above, the entry is not in Norris's hand.

207. *Wednesday, 10 November 1736* Middlesex John Fawcett Servant to Robert Pitts Esq[r] of Bethnall green maketh Oath that on this tenth day of November instant Samuell Gold of Lambeth Gardner did profanely [Swear *deleted*] Curse three Severall times in the Hamlet of Bethnall Green in the Parish of Stepney Saying each time God damn you in the hearing of this Deponent. John Fawcett [*mark*]. Sworn before me this 10 November 1736 Henry Norris. Signed a pper warr[t]: to Levy y[e] penalty 3[s] & dd it to Rob: Pitt Esq[r] to be put into y[e] hands of a pper officer.

208. *Tuesday, 16 November 1736* Elis[a]: Chandler Examined upon Oath being a Single woman & Mother of a bastard female Child called Hannah & She charged Richard Scandret of Mare Street Victualler to be the father, was born day before xmas day last.

209. *Thursday, 9 December 1736* Convicted my Coachman Tho: Lafford of Swearing in my hearing Saying by God & demanding y[e] penalty 1[s] he pd it & dd it to M[r] Sadleir to be pd y[e] Churchwarden for y[e] use of y[e] poor of Hackney parish.

210. *Tuesday, 4 January 1737* W[m] Gibbons complains ag[t] Rich[d] Upton Jn[o]: Wetherhead Geo: Eaton & Rich[d] Masling for an assault &c – made a warr[t]: for y[m].
Saturday, 8 January 1737 Eaton, Wetherhead & Masling were bro[t]: & agreed w[th] y[e] Complain[t] & discharged y[m].

211. *Tuesday, 4 January 1737* John Curtis bro[t]: in Custody by warr[t]: frm: Alex[a]: Garrat Esq chrgd on y[e] Oath of [*blank*] Weston Churchwarden for being a loose idle disorderly fellow & leaving his wife & family w[th]out maintenance whereby they are become chargeable to y[e] Parish. Committed him to Bridewell to hard labour.
Wednesday, 12 January 1737 [Discharged him *deleted*] Desired he might be dischgd at discharge of the Gaol. [*See* **243**, **910**].

212. *Thursday, 27 January 1737* Anne Fischer complains ag[t]: W[m]

Howard for an assault on her & beating her grievously this morning in Brookh°: Clopton. Made a warr[t]: for him.

213. *Wednesday, 16 February 1737* Susannah Baldwin complains ag[t] Elisabeth Wilson for an assault & beating her grievously. On her oath made granted a warr[t]: for Wilson.

214. *Wednesday, 23 February 1737* W[m] Gill bro[t]: before me chgd by [*blank*] on Suspicion of Stealing a brass pound weight but on hearing it discharged him for want of proof.

215. *Friday, 25 February 1737* James Bolton complains ag[t] Hen: Fouch for an assault last Tuesday in Church field & misusing him very much. Granted a Warr[t]:
Monday, 28 February 1737 The matter was agreed & dischargd y[e] warr[t]: at desire of y[e] Complain[nt]:

A list of names and dates (relating to burials in woollen) which appeared at this point in the manuscript, has been removed to the end, entry **357**.

216. *Monday, 28 February 1737* Thomas Keeling bro[t]: in Custody of Rob: Loyd charged by Jacob Crew for Suspicion of Stealing from him Severall Iron Smiths tools taken upon him going from Crews house towards London. On ex[a]: Keeling he says he knows nothing how y[e] goods came into his bag. Jacob Crew of Marestreet in Hackney Smith [and] Richard Orton of D° D° bound in £20 each to psecute & give evidence. Rob: Loyd the Constable of Hackney Gardner bound also in £20 to give evidence y[e] goods being put in his Custody & committed Tho: Keeling to Newgate.[1]

1. Keeling died in gaol awaiting trial. MJ/GBB/315/92.

217. *Friday, 29 April 1737* Dan[ll]: Atkins complains ag[t]. W[m] Pearson & Henry Coomes for assaulting him & knocking him down last night in Clapton. On his Oath taken granted a warr[t]: for both of y[m].
Same day Hen. Coomes bro[t]: in Cust°: of Jos: Hill headb°: & on hearing Dan: Atkins & Hen: Smith upon Oath it appeared y[t] Hen: Coomes took by force a Crutch from Hen: Smith & put it into y[e] hand of W[m] Pearson who therew[th] knockt Dan. Atkins down immediately. Bound over Hen: Coomes of [H *deleted*] Clopton Hackney Cordwainer by his own recognisance in £10 to appear at next Gen[ll]: Sessions of the peace to answer y[e] complaint.[1]

1. Coombs failed to appear at the May sessions and his recognizance was estreated. MJ/SBB/944, recog. 126.

218. *Sunday, 1 May 1737* Anne Godfrey complains of having lost Some linnen put to her to wash Stolen from her garden last friday afternoon ab[t]: 5 or 6 Viz: 3 linnen Shirts & 6 Shifts 2 Shirts y[e] pperty of M[r] Beard 1 shirt of M[r] Powell & y[e] Shifts of M[rs] Warner & Suspects they were taken by 3 men one whereof is a Blackman whose name She is informed is George Scipio & She knows not ye names of ye other 2. Made a warr^{t}: to attach Scipio.

Middlesex. The information of Anne Godfrey taken before Henry Norris one of his Majestyes Justices of the Peace for the Said County who upon her Oath Saith that last friday in the afternoon there were Stolen from her out of her Garden 6 Shifts the property of Mrs Warner & 2 Shirts the property of Mr Beard & 1 Shirt the property of Mr Powell & She does verily beleive they were Stolen by 3 men one whereof is a Black & She is informed his name is George Scipio but She does not know the name of the other 2 men. [*signed*] Ann Godfrey. 1 May 1737 Sworn before me Henry Norris.

Monday, 2 May 1737 Geo: Scipio being bro^{t}: in Custody of John Flatman upon my Warr^{t}: Anne Godfrey made oath to her loss at ye time ab^{t}: 5 or 6 a clock & was at the Same time told by Sarah Riddle a child of 7 year old y^{t} there were men in Mr Walkers garden, Mary House Same day told her y^{t} one of those men was black & a br^{o} Coat full of Rags. Deb: Plant another child Saw only a mans leg in ye Garden wch the children confirmed. Wm House near 14 deposes y^{t} he Saw ye Black in Mr Walkers garden last friday nearly ab^{t}: 4 or 5 a clock. Geo: Scipio alledges y^{t} he knows nothing of ye matter & was at Hackney last Thursday but not on friday. Geo: Bovet [Dow *deleted*] watchcasemaker at Mary Germains in Spitall fields makes oath y^{t} he was in comp^{a}: wth Scipio last friday [till *deleted*] ½ 11 till ½ 2 at ye 3 Crowns Dowg:hill. Wm Reed confirms ye Same y^{t} he was wth y^{m} till after 1. Geo: Hawksford Sworn Says y^{t} Scipio was at Hackney last friday & he met him in Chur: y^{d} between 6 & 7. Jno Blackwell Sworn Says he verily beleives he Saw him last friday at lest he Saw him 2 d^{s}: last week in Hackney whereas Scipio owns to have been there but 1 day. Geo: Scipio of S^{t}. Leonard Shoreditch chapman £80, Wm Sanderson of St Christophers London Linnen Draper £40, John Slade of St Leonard Shoreditch weaver £40, upon Condition that Geo: Scipio personally appeareth at the next General Session of the Peace to be held for the County of Middx to answer Ann Godfrey being charged by her on Suspicion of having feloniously taken out of her Garden in Hackney in the s^{d}. County three shirts & 6 Shifts the property of several persons & to be of the good behaviour & not depart the Court without License. Ann Godfrey of Hackney Wid^{o} £40 To prosecute Geo Scipio.[1]

1. Scipio's recognizance does not appear to have been returned to the sessions, nor has any indictment against him been traced. The affair was almost certainly compromised. As the offence is clearly stated to have been felonious, this suggests that both Norris and the prosecutor were acting improperly (see introduction).

219. *Thursday, 12 May 1737* Esther Young complains ag^{t}: her husband Richd Young for beating & abusing her & threatning to kill her on her Oath made a warr^{t}: for him.

220. *Monday, 16 May 1737* Oliver Fitsgerald complains ag^{t}: Wm Harrison for assaulting & Striking him and threatning to murder him in Well

Street Hack. On Oath made by him granted a warr^t: for W H. On hearing ye Cause he being bro^t: in Cust^o of [*blank*], O Fitsgerald Swore to ye Assault but it was made up & dischgd.

221. *Thursday, 19 May 1737* Tho: Newbery complains ag^t: Jno Parsley for an assault beating & kicking him & knocking him down wth a brick-batt & wounding him very much. On his Oath made thereof granted a Warr^t: for Parsley.
Same Day & on hearing ye cause it appeared as above but it appearing also y^t ye wound was by Mr Cottons opinion likely to be cured in a week ye matter was adjusted between y^m and ye warr^t: dischgd at ye desire of ye psecutor.

222. *Thursday, 26 May 1737* Middlesex Robert Iles of the Parish of S^t. John at Hackney in the County of Middlesex Farmer [and Elizabeth the wife of *deleted*] maketh Oath that William Harrison this day used such threatening words to him this Deponent that he goes in danger of his Life or of some bodily hurt that the said William Harrison will [cause or *deleted*] do cause or procure to be done unto him and that he desires the Peace of him not out of any Malice vexation or revenge but for the causes aforesaid. [*signed*] Robert Iles. Sworne before me the 26th [*apparently altered from* 27th] day of May in the year of our Lord 1737 [*signed*] Henry Norris.[1]
Same day Committed him W Harrison to Newprison for want of Sureties for the Peace & his good behaviour.[2] [*See* **224**].

1. The preceding part of this entry is not in Norris's hand.
2. The sessions book notes that Harrison was not to be discharged without reference to Norris, Tyssen and Garrett, or any two of them. MJ/SBB/944, p. 82.

223. *Tuesday, 14 June 1737* Jno Wollard complains ag^t: Wm Rogers for beating & abusing him in breach of ye Peace last Saterday in Homerton. On his Oath made a warr^t: for him.

224. *Tuesday, 21 June 1737* William Smith living in King Street in the Parish of St George in the County of Middx Cooper Bound in £20 [and] James Holland of the Parish of Christ Church in the said County Reed maker Bound in £20 upon Condition that William Harrison now in Custody of the Keeper of New Prison shall personally appear at the next Quarter Sess of the Peace to be held for the County of Middx to answer the Complaint of Robt Iles he having Sworn the peace against him and that he shall in the mean time be of the good behaviour &c. Taken June 21st 1737 and a Discharge Signed by H Norris & Saml Tyssen Esqr.[1] [*See* **222**].

1. This entry is not in Norris's hand. Harrison was discharged at the July sessions. MJ/SBB/945, recog. 114.

225. *Wednesday, 22 June 1737* Sarah Miller complains ag^t: John Shaw for beating & abusing her this morning in her lodgings near Mutton lane, on Oath made granted a warr^{t} for him.

226. *Friday, 24 June 1737* Wm Carter bro^{t}: in Cust^{o}: of Henry Hollis, George Marwick chgd by him wth Gathering & Stealing a parcell of Beans to y^{e} quantity of near $\frac{1}{2}$ a bushell out of a field in y^{e} Parish of S^{t}: Mary Le Bow. Wm Jagger made oath that on Suspicion of having lost Some beans y^{e} night before out of y^{e} field, y^{t} last night he wth Some others kept watch & found in y^{e} field sd Geo: Marwick wth 2 bags & his pockets filled wth beans gathered in ye field ye pperty of Wm Carter & the prisoner acknowledged ye Same. Sent to Bridewell to hard Labour the S^{d} Geo: Marwick.
Wednesday, 29 June 1737 Ordered Geo: Marwick to be discharged out of Bridewell at desire of the psecutor Wm Carter.

227. *Friday, 19 August 1737* Tho: Lely complains ag^{t}: Joseph Swaby & Wm Brown for assaulting him & beating him last Tuesday in ye Brick field at Marestreet. Made a Warr^{t}: for him.

228. *Tuesday, 30 August 1737* James Coo complains [ag^{t}: *deleted*] he had lost a Cloth or Rug out of his Coach ab^{t}: 14 d^{s}: ago his own pperty Vallue 2^{s} & Suspects y^{t} Tho: Wright had feloniously taken ye Same. Made out a Warr^{t}: for him.
Wednesday, 31 August 1737 On his being bro^{t}: before me. Middlesex The Information of James Coo of the Parish of Islington Stage Coach driver taken before me Hen: Norris one of his Majestyes Justices of the Peace for the Said County on [Monday *deleted*] Tuesday 30th day of August 1737 Who upon his Oath Saith that about 14 days ago he lost out of the Coach he drives a Rug covering for the Coachbox Seat the property of him the Said James Coo and that he vehemently Suspects that Thomas Wright of Homerton in the Parish of Saint John at Hackney did feloniously take the Same and he charges the Said Thomas Wright on Suspicion of stealing the same. [*signed*] James Coo. Sworn before me 30 August 1737 Henry Norris.
Same day James Coo of the Parish of Islington Stage Coach driver bound in £20 to psecute Thomas Wright for felony &c.
Same day Bound Tho: Wright of S^{t}: Jno: at Hackney Labourer in £40 Joseph Wright of D^{o} Victualler 20 [and] Edward Poole of D^{o} D^{o} 20, for the appearance of Tho: Wright at next Gen^{ll} Session &c to answer James Coo being charged on Suspicion of Stealing Rug out of his Coach &c.[1]

1. An attempt to indict Wright at the September sessions failed and the recognizance, which was signed by both Norris and Tyssen, was discharged. MJ/SBB/946, recog. 16.

229. *Tuesday, 6 September 1737* Geo: Howe desires leave to Sell drink at ye Plow in Mile end old Town & gave him leave to Licensing time.

230. *Thursday, 8 September 1737* Sarah Thompson complains ag^{t}: Joseph Whitehead for using threatning Speeches to her that She goes in fear of her life whereof She made oath in usuall form & made a Warr^{t}: for him.

231. *Wednesday, 21 September 1737* Mary Dudley [*entry incomplete*].

232. *Sunday, 25 September 1737* Wm Catlin bro^{t}: Frederick Eaton in Cust^{o}: of Wm Catherines & charged him on Oath wth Stealing a pair of old Stockings of Small vallue out of his Garden in Lond^{o}: Field wch he acknowledged. Sent him to Bridewell.

233. *Tuesday, 27 September 1737* Geo: Fox complains ag^{t}: his apprentice Wm Cumberland for being a disorderly & ungovernable Servt: & on his Oath made a warr^{t}: for him & on his appearance & fair promises it was made up. [*See* **188**, **731**].

234. *Tuesday, 4 October 1737*[1] Susan Ditty complains ag^{t}: Abraham Downham for assaulting & kicking her in a barbarous manner at her own door in Hummerton last night without any provocation. On oath made granted a warr^{t}.

1. This entry is dated 1736 in the manuscript, but its position suggests that 1737 is more likely.

235. *[Friday, 7] October 1737* Henry WebbLen [*sic*] [bro^{t}: *deleted*] did bring in Cust^{o}: of Hugh Warren, Sam^{ll}: Dent chgd on Suspicion of robbing him on ye highway last night near Newington Turnpike of a p^{r}: Silver Shoe buckles & knee buckles &c. On his oath sd [&c *deleted*] y^{t} last night ab^{t}: 8 a Clock as he was coming from Lond^{o} to Newington he was met by 3 psons near Kingsland turnpike who Stopt him & robbed him of a p^{r}: Silver Shoe buckles a p^{r}: of Silver knee buckles & 8 or 10^{s} in mo: & he violently Suspects Sam: Dent to be one of the 3 & ye person who actually put his hand in his pocket & took his mo: knowing him by his voice & lower p^{t} of his face. Bound Henry Weblen of S^{t}: Ethelburga Lond^{o}: Cabinetmaker in £40 to psecute at next Gen^{ll}: Q^{r} Sessions at Hicks hall &c & Sent Samuell Dent to Newgate. NB Sam^{ll}: Dent denyed any knowledge of ye matter & alledged y^{t} he was at home at his Cottage near Newington Causeway at ye time ye Robbery was committed & called a woman (who sd She lived at ye Palatine houses as a lodger) to prove ye same but it was not well made out. He Says he gets his living by his & a woman y^{t}: lives wth him Selling apples & Gingerbreads & drams. Medall found in Sam. Dents pocket large of Copper as 10^{s} p^{ce} Maria II D G Mag: Br: Fr: et Hib: Regina on one Side Velut inter ignes Luna minores on Reverse. There was found also in his pocket a $\frac{1}{2}$ Cr^{o}: & 1^{s} together 3^{s}:6^{D} & Some Copper $\frac{1}{2}$ pence. On inquiring how he came by y^{e} mo: y^{e} woman Said She had pawned Some linnen last Monday for 5^{s} & this was p^{t}: of it but they did not alledge y^{t} it was any of it taken in y^{e} trade wch they pretend to drive.[1]

1. Dent was acquitted at the October Old Bailey Sessions. MJ/GBB/315/142.

236. *Sunday, 30 October 1737* Geo: Sully complains y^{t} he was robbed last night of part of a Calf w[ch] was killed & y[e] 2 hind Quarters carryed away On oath made & y[t] he Suspected George Saintclair and y[e] People who live in y[e] 2 houses adjoyning to the Eastward & Westward of him to have Stolen y[e] Same made a Search warr[t]:

237. *Friday, 4 November 1737* W[m] Rogers & Jn[o]: Woodward bro[t]: in Cust[o] of Ch[a]: Gosdin Headb[o]: chgd by W[m] Shrubsall of Queen Street Lond[o]: & Ezek: Cotchett wth assaulting them last night in y[e] fields beating & bruising y[m]. On hearing y[e] matter disch[a]: Jn[o] Woodward who appeared innocent in this affair & ordered W[m] Rogers to find Sureties for his appearance at y[e] Sessions (& gave him 2 hours to do it) to answer compl[t]: of W[m] Shrubsall. William Rogers of S[t]: Jn[o] at Hackney Labourer in £20, Isaac Wintell of D[o] Victualler in 10 [and] Charles Gosdin of D[o], Victualler in 10 bound for y[e] appearance of W[m] Rogers at next Gen[ll]: Session &c to answer compl[t]: of W[m] Shrubsall for assaulting beating & bruising him.[1] [*See* **240**, **242**].

1. Rogers, a notorious deerstealer with a reputation for violence, was discharged at the December sessions. MJ/SBB/948, recog. 23.

238. *Tuesday, 8 November 1737* Dianah Grainger complains ag[t] Edw[d] Wright for assaulting & beating her. On her Oath made a Warr[t]: for him.
Same day On hearing y[m] it was agreed & he discharged.

239. *Tuesday, 15 November 1737* Richard Price complains ag[t]: James Grimsdale & James Harris for an assault on himself & his wife Eliz[a]: Price on y[e] 12:9ber near Newington.

240. *Wednesday, 30 November 1737* Benj[a]: Stevens of Epping Forrest underkeeper complains ag[t]: W[m] Rogers of Hummerton Labourer for Hunting & killing & carrying away unlawfully a Fallow deer out of the Forrest & on y[e] Oath of Jos: Mason made out a Warr[t]: for him.[1] [*See* **237**, **242**].

1. Rogers was the leader of a notorious deer-stealing gang. He was eventually arrested in December 1738 after a violent struggle and was subsequently tried and convicted at the Essex assizes on charges of assault/shooting at various keepers of Waltham Forest. He was sentenced to death. Barlow, *Dick Turpin and the Gregory Gang* (Chichester, 1973), pp. 29–30.

241. *Thursday, 1 December 1737* Joseph Miller & Samuell Smith bro[t]: in Custody of Robert Barnes Headb[o]: chgd by Margaret Parker for Stealing off her line in her yard 3 Shirts Vall: 4[s]. Marg: Parker made Oath to an inform[a]: of y[e] taking of 3 Shirts by 2 men whom She believes were y[e] prisoners & y[t] on her outcry they run away & dropt y[e] Shirts near y[e] Gate. W[m] Cox made Oath y[t] on hearing M[rs] Parkers outcry he saw y[e] two prisoners run from her Gate & pursued them thro Church Street where they were taken. The Prisoners denyed all knowledge of y[e] affair. Marg: Parker [and] W[m] Cox of Hackney Gardner, bound in £40 to psecute & give evidence & Sent y[e] prisoners to Newgate.[1]

1. Miller and Smith were acquitted at the December Old Bailey sessions. Samuel Sadleir acted as Margaret Parker's attorney and the prosecution costs of £1 4s. 4d. were paid by the parish, 'she being very poor'. MJ/GBB/315/148; P79/JN1/142/5.

242. *Wednesday, 30 November 1737* Middlesex The Information of Joseph Mason taken before me Henry Norris one of his Majestyes Justices of the Peace for the Said County who upon his Oath Saith that William Rogers of Hummerton Labourer on the 12th of August last past, in company with another person to this Deponent unknown, did in Epping Forrest near Sr Thomas Websters warren kill & carry away one Fallow Deer the property of his Majesty contrary to law. [*Signed*] Joseph Mason. Sworn before me this 30th November 1737 Henry Norris. [*See* **240**].

243. *Friday, 2 December 1737* Mary Curtis complains ag^{t}: her husband Jno: Curtis for assaulting her & abusing her very barbarously & threatning her life driving her out of ye house & neglecting to pvide for his family. On her oath taken made a Warr^{t}: for him. [*See* **211**, **910**].

244. *Friday, 2 December 1737* Hen: Johnson Philip Liscomb Jno Harris Jno Badger bro^{t}: before me on Suspicion of Stealing Lead from Mr Brewis house. Jos: Cottrell made Oath y^{t} he met on Wednesday Philip Liscomb &c but not to ye purpose. Jno Crawley made Oath y^{t} he met ye 3 first today between Bethnall Green & ye Globe in Mileend 2 [bein *deleted*] having each a Sack wch Seemed heavy as tho Lead were in it & on ex^{a}: w^{tt} was in y^{t} Sack Liscomb would Not say w^{tt} was in the Sack Saying he did not know. Jno Brooks on oath charged y^{m} on Suspicion of Stealing Lead from ye house late Mr Spencers. Sent ye 3 first to New-prison on Suspcion &c for further Ex^{a}:
Saturday, 3 December 1737 Found 2 Sacks & 2 Plaisterers Hammers for cutting up Lead & Committed Jno: Badger to Bridewell Suppose those tools dropt by y^{m} Some at my Gate & others in ye Field where they had been bro^{t} along.
Same day[1] Middlesex Thomas Williams Servant to M^{r}. Valentine Brewis maketh Oath that there hath been lately feloniously taken from the House late in the Occupation of Mrs Katherine Spencer in Grove Street in the parish of St John at Hackney in the said County of Middlesex several Parcels of Lead and that he Suspects the said Lead or some part thereof is concealed in the house of or out houses Known by the sign of the Shepherd and Shepherdess in the parish of St Dunstan Stepney otherwise Stebonheath in the said County of Middlesex. [*signed*] Tho. Williams. Sworn before me the 3d day of December 1737, [*signed*] Henry Norris.[2] [*See* **247**, **250**, **256**].

1. The remaining part of the entry is not in Norris's hand.
2. Liscomb, Johnson and Harris appear to have been committed to Bridewell rather than the New Prison. The sessions book notes that they were to be bailed only by Norris, Garrett or by Justice Richard Farmer. At the January sessions, Thomas Williams and John Crawley exhibited articles of the peace against Philip Liscomb and John Brooks exhibited articles of the peace against Henry Johnson; articles of the peace were also exhibited against John Harris, although the precise details are unclear. On 18

January 1738, Liscomb and Johnson were bound over to keep the peace for a year. Harris was similarly bound over 20 April 1738 (256). MJ/SBB/949, recog. 32, pp. 51, 52, 92.

245. *Thursday, 8 December 1737* Patr: Lindsay compl[ns]: ag[t]: W[m] Reeves for an assault last night & beating him being Sworn made a Warr[t].

246. *Tuesday, 13 December 1737* Mary Chittum complains ag[t]: her husband Charles Chittum for assaulting & beating her in a very grievous manner & kicking her & throwing her down Stairs & threatning to murder her – on oath made granted a warr[t]: for him.

247. *Thursday, 15 December 1737* Bail offered for Hen: Johnson. Jn[o]: Loyd Cordwainer over ag[t]: 3 Tons in Putney near y[e] River, Benj[a]: Biggs Carpenter in Windsor Str[t]: in Putney known to M[r] Fletcher a Haberdasher at y[e] Sun in Cheapside, to M[r] Marks a Glover in Cheap cornr Gutterlane, appointed y[m] Monday next to come at 12.[1] [*See* **244**, **250**, **256**].

1. The bail were acceptable and a recognizance was returned to the January sessions. It was discharged 18 January 1738 on Johnson entering a fresh recognizance to keep the peace for a year (see **244**). MJ/SBB/949, recog. 32, p. 52.

248. *Wednesday, 28 December 1737* Middlesex The information of John Shepherd of London field in Hackney Labourer taken before me Henry Norris one of his Majestyes Justices of the Peace for the Said County Who upon his Oath Saith that on Monday the 26 of this instant December his House Situate near London field was broken open in the night time about 7 or 8 a clock and there were Stolen out of his house a Guinea in gold a pair of Stays two womens Gowns Six Linnen Aprons three Cambrick handkerchiefs one Holland handkerchief all his own property & he doth vehemently Suspect that the Said Burglary and Felony were committed by Mary Clark and he is informed and doth verily beleive that part of the Said goods So Stolen are concealed in the house of Elisabeth [*recte* Eleanor] Hutchinson near Cambridge heath. John Shepherd [*mark*]. Sworn 28 December 1737 before me Henry Norris.
Same day Made out a Search warr[t]: for y[e] goods in Atchinsons [*altered from Hutchinson*] house.
Thursday, 29 December 1737 W[m] Catherines Headb[o]: attended wth a return of y[e] Warr[t]: & bro[t]: a p[r]: Stays found in Eleonor Hutchinsons possession w[ch] Mary Shepherd wife of Jn[o] Shepherd made Oath was her husbands & p[t] of y[e] goods Stolen & Hutchinson declared She bo[t]: y[m] on Monday of a woman a Stranger whom She beleives She Should know again. Bound over W[m] Catherines, Eleonor Atchinson [*altered from Hutchinson*] in £20, & Mary Shepherd [each £40 *deleted*] on pain of imprisonm[t] to give evidence at next Q[r] Sessions &c.
Wednesday, 11 January 1738 Jn[o] Shepherd bound in £20 to psecute y[e] Same.[1]

1. Clark was convicted of stealing to the value of 39s. at the January Old Bailey sessions. She was sentenced to transportation. MJ/GBB/315/166.

A list of names and dates (relating to burials in woollen) which appeared at this point in the manuscript, has been removed to the end, entry **358**.

249. *Wednesday, 25 January 1738* Jno: Stubbs complains ag^{t}: his Servt: Matthew Ford for embezling his mo: & running away from his Service contrary to his agreem^{t}: & without notice. On oath made granted a warr^{t} for him.

250. *Friday, 27 January 1738* George Pickstone of the Parish of St George in the County of Midd^{x} Butcher [and] Richard Birch of the same parish Housesmith each bound in the sum of Forty pounds upon Condition that John Harris shall personally appear at the next General Sessions of the Peace to be held for the County of Middlesex at Hicks hall in St John Street then & there to answer the Complaint of John Brookes he having Exhibited articles of the peace against him at the last Quarter Sessions of the Peace held for the s^{d} County and in the mean time to be of the good behaviour & not depart the Court without License. Taken & acknowledged before H Norris Esq Jan^{ry} the 27th 1738.[1] [*See* **244**, **247**, **256**].

1. This entry is not in Norris's hand. The process here is not clear. The recognizance does not appear to have been returned to the sessions. Harris entered into a recognizance to keep the peace for one year on 20 April 1738 (**256**). MJ/SBB/952, recog. 78.

251. *Sunday, 5 February 1738* Mary Grace complains of a Robbery committed in her house yesterday a Camlet gown & a [Silk *deleted*] Cotton gown her own pperty wth Severall other goods Stoln in her house in back lane at Bethnall green & Suspects Martha LittleJohn to be concerned in the Robbery also Mary her Daughter. On her Oath made granted a warr^{t}: for her.

252. *Tuesday, 28 February 1738* Tho: Williams complains ag^{t}: James Conyer for assaulting & beating him. On Oath made granted a warr^{t}: for him.

253. *Saturday, 11 March 1738* Mary Mayn complains ag^{t}: Jos: Whiffin for assaulting Kicking & beating her in a grievous manner. On Oath made granted a warr^{t}: for him.
Same day On hearing ye Cause it appeared y^{t} She was her Self the Aggressor & caused her own hurt & Jos: Whiffin in no fault So dismissed him.

254. *Friday, 24 March 1738* Jean Chambers complains ag^{t}: Wm Platt for assaulting & beating her. On her Oath made a Warr^{t}: for him.

255. *Wednesday, 19 April 1738* Jean Ross complains ag^{t}: Mary Wright for assaulting her in her house beating her & breaking her windows. On Oath made granted a warr^t^: for her.

256. *Thursday, 20 April 1738* Cornelius Dawkins Shoemaker of ye Parish of S^t^: Sepulchre in 3 Fox Court in Long Lane Smithfield [and] George Pickston [*altered from* Pixton] of ye Parish of S^t^: George in the East at the Head of Anchor & Hope alley near Greenbank Butcher bound each in £40 for Jno: Harris for his keeping ye peace towards Jno: Brookes & c & being of ye good behaviour for 1 year to come & discharged Jno: Harris out of new prison. [*See* **244**, **247**, **250**].

257. *Friday, 21 April 1738* Mary Townsend complains y^t^ She had lost a Camlet Cloak Stoln out of her house ye 15th of this instant Aprill & She violently suspects Eliz^a^: [Pryor *deleted*] Robinson to have Stolen ye same by Severall concurring circumstances. On her Oath made granted a warr^t^: for her.

258. *Tuesday, 2 May 1738* Gilbert Dudley complains ag^t^: Hen: Robiston for assaulting him & throwing water upon him. On his Oath made a warr^t^ for him.

259. *Tuesday, 4 July 1738* Jno: Stubbs complains ag^t^: George Macgee his late Servt: for defrauding him of milk to the Vallue of 20^s^ & upwards & unlawfully taking away 2 wood Pails a measure & Strainer & a Yoke. Upon his Oath made a warr^t^: for him.

260. *Tuesday, 11 July 1738* Eliz^a^: Allen complains ag^t^: George Sinclair for assaulting & beating her in breach of ye peace. On Oath made granted a Warr^t^: for him. [*See* **267**, **291**].

261. *Friday, 14 July 1738* Nathan Cooper complains of Green Goodwin for assaulting him on ye road to Hackney ye 13th July & punching him wth his Cartwhip. Upon his Oath made granted a warr^t^: for him. On hearing ye Cause at N Coopers desire discharged Green Goodwin.

262. *Saturday, 15 July 1738* Tho: May bro^t^: in Custody of Jno: Stevens Headb^o^: chgd by Sam. Harris for robbing his Garden of fruit & abusing & assaulting his wife. T: May acknowledged ye taking some fruit, Norman Herbert of Bromley, Sam: Baker at 7 Stars at Bromley, both upon Oath, dischgarged [*sic*] as Crased.

263. *Saturday, 15 July 1738* John Ditto complains ag^t^: Abraham LeSoeur & his Wife Mary Le Soeur for assaulting & beating him last Thursday in their house in Brick lane. On oath made granted a warr^t^: for y^m^.

264. *Wednesday, 26 July 1738* Patience Dale complains ag^t^: Tho: King for asssaulting & beating her. Granted a Warr^t^: for him on her Oath made.

Same day On hearing ye Cause upon his being bro^{t}: it was agreed & discharged ye Party.

265. *Friday, 28 July 1738* Mary Seele complains ag^{t}: Jonathan Bull for assaulting & beating her. On her Oath made granted a Warr^{t}: for him.

266. *Wednesday, 2 August 1738* Jno Jones complains ag^{t}: Jno Murphey for assaulting him. On oath made granted a warr^{t}:
Same day On hearing ye matter the ptyes agreed & were discharged.

267. *Saturday, 5 August 1738* Geo: Sinclair bro^{t}: in Cust^{o}: of Dan. Saxendale to answer ye assault upon Eliz^{a}: Allen. She Swore to his Assaulting her 10 July on Bethnall green Struck her Severall blows hurt forefinger of her left hand wch is in a great measure yet useless, at length it was agreed & discharged ye Warr^{t}. [*See* **260**, **291**].

268. *Tuesday, 8 August 1738* Mary Perry complains ag^{t}: James Hall for assaulting her yesterday at Oldford & beating her wth a Pitchfork & threatning her wth farther Mischief. On her Oath taken made a Warr^{t}: for him.

269. *Wednesday, 9 August 1738* Tho: Cross complains ag^{t}: Geo: Watts for assaulting & wounding him in the eye & finger. On his Oath made granted a Warr^{t}: for him.

270. *Friday, 11 August 1738* Daniel Quint made oath that Ralph Wright hath used such threatening words to him that he goes in Danger of his Life or some bodily hurt that he will do cause or procure to be done unto him. Peace warrant granted to apprehend him.[1]
Saturday, 12 August 1738 On ye party's being taken & bro^{t}: before me, heard the Cause & ye matter was agreed between y^{m} & discharged ye def^{t}: out of Cust^{o}: at desire of ye Pl^{f}:

1. The preceding part of this entry is not in Norris's hand.

271. *Tuesday, 22 August 1738* Richd Say bro^{t}: in Cust^{o} of Dan: Quint Headb^{o}: on R Farmer Esqr Warr^{t}: for a breach of ye Peace ag^{t}: Ch^{a}: Tilbury. On Dan. Quints Oath y^{t} Ch^{a}: Tilbury wth [*sic*] his being in Cust^{o}: & y^{t} he w^{d}: presently bring him before me he refused to come upon wch dischgd ye Warrt:

272. [*Wednesday, 23 August 1738* Ebenezer Brathwaite for Walter Morris *entry deleted*].

273. *Friday, 11 August 1738* John Crane was brought by John Stevens one of the Headboroughs of the parish of S^{t}. Mary of Stratford Bow in the County of Middx: by virtue of my Warrant Ann Damont having voluntarily before me on her Oath charged him with having gotten her with Child which Child is likely to be born a Bastard and to be Chargeable to the said parish and the said John Crane was bound in the sum of

£40 and the [*sic*] John Stevens in the like sum upon Condition that the said John Crane shall personally appear at the next General Sessions of the Peace to be held for the County of Middlesex at Hicks hall in St John Street to answer the s^{d} Complaint and also to abide & perform such order or orders as shall be made relateing the same pursuant to the Statute in that Case made & provided &c.[1]

1. Crane, a dyer, failed to appear to his recognizance in September and it was ordered to be estreated. In October, the estreat was cancelled and the recognizance was respited until the following quarter sessions. It is again marked as estreated in the sessions book for January 1739. MJ/SBB/954, recog. 229; MJ/SBB/955 p. 61, MJ/SBB/958, p. 8.

274. *Thursday, 5 October 1738* Sam. Johnston bro^{t}: Sarah Thompson in Cust^{o}: of Dan. Quid Headb^{o}: of Bow on a charge of picking his pocket of a purse wth 9^{s} & Some Cop^{r}: wch he Swore to. Geo: Abbott [and] Mary Bull Sworn was present w^{n} this hapned & both made appear the contrary. On hearing ye whole discharged ye defendant by consent of the psecutor.

275. *Monday, 16 October 1738* Nathan Cooper complains ag^{t}: Tho: Wilkinson for assaulting him at ye Tollgate 14:8ber on Hackney Road by pushing him in a violent manner & afterwards Striking him Severall blows. On his Oath made granted a Warr^{t}: for him.
Thursday, 19 October 1738 On hearing ye partyes it was agreed & dischgd ye Warrant.

276. *Wednesday, 18 October 1738* James Coniers bro^{t}: before me by a Bench Warr^{t} being indicted for an assault on Ja: Bolton.
Morgan Bynon of Hackney brewer bound in £20 [*altered from* £10] Jno: Masling of D^{o} Victualler in 20 [*altered from* £10] James Coniers of D^{o} D^{o} £40 [*altered from £20*] for ye appearance of Ja: Coniers at next Gen^{ll}: Sessions to answer to an indictm^{t}: preferred ag^{t}: him by Ja: Boton [*sic*] &c.[1]

1. James Coniers was convicted at the December sessions and fined 1s. MJ/SBB/956, recog. 1.

277. *Wednesday, 18 October 1738* Wm Trepass complains ag^{t}: Rob: Slater for assaulting him in his own house in Homerton. On his Oath made granted a Warr^{t} for him.
Same day On hearing ye cause the matter was agreed & discharged ye Warr^{t}:

278. *Tuesday, 24 October 1738* Edwd Marshall bro^{t}: in Cust^{o}: of Wm Catherines Headb^{o}: charged by Mary Pryor on Suspicion of Stealing a Silver Spoon ye goods of James Pryor at ye Should^{r} of Mutton in Hackney last Sunday morn: ab^{t}: 10 or 11 a Clock. Mary Pryor [and] Mary Taylor Sworn. Mary Pryor charges him on Oath wth a Strong Suspicion of his taking a Silver Spoon last Sunday between 10 & 11. She had a Spoon in her hand & laid it down & he came into ye Shop & put his hand

in a Suspicious manner und^{r} his Apron & She beleives at y^{t} time he Stole it & y^{t} She has absolutely lost it. Mary Taylor deposes y^{t}: at ye Cock in Church Street She bo^{t}: of him a p^{ce}: of a broken Silver Spoon & pd him 2^{s}:6^{D} for it being Sunday morning wch he then declared he found it by ye Sh^{o}: of Mutton. Ed. Marshall being ex^{a}: owns he did Sell her a p^{ce}: of a Spoon wch he Says he found near the Pond near Mutton lane end in Mare street.
Wednesday, 25 October 1738 Sent Marshall to New prison. [*See* **281**].

279. *Saturday, 14 October 1738* Edward Taylor Thomas Page Robert Johnson and Thomas Gray were brought by John Stevens one of the Headboroughs of Bow by vertue of a Bench warrant they standing indicted for breaking the Glass windows belonging to the dwelling house of Edmund Smith in the said parish and entered into the following recognizances. Edward Taylor of Bow labourer in £40, John Page of the same vict [and] Henry Hollis of the same vict each in £20. Thomas Page of Bow Labourer £40, W^{m} van Leute of Bow Scarlet Dyer [and] James Huggett of Stepney Farmer each in £20. Robert Johnson of Bow Labourer in £40, W^{m}. van Leute [and] James Huggett each £20. Thomas Gray of Bow Labourer in £40, W^{m}. van Leute [and] James Huggett each £20. To appear at the next General Sessions of the Peace to be held for the County of Middx to plead to the said Indictment.[1]

1. This entry is not in Norris's hand. The four men were tried on 4 December following. Taylor and Gray were convicted and fined 13s. 4d.; Johnson (who is described as a gardener in the indictment) and Page were acquitted. MJ/SBB/956, recogs. 2–5; MJ/SBP/14/423.

280. *Monday, 6 November 1738* Hannah Boucher complains ag^{t}: James Butler for assaulting her in a rude manner throwing her on a bed wth intention to lye wth her by force & doing very rude actions to her in her own chamber in Clapton. On her Oath made a Warr^{t}: for him.

281. *Thursday, 16 November 1738* James Pryor of Hackney Cook bound in forty pounds To prefer an Indictment against Edward Marshall charged by Mary the wife of James Pryor on suspicion of Stealing a Silver Spoon at the next General Sessions of the Peace and prosecute the Law with effect upon the same and also that his said wife shall give evidence upon the said Indictment.
Thursday, 30 November 1738 Mary Taylor of Hoxton Square wid^{o}: bound in £20 to appear & give evidence ag^{t}: Edwd: Marshall foregoing.[1] [*See* **278**].

1. Marshall was discharged by proclamation at the gaol delivery in December. MJ/GBB/315/234.

282. *Tuesday, 5 December 1738* Henry Swell complains ag^{t}: his Apprentice Jno: Spencer for behaving himself disobediently & disorderly & absenting himself [a night *deleted*] unlawfully from his Masters Service without leave. On his Oath thereof granted a Warr^{t} for him. On hearing ye matter & pmise of amendm^{t}: dismist him.

283. *Monday, 18 December 1738* Dav: Solomon, Rob: Clark, Napthali Franks, Simpson Levi, Solomon Solomons, all charged by Wm Hornby for a [Riot *deleted*] breach of the peace in his house last night & bro^{t}: pr Wm Saxendale in his Cust^{o}: as Headb^{o}: On hearing ye matter reccommended them to make up ye matter wth Hornby wch was done & all things on both Sides forgiven & ye persons dischgd.[1]

1. Napthali Franks (1715–1796) and his cousin David Salomons were members of a prominent and wealthy Anglo-American Jewish mercantile family. Their companions were almost certainly drawn from a similar background. Unfortunately, Franks' surviving correspondence throws little light on the origins of this particular escapade. Leo Hershkowitz and Isidore S. Meyer (eds), *Letters of the Franks family 1733–1748*, (American-Jewish Historical Society, Waltham, Mass., 1968).

284. *Saturday, 23 December 1738* John Wetherhead Grave Digger of Hackney and Katherine Smith Servant to Mr John Singleton Sexton of the said parish Complained upon Oath against James Cooke John Spencer Thomas Wingfield John Russell John Miles John Platt & John Cooke for making a very noise and disturbance in the said parish Church on Sunday the 17th Instant and Assaulted them in breach of his Majesties peace.[1]

1. This entry is not in Norris's hand. The accused all entered into recognizances before Norris and were discharged at the February sessions. MJ/SBB/959, recogs. 113–117.

285. *Tuesday, 16 January 1739* Eliz^{a}: White complains ag^{t}: Mary Clark for assaulting & wounding her on the Arm. On Oath made granted a Warr^{t}: for her.

286. *Tuesday, 9 January 1739* Cath: Baker complains ag^{t}: Jno: Patmore for assaulting her & cutting her gown maliciously. On her Oath made a Warrt: for him.

287. *Monday, 22 January 1739* Robert Smith bro^{t}: by Wm Katherines Headboro [for *deleted*] being charged by Thomas Southwell for putting down a parcell of pales belonging to Mr Thomas Rudge being part of the fence belonging to a Garden in Grove Street in the Hamlet of Bethnal Green in the parish of Stepney on Thursday morning the 18th Instant. Robert Smith Confessed the fact. Henry Vaughan appeared for M^{r}. Rudge and desired that the s^{d}. Smith might be ordered to make up some fence to prevent persons from going into the Garden and that will be all the Satisfaction he desires which he was accordingly ordered to do and also was ordered to pay 1^{s} to the use of the Poor of the said Hamlet where the s^{d} Offence was committed which he paid accordingly and was then discharged it being his first Offence.[1]

1. This entry is not in Norris's hand.

288. *Monday, 5 February 1739* Edwd Pimm complains ag^{t}: Jno Thompkin for assaulting & beating his wife Mary Pimm this day at Kingsland at his own house ye Wheatsheaf. On oath made granted a warr^{t}: for him.

289. *Friday, 16 February 1739* James Thompson complains ag^{t}: Elis^{a}: Gray for assaulting him & throwing Urine upon him last week on Oath made granted a warr^{t}: for her.

290. *Tuesday, 6 March 1739* Martha Nichols complains ag^{t}: Joseph Lucas for an assault. On Oath made granted a Warr^{t}: for him.
Saturday, 24 March 1739 Y^{e} pson was bro^{t}: in Cust^{o}: of Wm Griffith & on hearing ye matter ye ptyes not being willing to agree Viz: below. [*See* **292**].

291. *Thursday, 15 March 1739* Elis^{a}: Allen complains ag^{t}: Geo: Sinclair for an assault & beating her Sorely wth a Stick last night. On Oath made granted a warr^{t}: for him.
Sunday, 18 March 1739 Geo: Sinclair bro^{t}: in Cust^{o}: of Dan. Saxendale who declared Eliz^{a}: Allen was not able to come abroad wch was confirmed by Dan: Delorem who upon Oath Saith y^{t} last Wednesday Sinclair assaulted E Allen & Struck her a blow on ye breast without her having assaulted him. On hearing ye whole matter gave him 3 hours time to find Sureties wch he not doing Sent him to New Prison.
Wednesday, 21 March 1739 Discharged him out of prison at the desire of the Complainant El: Allen. [*See* **260**, **267**].

292. *Saturday, 24 March 1739* Bound over Jos: Lucas in £20 of Hackney Lab^{o}: Richd Speed in 10 of D^{o} brickl^{a}: [and] Tho: Shepperdson 10 of D^{o}, Gardner for appearance of sd Jos: Lucas att next Gen^{ll}: Q^{r} Session of ye Peace to answer compl^{t}: of Martha Nichols &c.[1] [*See* **290**].

1. Lucas was discharged at the April sessions. MJ/GBB/960, recog. 88.

293. *Tuesday, 10 April 1739* Francis Rosamond complains ag^{t}: James Holms for assaulting him & beating him. On his Oath made granted a Warr^{t}: for him.
Same day On ye pty's being bro^{t}: in Cust^{o}: & hearing ye Case they agreed ye matter & dischgd him.

294. *Wednesday, 25 April 1739* Everett Jackson bro^{t}: by Warr^{t}: of M^{r} R: Farmer chged on Oath of Mary Johnson for assaulting & beating her. Upon ye Complain^{ts}: desire was discharged.

295. *Friday, 4 May 1739* Wm Gray & Christ^{o}: Plaice complain [*altered from* complaining] ag^{t}: Jno Dumbleton for assaulting & beating y^{m} in breach of ye Peace &c. On Oath made granted a Warr^{t} for him.

296. *Saturday, 12 May 1739* Jno Price complains of his Mistress Dorcas Carter for [detai *deleted*] turning him out of her Service contrary to agreem^{t}: & detaining his wages. [*Entry deleted*].

297. *Wednesday, 16 May 1739* Mary Catgitt complains ag^{t}: Mary Clark for an assault on her in Mrs Gregory's house in Church Str^t: & Striking her divers blows & threatning her. On Oath made granted a Warr^t:

298. *Wednesday, 9 May 1739* The Information of John Stubbs living on the Green in the Hamlet of Bethnal Green in the County of Middlesex Dary Man Taken the 9th day of May 1739. Who upon his Oath sayes that on Sunday night last or the next morning a Door belonging to a room in his dwelling house at Bethnal Green aforesaid was broke open and that there was taken out of the said room a large Copper boiler and a box Iron and that about a Week before he [had taken *deleted*] lost out of the said room about twenty shillings in money & a Linnen Sheet out of a Chest that stood in an other room in the same house & several other things and he this Informant charges one James Darlington who had been his Servant on Violent Suspicion of having Feloniously taken the above mentioned goods and money out of his said house and further sayes not. John Stubbs [*mark*]. Sworn before us the day and year first above written [*signed*] Henry Norris.[1]

1. This entry is not in Norris's hand. Darlington was tried at the June Old Bailey sessions for breaking and entering the house and stealing goods to the value of 13s. (a capital charge). He was found quilty of the theft only (thus reducing the gravity of the charge) and was sentenced to transportation. MJ/GBB/316/6.

299. *Thursday, 14 June 1739* Ruth Clemms complains ag^t: Tho: Parton for Assault on her & tearing her Cloths & cramming her Mouth full of dirt. On her Oath made granted a warr^t: for him.
Saturday, 16 June 1739 On hearing ye matter it was agreed between them & discharged.

300. *Wednesday, 20 June 1739* Margaret Bridgman complains of her husband Matthew Bridgman for beating her in a cruell manner & threatning to murder her. On her Oath taken granted a Warr^t for him.
Same day On hearing ye Cause he acknowledged ye beating her & She charged him wth threatning her life & demanded Sureties for ye peace and took her Oath accordingly. He offering Sureties [bound Matthew Bridgman of *blank* in £40, *blank* £20, *blank* £20 *deleted*] he went away in Cust^o: to pcure them but as ye Officer Bolton alledged Run away & made his escape.

A list of names and dates (relating to burials in woollen) which appeared halfway through the previous entry in the manuscript, has been removed to the end, entry **359**.

301. *Thursday, 28 June 1739* Catherine Macguire complains ag^t Jno Shaw for assaulting & beating her. On her Oath made granted a Warr^t: for him.

302. *Monday, 18 June 1739* Francis Trumble brought by Henry Harrill one of the Headboroughs of the parish of St John at Hackney and charged by Thomas Browne on Oath on Violent Suspicion of having about Six of the clock in the Evening of this day Assaulted him in a certain Field or open place near the Kings high Way near Brook house in the said parish and Feloniously took from him a Silver Watch his property. Committed to new Gate. Thomas Browne of Hackney Cloth Worker bound in £100 to prosecute. Edward Dixon Gardener, Samuel Pamplin Lab[r], Joseph Rotherford D[o], Thomas Harris D[o], Edward Batty Vict[r], Henry Harrill Butcher [all] of Hackney, Edward Hawkins Lab[r], Job Griffin D[o], William Evans D[o], [all] of Stoake Newington, Bound in £50 each to give evidence against the said Fran[s]. Trumble.[1]

1. This entry is not in Norris's hand. A much fuller account of the capture is given in the *Old Bailey Proceedings*. Trumble, a cabinet maker, was convicted of highway robbery at the July Old Bailey sessions and sentenced to death. His defence amounted to a plea of mental instability, falling short of actual lunacy (which at this time was generally accepted to be the total inability to distinguish between right and wrong). He was pardoned. MJ/GBB/316, 17, 31. *O.B. Proc.*, July 1739, R *v* Trumble. Nigel Walker, *Crime and insanity in England* (Edinburgh, 1968).

303. *Saturday, 7 July 1739* Mary Cornish complains ag[t] Mary Overton for assaulting & kicking her. On oath made granted a Warr[t] for her.

304. *Friday, 20 July 1739* Sarah Hutchinson complains ag[t]: Eliz[a]: Richardson Jean Bennett Edward Upperton Jn[o]: Upperton & Hannah Upperton. On her Oath made a warr[t]: for y[m].

305. *Monday, 23 July 1739* Elis[a]: Liddall complains ag[t] Abigail Cawdell for assaulting & Striking her wth a large key & wounding her near y[e] Eye. On her Oath taken granted a warr[t]: for her.
Friday, 27 July 1739 On hearing the matter of the Parties She the Def[t]: acknowledged the assault & offered Sureties to appear at ye next Gen[ll]: Sessions of the Peace. Bound Abigail Cordwell of Hackney Spinster in £40, Matthias Cordwell of Castle Street Spittallfields Stocking weaver 20, Wm Balmes of Castle Street Victualler 20, for her appearance &c.[1]

1. Abigail Cordwell was discharged at the August sessions. MJ/SBB/964, recog. 28.

306. *Monday, 6 August 1739* Frances Webb complains ag[t]: [*entry incomplete*].

307. *Wednesday, 8 August 1739* Christ[o]: Fox & Jn[o]: Page bro[t]: in Custody of James Bolton chgd by Josiah Eberall. [August *deleted*] Josiah Eberall upon oath sayes that the said Fox & Page play'd with him at Skittles at M[r] Panks lost 9[s]:6[d] in money a Silver Watch and a pair of Silver Shoe Buckles. Christopher Fox in Montague Street White Chappel Butcher £20, Joseph Gibbs in the Hay Market White Chappel Butcher [and] James Bolton of Hackney Cordwainer £10 each. John Page in Mag Pye Alley Bishopsgate Street in the parish of S[t] Botolph without Bishopsgate London Butcher £20, Joseph Gibbs [and] James Bolton £10 each. Each of them to appear at the next General Sessions of the Peace to be held for the County of Middx for a Breach of good Behaviour in playing unlawfully at a game called Skittles & Cards in the parish of Hackney [at whi *deleted*] and to answer the Complaint of Josiah Eberall who then lost nine shillings & Six pence in money a Silver Watch and a pair of Silver Buckles & a green plush Coate w^{t} [*illegible*] Buttons & to be of the good behaviour & not depart the Court without License.[1]

1. Apart from the first sentence, this entry is not in Norris's hand. Page and Fox failed to appear at the August sessions and their recognizances were estreated. MJ/SBB/964, recogs. 26, 27.

308. *Monday, 20 August 1739* Hearty Heart complains ag^{t}: Geo: Spencer for assaulting & beating him wth a Stick in a violent manner & wounding him in his right eye. Upon his Oath taken granted a Warr^{t}: for him.

309. *Tuesday, 18 September 1739* Elis^{a}: Catlin complains ag^{t}: John Wheeler for assaulting & beating her on Cambridge heath. On oath made granted a Warr^{t}: for him.

310. *Thursday, 20 September 1739* Judith Edw^{ds}: [& Ma: Schofield *deleted*] complains ag^{t}: Jos^{h}: Hodges & Mary Cross for assaulting her & beating her. On her Oath made a Warr^{t}: for them.
Friday, 21 September 1739 Jos: Hodges & Mary Cross bro^{t}: in Cust^{o}: of Wm Cawn Headb^{o}: who made oath y^{t} he [*altered from* she] gave J Edwards notice y^{t} he had ye prisoners in Cust^{o}: & She came wth them p^{t}: of ye way but then turned back & refused to come to make her complaint good, for wch reason I discharged ye prisoners.

311. *Saturday, 22 September 1739* Mary Kingsland complains of [y^{e} *deleted*] her husband Wm Kingsland for assaulting her & beating her in a very grievous manner & threatning her life. On her oath made granted a warr^{t}: for him.

312. *Friday, 26 October 1739* Mary Williams complains ag^{t}: John Squire & Francis Rosamond for assaulting her Sundry times & breaking her earthen ware to the vallue of 8^{s}. On Oath made granted a Warr^{t}: for them.
Monday, 5 November 1739 Francis Rosamond being bro^{t}: & ye matter heard he made ye woman Satisfaction & was dischgd at her request.

313. *Tuesday, 27 November 1739* Richard Grately complains (in behalf of Mary Ogilby) of Sarah Always for assaulting ye said Mary Ogilby & throwing her down & grievously wounding & bruising her. On Oath made granted a Warr^{t}: ag^{t}: her. On hearing ye Cause Mary Ogilby made oath to ye assault & her hurt & refused to make it up. Gave her time to pcure Sureties wch she did not do
Wednesday, 28 November 1739 so on ye 28:9ber [committed her to New prison for want of Sureties *deleted* Mar *deleted*] Sarah Always of Hackney Wife of Jeremiah Always of [the parish of *deleted*] Putney near Wandsor [*sic*] bound on pain of Imprisonment, Thomas Read of S^{t}:

Leonard Shoreditch Hog butcher bound in £10, Francis Poulter Victualler [of *deleted*] at Jacobs Well in St Leonard Shoreditch in £10.[1]

1. Always was indicted at the December sessions; she was convicted and fined 1s. on 14 January 1740. MJ/SBB/966, recog. 100; MJ/SBP/14/521.

314. *Saturday, 8 December 1739* Richd Wilford complains ag^{t}: Joseph Green for assaulting & Striking him. On Oath made granted a Warr^{t}: for him.

315. *Monday, 31 December 1739* Tho: Fletcher charges Mary Main wth assaulting him this evening in ye house of Mr Masling at ye Rising Sun Church Str^{t}: wch he made Oath to. Mary Main chgs Tho: Fletcher wth assaulting her last Wednesday at ye same house & laying her upon ye fire wch She made Oath to being bro^{t}: in Cust^{o}: of [*blank*] Griffith Headb^{o}: [Wm Fletcher *deleted*] Sent Mary Main to new prison for want of Sureties but was bro^{t}: back & on agreem^{t}: made between the pties dischgd. Rowland Mitchell [bound *deleted*] Whitster of Hackney in £5 Wm Griffith Gardner of D^{o}. 5 [*and*] Th^{o}: Fletcher D^{o} D^{o} 10, bound for appearance of Tho: Fletcher &c.[1]

1. Fletcher was discharged at the January sessions. MJ/SR/2729, recog. 101.

316. *Wednesday, 2 January 1740* Edward Pimm complains ag^{t}: Thomas Chelsum [*recte* John Chesson] on suspicion of Stealing a Cheesecutting knife Vall: 4^{D} a box Iron knives & forks & other things. Edwd: Pimm made Oath to loss of ye things. Dan. Tappee made Oath y^{t} ye Prisoner Thomas Chessum owned the Cutting knife as his wch he did not now deny. Sent to Newprison. Edward Pimm of Kingsland Victualler bound in £40 to psecute. Dan Tappee Servt: to Edw: Nutt of Shacklewell in £40 to be a witness.[1]

1. An attempt to indict John Chesson failed at the January sessions. MJ/SBP/14/524.

317. *Friday, 4 January 1740* Rebecca Child wife of Anthony Child complains ag^{t}: her husband Ant: Child for assaulting & beating her & threatning her life wch She made Oath of & y^{t} She goes in danger of her life. Granted a Peace Warr^{t}: ag^{t}: him.[1] [*See* **977**].

1. Child entered into a recognizance the following day (**977**) which was discharged at the February sessions on his entering a fresh one (probably to keep the peace for a year). MJ/SR/2731, recog. 68.

318. *Tuesday, 15 January 1740* George Pritchard charged John Pateman on Oath with having beate Mary his wife on the 26th December last in such a violent manner that she voided blood and languished 'till the 14th Instant & then Dyed. Johanna Pritchard his Daughter saw her. Granted a Warrant to apprehend him.[1]

1. This entry is from a loose piece of paper in the notebook volume. Norris committed Pateman to Newgate the following day, to await trial for murder. However, a coroner's inquisition found that Pritchard had died of natural causes, which made it extremely unlikely that a grand jury would find that Pateman had a case to answer.

There was no attempt to indict him and he was therefore discharged at the delivery of the gaol later that month. MJ/SR/2730; MJ/GBB/316/58.

319. *Friday, 1 February 1740* Letitia Goose complains ag^{t} Susan Banister for assaulting & striking her. On Oath made granted a warr^{t}: for her.

320. *Saturday, 2 February 1740* Joseph Bourn complains ag^{t}: [Thomas *deleted*] John Coats & Thomas Stacey & others for assaulting him at ye Hackney Tollgate & forcibly passing ye Toll Gate wth their Teams without paying on ye 23 Jan: & on his Oath made a Warr^{t}:
Saturday, 16 February 1740 Jno Coats appearing wth Bourn acknowledged ye charge & Said y^{t} Robin Hanwell, Wm Martin [and] Sim: Horn were in Comp^{a}: wth him at Same time & were guilty of ye same. Jno: Coats made it up wth Mr Bourn & dischgd him. [*See* **1132**, **1140**].

321. *Tuesday, 12 February 1740* Nathan Cooper complains ag^{t}: Wm Pooll for assaulting him at ye Tollgate & Striking him wth a whip. On Oath made granted a Warr^{t}: for him.

322. *Sunday, 24 February 1740* Robert Chambers complained y^{t} there was Stolen out of ye house of Charity Chambers ab^{t} 6/ms ago 6 China Plates & 4 Silver tea Spoons being her pperty & y^{t} he Suspects ye Same to be concealed in ye house of M^{rs} [*blank*] Jackson in Church Str^{t}: in ye Apartm^{ts}: of Hannah Crow on Oath made made a search warr^{t}: for y^{m}.

323. *Tuesday, 26 February 1740* Tho: Kirk bro^{t}: in Cust^{o}: of Mr James Bolton Alice Racket & chgd her wth Stealing from him a knife vallue 6^{D} wch She acknowledged. Sent her to Bridewell.

324. *Tuesday, 8 April 1740* Robt Day complains ag^{t}: Mary Wilson for assaulting & beating him &c. On Oath made granted a warr^{t} for her.

325. *Thursday, 10 April 1740* Mary Mouse complains ag^{t} Samuell Flinton & Martha Flinton for assaulting her & beating her in her house at Newington. On Oath made granted a warr^{t} for them.

326. *Monday, 28 April 1740* Jno Pavet complains ag^{t}: Hen: Elsley his Apprentice for being disorderly & absenting himself Severall d^{s} & nights – On oath made granted a warr^{t} for him.

327. *Wednesday, 7 May 1740* Elisabeth Gray complains ag^{t}: Jacob Hide for assaulting her & bruising her. On Oath made granted a Warr^{t} for him.

328. *Saturday, 24 May 1740* Thomas Jarratt bro^{t}: in Cust^{o}: of Nathan Cooper charged wth assaulting him at ye Tolgate in execution of his office. On hearing ye Cause ye ptyes agreed & discharged ye person.

329. *Thursday, 29 May 1740* Jno Stubbs complains ag^{t}: Jno: Keeton for assaulting Mary Cornish in Mare Street riding ag her throwing down her load of Milk & Spilling it & hurting her much. On ye oath of Mary Darlington made a warr^{t} for him.

A list of names and dates (relating to burials in woollen) which appeared at this point in the original manuscript has been removed to the end, entry **360**.

330. *Tuesday, 10 June 1740* Anne Shaw complains ag^{t}: her husband Joseph Shaw for assaulting her and threatning to murder her. On Oath made granted a Warr^{t} for him.

331. *Friday, 13 June 1740* Jno Bell bro^{t}: in Cust^{o}: of Ch^{a}: Gosdin by warr^{t} of Hen. Trent Esq chgd on Oath of Jno Coughlin on Suspicion of Stealing Sev^{ll}: p^{cs}: Timber Vall: 40^{s} his pperty. Jno Coughlin made oath he lost Severall p^{cs}: of Timber ab^{t} 10 or 11 taken from y^{e} Wall of his own h^{o}: in Drury lane in this County Vall: ab^{t} 40^{s} ab^{t}: $2\frac{1}{2}$ years ago in day time. Chaplin Harris made Oath y^{t} he Saw y^{e} prisoner Bell to unchain y^{e} Timber in question & take y^{m} away ab^{t} $2\frac{1}{2}$ years Since. Jno: Bell alledges being ex^{a}: y^{t} Coughlin had bo^{t}: y^{e} Timber of him but on his not paying for it he Sued him at law & y^{t} by consent of Coughlin he did take away y^{e} timber in question to make him Satisfaction for y^{e} law charges, & part of this proved to be true by acknowledgm^{t} of Coughlin. [*See* **333**].

332. *Tuesday, 24 June 1740* Mary Saunders bro^{t}: in Cust^{o}: of J^{a}: Martin chgd by Francis Studley & Ralph Field Overseers of ye Poor of ye parish of Braughing in Hertfordshire for running away & leaving a child on ye Parish wch is become chargeable. Elis^{a}: Wright Sworn Says ye childs cloths pduced by Ralph Field [were *deleted*] as found on ye child deserted belonged to M Saunders. Ralph Field swore ye things were found on ye Child. [Mar *deleted*] Elis^{a}: Wright Says y^{t} Mary Saunders told her y^{t} She was about 14 d^{s}: ago in the S^{d} [M *deleted*] Parish whereas M Saunders denyes to have been there within 3 wks & did not own to have left ye Child but was willing to go away wth the Overseers to ye Parish of Braughin & did go wth y^{m}.

333. *Friday, 13 June 1740* Jno: Coughlin bound in £40 of S^{t}: And: Holborn Carpent^{r}, Chaplin Harris 20 of S^{t}: Jno: Hackney Perrukem^{a}: ye former to psecute Jno: Bell for felony chgd ye other to give Evidence. *Saturday, 14 June 1740* Jno: Bell of S^{t}: Mary Whitechappell in W^{t}Chappell road next the Coachm^{a}: dealer in Timber bound in £200, Jno Horne of St Martins in ye fields Carpenter in Thackham Court near St Martins Church in £100 [and] Jonathan Oldham of S^{t}: Andrews Holborn Painter in Hand Court in £100 for ye appearance of Said Jno Bell at next Sessions of Goal delivery at Old Bailey for County of Middlesex to answer an indictm^{t} for felony to be preferred ag^{t} him by Jno Coughlin &c.[1] [*See* **331**].

1. The sessions roll shows that the recognizance was taken before Norris and Tyssen.

An indictment against Bell was thrown out by the grand jury in July. MJ/GBB/316/108; MJ/SR/2740.

334. *Monday, 14 July 1740* Geo: King complains ag^{t}: Walter Mackensie for assaulting him & pissing on him challenging him to fight – On his oath made a Warr^{t}: for him.

335. *Tuesday, 15 July 1740* Richard Insckoo complains ag^{t}: Nich^{o}: North for assaulting him beating him & taking away Cherries from him by force & kicking his basket down whereby he lost 6 or 8^{lb} Cherryes & Several halfpence. On oath made granted a Warr^{t} for him.

336. *Thursday, 4 September 1740* Edward Dixon bro^{t}: Sarah Chandler in Cust^{o}: of Wm Cawn & charged her wth being found in his Garden fenced in &c. Abraham Parker made Oath that this morning between 5 & 6 he took her in his Masters garden wth fruit in her Apron Viz: Plumbs & Apples wch he beleives to be his Masters. Edwd: Dixon made Oath y^{t} he beleives ye Said fruit taken on her to be his & y^{t} he has lately lost fruit Stolen Severall times out of his Garden. Upon Examination of ye Prisoner She acknowledged the charge but alledged the fruit was the fallings under the trees & nott by her gathered. On considering y^{e} whole & y^{e} psecutors desiring it might be forgiven dismissed her wth a reprimand.

337. *Sunday, 14 September 1740* Judith Coward bro^{t}: in Cust^{o}: of Geo: Kello charged by Tho: Cade wth Stealing from him a Fan Vall: $1\frac{1}{2}^{D}$ a p^{r}: old Stockings Vall: 1^{D} & Severall other Small things the whole to Vallue of 10^{D} wch he made Oath & She acknowledged y^{e} taking & Stealing them. Committed her to Bridewell Labour.

338. *Monday, 10 November 1740* Hannah Atkinson Widow brought by Henry Hollely one of the Headboroughs of the Hamlet of Mile End old Town & charged by James Huggett the Younger with having this morning pilferred from him a small parcell of Turnipps in the Parish of Saint Mary of Stratford Bow his property. To support the charge Joseph Windsor on oath sayes he saw the above named Hannah Atkinson about seven this morning have Turnipps in her apron in the s^{d} Mr Huggetts field. Robert Smith on Oath confirms what the said Windsor said. She Confessed the Fact but alledged she did it for need. Committed to the House of Correction.[1]

1. This entry is not in Norris's hand.

339. *Sunday, 23 November 1740* Daniell Bonam bro^{t}: in Cust^{o}: of Hen: Harrill Headb^{o}: chgd by Jno Burton for pilfering Turneps out of his field last night ab^{t}: 11. Fran^{cis}: Boucher made oath y^{t} he last night ab^{t}: 11 took ye prisoner wth a Sack wth Turneps in it & cutting more into it. The prisoner confessed it. Sent him to Bridewell.

340. *Monday, 24 November 1740* Middlesex Francis Pank of Tilers Ferry in Hackney maketh Oath that Abraham Downam of Homerton in the Said Parish did this day threaten the life of him the Said Francis Pank & that he this Deponent apprehends that he goes in danger of his life or of Some bodily hurt that the Said Abraham Downam will do or procure to be done to him & that he desires the peace not for any private malice vexation or revenge but for very fear & for needfull Safety of his Person. Francis Pank [*mark*]. Sworn before us this 24th November 1740, Henry Norris.

341. *Monday, 17 November 1740* Ab: Rogers bro^{t}: before me & Mr Tyssen in ye Vestry in Cust^{o}: of James House Watchman who Said he was bro^{t}: to y^{m} by Jno Upton & Sam: Taylor & dd to their Cust^{o}: but they not appearing nor any matter ag^{t}: him he was discharged.

342. *Sunday, 28 February 1741* Letitia Hughs complained ag^{t} Mary Hardy for assaulting her & made Oath to it on wch granted a Warrant for her.

343. *Tuesday, 20 January 1741* Helen Nutbrown complains ag^{t}: her husband for beating her very grievously & threatning her life, Miles Nutbrown. On her oath made a Warr^{t}: for him.
Wednesday, 21 January 1741 being bro^{t}: in Cust^{o}: of Ch^{a}: Gosdin the Wife Helen charged him as above on wch I demanded Sureties for his appearance at the next Sessions. Rich^{d}: Spurling bound in £10 of S^{t}: John Hackney Cooper, Edward Martin 10 of D^{o} Labourer [and] Miles Nutbrown 20 of D^{o} D^{o}. Recogn not pd, bound to appear & answer ye Complaint.[1] [*See* **127**, **996**].

1. Nutbrown was discharged at the February sessions. MJ/SR/2752, recog. 107.

344. *Monday, 26 January 1741* Jno Bell complains ag^{t}: Tho: Cook for assaulting & Striking him in ye face wth a poker. On his Oath made granted a Warr^{t}: for him.
Tuesday, 27 January 1741 being bro^{t}: in Cust^{o}: of Mr Gosdin heard the Parties & reccommended an agreem^{t}: wch was made & ye Complain^{t} recd Satisfaction for ye injury & at his desire discharg'd ye Warr^{t}:

345. *Thursday, 29 January 1741* James Strutty bro^{t}: before me in Cust^{o}: of Dan. Wingfield chgd by him on Suspicion of being a Convict ordered for transportation wch Strutty also acknowledged & y^{t} he had made his escape. Put him in Cust^{o}: of Dan: Bromwell Const^{a}: to convey to the Italian Merch^{t}: Capt: Perry from whence he escaped & to take the Capt: rec^{t}:

346. *Saturday, 21 March 1741* Eliz^{a}: Ingram & Jean Kidd bro^{t}: in Cust^{o}: of Jno: Page Headb^{o}: of Bow chgd wth Pilfering out of ye Garden of Wm Stevens Some Cabbage Sprouts. Sam Edger Sworn Says y^{t} this morning he took both these women in Wm Stevens garden at Oldford in ye Parish of Bow gathering Cabbage Plants ye pperty of Wm Stevens. Committed y^{m} to Bridewell.[1]

1. Ingram and Kidd are both listed in the House of Correction calendar of April 1741 as to be discharged on paying fees of 1s. each. Marginal notes identify each as 'poor'. MJ/CP/P/68.

347. *Thursday, 2 April 1741* Hen: Flower complained y^{t}: [*altered from* ag^{t}:] he was robbed on Tuesday night of a Cane & Some mo: & Snufbox & y^{t} he Suspects the goods or part thereof are concealed in ye House of [*blank*] Paul of Virginia Street. Granted a Search Warr^{t}:-
Same day Francis Paul Batchelor bro^{t}: in Cust^{o}: of James Rammett Headb^{o}: Hen. Flower, Elis^{a} Spicer [and] Hannah Spicer Sworn declared that ye 1 1st were robbed on Tuesday as above but there appearing no circumstance to charge ye prisoner – dismist him.
Same day Henry Flower of the Parish of S^{t}: John at Hackney Gent: maketh Oath that on Tuesday last the 31st March last coming in the evening from London towards Hackney he met with two men in a field near the Shoulder of Mutton who robbed him of a Cane with a Gold head an Iron Snufbox & Some money and that he has just cause to Suspect that the said goods or part thereof are concealed in the dwelling house or outhouses of [*blank*] Paul in Virginia Row in the Hamlet of Bethnall green in the County of Middlesex. [*signed*] Hen: Flower. Sworn before me this 2 Aprill 1741, Henry Norris.

348. *Sunday, 12 April 1741* Nathan Cooper charges David Morris wth assaulting him on his duty wch he made Oath to.
Monday, 13 April 1741 bound him in Recogn: in £40 of S^{t}: Ja. Clerkenw: Coachm^{a}: Jno Dell of S^{t}: Giles Crippleg: 20 Stocking presser, Griffith Evans of S^{t}: B^{o}: Aldersgate: 20 Coachm^{a}: for appearance at next gen^{ll}: Sessions.[1]

1. Morris, together with James White and William White the Elder, was indicted at the May sessions for assaults on Nathan Cooper and on Richard Stokes. Morris and William White were convicted and fined 1s. on each charge on 12 October 1741. No verdict against James White is recorded. MJ/SBB/978, recog. 81; MJP/SBP/14/660.

349. *Thursday, 4 June 1741* Frances Shepherd complains ag^{t}: Eliz^{a}: Windsor for assaulting & beating her wth a broomstick. On Oath made granted a warr^{t}: for her.

350. *Saturday, 2 May 1741* Alice Sale complains ag^{t} Jno Swift for assaulting & kicking her & bruising her by ye Sh^{o}: of Mutton in ye field yesterday. On her Oath taken granted a Warr^{t}: for him.

351. *Thursday, 9 July 1741* Arthur Ellis of Hackney, Lab^{o}: complains y^{t} had lost taken out of his house in Well Str^{t}: in Hackney a gown of silk & Petticoat of Stuf & other things & he apprehends they may have been stolen by Frances Shepherd of Well Str^{t} wife of [*blank*] Shepherd. On his Oath granted a Warr^{t}: to search her h^{o}:

352. *Saturday, 11 July 1741* Nath^{a} Bamford complains ag^{t}: Wm Miles for threatning his Life on his Oath taken in ye form granted a Warr^{t} for him.

353. *Sunday, 12 July 1741* James Huggett J^{r}: bro^{t}: in Cust^{o}: of Noah Payne Headb^{o}: [Edw *deleted*] Abell Brierly & Eliz^{a}: Cox & chgd on Oath by Jno Nevill being found this morning between 12 & 1 Stealing beans in the ground of S^{d} Ja: Huggett in ye Hamlet of Mile end old town allotted them to pay each 20^{s} to Mr Huggett to make Satisfaction wch they declared themselves unable to pay. So made a Warr^{t}: to Jos: Wright Headbo: to whip y^{m}.

354. *Friday, 17 July 1741* Thomas Hacknett Servt to Mr Edward Nutt of the Parish of St John at Hackney in the County of Middlesex Farmer Maketh Oath that on the 16th day of this Instant July a person who calls himself by the name of John Fowell was in a Field belonging to his said master called Shacklewell Field in the parish aforesaid and had then & there gathered in a parcell of Beans the property of his said Master. Thomas Hacknett [*mark*]. Sworne before me July ye 17th 1741 [*signed*] Henry Norris.[1] Upon this awarded him to pay 10^{s} wch he refusing to do ordered him by Warr^{t} to Hen: Harril Headb^{o}: to be whipped.

1. The preceding part of this entry is not in Norris's hand.

355. *Thursday, 30 July 1741* Thomas Booth complains ag^{t}: Thomas Snow & Edwd: Anderson for assaulting his wife Anne Booth & beating her in his garden in Grovestreet. On his Oath taken granted a Warr^{t} for y^{m}.

The following lists (**356–60**) *of names of dates (relating to burials in woollen) are collected from various places in the original manuscript.*

356. *Friday, 31 October 1735* Elis^{a}: Blevin for Ed. Jones & Est: Jarin. Sarah Oatwell for Ursula Bridgman.
Saturday, 8 November 1735 E Blevin for Elis: Clare, Jno Westrup, Jam: King, Jno Jones. Marg Jackson: for Geo: Free.
Saturday, 15 November 1735 E Blevin for Jam. Bridgfoot. A Raggett – Eli: Green.
Saturday, 22 November 1735 Sa: Dobbs – Wm Cowper.
Saturday, 3 January 1736 Ed. Okey, Ma: Collins, Jno Graves, Wm DunCom, Ri: Newcome.
Monday, 19 January 1736 An. Page – Tho: Page.
Wednesday, 4 February 1736 Anne Fisher – Ma: Owen, Reb: Wightman, Joan Hooper.
Tuesday, 17 February 1736 D^{o} – Tho: Pryor, Esther Smith, Amey Davis.
Monday, 8 March 1736 Anne Raggitt – Wm Green.
Thursday, 6 May 1736 El: Blevin for Elis^{a}: Jackson Mild: Colson Hen: Lillie & Jno Thomas.
Monday, 10 May 1736 Susan Foulcher for Benj^{a}: Vandepus.
Friday, 14 May 1736 El: Martin for Jos: Martin.
Saturday, 15 May 1736 El: Blevin for El. Wood Syb: Fitsgerald Jane Faithfull.
Monday, 24 May 1736 D^{o} – Ja: Sadleir Eli: Kew El: Bugby.
Friday, 4 June 1736 Sar: Oatland – Elis^{a}: Archer.

Saturday, 5 June 1736 E Blevin – Enoch Wratten & John Harrill.
Monday, 21 June 1736 D^{o} – Rob: Revill Jno Stillingfleet Jno Woodfield.
Monday, 28 June 1736 D^{o} – Sa: Townsend & Jane Adams.
Saturday, 3 July 1736 D^{o} – El: Mayhew.
Tuesday, 6 July 1736 Sa: Dobbs pr Tho: Marvell.
Saturday, 10 July 1736 E Blevin pr Tho: Vandeclus Wm Buckell Jno Wallis Jam: Coppin. Anne Fisher pr Wm Harwood.
Thursday, 15 July 1736 Mary Wasley pr Jno: Curtis.
Friday, 16 July 1736 Mar. Askwith – Elis^{a}. Askwith.
Thursday, 22 July 1736 E Blevin – Alex^{a}: Gould & Jno Brewer.
Friday, 23 July 1736 Sus: Foulser – Wm Jones.
Thursday, 29 July 1736 Mary Wasley for Reb: Neale.
Thursday, 5 August 1736 Elis^{a}: Blevin for Sus. Heathcoat Sam: Sammon Math. Walker Anne Corn & Jno Wright.
Friday, 13 August 1736 Ma: Wasley for Sarah Pearson Jam: Lampier Mar: Cookman.
Saturday, 21 August 1736 E Blevin for Sarah Bell & Jos: Marvell.
Thursday, 26 August 1736 Marg: Cota for Fran. Loy.
Friday, 27 August 1736 H Harrill – Marg: Baldry. M Wasley – F: Tyssen Sar: Lamprier Eliz: Milner Jane Eady & Eliz: Stanton.
Monday, 30 August 1736 Sarah Dobbs for Jam: Morphew.
Saturday, 4 September 1736 E Blevin for Anne Stephenson Ma: Moulten Ruth Bollard Ma: Green & Jno. Inott.
Saturday, 11 September 1736 M Wasley for Wm Pamplin Jno Dixon Rach: Maslin Anne Miles.
Monday, 4 October 1736 E Blevin for Kath. Maslin & a Child unknown.
Friday, 8 October 1736 Sar. Oatwell – Elis^{a}: Thompson. M Wasley – Gab: Rawlinson.
Saturday, 16 October 1736 E Blevin – Tho: Hedges.
Friday, 29 October 1736 M Wasley – Ma: Winter.
Thursday, 4 November 1736 Alice Rice – Ma: Rice.
Friday, 5 November 1736 M Wasley – Fran. Dolby & John Maslin.
Monday, 8 November 1736 Sar: Palmer – Sam. Newton.
Wednesday, 10 November 1736 E Blevin – M Booth E Wilson.
Friday, 19 November 1736 M Wasley – Cath: Aug: Ranger Sar. Hill Sar: Jones.
Monday, 22 November 1736 S Dobbs – Wm Coleman.
Wednesday, 24 November 1736 E Blevin – Sam. Barnard Han: Barston Marg: An: Arundell.
Saturday, 27 November 1736 E Panter – Ma: Cole.
Monday, 29 November 1736 E Blevin – Jno Rows.
Tuesday, 30 November 1736 M Burroughs – Geo: Dudderidge.
Thursday, 9 December 1736 M Wasley – M Parsons.
Thursday, 16 December 1736 D^{o} – G Turner.
Monday, 20 December 1736 Marg: Buck – Rab. Biggerton.
Friday, 31 December 1736 M Wasley – Wm Nicholes.
Monday, 10 January 1737 E Blevin – El: Somers Magd: Buscarlet Ma: Foster El Samon.
Thursday, 13 January 1737 M Long – Reb. Demesa.

Friday, 21 January 1737 M Wasley – Wm Sandford Est: Masling

357. *Thursday, 27 January 1737* Elis^a: Blevins affidavit for Hen: Samwall.
Saturday, 5 February 1737 Mary Wasley for Sam. Alderman, Anne Hutchison, Richd Cook.
Monday, 7 February 1737 El Windsor for El Mason.
Thursday, 10 February 1737 M Wasley – Wm Page, Sar. Smith, Wm Rayner.
Monday, 14 February 1737 Ma. Hendricks – M Hendricks J^r.
Tuesday, 15 February 1737 E Hyde – Jos: Hyde.
Friday, 18 February 1737 M Wasley – G E Blocker.
Wednesday, 23 February 1737 D^o – Fr: Harris.
Thursday, 24 February 1737 E Blevin – Jno Cubbage, Wm Harris, M^a: Craft, M^a: Fox.
Saturday, 26 February 1737 Anne Clark – Tho: Clark.
Friday, 4 March 1737 M Wasley – Elis^a: Vanne.
Friday, 11 March 1737 D^o: – Ma: Gregory
Tuesday, 15 March 1737 Tim. Raseborough – Jno Raseborough
Thursday, 17 March 1737 Ma. Gallatt – Jno Gallatt.
Saturday, 19 March 1737 M Wasley – Kath. Taylor, Martha Johnson, Wm Newton. E Thornton – [W^m] Dickins.
Monday, 21 March 1737 E Panter – Anne Collin.
Thursday, 24 March 1737 M Wasley – Ed Whitford & Hans Fred. Webber.
Saturday, 2 April 1737 Jno Price – Jno Price. M^a: Wasley – Tho: Gillam.
Monday, 11 April 1737 E Blevin – Wm Peters, Ma: Merriday, Garrett Kew.
Saturday, 23 April 1737 M Wasley – Sus: Charlton, Ma: Archer, Ma: Smith.
Thursday, 28 April 1737 Anne Cox – Mary Eldridge.
Saturday, 7 May 1737 E Blevin – Tho: Blackway, Crister Turk, Anne Humphreys & Letitia Wooten.
Thursday, 12 May 1737 M Wasley – El. Powell, El: Tingoo.
Friday, 13 May 1737 Mary Gillett – Mary Eaton.
Monday, 23 May 1737 E Blevin – Jno Bartlett, A Pank, G Shallard.
Tuesday, 24 May 1737 G Jenks – [E. Fame].
Saturday, 28 May 1737 M Wasley – Tho: Towers, Moor Foucher.
Thursday, 2 June 1737 D^o – G Gravit. Mary Tooly – J Tooly.
Friday, 10 June 1737 M Wasley for Jno Lamb Rich. Cooper, Wm Thomson, Mary Hampton.
Thursday 23 June 1737 D^o – M Tilyard, R Peacock, J Rust.
Wednesday, 29 June 1737 Anne Archer pr Jno: Moore.
Friday, 1 July 1737 Fran: Rob^ts – Wm Burtwell. E Blevin – Ma: Vawin, Jno Eyles, Est. Molen.
Thursday, 7 July 1737 D^o – Rich: Mare.
Wednesday, 13 July 1737 M Wasley – Wm Brown, A Davis.
Saturday, 16 July 1737 E Blevin – J Ashby.
Wednesday, 20 July 1737 R Moore – James Edw^ds.

Friday, 29 July 1737 T Cade – Kat. Kitt.
Friday, 12 August 1737 M Wasley – G Socklynge, M Bates, M Ford.
Friday, 19 August 1737 D° – M Sanders, W Buck.
Saturday, 27 August 1737 S Letton – J Conyers.
Saturday, 3 September 1737 El. Lund – Ja. Lund.
Saturday, 10 September 1737 M Wasley – Sam: Warren, Mary Hadder, Ma: Baxter. Mary Dallistone – [Mary *deleted*] Benj Burroughs.
Friday, 16 September 1737 M Wasley – Ja. Dodd, Jn° Wilson, Ab. Harwood, Eli: Bone.
Thursday, 29 September 1737 D° – H Crofts, Elis[a]: Bunn.
Friday, 14 October 1737 E Blevin – Ma: Picket, Tho: Clayton, Tho: Taylor.
Friday, 21 October 1737 M Wasley – J Chapman.
Tuesday, 1 November 1737 M Burroughs – D Skate.
Thursday, 3 November 1737 M Wasley S Raincroft, W[m] Dumbelton, A Oneal.
Thursday, 10 November 1737 D° – M Pain, [*blank*] Thorogood.
Friday, 11 November 1737 Marg: Gosdin – Thos: Stoaks.
Wednesday, 23 November 1737 E Blevin – Geo: Wildey, Jane Brasier, Ma. Merrall, El: Oakley, Ed. Saunders.
Saturday, 26 November 1737 A Shaw – Tho: Clark.
Thursday, 1 December 1737 M Wasley – E Ford, J Parsloe, T Smart, E Bradley, S Pank.
Thursday, 8 December 1737 D° – Hope Ja: Betts, A Greenwood, W[m] Baker, Jn° Woollard, Sa. Ward, Jn° Woollington, Is: Bull.
Saturday, 17 December 1737 E Blevin – J Strype, M Eleonor, E Mager, M Fisher, Tho: Archer, R Dobbs.
Monday, 26 December 1737 M Wasley – J Womsley, G Fox, A Tisoe.
Tuesday, 27 December 1737 E Lort – S Newcome

358. *Monday, 2 January 1738* El. Blevins affidavit for Mary Beux & El: Holmes. Jud. How – Geo: How.
Tuesday, 3 January 1738 Mary Wasley – Ma: Morgan.
Monday, 9 January 1738 D° – Ma: Wilk: Jones Jam. Deakins Pet. Cleyn.
Friday, 13 January 1738 D° – C Benbridge.
Saturday, 21 January 1738 D° – A Clark S Pamplin E Morrison
Saturday, 28 January 1738 D° – T Slater Z Moyse F [Moyse *deleted*] Walker.
Friday, 3 February 1738 D° – T Oylman.
Saturday, 11 February 1738 D° – E Blevin M Johnson.
Wednesday, 15 February 1738 D° – A Fonser.
Friday, 17 February 1738 D° – J Window M Roberts.
Monday, 20 February 1738 D° – A Paine.
Saturday, 25 February 1738 D° – T Hall C: Burgoin.
Friday, 3 March 1738 D° – M Mason S Hillard.
[*Friday, 10*] *March 1738* D° & Anne Pasfield for R Saunders.
Monday , 13 March 1738 A Pasfield for Dav. Bently & H Samuell.
Wednesday, 15 March 1738 M Goodwin – S Apted.
Thursday, 16 March 1738 F Shepherd for Tho: Armstrong.

Saturday 18 March 1738 M Wasley – W Lamb, Th: Rutherford A Door M Woodyeard J Hale J Costed J Barbut.
Tuesday, 21 March 1738 Sus: Taylor for A Taylor.
Thursday, 23 March 1738 M Wasley – L W^{ms} & B. Jones.
Wednesday, 29 March 1738 D^{o} – J Whaeley A Belknap J Jewell
Tuesday, 4 April 1738 Sa: Fletcher – Reb: Fletcher.
Friday, 7 April 1738 M Wasley – E Ball, Js: Gage S Harrill E Marslin T. Fort M McAdams.
Friday, 14 April 1738 A Pasfield – J Robinson.
Wednesday, 19 April 1738 D^{o} – Anne Jones.
Monday, 24 April 1738 M Wasley – Wm Ogier.
Wednesday, 3 May 1738 D^{o} – M Disberough
Tuesday, 9 May 1738 El: [*Parsons* deleted] for Anne Pheasant.
Friday, 19 May 1738 A Webb – Jno: Webb. A Pasfield – E Clark L Gibbons.
Monday, 22 May 1738 M Wasley for J Helling.
Thursday, 25 May 1738 M Hind – Jane Hind & Mary Lack.
Friday, 2 June 1738 M Wasley – R James S Cocke H Crafts J Annable.
Thursday, 8 June 1738 D^{o} – F D'Agand Is^{b}: Eaton.
Tuesday, 13 June 1738 F Shepherd – J Wilmot.
Friday, 16 June 1738 A Pasfield – C Masling.
Wednesday, 21 June 1738 D^{o} – J Byfield J Marshall J Matchett J Woodin. Wm Harrison – Ma: Harrison.
Saturday, 1 July 1738 M Wasley – M Archer L Norwood.
Thursday, 6 July 1738 A Pasfeild – E Okey J Green.
Saturday, 15 July 1738 [B Grove *deleted*] M Wasley – B Grove M Bull.
Friday, 21 July 1738 D^{o} – M Vigne E Crouch M Soaper.
Saturday, 22 July 1738 E Brathwaite – M Cooper.
Friday, 28 July 1738 M Wasley – A Lotton M Rawlinson M Clyne.
Saturday, 29 July 1738 D^{o} – E Simons.
Tuesday, 15 August 1738 A Pasfeild – J Baker Wm Johnson Jno Trott.
Wednesday, 23 August 1738 E Brathwaite – W Morris.
Thursday, 24 August 1738 M Wasley – M Bennett M Hide S Singleton.
Wednesday, 30 August 1738 A Pasfield – D Pyle J Holmes M Smith.
Monday, 4 September 1738 D^{o} – T King J Pratt M Panks J Panks A Griffith.
Thursday, 14 September 1738 M Wasley – W Swell E Evans A Batram W Salmon.
Monday, 25 September 1738 A Pasfield – W Clark S Bignall T Rudd.
Monday, 2 October 1738 D^{o} – K Morton A Sprigins J Crowe H Atwood.
Monday, 9 October 1738 S Newington – A Stacey.
Friday, 13 October 1738 M Wasley – J Marvill M Vaughan.
Monday, 16 October 1738 A Pasfield – P Newcome L Parsons. S Newington – E Bush.
Tuesday, 24 October 1738 A Pasfield – C Whichcote.
Monday, 30 October 1738 S Dobs – E Coleman.
Friday, 3 November 1738 A Pasfield – E Grinley E Dufoor T Rich^{ds}.
Wednesday, 8 November 1738 M Wasley – J Collings Ja: Porter.
Saturday, 11 November 1738 D^{o} – J Kirk E Bullock R Bowers.

Wednesday, 15 November 1738 A Pasfield for R Johnson W Atkins.
Saturday, 18 November 1738 M Walsey [*sic*] – J Holland E Everett J Betts.
Monday, 27 November 1738 A Pasfield – S Palley E Austin.
Wednesday, 29 November 1738 M Wasley – E Watson.
Monday, 4 December 1738 E Panter – T Nichols.
Tuesday, 5 December 1738 A Pasfield – J Landery M Tedman.
Monday, 11 December 1738 Sarah Swaby – Tho: Swaby.
Tuesday, 12 December 1738 A Pasfield – J Singleton W Saunders.
Friday, 22 December 1738 M Wasley – S Eden.
Tuesday, 26 December 1738 A Pasfield – M Stretton H Preston T Masling A Wood.
Friday, 29 December 1738 H Alderman – W Cock.
Tuesday, 2 January 1739 A Pasfield – H Sherwood.
Thursday, 4 January 1739 M Wasley – W Newton.
Friday, 5 January 1739 James Edward Bettell – Carolina Bettell.
Thursday, 11 January 1739 A Pasfield – A Taylor M Socklin.
Monday, 15 January 1739 M Goodwin – J Goodwin.
Tuesday, 16 January 1739 A Pasfield – S Wint H Harding J Hodges E Owen.
Tuesday, 23 January 1739 E Panter – D Bennett.
Tuesday, 30 January 1739 A Pasfield – J Tisoe R Dyson S Dudley
Friday, 2 February 1739 M Wasley – J Edwards.
Saturday, 10 February 1739 A Pasfield – T Burt J Thomson A Caseson
Tuesday, 13 February 1739 A Cox – E Cox.
Saturday, 17 February 1739 M Davis – A Ball.
Sunday, 25 February 1739 S Fletcher – S Barnard.
Tuesday, 27 February 1739 A Pasfield – B Smith S Barnard. A Soden – W Holms.
Saturday, 10 March 1739 D Roswell – M Carter.
Tuesday, 13 March 1739 [M Wasley *deleted*] A Pasfield – B Annable G Suthera B Wood J Crynes.
Thursday, 15 March 1739 A Davis – J Ganner.
Friday, 23 March 1739 M Wasley – T Thornton T King.
Saturday, 31 March 1739 A Pasfield – J Falkner D Scot H Norris R Miles T Jackson R Iles W Rogers.
Friday, 6 April 1739 M Wasley – G [R *deleted*] Lane, A Barnes.

359. *Saturday, 14 April 1739* M Wasley for Kath: Wilmer.
Thursday, 19 April 1739 A Pasfield – J Barrow J Polley.
Friday, 27 April 1739 M Wasley – Thomas [*blank*]. A Pasfield – W Robinson.
Wednesday, 9 May 1739 A Furly – Is[a]: Huggins.
Friday, 11 May 1739 J Wethered – Tho: Francis.
Wednesday, 23 May 1739 A Pasfield – M Tomkins J Crew F Roberts E Pearson.
Wednesday, 30 May 1739 M Wasley – E Hougham E Ware.
Friday, 1 June 1739 A Oncle – W Oncle.
Saturday, 2 June 1739 M Wasley – F Shurwood.

Wednesday, 6 June 1739 E Howard – A Howard.
Monday, 11 June 1739 M Wasley – F Jackson S Skinner J Walker J Mather.
Saturday, 16 June 1739 M Searcher – R Room.
Monday, 18 June 1739 A Pasfield – W Eaton J Bartbum E Scandrett.
Saturday, 30 June 1739 M Wasley – J Dixon E White.
Thursday, 5 July 1739 D[o] – W G Underhill M Pick.
Monday, 9 July 1739 D[o] – J Wing.
Thursday, 12 July 1739 A Pasfield – Jn[o] Flower J Newcome.
Monday, 23 July 1739 D[o] – E Thomson E Preston J Rust.
Monday, 30 July 1739 D[o] – W Godson W Hayes E Cotton.
Thursday, 9 August 1739 A Pasfield – E Precher W Dobbs
Saturday, 18 August 1739 C Ball – E Brown.
Monday, 20 August 1739 A Pasfield – A Layman W Stife S Webb.
Monday, 27 August 1739 D[o] – R Wilks T Clayton E Lukey E Atwood S Brasier T Gibson.
Friday, 21 September 1739 M Wasley – E Taylor E Limpous S Gilding.
Monday, 1 October 1739 A Pasfield – W Fletcher J Roston.
Thursday, 4 October 1739 S Fletcher – J Fletcher.
Monday, 8 October 1739 A Pasfield – W Fletcher W Cattlin.
Saturday, 20 October 1739 D[o] – M Morphew M Yerbury T Monk M Trott E Gibbs. C Small – C Shaw.
Monday, 22 October 1739 C Gosding – H Hyde.
Friday, 26 October 1739 A Pasfield – S Peters T Pratt, E Taylor W Thomson.
Wednesday, 31 October 1739 A Pasfield – E Maynard M Murell R Upton A Norwood J Upham & E Hannah.
Thursday, 8 November 1739 M Wasley – T Collyer J Pots S Pheasant.
Monday, 12 November 1739 E Skettle – T Skittle.
Wednesday, 14 November 1739 M Wasley – E Powell K Parsons F Ward. J Burk – J Murphey.
Friday, 23 November 1739 A Pasfield – P Comb E Howson E Harding.
Saturday, 8 December 1739 D[o] – N Potts J Rose M Bishop J Stretton M Ratclif.
Wednesday, 12 December 1739 M Goodwin – E Bromley.
Saturday, 22 December 1739 M Wasley – S Kidman W Chandler M Portway E Grey.
Wednesday, 26 December 1739 A Pasfield – G Stanton. Elis[a]: Odie – Alice Rice.
Saturday, 5 January 1740 A Pasfield – M Worthey E Morris D Brown R Sutton.
Thursday, 10 January 1740 D[o] – P Lynham J Jackson M Norris H Cooper.
Monday, 14 January 1740 D[o] – T Nutbrown.
Saturday 19 January 1740 M Wasley – J Wintall.
Thursday, 24 January 1740 A Pasfield – M Royston M Thomson.
Monday, 4 February 1740 D[o] – J Milner M Wright.
Friday, 8 February 1740 M Wasley – M Brouman [D] Adams. C Small – J Small.

Saturday, 16 February 1740 A Pasfield – S Enderbury S Woodyard H Brown J Potts.
Monday, 25 February 1740 M Wasley – M Blanchard R Hampson J Arundell J Chaucer R Deale.
Monday, 3 March 1740 D° – W Mayne A Price.
Saturday, 8 March 1740 A Pasfield – R Aldwinckle E Socklyng J Harris W Launder.
Monday, 24 March 1740 D° – E Wootton M Kirby M Fox G Lane E Bruce.
Tuesday, 1 April 1740 D° – S Bodycoat T Garnham W Edw[ds] J Spiggs.
Wednesday, 2 April 1740 E Brathwaite – M Combauld.
Saturday, 5 April 1740 M Wasley – J Wildey A Walker J Guy.
Friday, 11 April 1740 D° – R Blackburn R Day.
Monday, 21 April 1740 A Harrison – Wm Harrison.

360. *Friday, 25 April 1740* A Pasfield for T Williams J Sucklin A Rolf M Roffe S Johnson S Holbrook T Pain.
Monday, 28 April 1740 E Panter – E Bennett.
Saturday, 3 May 1740 A Pasfield – T Harris T & A Humphreys.
Tuesday, 6 May 1740 D° – E Carsey A Bently R Giglis M Stent R Huntly & M Wood.
Tuesday, 13 May 1740 D° – W Crichton.
Friday, 23 May 1740 M Pettit – J: Butler.
Monday, 26 May 1740 M Wasley E Shadwell J Eyles T Wasley J: M Titcome.
Wednesday, 4 June 1740 A Pasfield – A Wright R Wright J Richson M Chamberlain R Fowler A Uncles.
Saturday, 10 June 1740 D° – J Moargue J Houghton E Yarrow A White H Buckle.
Saturday, 17 June 1740 D° – A Crosfield D Findley W Pritchard M Dollins E Jenison J Monington S Flint.
Wednesday, 21 June 1740 M Wasley – J Du Cane.
Saturday, 7 July 1740 A Pasfield – R Burton E Tomkins M Booth J Fordham.
Friday, 22 August 1740 D° – J Guy M Speering T Lee M Arthur E Winstanley.
Saturday, 30 August 1740 M Wasley – W Stoaks R M[c]Gill T Fillis A Rowson.
Monday, 8 September 1740 D° – K Walkington J Hardy G Peacock S Harris.
Tuesday, 16 September 1740 A Pasfield – E Grimault A Shepey J Hyde.
Monday, 29 September 1740 D° – R Johnson S Wilkinson M Jeffreys H Boon.
Monday, 20 October 1740 D° – A Perkins A Buckley J Byfield.
Friday, 31 October 1740 M Wasley – J Buckle G Royston A Paine W Brewer Jn° Worrin M Buck. M Tigh – T Barrow.
Saturday, 8 November 1740 A Pasfield – J Eastwick R Emerton J Terrey R Pain.
Friday, 14 November 1740 M Wasley – S Stife S Rob[ts]: T Davis C

Sherburn.
Monday, 24 November 1740 A Pasfield – M Young M Hancker S Collins M Brooks W Mitchell.
Monday, 8 December 1740 M Wasley – S Kidman J Osman A Hargrove T Finchley.
Tuesday, 23 December 1740 M Wasley – M Martin E Pym A Sowden M Urbin S Urben.
Tuesday, 30 December 1740. D° – M Howard M Coker.
Monday, 19 January 1741 Anne Pasfield – M Newcome S Poole C Butler J Archer.
Monday, 26 January 1741 D° – A Buckle S Gregory M Trevett W Gurton.
Monday, 2 February 1741 M Wasley – R Champion J Trepass E Blanchet A Tapps J Curtice.
Monday, 9 February 1741 D° – A Holloway J Wright.
Saturday, 14 February 1741 A Pasfield – J Pritchard.
Tuesday, 24 February 1741 S Fletcher – S Fletcher.
Friday, 6 March 1741 A Pasfield – P Gunn R Foster M Joseph W S Giding.
Wednesday, 11 March 1741 D° – J Burton A Kingsley M Anderson B Summers.
Saturday, 21 March 1741 D° – H Gany.
Monday, 23 March 1741 W Davis – M Davis.
Wednesday, 8 April 1741 A Pasfield – H Green J Bruff.
Tuesday, 14 April 1741 M Wasley – T Hickman E Keif S Pettiver R Walker G Parker J Masling J Hedge.
Friday, 17 April 1741 D° – J Blondell, P Palmer, H Kingslow, P Bowles.
Monday, 20 April 1741 A Lightwood – H Corting.
Friday, 24 April 1741 M Wasley – J Crookshank J Goodwin T Lake.
Wednesday, 29 April 1741 Jn°: Wicks – F Wickes.
Saturday, 2 May 1741 A Pasfield – E Clay T Mears M Davis W Cooper R Rousham.
Monday, 4 May 1741 F Watson – W Watson.
Friday, 8 May 1741 A Pasfield – A Cox R Ross J Roffe J Irwin M Chandler J Ward J Bourn.
Monday, 18 May 1741 A Pasfield – E Fox.
Wednesday, 20 May 1741 D° – J Boon P Boon.
Tuesday, 26 May 1741 D° – T Bird B Alvard S Bryant M Bourn.
Tuesday, 9 June 1741 D° – B Tebbell W Buck W Cox.
Friday, 19 June 1741 M Wasley – A Robertson R Stevens M Emerson E Sheston.
Friday, 26 June 1741 D° – S Stretton R Barns
Monday, 20 July 1741 D° – J Knight M Blemeny.
Wednesday, 22 July 1741 E Crew – S Delmere.
Tuesday, 4 August 1741 A Pasfield – A Green S Costed.

HACKNEY PETTY SESSIONS BOOK

361. Beadles Duty settled at the Election of Henry Harrill – To attend Justices at their Petty Sessions attend at all Vestry and Parish Meetings carry out Summonses on all necessary occations and waite on the Justices on Saturday moring [*sic*] to know when they will please to meet. To assist Churchwardens and Overseers of the Poor in Collecting their several Rates and in Releiving the Poor, attend at the Great Door of the Church every Sunday in the forenoon and afternoon. To Inquire of all Foreign poor and bring in an account of them to the Justices at their Petty Sessions as soon as they become Intruders. To bring in a List of all new [house Keepers *deleted*] Inhabitants both House Keepers and Lodgers to the Justices at their Petty Sessions twice in every year viz[t] next Petty Sessions after Lady day and the next Petty Sessions after Michaelmass. To Convey Foreign Poor with Passes to their Settlements. To apprehend Vagrants and Wandering Beggars and carry them before the Justices in order that they may be Punished.[1] [*See* **449**].

1. This entry appears at the commencement of the petty sessions book.

The Mermaid Tavern, Friday, 29 October 1731
Justices present: Henry Norris, Samuel Tyssen

362. Signed a warrant to apprehend John Knight, Joseph Cooper & Mary Carpenter to give an account of their Settlements on the Oath of Francis Davis. [*See* **377**, **382**, **438**, **441**, **563**, **994**].

363. Signed a Warrant to discharge Grace Chandler out of the House of Correction committed for refuseing to Labour for her family whereby they became chargeable to the Parish upon the Humble Peticon of her Daughter.[1] [*See* **364**, **396**, **401**].

1. Grace Chandler had been committed by Norris and Tyssen three days previously. MJ/SR/2564, House of Correction Calendar, no 28.

364. Ordered That M[r] Thomas Wood the Churchwarden do Pay to Henry Batt Headborough three shillings for his trouble and Expences in taking care of and conveying Grace Chandler to the House of Correction for refuseing to worke for the maintenance of her selfe and family. [*See* **363**, **396**, **401**].

365. Granted a Warrant to apprehend to Thomas Cooke, James Bolton having sworn the Peace against him. [*See* **30**].

366. The following persons were Summoned to appear before the said Justices this day to Shew cause why they have neglected to Perform their Statute on the Highwayes belonging to the Parish of S[t]. John at Hackney for the year 1731 and also why they have refused or neglected to pay M[r]. Robert Aldwinckle and M[r] Edward Nutt the Present Survey[rs]. for their defaults viz[t] –

Church Street: Giles Lopas paid 12s.; Mary Harris Excused; Sarah Cole paid 6s.; W[m] Hinchman paid 4s. 6d.; *Henry Riddell to pay 4s. 6d.; *Joshua Buckley to pay 3s.; Elizabeth Morris paid 6s.; Francis Eaglesoe paid 6s.; Hannah Ashley paid 4s. 6d; W[m]. Thornton paid 4s. 6d.; Rich[d]. Hoggins paid 4s. 6d.; Mary Wingood paid 4s.; John Herbert paid 3s.; Marg[t] Parker paid 3s.; Sarah Palmer Excused; *Daniel Card to pay 4s. 6d.; Thomas Bishop paid 3s.; Edward Ward paid 4s. 6d.; Jane Beale paid 2s. 6d.; John Coster paid 4s. 6d.; Marresia Boett paid 9s.; Elizabeth Watts paid 9s.; W[m]. Yellowley paid 9s.; Deborah Drury paid 6s.; Mary Taylor gone away; John Pincock paid 6s.; Richard Pescod not Sumoned; Matt[w]. Chester paid 4s. 6d.; *Franc[s]. Carrenton to pay 4s. 6d.; Ann Weatherhead Excused; Joseph Ingleton paid 4s. 6d.; *James Albonelo to pay 1s. 6d.; Wid[o]. Fletcher paid 4s. 6d.; Tho[s]. Stanley not Sumoned; Thomas Graves paid [*apparently altered from* to pay] 4s. 6d.; Samuel Bennett paid 6s.; *John Weatherhead to pay 4s. 6d.; Edw[d]. Gibbons paid 4s. 6d.; *Peter Lambeth to pay 3s.; W[m]. Gibbons paid 4s. 6d.; Ann Fisher Excused; James England Poor & Lame; Sarah Wills paid 4s. 6d.; *Geo: Sherrard to pay 4s. 6d.; *James House to pay 4s. 6d.; John Lightwood not Sumoned; George Gravett Excused; William Stanley Excused.

Mare Street: *George Layton to pay 1s. 6d.; Elij[a] Loveday not sumoned; Samuel Shaw paid 4s. 6d.; *George Lane to pay 3s.; Wid[o]. Austin Excused; Charles Lawrence not to be found; Hannah Speed not sumoned; Thomas Jennings gone away; *Sarah Thompkins to pay 1s. 6d.; *James Allen to pay 3s.; *James Beale to pay 4s. 6d.; Alice Gates not sumoned; John Steward Excused this year; Richard Stoakes paid 6s.; John Everton Excused; *John Ward to pay 4s. 6d.; Miles Nutt-browne not sumoned; Robert Ballenger Excused; James Sherwood not Sumoned; *William Kingsland to pay 4s. 6d.; John Rouse paid 1s. 6d.; *Giles Lomas to pay 4s. 6d.; Richard Eades gone away; John Burrowes not Sumoned; Timothy Peters paid 4s. 6d.; *John Porter to pay 4s. 6d.; Jo: Schooling paid 2s.; *Rich[d]. Hatt to pay 4s. 6d.; *James Wooton to pay 4s. 6d.; *William Main to pay 4s. 6d.; William Finch to be sumoned againe; Abraham Clarke paid 4s. 6d.; John Ramsey Excused this year; W[m]. Street paid 1s. 6d.; Rob[t]. Bell not sumoned.

Homerton: *Katherine Davey to pay 3s.; Joseph Parsloe paid 4s. 6d.; *William Rogers to pay 4s. 6d.; Oliver Lyde Excused; John Wasley paid 3s.; Sarah Bennett Excused Pention[r]; Samuel Barnard paid 9s.; Mary Powell paid 3s.; W[m]. Pratt paid 3s.; *Edw[d] Whitaker paid 4s. 6d.; *John Townsend to pay 6s.; Elizabeth Jenkins paid 3s.; Rich[d]. Gears Excused y[s] year; *John Webb to pay 4s. 6d.; Tho[s]. Baker not sumoned; *W[m]. Panter to pay 1s. 6d.; *Rob[t] Newington to pay 3s.; *Tho[s]. Bartrum to pay 4s. 6d.; Jere Kemp paid 4s. 6d.; *Mary Overy to pay 1s. 6d.;

*Nath^{a}. Root to pay 4s. 6d.; *Samuel Stockell to pay 9s.; Robt Green paid 4s. 6d.; Kath^{e}. Ashby paid 9s.; Thos. Nash paid 4s. 6d.; Ann Stracey paid 3s.; *Edwd. Bush to pay 4s. 6d.; *Phelatia Salmon to pay 4s. 6d.; Wm Udall paid 1s. 6d.; Robt. Roome paid 4s. 6d.; *Frances Green to pay 4s. 6d.; John Bird not Sumoned; *Ann Bartrum to pay 4s. 6d.; Chas. Hancock paid 9s.; John Taylor paid 3s.; James Betts paid 9s.; *Rich^{d}. Giglis to pay 4s. 6d.; *George Edmonds to pay 3s.; *Thos. Cooke to pay 4s. 6d.; *Mark Scott to pay 1s. 6d.; Henry Harrill Excused; Wid^{o}. Whitehurst Excused; *William Preston to pay 4s. 6d.; *Saml Bodycoate to pay 4s. 6d.; John Dry paid 9s.; Henry Cumberland p^{d} 3s.

Clopton: Henry Page Excused; *[*blank*] Bergaine to pay 9s.; Robt Thompson not sumoned; *John Windum to pay 4s. 6d.; John Cawne paid 4s. 6d.; *Marg^{t}. Gelding to pay 6s.; Wm Hewson to be Excused on Condition he opens the Drains in Clopton; Samuel Stower gone away; W^{m}. Stretton Junr Excused; *Wid^{o}. Piller to pay 4s. 6d.; *William Darville to pay 3s.; Matt^{w}. Willson paid [*apparently altered from* to pay] 4s. 6d.; *W^{m}. Boatman to pay 4s. 6d.; Thos Sowden paid 3s.; *John Wilmer to pay 1s. 6d.; *John Hilliard to pay 3s.; W^{m}. Harris Excused; Christop Place; *Joseph Bourne to pay 1s. 6d.; *W^{m}. Knight to pay 4s. 6d.; Philip Osborne will pay; Jane Wright not sumoned; Isaac Portway p^{d} 1s. 6d.; *Jonat^{h} Adams to pay 1s. 6d.; Fran^{s}. Wheeler not sumoned; Edmund Matthew p^{d} 6s.; Edward Cressell gone away; Thos. Nicholls to worke 3 days; Joseph Cooper paid 4s. 6d.; *Wid^{o}. Smith to pay 1s. 6d.; Thomas Archer paid 4s. 6d.; *Rich^{d}. Hawkins to pay 1s. 6d.; *Thos. Gillam to pay 6s.; *Thos. Townsend to pay 6s.; *W^{m}. Gatley to pay 6s.; Rich^{d}. Feasant Excused; *Thos Fouch to pay 4s. 6d., *John Bracey to pay 4s. 6d.

Newington: Henry Donmer p^{d} £1 12s.; *Robt. Tattersell to pay 3s.; James Samples paid 4s. 6d.; *Robt. Whichler to pay 1s. 6d.; *John Whitehead to pay 3s.; Alice Gates Excused; *Ann Thompson to pay 4s. 6d.; John Hardy paid 4s. 6d.; James Hall paid 3s.; Eliz^{a}. Robinson paid 1s. 6d.; *Thos. Fryer to pay 3s.; *Eliz^{a}. Hadley to pay 3s.; Thos. Pettett paid 4s. 6d.; *Robt. Walberton to pay 3s.; John Copley paid 4s. 6d.; *Thos. Barnard to pay 4s. 6d.; Mary Mare not to be found; John Wells gone away.

Shacklewell: Wid^{o}. Clarke paid 4s. 6d.; James Mortimer not sumoned; Thomas Askew paid 1s. 6d.

Kingsland: *Thomas Battmaker to pay 3s.; *Edwd. Mitchell to pay 3s.

Dorleston: Thomas Hilliard paid 6s.

Grove Street: John Rooke paid 9s.; W^{m}. Browne paid 9s.

Well Street: W^{m}. Hyde paid 3s.; *John Home to pay 3s.; Wid^{o}. Johnson paid 1s. [6d.]; Joseph Read paid 9s. [0d.]; *Wid^{o}. Wright to pay 1s. 6d.; James Pryor paid 3s.; Peter Me[ij]ender not sumoned; Samuel Fenner paid 3s.; Thomas Collee paid 3s.

367. Ordered That a warrant be made out against the several Defaulters contained in the preceeding List to Levy on their several Goods and Chattells one shilling and Six Pence pr day for each and every day they and each of them have made default to be laid out and imployed for the use of the Highwayes aforesaid.

368. Ordered That Edward Mitchell a Barber liveing at Kingsland do deliver to Samuel Sadleir our Clerk a proper Certificate of his Settlem^{t}. before our next meeting and in failure therein that an Order be then made out to remove him and his family thither.[1] [*See* **375**].

1. Mitchell appears as rated to the highways at **366**, above.

369. Adjorned to this place to Monday the 8th day of November 1731 at nine in the morning.

The Mermaid Tavern, Monday, 8 November 1731
Justices present: Henry Norris, Samuel Tyssen, Alexander Garrett

370. Allowed an Indenture whereby John Dryden a poor Child of the Parish of S^{t}. John at Hackney aged twelve years was bound apprentice to James Huggett Junr. of the parish aforesaid yeoman.

371. Signed a Warrant of Distress against the Defaulters that have neglected to performe their Statute worke on the Highwayes pursuant to an Order made at the last meeting.

372. Ordered That Samuel Sadleir do transcribe the accounts of M^{r}. James Grier late Churchwarden and lay them before us this day month.

373. Ordered That Marg^{t}. Cavennough aged fourteen years and a halfe a Poor Child of this parish to forthwith go upon liking to M^{r}. George Cheere a Baker in [*deletion*] Mare Street. [*See* **409**].

374. Ordered That M^{r}. Thomas Wood the Churchwarden do Pay to Thomas Odey 1^{s} 6^{d} for the present & to continue to pay him the same sume weekly for three weeks to come from this day he being very antient and at present incaple [*sic*] of Labouring for his maintenance.[1]

1. Odey was not settled in Hackney but in Sudminster (?Southminster), Essex. He was called for examination in 1736; his widow obtained a certificate in 1739. H.A.D., P/J/P/68; P79/JN1/398.

375. Signed an Order to remove Edward Mitchell Mary his wife and Edward his Son from the Parish of S^{t}. John at Hackney to the Parish of S^{t}. James in the City and Liberty of Westminster the place of their Settlement. The said Edwd. Mitchell peticoned the Justices that they would allow him ‘till Saturday sennight to bring a Certificate. Ordered That the s^{d}. warrant be not executed ’till this day fortnight. [*See* **368**].

376. Ann Fisher made Oath that Katherine Banks lately Deceased was buryed in Sheeps wool only.

377. John Knight made Oath that his last Settlement is in the Parish of

Walthamstow in the County of Essex. Ordered That he bring a Cert by this day fortnight. [*See* **362**, **994**].

378. Ordered That Mr. Thomas Wood Churchwarden do pay to Margaret Pouter Wido. two shillings pr week for two weeks to come from this day she having lately lost her husband and having two Children to provide for and being in want. [*See* **456**, **475**].

379. Ordered That Do. do pay [*deletion*] towards the maintenance of Thomas Wingfeilds four Children two shillings & Six Pence pr week for four weeks to come from this day his wife being Ill and going into St. Thomas's Hospital for Cure.

380. Ordered That Do. do pay to Richard Evans five shillings to put him in a way to get his living he being Lame & in want being for ten weeks to come from this day. [*See* **2**].

381. Ordered That Do. do pay towards the maintenance of John Braceys wife bed ridden One shilling pr week from this day until further Orders. [*See* **402**, **682**].

382. Mary Carpenter Wido. made Oath that her last legal Settlement is in the parish of St. Mary Islington in the County of Middx. Ordered That the said Mary Carpenter do deliver a Cert from the sd. parish owning her to be a legal Inhabitant thereof by this day fortnight and in case she failes therein that an Order be made out to send her thither. [*See* **362**, **438**, **441**].

383. Adjourned to this place to this day sennight nine in the morning.

The Mermaid Tavern, Monday, 15 November 1731
Justices present: Samuel Tyssen, Alexander Garrett

384. The following persons were Sumoned to appear this day to give an account of the place of each of their last legal Settlements: John English, Exmd & allowed one week to bring a Cert; Robert Wormlayton; *Francis King, Examd & allowed one week to bring a Cert; John Robinson; Mary Plant; Mary Wormlayton; *Robert [Whistler *deleted*] Whichley, Examd & allowed one Month; *Thomas Rowley, Examd and allowed one month to bring a Certificate. [*See* **393**, **394**, **422**, **436**, **994**].

385. Mary Percival rated twenty shillings reduced to ten shillings being not off ability to pay more. Katherine Ashby rated thirty shillings reduced to twenty shillings she having two hundred pounds pr ann Empty; Bridgman Browne for a Shop 6s, for land late Parsons's 15s, for land late Do 40s, [total] 61s; abated 5s being overcharged for ten pounds pr ann. Elizabeth Northey rated one pounds thirteen shillings & nine pence but it appearing upon the evidence of Mr. Northey that it is but one house and that she is a Lodger wth. Mrs. Dixon Ordered That she be discharged from the s^{d} assessment. Martha Baxter rated 4^{s} not relieved being of Ability to pay. John Harbert rated 4^{s} not relieved being of ability to pay. Henry Richard rated 2^{s} 6^{d} not relieved. William Fenton rated 4^{s} not relieved. Benjamin Cooper rated 20^{s} reduced to 10^{s} not being of ability to pay more. Thomas Sowden rated 4^{s} reduced to 2^{s} 6^{d}. Elizabeth North rated 3^{s} not relieved. Henry Haggard Esq £1 13^{s} 9^{d}, D^{o} Land, appealed against by S^{r}. Edward Hill, reduced to 12^{s} 6d for three Quarters. Thomas Townsend 12^{s} reduced to 8^{s} being in low Circumstances.

386. Children to be Clothed: Mary Kirby for Susannah Stanley, Nicholas Cavenough & William Pegram, £1 16s 0d; Rebeckah Webb for Sarah Emmersome and Ann Wood, £1 4s 0d; Ann Cumber for Sarah Hardy, 12s; Rachael Moor for Marg^{t}. Cavennough, Mary Pegram, Hannah Whaley, Henry Tilliock & 4^{s} for Thomas Kemp, £2 12s 0d; Margaret Haynes for Susannah Twitchell, 12s; Katherine Parsons for Sarah Cavennough, 12s; James Boolen for Elizabeth his Daughter, 12s; Mary Burt for W^{m}. Silvester & Mary Silvester, £1 4s 0d; Mary Dean for Richard Ives, 12s; Susannah Flaxmore for Francis Rosamond & Mary Rosamond, £1 4s 0d; for John Coliver, a Base Child, 12s; Elizabeth Johnson for Elizabeth Johnson & Henry Johnson, £1 4s 0d; Elizabeth Peters for John Willson, Samuel Coleman, Edward Willson, Mary Coleman & Hannah Dudley £3; Elizabeth Miles for Susannah Holbrook, 12s; Ann Bolton for her two Children, £1 4s 0d; [total] £17 12s 0d.

387. Ordered That that [*sic*] the sume of twelve shillings be laid out by M^{r}. George Harrison and M^{r}. David Taylor the Present Overseers of the Poor of the Parish of S^{t}. John at Hackney in the County of Middx: towards the Clothing of the several Children contained in the Preceeding List amounting to the sume of Seventeen Pounds & twelve shillings and it is further Ordered that M^{r}. Thomas Wood the Present Churchwarden of the s^{d}. Parish do forthwith pay to the said George Harrison and David Taylor the s^{d} Sume of Seventeen Pounds & twelve shillings for that purpose.

388. Ordered that Mr Thomas Wood Churchwarden do pay twenty shillings towards the Clothing of Samuel Winstanley a poor Child belonging to this Parish put out apprentice to a Horn Turner of the Parish of St Botolph without Bishopsgate London a member of the Clothworkers Company.

The Mermaid Tavern, Monday, 22 November 1731
Justices present: Henry Norris, Samuel Tyssen, Alexander Garrett

389. The following Persons were Sumoned to appear this day to give an account of the places of their last legal Settlements: *William Eden, not to be found; *Robert [Price *deleted*] Rice, Examd & appearing to be a Freeholder was Excused from bringing a Cert; *Thomas Hunt, delivered a Certificate; Alexander Willson, ordered that a warrant be made out to apprehend him he not attending upon the Sumons on the oath of James Bolton.[1] [*Marginal entry*: Delivered a Certificate].

1. Rice was not a freeholder in Hackney, but in Attlebridge, Norfolk. Hunt (of Homerton) was rated to the highways. Wilson (also of Homerton) was excused poor rates the following year, as a certificated man without a settlement in Hackney. H.A.D., P/J/P/68, P/J/H/14, P/J/P/86.

390. Ordered That M[r] Thomas Wood Churchwarden do pay to Dianah the wife of Thomas Jenningson 2[s] pr week for four weeks from this day her said husband having left her and her 2 Children in want.[1] [*See* **529**, **550**, **580**, **610**].

1. Unless there were two women of similar name in virtually identical circumstances, this must be Dianah the wife of John Jennison, whose examination is noted at entry **723**. H.A.D., P/J/P/68.

391. John Davis Churchwarden of the Parish of S[t]. John at Hackney and William Davis one of the Headboroughs of the said Parish gave Informacon upon their several Oaths against the several Persons whose names are hereunder written for severally exerciseing their worldly Trades on Sunday the 21st of this Instant November in the parish aforesaid: viz Joseph Hill at the Crooked Billett in Clopton vict; John Duncalfe at the 3 Rabbitts D[o] vict; [*blank*] Groves in Clopton Chandler; Edward Poole at the Peacock in Homerton vict; Susannah Warren at the Faulcon in Homerton vict. Signed a Summons requiring each of them to attend this day sennight at nine in the morning to shew cause why they should not be Convicted of the said Offence. [*See* **404**, **405**, **406**, **407**, **408**, **431**].

392. Ordered That M[r] Thomas Wood Churchwarden do pay to Mary White 2[s] 6[d] for the Present & to continue to pay her the same sume weekly for eight weeks to come from this day she being very Ill & having a young Child to provide for. [*See* **457**, **506**].

393. Mary Plant wid[o]. brought by Henry Batt Headborough by virtue of a Warrant Granted by Henry Norris Esq for not attending to give an account of her Settlem[t]. It appearing that her Settlem[t]. is in the parish of Stoake Newington – Ordered That she deliver a Certificate thereof by this day fortnight and in Default thereof that she be removed thither by a pass. [*See* **384**, **422**].

394. Mary Wormlayton bro[t]. by D[o]. Exam[d] & allowed one Week. [*See* **384**, **422**, **436**].

395. Elizabeth Robinson Wid[o]. brought by D[o]. delivered a Certificate owning her late Husband to be [selled *deleted*] settled in the Parish of Wellington in the County of Sallop. Ordered That in case she shall remove out of this Parish that her Cert be delivered to her.

396. Ordered That M[r] Thomas Wood Churchwarden do pay to Grace

Chandler 2s 6d pr week for the present and continue to pay her the same sume weekly for three weeks to come from this day she being very Sick & in want. [*See* **363**, **364**, **401**].

397. Ordered That Mary Pegram aged 13 years a poor Child of this Parish be bound apprentice to Joseph French of the parish of St. Mary at Newington in the County of Surry pin maker for the usual Term and that Mr. Thomas Wood the Churchwarden do pay to him the sume of forty shillings with her. [*See* **416**].

398. Ordered that Mr Thomas Wood Churchwarden do pay to Samuel Sadleir his Bill for business done by him for the parish amounting to the sume of five pounds Sixteen shillings & eleven pence, from July the 28th 1731 to the 22d day of November following.

399. Adjorned to this day sennight to this place at nine in the morning.

The Mermaid Tavern, Monday, 29 November 1731
Justices present: Henry Norris, Samuel Tyssen, Alexander Garrett

400. Persons sumoned to give an accot of their Settlements, viz: *William Rutley; John Ellis; John Wormlayton; Henry Nicholls; *Samuel Thompson gone away; William Carey; *George Fox Examd & allowed 2 weeks. [*See* **435**, **437**, **441**, **451**, **464**, **480**, **505**].

401. Ordered That Mr. Thomas Wood the Churchwarden do pay to Elizabeth Crew five shillings for nursing & maintaining Grace Chandler for four weeks she being in Want. [*See* **363**, **364**, **396**].

402. Ordered That Do. do Pay towards the maintenance of John Braseys wife one shilling pr week for 4 weeks from this day she being bed ridden and in Want. [*See* **381**, **682**].

403. Ordered That Do. do Pay to Mary Anderson Wido. 1s 6d for the Present & the same sume weekly for three weeks to come from this day she being sick & in want. [*See* **613**].

404. Edward Poole at the Peacock victr convicted on the Oaths of John Davis & Wm. Davis four persons Drinking of Geneva on Sunday the 21st of November 1731 in the Parish of St. John at Hackney. [*Marginal entries*: To pay 5s. Paid]. [*See* **391**].

405. John Duncalfe at 3 Rabbitts in Clopton Confessed the fact. Convicted. [*Marginal entry*: Paid 5s]. [*See* **391**].

406. Joseph Hill at the Crooked Billett in Clopton Convicted on Oaths of Jno. Davis & Wm. Davis. [*Marginal entry*: Paid 5s]. [*See* **391**].

407. Samuel Groves Chandler in Clopton on the Oaths of Do – Convicted – Elizabeth his [appeared *deleted*] wife appeared and Confessed that her said husband used commonly the selling of English Brandy by retaile to be Drank in his Shop in the said parish. Ordered That the said Samuel Groves be and he is hereby Convicted of the said Offense and it is hereby further Ordered that a Warrant be forthwith made out to Levy the sume of 20[s] for the said Offence as the Law directs. [*Marginal entry*: Paid 20[s]]. [*See* **391**, **431**].

408. Susannah Warren Wid[o]. at the Faulcon in Homerton Sumoned but did not attend the Evidence not be[g]. clear she was not Convicted. She afterwards appeared & confessed the fact & ordered to Pay 5[s]. [*See* **391**].

409. Ordered That Margaret Cavennough aged fifteen years a poor Child of this Parish be bound out to M[r]. [James *deleted*] George Cheere of the same Parish Baker 'till she is 21 years of Age or day of marriage and that M[r] Thomas Wood the Churchwarden do pay him forty shillings with her to be laid out in Clothing for her. [*See* **373**].

410. Robert [Walberton *deleted*] Worberton brought by Henry Batt Headborough by vertue of a warrant Granted by Henry Norris Esq[r] for refusing to attend to give an account of his Settlem[t]. Examined and the Settlement appearing to be in the Parish of Stoake Newington and allowed two weeks to bring a Certificate. [*See* **558**].

411. Ordered That M[r]. Thomas Wood Churchwarden do pay to Lyonell Theed 2[s] 6[d] for the Present and continue to pay him the same sume weekly for three weeks to come from this day he being very Sick & Weak.[1]

1. Theed, together with his wife Mary, had been receiving regular relief from May 1730 until February 1731. P79/JN1/227.

412. Ordered That D[o]. do Pay to Elinor Kingsland Wid[o]. 1[s] pr week from this day until further Orders she being incapable of Getting her living and in Want.[1] [*See* **538**].

1. Elinor Kingsland was not settled in Hackney but in Bideford, Devon. Her husband had been examined in 1728, and she was herself examined in 1737. H.A.D., P/J/P/68.

413. Signed a warrant to apprehend Samuel Bodycoate to bring a Cert he having Intruded himselfe into the parish to dwell there as a parishoner thereby being likely to bring a burthen & charge upon the said Parish. [*See* **418**, **441**].

414. Ordered That M[r]. Thomas Wood Churchwarden do Pay to James Bolton Headbo[r] three shillings and also to Henry Batt Headborough three shillings for Extraordinary Services by them done for the Parish.

415. Ordered That M[r]. William Weston and M[r]. Francis Wigley the Late Overseers of the Poor of the Parish of S[t]. John at Hackney do forthwith make up and perfect their acco[ts] in writing of all monys by them received and Paid in the discharge of the s[d]. Office, and being so stated to Lay them before us at a Petty Sessions to be held in this place on Monday the [16 *deleted*] 13th day of December next at nine in the morning. [*See* **421**].

416. Allowed an Indenture of apprenticeshipp whereby Mary Pegram aged thirteen years a Poor Child of this parish was bound to Joseph French of the Parish of S[t]. Mary Newington in the County of Surry Pinn Maker. [*See* **397**].

417. Adjorned to this day fortnight to this place at nine in the morning.

The Mermaid Tavern, Monday, 13 December 1731
Justices present: Henry Norris, Samuel Tyssen, Alexander Garrett

418. Samuel Bodycoate brought by Henry Batt Headborough by vertue of a Warrant to shew cause why he hath not delivered a Certificate. Examined & allowed one Month and that an Order be forthwith made out to remove him and his Son to the place of their last legal Settlement and in case he faile to bring a Certificate in that time that the order be then put in force. [*See* **413**, **441**].

419. Ordered That M[r] Thomas Wood the Churchwarden do Pay to Katherine Browne Wid[o]. very Poor and two Children to provide for ten shillings to put her in a way to get her living she having Promised not to ask for any assistance for three years to come.

420. Thomas Collings applyed to the Justices for a License to keep the Plow ale house in Homerton – It appearing to the said Justices that Alexander Willson at the sign of the Black horse in Homerton was Licensed in the room of Charles Harper who formerly kept the s[d]. Plow Ale house, Ordered That the said Thomas Collins shall not have a License to retaile ale & Beer in the said House and the said Thomas Collings was then Commanded by the said Justices not to be Guilty for the future of retaleing ale & Beer &c under the penalty contained in the several acts of Parliament in that case made & provided.

421. M[r]. William Weston and M[r]. Francis Wigley Overseers of the Poor of the Parish of S[t]. John at Hackney for the year 1730 pursuant to an Order of the last meeting laid their acco[ts] before the said Justices by which it appears that they Received four hundred and Seven pounds ninteen [*sic*] shillings and Eight Pence and that they have paid three hundred ninety Six pounds twelve shillings and Seven Pence so that their remains due from them to the Parish to ballance the said Accounts the Sume of Eleven Pounds Seven shillings and One Penny. Rec[d] £407 19s 8d, Paid £396 12s 7d, [Balance] £11=7s=1d. Ordered That the said William Weston and Francis Wigley do forthwith Pay to George Harrison and David Taylor the present Overseers of the Poor of the said Parish the said ballance of their accounts being Eleven pounds Seven shillings & One Penny to be by them laid out and imployed for the use of the Poor of the said Parish. [*See* **415**].

422. Ordered That Orders be forthwith made out to remove Mary Plant and Mary Wormlayton to the Places of their last legal Settlement for not delivering Certificates of their Settlements pursuant to an Order of the 22ᵈ of November last. [*See* **384**, **393**, **394**, **436**].

423. Ordered That Mr Thomas Wood Churchwarden do pay to Martha Stent wid° Six Pence pr week for Eight Weeks to come from this day she being old & poor.

424. Ordered That D°. do pay to Elizabeth the Wid°. of Charles Stamper 2ˢ for the Present & continue to Pay her the Same Sume weekly for four weeks to come she being big with Child. [*See* **439**, **460**, **548**].

425. Ordered That Mʳ Thomas Wood Churchwarden do pay to Mary the wife of Samuel Johnson two shillings & Six Pence she being in Great Want and having two Children to provide for and her husband having left her in want.[1] [*See* **433**].

1. Mary Johnson's examination, taken this day, indicates that she was not settled in Hackney but in Boden, Cheshire. H.A.D., P/J/P/68.

426. Henry Batt and William Davis made Oath that Thomas Pouter who keeps a Brandy Shop in Church Street in the Parish of Sᵗ John at Hackney in the County of Middlesex useth commonly the selling of Brandy and Distilled Liquors to be drank in his said Shop by retale and did this Present day sell to the said Henry Batt & William Davis one Quartern of Liquor or Spirits called Geneva for three halfe Pence and Sufferred them to drink it in his said Shop. Ordered That the said Thomas Pouter be and he is hereby convicted of retailing Distilled Liquors without a License and it is further Ordered that he be Sumoned to appear before the sᵈ Justices at the next meeting to be held on Monday next at ten in the forenoon to Shew cause why he should not be Proceeded against as the Law directs. Warrant Signed by Henry Norris & Samuel Tyssen Esqʳˢ. [*See* **429**].

427. Adjourned to this Place to Monday next at ten in the forenoon.

The Mermaid Tavern, Monday, 20 December 1731
Justices present: Henry Norris, Samuel Tyssen, Alexander Garrett

428. Mary Thompson made Oath that Ann Webb of the Parish of Hackney lately Deceased was buried in Sheeps Wool only.

429. Thomas Pouter who keeps a Brandy Shop in Church Street in the Parish of Hackney attended pursuant to notice given him for that purpose to shew cause why the penalty should not be Levy'd upon his goods which he was adjudged to pay at the last meeting he being then

Convicted of usually Selling Brandy and other Distilled Liquors to be Drank in his s[d] House And confessed that he hath not any License to retale those Liquors and also hath for a considerable time past frequently Sold Brandy & Distilled Liquors in his said House by retaile to be Drank there. Upon which the said Justices commanded M[r]. John Davis one of the Churchwardens of the said Parish to put the Warrant against him in Execution and he accordingly in the presence of the said justices Demanded of him the Sume of Twenty shillings pursuant thereto. [*See* **426**].

430. Ordered That M[r]. Thomas Wood Churchwarden do pay to Elizabeth the wife of Thomas Bartmaker ten shillings towards Supporting her in the time of her laying Inn she being very Big wth. Child and her said husband being very Infirm and in Chelsea Hospital and having one Child to provide for and she being in want. [*Marginal entry*: not paid *It is not clear whether the word 'not' has been deleted*]. [*See* **432**, **525**, **537**, **557**].

431. Samuel Groves applyed to have a License to retaile Distilled Liquors at his house in Clopton. The said Justices absolutely refused him and Commanded him at the same time not to presume to take upon him to retale any of those Liquors under the several penaltys contained in the Laws in that Case made and provided. [*See* **391**, **407**].

432. Ordered That M[r]. Thomas Wood Churchwarden do pay to Elizabeth the wife of Thomas Bartmaker three shillings for one week past [and continue to pay her 2[s] pr week for four weeks to come from this day *deleted*]. [*See* **430**, **525**, **537**, **557**].

433. Ordered That D[o]. do Pay to Mary the wife of Samuel Johnson the Sume of twelve shillings her said husband having ran away & left her and her two Children in great want she promising to go out of the Parish and never to trouble the Parish any more. [*See* **425**].

434. Allowed an Indenture of Apprenticeshipp whereby Ann Pegram aged Sixteen years was bound to Ann Shilling of the Parish of S[t]. Mary White Chappel Dealer in Hoggsheads and Earthen Ware.

435. Ordered That a Warrant be made out to apprehend William Rutley for not attending to give an Account of his Settlement. [*See* **400**, **437**, **441**, **505**].

436. Signed an Order to remove Mary Wormlayton to Stoake Newington.[1] [*See* **384**, **394**, **422**].

1. The removal order does not appear to have been enforced. Mary Wormlayton obtained a certificate in 1731 and was still living in Hackney in 1736 (**189**). She is presumably the Widow Wormlayton of Newington who was listed in 1733 as 'very poor'. P79/JN1/398; H.A.D., P/J/H/14.

The Mermaid Tavern, Monday, 3 January 1732
Justices present: Henry Norris, Samuel Tyssen, Alexander Garrett

437. Ordered That a Pass be forthwith made out to remove William Rutley & his wife & children to the Parish of S^{t}. Michael Royal in the City of London. [*See* **400**, **435**, **441**, **505**].

438. Ordered That a Pass be forthwith made out to remove Mary Carpenter to the Parish of S^{t}. Mary Islington in the County of Middlesex. [*See* **362**, **382**, **441**].

439. Ordered That M^{r}. Thomas Wood the Churchwarden do pay to Elizabeth the wid^{o}. of Charles Stamper 5^{s} for the present and continue to pay her 2^{s} pr week for three weeks from the 13 Instant she having lately laid in & having two Children to provide for. [*See* **424**, **460**, **548**].

440. Adjourned to Monday the 17th Instant to this place ten in the forenoon.

The Mermaid Tavern, Monday, 24 January 1732
Justices present: Henry Norris, Samuel Tyssen, Alexander Garrett

441. Signed Orders to remove the following Persons to the Places of their last legal Settlement vizt, Samuel Bodycoate & his Son, W^{m}. Rutley & his family, and Mary [Plant *deleted*] Carpenter.[1] Signed by Henry Norris & Samuel Tyssen Esq^{s}. [*See* **362**, **382**, **400**, **413**, **418**, **435**, **437**, **438**, **505**].

1. The orders against Bodycoate (of Homerton) and Carpenter (of Clapton) do not seem to have been enforced. Bodycoate, who is listed as rated to the highways at **366** above, obtained a certificate in 1736. Carpenter, who was also rated to the highways, obtained a certificate in 1731 and was still listed in the rate book at her death in 1733. Rutley obtained a certificate in 1731 but was removed (**505**) and must therefore have been indigent. P79/JN1/398; H.A.D., P/J/H/14.

442. Ordered That M^{r}. Thomas Wood the Churchwarden do pay to M^{r}. Thomas Saunders apothecary three shillings & Six Pence for Physick for [the *deleted*] a Poor woman.

443. Ordered That D^{o}. do Pay to Thomas Hilliard 2^{s}:6^{d} for the Present and continue to pay him the same Sume for two weeks to come he being out of Business and having a Wife and two Children to provide for.

444. Ordered That D^{o}. do pay to Samuel Sadleir his Bill for Business done for the Parish amounting to the Sume of three pounds nineteen shillings & ten pence in full to this day.

445. Elizabeth Fletcher appealed against 4^{s} not relieved.

446. Ordered That Sarah Emmersome aged 15 years be bound to John

Turner of St John Wapping Waterman and that Mr Thomas Wood the Churchwarden do pay him forty shillings with her. [*See* **458**].

447. Ordered That Sarah Hardy 14 years old a poor Child of this Parish be bound apprentice to Joseph Hall of the Parish of S^t. Mary Magdalen Bermondsey in the County of Surry pack thread Spinner and that Mr Thomas Wood the Churchwarden do pay forty shillings to him with her. [*See* **458**].

448. Ordered that M^r. Thomas Wood the Churchwarden do Pay to Elizabeth the wife of Timothy Peters nine shillings and Seven Pence which she laid out for Clothing for Sarah Chandler and four shillings for nursing of her for two weeks.

449. Ordered That D^o. do pay to Samuel Sadleir the sume of three Pounds thirteen shillings & nine Pence which he Paid for a Coate & Hatt for Henry Harrill the new Beadle.

450. Ordered That D^o. do pay to Ann the wife of Edward Jarsey 1^s:6^d pr week from this day until further Orders her husband being Sick & she being Poor & having one Child to provide for. [*See* **541**].

The Mermaid Tavern, Monday, 7 February 1732
Justices present: Henry Norris, Samuel Tyssen, Alexander Garrett

451. George Fox attended upon his Summons and acquainted the Justices that he hath endeavoured to procure a Certificate and that in about a fortnights time he shall be able to have it and prayed time for that purpose. Ordered That the s^d George Fox have leave 'till the next meeting to deliver it. [*See* **400**, **464**, **480**].

452. George Gillman attended Pursuant to his Summons and gave an Account of the Place of his last legal Settlement upon Oath allowed two weeks to bring a Certificate. [*See* **471**].

453. Complaint having been made against John Collins Headborough and Watchman for refusing to assist M^r. Brian Oram in the securing of two thieves on the thirty first of January last past. Ordered That they be Summoned to attend at the next meeting to answer the said Complaint. [*See* **35**, **469**].

454. Complaint having been made against the Constables & Headboroughs for neglecting their Duties in not attending at the several Watch-houses as they are severally by Law Obliged. Ordered That they be Summoned to attend at the next meeting to answer the said Complaint.

455. Ordered That M^r. Thomas Wood the Churchwarden do pay to

John Kirby ten shillings for nursing & maintaining Thomas Dodds afflicted with the foul Desease for two weeks.

456. Margaret Pouter widow of Joseph Pouter gave an account upon Oath that she hath [*deletion*] often heard her said late husband declare that he was borne in the Parish off [*sic*] Thackstead in the County of Essex and that he did not afterwards gain any legal Settlement elsewhere and she hath son by the s^{d}. Joseph Pouter about three years old named John and she hath not since his Decease gained any legal Settlem^{t} in his own right. That [*deletion*] there is a woman lives near the Naggs head ale house that knows it to be true she living at Thackstead at the time of his Birth – and she can direct [*deletion*] another woman in Shoreditch who knew the Settlement to be in [Shoredi *deleted*] Thackstead afores^{d}. Ordered That the said Margaret Pouter and her Son John Pouter be forthwith removed to the said Parish of Thackstead in the [*deletion*] County of Essex It appearing to be the Place of their last legal Settlement.[1] [*See* **378**, **475**].

1. The order was not signed until 22 February. Thaxted appealed unsuccessfully. MJ/SBB/900, p. 92.

457. Ordered That M^{r}. Thomas Wood the Churchwarden do Pay to Mary White One shilling and Six pence for the present and continue to pay her the same sume weekly for four weeks to come from this day she being in want and having one Child to provide for. [*See* **392**, **506**].

458. Allowed an Indenture whereby Sarah Emmersome aged fifteen years a Poor Child of this Parish was bound to John Turner of the Parish of S^{t}. John Wapping in the County of Middlesex Waterman and also an other Indenture whereby Sarah Hardy aged fourteen years a poor Child of this parish was bound to Joseph Hall of the Parish of S^{t}. Mary Magdalen Bermondsey in the County of Surry pack thread Spinner. [*See* **446**, **447**].

459. Ordered That Mr Thomas Wood the Churchwarden do pay to Susannah Durrant Widow four shillings for the Present and continue to Pay her two shillings pr week for Six Weeks to come from this day she having lately laid in and having two Children to Provide for. [*See* **527**].

460. Ordered That Mr Thomas Wood the Churchwarden do Pay to Elizabeth the Widow of Charles Stamper ten shillings to put her into a way of business she having two Children to provide for. [*See* **424**, **439**, **548**].

The Mermaid Tavern, Monday, 14 February 1732
Justices present: Henry Norris, Samuel Tyssen, Alexander Garrett

461. The said Justices began to audit the accounts of M^{r}. James Grier late Churchwarden & Overseer of the Poor of the Parish of St John at Hackney for the year 1730 but not having time to go through the same they adjourned to Saturday next at four in the afternoon to perfect the same.

The Mermaid Tavern, Monday, 28 February 1732
Justices present: Henry Norris, Samuel Tyssen, Alexander Garrett

462. The Persons whose names are underwritten were Sumoned to give an Account of the Places of their last legal Settlement: William Pescod; Thomas Wadsworth, Mr Wm Weston engaged for his bringing a Certificate; Christop: Turk; Mary Heath Wid^o^. of John Heath Cert delivered anno 1711; William Griffith; Edward Preston. [*See* **478**, **490**, **491**, **492**, **499**, **516**, **517**].

463. Ordered That Mary Rosamond aged thirteen years a poor Child of this Parish do go upon liking to Ann Mills a Band box maker living in little Grays Inn Lane in the parish of S^t^. Andrew Holborn in the County of Middx. [*See* **487**, **497**].

464. It appearing that George Fox hath endeavoured to get a Certificate and that he will be able in a very little time to procure it, Agreed That the consideration of what is necessary to be done relateing thereto be [further *deleted*] referred to the next meeting. [*See* **400**, **451**, **480**].

465. Rowland Child of Lambeth attended upon his Sumons for keeping a Puppett show at the Mermaid ale house contrary to Law and Confessed before the Justices that he began to Shew on Fryday last was sennight and desired leave to show for three or four dayes. The [*deletion*] Justices taking the said affair into their considerations adjudged him to be a Vagrant and charged him immediately to disist from Acting and told him if he acted again they would [*deletion*] commit him to the House of Correction as they [*sic*] Law directs. [*See* **466**, **467**].

466. Joseph Ratcliffe who keeps the said house attended upon his Summons for suffering the said Rowland Child to act a Puppett Show there contrary to Law. Upon his making a proper submission and begging Pardon for what he hath done and promising never to be Guilty for the future. The said Justices forgave him. [*See* **465**, **467**].

467. Palmer the Fidler attended upon his Summons for playing at the said Puppet Show and also going round the Towne with the said Rowland Child playing upon his Houghboy contrary to Law. The Justices upon his submitting himselfe and begging Pardon and Promising not to be Guilty for the future Excused him. [*See* **465**, **466**].

468. The Constables and Headboroughs attended to answer a Complaint Exhibited against them for not [attended *deleted*] attending at the several Watch-houses. They Promising to attend constantly and carefully do their duties for the future the Justices Excused them for what is past.

469. John Collins one of the Headboroughs of the Parish of S^t^. John at Hackney attended upon his Summons to answer a Complaint Exhibited against him by Mr Brian Oram for refuseing to get up in the night on the thirty first of January last to secure two footpads [that *deleted*]. Upon his making it appear to the Justices that he was Sick otherwise he would willingly have attended The Justices were pleased to Excuse him. [*See* **35**, **453**].

470. John Collins appealed against twenty shillings which he is rated to the poor. Reduced to Seven shillings and Six pence he being in low Circumstances.

471. George Gillman who was Ordered to bring a Certificate at a meeting held on the 7th of this Instant attended and acquainted the Justices that he Occupies two tenements in Homerton in the Parish of Hackney for which he is to pay twelve Pounds pr ann and therefore desired to be Excused from bringing a Certificate.[1] [*See* **452**].

1. By renting to the value of £10 or more (even though two properties were involved) Gillman acquired a settlement in Hackney.

472. Ordered That Thomas Kemp aged fourteen years a Poor Child of this Parish be forthwith bound Apprentice to William Hewitt of the Parish of S^t^. Leonard Shoreditch narrow Weaver and that M^r^. Thomas Wood the Churchwarden do Pay forty shillings with him. [*See* **479**].

473. William Tolley attended and desired leave to keep an Ale house at the Bird in hand at Newington in this parish. Agreed that he have a License granted for that purpose at the next General meeting to be held [for that p *deleted*] at the Court house in White Chapple.

474. Ordered That an Order be forthwith made out to remove Rebecca Newgent wife of Patrick Newgent and her three Children from this Parish to the parish of Conton in the County of Nottingham her said husband being an Irishman and the said Parish of Conton being the Place where her late husband John Machum was last legally Settled.[1]

1. Rebecca Newgent was chargeable to the parish. Conton appealed that part of the order relating to her and the child of her second marriage, probably arguing that remarriage had extinguished her rights of settlement in Conton. Under normal circumstances this would have been correct, since a wife took her husband's place of settlement as her own, as did any children of the marriage. However Patrick Newgent, as an Irishman, could not confer a settlement on his wife and her status therefore remained unchanged. No result of the appeal has been traced and it was probably withdrawn. MJ/SBB/900, p. 86.

475. Ordered That Mr Thomas Wood the Churchwarden do pay to Abigail Ronsum three shillings for Lodging Margaret Pouter for three weeks. [*See* **378**, **456**].

476. Ordered That D^o^. do pay to Elizabeth Stanley wid^o^. one shilling for the present and continue to pay her the same sume weekly till further orders.

477. Signed a warrant to apprehend John [*recte* Pelatia] Salmon and Elizabeth Best for refuseing to attend to give an account of the places of their last legal Settlement when duely Summoned for that purpose they having Intruded themselves into this parish contrary to Law and are likely to become chargeable thereunto if not timely prevented Oath having been made thereof. [*See* **481**, **482**].

478. Ordered That a Warrant be made out to apprehend William Pescod Christop: Turk William Griffith and Edward Preston to give an account of the Places of their last legal Settlements they having intruded themselves into this [said *deleted*] parish to Inhabit as parishion^rs contrary Law and having refused or neglected to attend to give an Account thereof although duely Summoned for that purpose Oath having been made thereof they being likely to become burthensome and chargeable to the Parish. [*See* **462**, **490**, **491**, **499**, **516**, **517**].

The Mermaid Tavern, Saturday, 4 March 1732
Justices present: Henry Norris, Alexander Garrett

479. Allowed an Indenture whereby Thomas Kemp aged fourteen years a Poor Child of this parish was bound apprentice to W^m. Hewitt of the parish of St Leonard Shoreditch in the County of Middx Narrow Weaver. [*See* **472**].

The Mermaid Tavern, Monday, 13 March 1732
Justices present: Henry Norris, Samuel Tyssen, Alexander Garrett

480. George Fox brought a Certificate from the Parish of Woodford in the County of Essex owning him and his wife to be Inhabitants of the said parish.[1] [*See* **400**, **451**, **464**].

1. George Fox, farrier of Homerton, was rated to the highways. H.A.D., P/J/H/14.

481. Pelatia Salmon bro^t. by W^m. Davis Headborough by Warrant for refuseing to attend to give an Account of his Settlement allowed 2 weeks to bring a Certificate.[1] [*See* **477**].

1. Salmon, who was rated to the highways (**366**), had been examined two years earlier. He delivered a certificate (issued in 1731) and had left Hackney by 1733. P79/JN1/398; H.A.D., P/J/H/14, P/J/P/68.

482. Elizabeth Best brought by D^o. and gave an account of the place of her last legal Settlement and allowed two weeks to bring a Certificate. [*See* **477**].

483. Margaret Willson made Oath that John Willson lately Deceased was buryed in Sheeps wool only.

[**484.** Ordered That Amy Fisher aged fourteen years a Poor Child of this Parish be forthwith bound to M^{r}. *entry incomplete and deleted.*]

485. Ordered Ann Wood aged 13 years do go upon likeing to Lucas Mans living in King Street the corner of Monmouth Street Shoemaker in the parish of Christ Church. [*See* **503**, **514**].

486. Luke Townsend rated 4^{s} not releived.

487. Ordered That Mary Rosamond aged thirteen years a poor Child of this Parish be forthwith bound apprentice to Ann Mills of the Parish of S^{t}. Andrew Holborn in the County of Middlesex Band box maker and that Mr Thomas Wood the Churchwarden do pay forty shillings with her. [*See* **463**, **497**].

488. John [*deletion*] Price applyed to keep an ale house at the Dolphin in Kingsland – Agreed upon his bringing a Certificate that a License be granted him at the next General Meeting for Licensing.[1]

1. Price obtained a certificate. P79/JN1/398.

489. Stephen Carr applyed to keep an ale house at the Kings head at Kingsland Agreed upon his bringing a Certificate that a License be granted him at the next General Meeting for Licensing.
[*See* **498**].

490. Christopher Turk Exam^{d} touching his Settlem^{t}. & allowed two weeks to bring a Certificate. [*See* **462**, **478**, **499**, **517**].

491. W^{m}. Pescod Examd & allowed one week to bring a Cert and in case he doth not Comply with this Order that he be removed. [*See* **462**, **478**, **499**, **516**].

492. W^{m}. Griffith Exam^{d} Settlem^{t} in this Parish. [*See* **462**].

493. Ordered That Mr. Thomas Wood the Churchwarden do Pay to Thomas Matterson one shilling for the present and continue to pay the same weekly for four Weeks to come he being very Infirm. [*See* **523**].

494. Ordered That Mr Thomas Wood Churchwarden do pay to [Thomas *deleted*] John Bartmakers wife five shillings her husband being Sick & two Children to provide for.

495. The said Justices Examd the accounts of M^{r}. James Grier late Churchwarden and Overseer of the Poor of the Parish of Hackney for the year [*deletion*] 1730 and their [*sic*] appears to be due from the parish to him to ballance the poors account one pound ten shillings and four pence farthing and that there is also due to him on the Church account fifty six pounds twelve shillings and ten pence halfe penny and that there is due from him to the parish to ballance the Turnpike account thirty five pounds thirteen shillings and two pence farthing So that upon the whole there remains due to him from the Parish the sume of twenty two pounds ten shillings and a halfe penny. Ordered That M[r] Thomas Wood the present Churchwarden & Overseer of the Poor do forthwith pay to the said M[r] James Grier the said Ballance.

The Mermaid Tavern, Monday, 3 April 1732
Justices present: Henry Norris, Samuel Tyssen

496. *Thomas Saunders Exam[d] & 1 month allowed to bring a Certificate [*Marginal note*: Excused from bringing a Cert not being likely to be chargeable being a pentioner at Chelsea Colledge. Elizabeth Townesend. *Christopher [*deletion*] Coates allowed 'till the next meeting to informe himselfe of his Settlem[t]. *Thomas Howell not to be found. *Thomas Davis Examd & allowed one Month to bring a Cert. *George Tarrant Examd & allowed one Month to bring a Cert. The several Persons above named were Summoned to attend this day to give an account of the places of their last legal Settlements.
[*See* **535**, **545**, **547**, **563**].

497. Allowed an Indenture of Apprenticeshipp whereby Mary Rosamond aged fourteen years a poor Child of this parish was bound apprentice to Ann Mills of the parish of S[t]. Andrew Holborn in the County of Middlesex. [*See* **463**, **487**].

498. Upon reconsidering the application of Stephen Carr to be Licensed and he having misbehaved himselfe since his application and not being a proper person to keep an ale house, Ordered That he be not Licensed. [*See* **37**, **38**, **39**, **489**].

499. Ordered That orders be forthwith made out to remove Christop. Turk & William Pescod to [*deletion*] the places of their last legal Settlements. [*See* **462**, **478**, **490**, **491**, **516**, **517**].

500. Solomon West rated 4[s] Excused this year being Sick & Poor.

501. Signed a warrant to apprehend George Nelson upon the Oath of Joseph Wright for assaulting and beating him & tearing his Shirt.

502. Sibella Hunt made Oath that John Norris lately deceased was buryed in Sheeps Wool only.

503. Ordered That Ann Wood aged thirteen years a Poor Child of this Parish be forthwith bound apprentice to Lucas Mans of the Parish of Christ Church in the County of Middlesex Shoemaker and that M[r]. Thomas Wood the Churchwarden do pay him forty shillings with her. [*See* **485**, **514**].

504. Ordered That Mr Thomas Wood the Churchwarden do pay to Rebeckah Johnson Widow an additional allowance of one shilling pr week for four weeks to come she being very Sick & weak. [*See* **528**, **559**].

505. Ordered That D°. do Pay the Expences in Passing William Rutley & family to S[t]. Michael Royal London amounting to Six shillings & Six Pence. [*See* **400**, **435**, **437**, **441**].

506. Ordered that D°. do Pay to Mary White one shilling and Six Pence for the present and continue to pay her the same sume weekly until further Orders she being Infirm and having one Child to provide for. [*See* **392**, **457**].

507. Ordered that D°. do Pay to Samuel Sadleir his Bill for Business done for the Parish amounting to the Sume of Seven Pounds [*deletion*] eleven shillings and [Eight pence *deleted*] five pence.

508. Ordered That D°. do Pay to Joseph Wright his Bill for the use of his room for the Justices to sit in to do the parish business from May the 11th 1729 to August the 10th 1730 and for Coffee and bread & butter amounting to the Sume of four pounds nineteen shillings and nine pence.

509. Ordered that D°. do Pay to M[r]. Thomas [Port] Goldsmith his Bill for a new Silver Head for the Beadles Staff, a new Staff, Doing up the Old head & new Sitting it and Engraveing two Inscriptions &c amounting to the Sume of Five pounds Six shillings.

510. Allowed and Confirmed six months additional assessment for the Poors Rate of the Hamlet of Bethnal Green amounting to the Sume of three hundred & thirty Six Pounds twelve shillings and five pence.

511. Signed a Warrant to Levy the Poors Rate upon the several persons whose names are hereunder written upon the Oath of M[r]. Thomas Wood Churchwarden and Overseer of the Poor for the year 1731. Francis Eaglesoe 8s.; William Thornton 4s. [*Marginal entry*: Excused poor]; Henry Richard 2s. 6d.; Mary Tayler 3s. [*Marginal entry*: Gone]; Thomas Masling Sen[r] 14s.; John Singleton 8s.; Thomas Shepperson 4s.; Solomon West 4s. [*Marginal entry*: Excused]; Miles Nuttbrowne 6s. [*Marginal entry*: Gone]; William Kingsland 10s. [*Marginal entry*: Excused]; Giles Lomas 5s. [*Marginal entry*: Excused]; Robert Bell 6s.; William Crotchrode 15s.; Luke Townsend 4s.; John Herbert £2 7s.; James Greenhouse 8s.; Jeremiah Kemp 8s.; John Bolton 8s. [*Marginal entry*: Excused]; Henry Hedger 6s.; William Udall 5s. [*Marginal entry*: to take 2s. 6d.]; Henry Godwin £1 16s. 9d. [*Marginal entry*: to take 18s. 4½d.]; Thomas Marsh 4s. [*Marginal entry*: gone]; [*blank*] Bergaine 10s.; Matthias Jackson 6s.; Job Everton £1 [*Marginal entry*: gone]; Thomas Archer 4s. [*Marginal entry*: Excused]; William Gatley 6s.; Ann Bartholomew 4s.; Thomas Barnard 5s.; Mary Mare 10s. [*Marginal entry*:

gone]; Ambrose Burchell 8s.; Lambert Lance 4s.; William Carter 8s.

512. Signed a warrant to Levey the Poors Rate upon the goods of the several Persons whose names are hereunder written upon the Oaths of Mr George Harrison & Mr David Taylor Overseers of the Poor for the year 1731. Francis Eaglesoe 8s.; Daniel Card 6s. [*Marginal entry*: paid]; Thomas Masling 14s.; Eliz[a]. Fletcher 4s. [*Marginal entry*: paid]; Roger Rotherford 4s. [*Marginal entry*: paid]; Solomon West 4s. [*Marginal entry*: Excused]; William Kingsland 10s. [*Marginal entry*: Excused]; Giles Lomas 5s. [*Marginal entry*: Excused]; Robert Bell 6s.; Luke Townsend 4s.; John Harbert £2 7s.; Jeremiah Kemp 8s.; Matthias Jackson 6s.; Thomas Archer 4s. [*Marginal entry*: Excused]; William Gatley 6s.; Jeremiah Woodley £3 5s.; Ann Bartholomew 4s.; Thomas Barnard 5s.; James Mortimer £2 10s. [*Marginal entry*: paid].

The Mermaid Tavern, Monday, 1 May 1732
Justices present: Henry Norris, Samuel Tyssen, John Oakey

513. A List of the names of the Persons returned by the Vestry to his Majesties Justices of the Peace for them to appoint Overseers of the Poor for the year 1732: **John Townsend [*marginal entry*: appointed]; *Joseph Sureties; *John Oswald; *James Huggett Jun[r]; *John Cox; *John Whittle; **Hezekiah Walker [*marginal entry*: appointed]; Benjamin Mendez Decosta [*marginal entry*: Fined]; Jacob Mendez Decosta [*marginal entry*: Fined].

514. Allowed an Indenture of apprenticeship whereby Ann Wood aged [fourteen *deleted*] thirteen years a Poor Child of this parish was bound to Lucas Mens of the Parish of Christ Church in the County of Middlesex Cordwainer. [*See* **485**, **503**].

515. Signed warrants to appoint and Confirme Richard Sturley Churchwarden and Samuel Shephard Richard Long and John Went Overseers of the Poor of the Hamlet of Bethnal Green in the County of Middlesex for the year 1732.

516. Signed an Order to remove William Pescod and Ann his wife to the Hamlet of Mile end old Town in the County of Middlesex.[1] [*See* **462**, **478**, **491**, **499**].

1. Pescod was first examined in 1726. The removal order does not appear to have been enforced. Pescod continued to live in Hackney (**195**) and was rated to the highways. He obtained a certificate during 1732, and was examined yet again in 1744. P79/JN1/398; H.A.D., P/J/H/14, P/J/P/68.

517. Signed an Order to remove Christopher Turk to Chatham in the County of Kent. [*See* **462**, **478**, **490**, **499**].

518. Signed a warrant to nominate and appoint M[r]. John Davis Churchwarden of the Parish of S^{t}. John at Hackney to be one of the Overseers of the Poor of the said Parish for the year 1732.

519. Signed a warrant to nominate and appoint M^{r}. Hezekiah Walker a Substantial Inhabitant of the Parish of S^{t}. John at Hackney in the County of Middlesex to be one of the Overseers of the Poor of the said Parish for the year 1732.

520. Signed a Warrant to nominate and appoint M^{r}. John Townsend a Substantial Inhabitant of the Parish of St John at Hackney in the County of Middlesex, to be one of the Overseers of the Poor of the said Parish for the year 1732.

521. Signed warrants to nominate and appoint Francis Davis and Henry Harrill Overseers of the Poor of the Parish of S^{t}. John at Hackney for the year 1732.

522. The following Persons were Sworne. Constables: Morgan Bynon, Thomas Howson, John Brewer. Headboroughs: William Davis, Henry Harrill, William Platt, John Southern Junr, Henry Donmer, Robert Loyd. Ale Conners: Daniel Card, Richard Hedge, Peter Clyne.

523. Ordered That M^{r}. John Davis the Churchwarden do pay to Thomas Mattison two shillings for the present and continue to Pay him two shillings pr week for Eight weeks to come from this day he being in a very very [*sic*] weak Condition. [*See* **493**].

524. Ordered That Elizabeth Harris aged 14 years a poor Child of this parish do go upon liking to Joseph French [Joseph French *deleted*] of the parish of S^{t}. Mary Magdalen Bermondsey pin maker.

525. Ordered That Mr John Davis Churchwarden do pay to Elizabeth the wife of Thomas Bartmaker three shillings for two weeks to come from this day she having two children to provide for. [*See* **430**, **432**, **537**, **557**].

526. Ordered That D^{o}. do pay to Margaret Bolton wife of John Bolton 1^{s} for the present and to continue to pay her the same sume for two weeks to come her husband being in Goal and she in want.

527. Ordered That D^{o}. do Pay to Susannah Durant Wid^{o}. 2^{s} for the Present and continue to pay her the same sume for two weeks to come from this day she having two Children to provide for. [*See* **459**].

528. Ordered That D^{o}. do Pay to Rebeckah Johnson Wid^{o}. two shillings for the Present and continue to pay her the same sume weekly for two weeks to come towards the maintenance and the maintenance of Ann Jones. [*See* **504**, **559**].

529. Ordered That D^{o}. do Pay to Dianah the wife of Thomas Jennison four shillings for the present and continue to pay her two shillings pr week for Six weeks to come from this day her said husband having left her and two Children in Want. [*See* **390**, **550**, **580**, **610**].

530. Ordered That D°. do pay to Ann Grosier 7s:6d. for nursing Thomas Usher a poor man at Kingsland very much bruised and in a very weak Condition for three weeks. [*See* **37**, **38**, **39**].

The Mermaid Tavern, Monday, 22 May 1732
Justices present: Henry Norris, Alexander Garrett, John Oakey

531. Mr. Edmund Matthews Sworne to Execute the Office of Headborough for the year ensueing.

532. Mr. James Martin Sworne to Execute the Office of Headborough for the year ensueing in the Room of Mr David Lawrence.

533. Mr. Wm. Griffith Sworne to Execute the Office of Headborough for the year ensueing in the room of Mr Henry Yeldall.

534. Mr George Fowler Sworne to Execute the Office of Headborough for the year ensueing in the room of Mr. Nehemiah Lyde a Lodger.

535. Ordered That a warrant be made out to apprehend Elizabeth Townsend she refusing to attend to give an account of the place of her last legal settlement she being likely to become chargeable to the parish. [*See* **496**, **545**, **547**].

536. Upon the affadts. of Benja. Carter & Joseph Rose Roger Beeston & Lettice his wife that Thomas Baxter of the Parish of St. John at Hackney in the County of Middx useth commonly the selling of Distilled Liquors by retaile to be drunk in his Shop [and did *deleted*] without being thereunto Lawfully Licensed he was convicted. Ordered That a warrant of Distress be made out against the next meeting to be then signed to Levy the sume of twenty shillings on his goods & Chattells for his said Offence for the use of the poor of the said Parish of St John at Hackney it being the first Conviction. [*See* **44**].

537. Ordered That Mr John Davis the Churchwarden do pay to Eliza. the wife of Thomas Bartmaker one shilling for one week past and continue to pay her the same sume weekly for Eight weeks to come [*deletion*] she having two Children to provide for. [*See* **430**, **432**, **525**, **557**].

538. Ordered That D°. do pay Martha Baxter Wid°. one shilling pr week from the 28th day of May last until further Orders towards the maintainance of Elinor Kingsland Wid°. incapable of working for her living. [*See* **412**].

539. Ordered That D°. do pay Mary Kirby eight shillings for nursing & maintaining Thomas Cawne for two weeks he being Lunatick.

540. Ordered That D°. do pay to Robert Piggott One Pound two shillings & Six Pence for the nursing & maintainance of a Poor Traveller for four weeks that fell in Labour at his Door at Newington.

The Mermaid Tavern, Monday, 5 June 1732
Justices present: Henry Norris, Samuel Tyssen

541. Ordered That Mr John Davis the Churchwarden do pay to Ann the wife of Edward Jarsey she being Sick & weak two shillings pr week for five weeks to come from this day. [*See* **450**].

542. Thomas Howson one of the Constables of Hackney gave an Informacon upon Oath against Ludlow Browne victualler at the sign of the Kings head at Kingsland in the parish of S^{t}. John at Hackney for exerciseing his Trade or Ordinary calling on Sunday the fourth of June Instant in the time of Divine Service and upon hearing what the s^{d} Ludlow Browne could alledge in his Defence Ordered that he be convicted of the s^{d}. Offence and that a Warrant be made out to Levy the sume of five shillings for the use of the Poor of the said Parish.

543. Signed a warrant to Commit Stephen Carr to new Prison for assaulting James Martin one of the Headboroughs of the parish of S^{t}. John at Hackney and Stabbing him in his right hand with a pitching fork in the Execution of his said Office and also for Assaulting and beating [him *deleted*] Ludlow Browne on the Oaths of the s^{d}. [Stephen Carr *deleted*] James Martin and Ludlow Browne to be detained there for want of Sureties until he shall be thence discharged by due course of Law. [*See* **46**, **552**].

544. Thomas Howson one of the Constables of Hackney gave an Informacon against Edward Fox, Stephen Patmore, & Edward Cooper of the Parish of S^{t}. John at Hackney vict^{rs} for Exerciseing their Worldly Trade & business on Sunday the 4th of this Instant June in the time of Divine Service. Ordered That they be Sumoned to attend at the next meeting to shew cause why [she *deleted*] they should not be Convicted of the above Offences & the Penalty Levy'd upon them. [*See* **551**].

545. Took the examinacon of Elizabeth Townsend Singlewoman upon Oath touching a Male Bastard child named William Born of the Body of Elizabeth Townsend in the parish of S^{t}. John Hackney [who *deleted*] now living and likely to become Chargeable to the s^{d}. Parish. Ordered That an adjudication be forthwith made out against W^{m}. Ward the putative father thereof. [*See* **496**, **535**, **547**].

The Mermaid Tavern, Monday, 19 June 1732
Justices present: Henry Norris, Samuel Tyssen

546. Edward Kingsclow made Oath that the Place of his last legal Settlement is in the parish of St John at Hackney and desired he might have a Certificate to the Parish of Walthamstow. Agreed that he be allowed a Certificate.

547. Upon the Examinacon of Elizabeth Townsend Spr touching her base Child Ordered That the further consideracon of making out an adjudication against the Putative father be referred 'till the next meeting. [*See* **496**, **535**, **545**].

548. Ordered That M^r^. John Davis the Churchwarden do Pay to Elizabeth Stamper Wid^o^. Eight shillings towards the burying her two Children. [*See* **424**, **439**, **460**].

549. Ordered That Mr John Davis Churchwarden do pay to Elizabeth George two shillings towards her present Subsistance she being big with Child & one Child to provide for.[1] [*See* **576**, **577**].

1. Elizabeth George was not settled in Hackney but in Buckinghamshire. P79/JN1/218.

550. Ordered That D^o^. do pay to Dianah Jennison 2^s^ for the Present & continue to pay her the same sume Weekly for eight weeks to come from this day she having two Children to provide for. [*See* **390**, **529**, **580**, **610**].

551. Persons sumoned for Exercising their Trades on the Sunday the fourth Instant in the time of Divine Service: Edward Fox paid, Stephen Pattmore did not attend [*Marginal entry*: Summoned], Edward Cooper paid, [all] Convicted upon the Oath of Mr Thomas Howson Constable. Ordered That a Warrant be made out to Levy the Penalty of 5^s^ upon Stephen Pattmore for the said Offence. [*See* **544**].

552. Mr James Martin one of the Headboroughs of the Parish of S^t^. John at Hackney acquainted the Gentlemen that he hath received a great deal of Damage by the wound which he rece^d^. from Stephen Carr and desired the favour of them to let the prosecution of the said Carr be at the Expence of the Parish he being at the time when he rec^d^. the s^d^. Wound keeping the peace in the house of Ludlow Browne. [*See* **46**, **543**].

553. Upon the Complaint of W^m^. Griffith one of the Headboroughs of the Parish of St John at Hackney that John Bright and Joseph Windsor refused to assist him to carry John Wheeler to new Prison whom he had in his custody by virtue of a Warrant from Henry Norris & Samuel Tyssen Esq^rs^. for that purpose. Ordered That the said John Bright and Joseph Windsor be Sumoned to attend at the next meeting to answer the said Complaint exhibited against them.[1] [*See* **48**, **560**].

1. Wheeler had been committed on a charge of wife-beating (**48**).

554. Ann Fisher made Oath that Robert Turner was buryed in Sheeps wool only.

The Mermaid Tavern, Monday, 24 July 1732
Justices present: Henry Norris, Alexander Garrett

555. The following vict^{r}s were sumoned to appear this day to answer a Complaint Exhibited against them by M^{r}. John Davis Churchwarden on the Eighth day of this Instant July for having severaly Exercised their trades or ordinary Callings in the parish of St John at Hackney in the County of Middx on Sunday the Second day of this Instant and to shew cause why they should not be convicted and the penalty Levy'd on each of them as the Law directs, vizt: John Baxter Chandler at Cambridge Heath grinding of Coffee Ordered that a warr^{t} be made out to Levy the penalty of 5s [*Marginal entry*: Philip Betty Jur], John Oswald Victualler at the Shoulder of Mutton in Mare Street [*Marginal entry*: 5s. paid], Ralph Lightwood vict at the Swan at Cambridge Heath convicted ordered that a Warr^{t} be made out to Levy 5^{s}. being penalty [*Marginal entries*: Philip Betty Jur *and* paid], *Charles Gosdin vict at the Green Dragon in Well Street [*Marginal entry*: 5s. paid], *James Matchin vict at the two black boys in Well Street confessed the fact [*Marginal entry*: 5s. paid], *Richard Brattle vict at the Red Cow at Dorleston confessed he had two boys drinking [*Marginal entry*: 5s. paid], *John Price vict at the Dolphin at Kingsland confessed the fact [*Marginal entry*: 5s. paid], *Robt. Piggott vict at the Coach & Horses at Newington confessed the fact [*Marginal entry*: 5s. paid], Thomas Ward vict at the Bird Cage on Stanford Hill convicted ordered that a warrant be made out to Levy 5s. penalty [*Marginal entries*: Philip Betty Jur *and* 5s paid *with paid deleted*]; Jacob Crew vict at the Naggs head at the Wick confessed the fact [*Marginal entry*: 5s. paid].

556. Ordered that M^{r}. John Davis the Churchwarden do pay to Samuel Sadleir his Bill for business done for the Parish amounting to the sume of Eight pounds Eighteen shillings from Aprill the 11th 1732 to this day.

557. Ordered That D^{o}. do pay to Elizabeth the wife of Thomas Bartmaker 1^{s}. pr week from this day until further Orders her said husband being Lame and she having two Children to provide for. [*See* **430**, **432**, **525**, **537**].

558. Signed an Order to remove Robert Worberton Sarah his wife and Ruth and Adam their two Children from the Parish of S^{t}. John at Hackney to the parish of Stoake Newington in the County of Middlesex.[1] [*See* **410**].

1. It is not clear whether this order was enforced. Worberton produced a certificate dated 1732 and was rated to the highways (**366** above as Walberton). P79/JN1/398.

559. Ordered That Mr John Davis the Churchwarden do pay to Rebecca Johnson Wid^{o}. Sixpence pr week from this day until further Orders she being very Infirm. [*See* **504**, **528**].

560. Richard Willshire, John Bright, and Joseph Windsor attended pursuant to their Sumons for refuseing to assist W^{m}. Griffith one of the Headboroughs of the Parish of S^{t}. John at Hackney in carrying one John Wheeler whom he had in his Custody [*deletion*] to New Prison by virtue of a Warrant from Henry Norris and Samuel Tyssen Esq^{rs}. They having satified [*sic*] the s^{d}. Headborough and beged [*sic*] pardon for the s^{d}. Offence They were discharged. [*See* **48**, **553**].

561. Henry Harrill made Oath that he Sumoned Joseph Lucas to attend this day to answer the Complaint of the Churchwardens & Overseers of the Poor of this Parish for intruding himselfe and his family into this Parish and are likely to bring a burthen and charge upon the parish and also to give an account of the Place of his last legal Settlement. Ordered That a warrant be made out against him and that he be brought before the s^{d} Justices at their next meeting to answer the said Complaint.

562. Ordered That Mr John Davis the Churchwarden do Pay to Mary Wingood twelve shillings for nursing maintaining and Lodging two Poor Travellers that were taken dangerously Ill.

The Mermaid Tavern, Monday, 7 August 1732
Justices present: Samuel Tyssen, Alexander Garrett

563. The following Persons were Sumoned to attend this day to give an account of the places of their last legal Settlements, viz: *John Fulsher Exam^{d} & allowed two weeks; *Henry Gregory Exam^{d} & allowed two weeks; Thomas Howell not to be found; [Robert Rice *deleted*]; Usley Care not to be found; *Thomas Fletcher Brought a Certificate; Joseph Cooper warrant to be made out against him; *Benjamin Burrough Settlement here, rents £18 pr ann to be rated in the next book.[1] [*See* **362**, **496**].

1. Fulsher (of Homerton) and Gregory (of Clapton) were both rated to the highways. Gregory had left Hackney by 1733. H.A.D., P/J/H/14.

564. Allowed and Confirmed a Rate for the relief of the Casual Poor of the Parish of S^{t}. John at Hackney for the year 1732 amounting to the sume of two hundred twenty Six Pounds twelve shillings and ten pence halfe Penny.

565. John Baxter attended to answer a Complaint exhibited against him by Philip Betty Gentleman High Constable of the Tower Division for exerciseing his Trade or ordinary Calling in the Parish of St John at Hackney on Sunday the 2d of July last. It appearing to the Justices that he was only grinding of some Coffee for the use of his family agreed that he be discharged from the said Complaint.

566. Dorothy Bayley wife of Samuel Bayley applyed to obtain the discharge of her said Husband out of new Prison committed for begetting Mary White Singlewoman with Child of a female Bastard Child chargeable to this Parish and it appearing upon the Oath of Saml Longbottom one of the Keepers of the said Prison that the said Samuel Bayley hath been Ill of a Fever for a considerable time past and is now in such a Condition that his life is in Danger. Agreed that he be discharged [that *deletion*] there being no likelyhood of getting the charges the Parish hath been at.

567. Ordered That M^{r}. John Davis the Churchwarden do pay to Jane Jackson ten shillings towards her subsistance and putting her into a way to get her living she having been Sick for a considerable time past and being now in a very weak Condition.

568. Ordered That Amy Butling afflicted with the Rhumatysm be put into St Thomas's Hospital for Cure. [*See* **569**, **588**].

569. Ordered That Mr John Davis the Churchwarden do pay to the said Amy Butling two shillings & Six pence towards her Subsistance. [*See* **568**, **588**].

570. Ordered That D^{o}. do pay to John Raby 1^{s} for the Present and continue to Pay him the same Sume weekly for four weeks to come from this day he being Lame & poor. [*See* **571**, **681**].

571. Ordered that D^{o}. do pay to David White nine shillings and three pence for nursing & Lodging of John Raby a poor man for Seven Weeks to this day. [*See* **570**, **681**].

572. Richard Morris brought by George Fowler one of the Headboroughs of the Parish of S^{t}. John Hackney for assaulting Edwd. Richardson [by *deleted*]. Discharged both Parties being agreed.

573. David Wight made oath of his Settlement & allowed two weeks to bring a Certificate.

The Mermaid Tavern, Monday, 21 August 1732
Justices present: Henry Norris, Samuel Tyssen

574. Ordered That W^{m}. Silvester and Sarah Silvester two Poor Children of this Parish [do *deleted*] be put out apprentice and that by the next meeting the Beadle do endeavour to Procure a Master for each of them. [*See* **578**, **587**, **590**, **596**, **601**].

575. Ordered That M^{r}. George Harrison & M^{r}. David Taylor the late Overseers of the Poor of this Parish do forthwith make up their accounts in Writing and lay them before us at the next meeting. [*See* **586**].

576. Ordered That M^{r}. John Davis the Churchwarden do pay to Mary Kirby thirty shillings for nursing and maintaining Elizabeth George for four weeks in her laying Inn and Eight shillings for nursing & maintaining her daughter Sarah for four weeks to this day. [*See* **549**, **577**].

577. Ordered That D°. do pay to Elizabeth George two shillings pr week for four weeks to come from this day she having two Children to provide for. [*See* **549**, **576**].

578. Ordered That William Silvester do forthwith go out upon likeing to Thomas Price a Weaver living in new Court in Agel [*sic*] Alley in Bishopsgate Street. [*See* **574**, **587**, **590**].

579. Ordered That for the future the full & whole charge of binding out Parish Children shall from time to time be paid by the Churchwarden.

580. Ordered That M[r]. John Davis the Churchwarden do pay to Dianah Jennison two shillings for one week past and continue to pay her the same sume weekly for Eight weeks to come from this day her husband having ran away and left her two young Children to provide for. [*See* **390**, **529**, **550**, **610**].

581. Ordered That D°. do pay to Tomassin the wife of John Wheeler two shillings for the present and continue to pay her the same sume weekly for four weeks to come her said husband having ran away and left her two Children to provide for. [*See* **582**].

582. Granted a warrant to apprehend John Wheeler for assaulting beating & bruising [her *deleted*] Tomassin his wife and also to answer the Complaint of the Churchwardens & Overseers of the Poor of this Parish for running away from his said wife and Family without making any provision for her whereby they are become burthensome and chargeable to the said Parish on the Oath of the s[d]. Tomassin Wheeler.[1] [*See* **9**, **48**, **89**, **119**, **129**, **553**, **560**, **581**, **680**].

1. Wheeler entered into recognizances on both charges before Justice Anthony Chamberlain on 19 October 1732. He was discharged at the December sessions. MJ/SR/2584, recogs. 127, 128.

583. Ordered That M[r]. John Harcourt and M[r]. Markham Spearing the present Survey[rs]. of the Highwayes of this Parish have notice to attend the next [General *deleted*] meeting to shew cause why they have not caused the several Occupiers of Land to Scower the Ditches.

584. Ordered That Francis Rosamond, George Stretton & Richard Alderman be Summoned to attend at the next meeting to answer Thomas Pampling for assaulting him.

The Mermaid Tavern, Monday, 18 September 1732
Justices present: Henry Norris, Samuel Tyssen, Alexander Garrett

585. M[r]. James Grier late Churchwarden applyed to have the ballance of his accounts paid him. Ordered That it be under consideration at the next meeting in what manner he shall be reimbursed.

586. Pursuant to the Order of the last Meeting M^r^. George Harrison & Mr David Taylor the late Overseers of the Poor of this Parish laid their accounts before the above named Justices by which it appears that they received four hundred thirty nine pounds eight [*deletion*] shillings & one halfe penny and that they have paid four hundred twenty four pounds and nineteen shillings & that there remains due from them to ballance the said accounts fourteen pounds nine shillings and a halfe penny. The above accounts were Confirmed and allowed by the above named Justices. Ordered that the said late Overseers do forthwith pay the s^d^ Ballance to M^r^. John Davis the present Churchwarden and Overseer of the Poor. [*See* **575**].

587. Ordered That W^m^. Silvester a Poor Child of this Parish aged 15 Years & a halfe be bound to Thomas Price a weaver living in the Parish of Bishopsgate London and that M^r^. John Davis the Churchwarden do pay the usual allowance of Forty shillings with him. [*See* **574**, **578**, **590**].

588. Ordered That Mr John Davis the Churchwarden do pay to Amy Buttling one shilling for the present & continue to pay her the same sume weekly for four weeks to come from this day. [*See* **568**, **569**].

589. Ordered That M^r^. John Davis the present Churchwarden & Overseer of the Poor of the parish of S^t^. John at Hackney in the County of Middlesex do forthwith pay to M^r^. James Grier Churchwarden & Overseer of the Poor of the s^d^. parish in the year 1730 the sume of twenty two pounds ten shillings and a halfe penny being the Ballance due to him from the Parish in the discharge of his said Office.

The Mermaid Tavern, Monday, 6 November 1732
Justices present: Henry Norris, Samuel Tyssen, Alexander Garrett

590. Allowed an Indenture of apprenticeshipp whereby William Silvester aged fifteen years a poor Child of this parish was bound to Thomas Price of the parish of St Botolph without Bishopsgate London Weaver. [*See* **574**, **578**, **587**].

591. Ordered That M^r^. John Davis the Churchwarden do pay to Richard Tyler two pounds twelve shillings for nursing and maintaining Ann Hyde a changling[1] for twenty Six Weeks from Lady day last to Michaelmass day then next following. [*See* **593**].

1. Changeling: half wit, imbecile, idiot, *O.E.D.*

592. Ann Fisher made Oath that Martha Potts & W^m^. [Stretton] lately deceased were buryed in Sheeps Wool only.

593. Ordered That M^r^. John Davis the Churchwarden do pay to Rich^d^. Tyler twelve shillings for nursing Ann Hyde for Six Weeks from Michaelmass last to the tenth of this Instant November. [*See* **591**].

594. Ordered That D^{o}. do pay to William George ten shillings towards Putting him in a way of Business for to maintain him his wife & two Children.

595. Ordered That D^{o}. do pay to Samuel Sadleir his Bill for Business done for the Parish amounting to Six Pounds thirteen shillings & two pence from August the fourth last to this day.

596. Ordered That Sarah Silvester aged 14 years a poor Child belonging to this parish be bound apprentice to W^{m}. Bradley of the parish of St George in Bloomsbury in the County of Middlesex Labourer and that Mr John Davis the Churchwarden do pay him the usual allowance of Forty shillings. [*See* **574**, **601**].

597. Adjourned to Saturday sennight nine in the morning to this place to hear the defaulters that have neglected to perform their Statute worke on the Highwayes.

The Mermaid Tavern, Saturday, 18 November 1732
Justices present: Samuel Tyssen, Alexander Garrett, Anthony Chamberlaine

598. The several Defaulters resideing within Church Street, Mare Street Well Street Grove Street & Homerton within the parish of St John at Hackney who have not performed their Statute worke on the Highwayes belonging to the s^{d} Parish for this present year 1732 were sumoned to attend this day [summoned to attend *deleted*] to shew cause why they have refused or neglected to pay the penalty they have each of them incurred for their default whose names are particularly menconed in a Summons under the hands and Seals of Henry Norris and Samuel Tyssen Esq^{rs} two of his Majesties Justices of the Peace for the County of Middx resideing within the s^{d} parish bearing date the 14th day of November Instant. Ordered That a Warrant of Distress be made out to Levy the several Penaltys on those Persons who did attend but could not make any reasonable Excuse for not having Paid the s^{d}. Penalties and also on those who did not attend pursuant to the s^{d}. Summons Henry Harrill one of the Headboroughs of the s^{d}. Parish having made Oath that they were duly Sumoned as is particularly menconed in the Summons above menconed.

The Mermaid Tavern, Monday, 11 December 1732
Justices present: Henry Norris, Samuel Tyssen

599. Ordered That M^{r}. John Davis the Churchwarden do pay to M^{r}. Thomas Cotton apothecary his Bill for physick for a Poor Person taking ill wth. the Spotted Fever[1] amounting to One pound three shillings.

1. Probably typhus, but the term was also used of epidemic cerebro-spinal meningitis and petechial fever, *O.E.D.*

600. Allowed an Indenture of apprenticeship whereby William Pegram aged thirteen years a poor Child of the Parish of St John at Hackney was bound apprentice to Thomas Wood of the said Parish Farmer.

601. Allowed an Indenture of Apprenticeship whereby Sarah Silvester aged fourteen years a poor Child of the Parish of St John at Hackney was bound apprentice to William Bradley of the Parish of St George near Hanover Square in the County of Middx: Labourer. [*See* **574**, **596**].

602. Signed a Warrant to apprehend Soloman Price for leaving his family a charge to the Parish on the Oath of M^r^. John Davis Churchwarden.

603. Ordered That Mr John Davis the Churchwarden be allowed 2^s^ which he paid by our Order to Katherine Browne in Want on the 21st of November last.

The Mermaid Tavern, Monday, 8 January 1733
Justices present: Henry Norris, Alexander Garrett

604. Complaint being made that the several Headboroughs of the Parish of S^t^. John at Hackney have been very negligent in the discharge of their Duties at the several Watch-houses on the foot way within the said parish Ordered that they be summoned to attend at the next meeting to answer the said Complaint.

605. M^r^. Hezekiah Walker and M^r^. John Townsend the present Overseers of the Poor of the Parish of S^t^. John at Hackney attended [*altered from* attending] pursuant to their Summons and laid before the said Justices their book of assessment for the relief of the Settled poor of the said parish for this present year by which it appears that they have collected £269:4^s^:9^d^ and that they have paid £200 and upwards. Ordered That they do as soon as Possible compleat their said Collection.

606. Mary South Spr serv^t^ to Edward Batty Vict^r^ at the White Hart in Clopton in the Parish of S^t^. John at Hackney brought by Henry Harrill one of the Headboroughs of the said Parish and charged upon the Oath of her said Master on violent Suspicion of having feloniously taken out of a Chest of Drawers which Stood in the Bed Chamber of the said Edwd. Batty 33 Guineas in Gold and about five pounds in Silver the Property of the s^d^. Edwd. Batty and Ester the wife of W^m^. Hewson bro^t^ by the same Officer for being accessary to the s^d^. felony in receiving the said money knowing the same to be Stolen. The said Mary South confessed the same & was Committed to Newgate and the s^d^. Ester Hewson was committed to new prison and the following persons were bound to prosecute the said Mary South [and in the same sums] to prosecute Ester Hewson: Edward Batty of Hackney Vict^r^ in £80, Thomas Hodgson of the same Gent £40, Samuel Woolmer of the same Gardner £40. [*See* **60**, **63**.]

607. Signed a warrant to Levy the Penalty on those defaulters who have neglected to perform their Statute worke on the Highways within the Parish of S^t^. John at Hackney on the Oaths of Mr John Harcourt & Mr Markham Spearing the present Survey^rs^.

The Mermaid Tavern, Monday, 22 January 1733
Justices present: Henry Norris, Samuel Tyssen

608. Signed the following Order upon Mr Thomas Wood – Middx:ss To M^r^. Thomas Wood Churchwarden and Overseer of the Poor of the Parish of S^t^. John at Hackney in the County of Middlesex for the year 1731. These are in his Majesties name to require you forthwith upon Sight hereof to pay to M^r^. John Davis the present Churchwarden and Overseers of the Poor of the said Parish of S^t^. John at Hackney the sume of Eleven Pounds Eighteen shillings and nine pence which you have Collected and received of the Inhabitants of the said Parish and is remaining in your hands beyond your disbursements in the discharge of your said Office of Churchwarden and Overseer of the Poor of the Parish aforesaid and in Case you do not comply with this our Order We will proceed against you according to Law Given under our hands & Seals the 22^d^ day of January Anno Dmo 1733. [*signed*] Henry Norris, Samuell Tyssen.

609. Ordered That Mr John Davis the Churchwarden do pay to George Sherrard Eight shillings for nursing and maintaining Elizabeth Thornton for four weeks very sick & Weak.

610. Ordered That D^o^. do pay to Dianah Jennison two shillings she and her Children having been Sick for a considerable time. [*See* **390**, **529**, **550**, **580**].

611. George Fowler Headborough for [Well Street and *deleted*] Grove Street complained that there are so few persons residing within his ward that he cannot possibly perform his Duty at the Watch and therefore prayed to be allowed some men from the rest of the Headbor^s^. Ordered That he be allowed two Watchmen from each Headborough.

The Mermaid Tavern, Monday, 5 February 1733
Justices present: Henry Norris, Samuel Tyssen, Alexander Garrett

612. Margaret Lee wid^o^. of William Lee made oath that her late husband was last legally settled in the Parish of S^t^. John at Hackney in the County of Middlesex and that she hath not since gained any legal Settlement elswhere.

613. Ordered That Mr John Davis the Churchwarden do pay to Mary

Anderson Wid°. five shillings towards her present Subsistance she having been sick and weak. [*See* **403**].

614. Allowed an Indenture whereby Elizabeth Johnson aged fourteen Years a poor Child of the Parish of St John at Hackney was bound apprentice to Elizabeth Emerton of the Parish of St Mary Islington in the County of Middlesex milliner.

615. Signed a Warrant to remove Lionel Theed to the House of Correction to hard Labour for leaving his wife and Child without making provision for them whereby they have been and continue to be burthensome and chargeable to the said parish on the Oath of Mr John Davis Churchwarden. [*See* **620**].

616. John Morris at the Kings Arms at Kingsland applyed for a License in the room of W^m^. Boardman gone away from thence. Agreed That he have a License at the next General Meeting for that Purpose.

617. Allowed a Bill of Henry Harrill Beadle for conveying W^m^. Tallis from Hackney to Walton in the Parish of Kimcoate in Leicestershire amounting to two Pounds Eighteen shillings and three Pence.

618. Adjourned to this day fortnight 9 in the morning.

The Mermaid Tavern, Monday, 19 February 1733
Justices present: Henry Norris, Alexander Garrett, Samuel Tyssen

619. William Austin brought by Henry Harrill one of the Headboroughs of the Parish of St John at Hackney by vertue of a Warrant granted by Henry Norris Esqr for assaulting and Strikeing Eliz^a^. North. Discharged both parties being agreed. [*See* **64**].

620. Robert Lloyd Headborough of Hackney Gardener Bound in £20 To appear at the next General Quarter Sessions of the Peace for the County of Middlesex to be held at Hicks hall in St John Street to answer the Complaint of Henry Norris Samuel Tyssen and Alex^a^. Garrett Esq^rs^ three of his Majesties Justices of the Peace for the s^d^. County for willfully sufferring one Lyonel Theed to Escape out of his Custody whom he was to have conveyed to the House of Correction by virtue of a Warrant under the hands & Seals of the s^d^ Justices and not Depart the Court without License. Coram Henry Norris Alex^a^. Garrett [and] Samuel Tyssen arm. [*marginal note*: returned – Aprill the 3d 1733].[1] [*See* **615**].

1. Theed had been comitted as a vagrant. Lloyd was indicted at the April sessions; he pleaded guilty and was fined 1s. on 8 May. MJ/SR/2592, recog. 85.

621. Ordered That a Warrant of Distress be made out against the Several Persons whose names are hereunder Written to Levey the poors Rate upon them they have refused or neglected to pay the same at the Complaint of Mr John Davis Churchward^n^ & Overseer.

Church Street: Thomas Masling Sen[r] 6s.; Matthias Woodyard 10s.; John Singleton 4s.; W[m] Gibbons 2s.; James Thompson 4s.
Mare Street: John Whittle 10s.; W[m]. Shepherd 2s.; Eliz[a]. Severn 7s. 6d.; James Bayes 3s.; Thomas Shepperson 2s.; Giles Lomas 2s. 6d.; Robert Bell 2s.
Homerton: Samuel Barnard £1; Wm Crotchrode 5s.; John Osman 2s.; W[m]. Platt 4s.; Jeremiah Kemp 4s.; Henry Vaughan 4s.; Joseph Skearing 7s.; Elizabeth North 1s. 6d.; Frances Green 5s. 6d.; Henry Godwin £1 1s. 6d.; Ann Bartrum 2s.; James Simms 2s. 6d.
Clopton: W[m]. Jones 3s.; Thomas Sowden 1s. 3d.; Edmund Matthews 6s.; Samuel Holdsworth 4s.; Rich[d]. Hedge 2s.; Thomas Archer 2s.; W[m]. Gateley 3s.
Newington: Thomas Barnard 2s. 6d.; Eliz[a]. Thompson 7s. 6d.
Shacklewell: John Rice 5s.; Lambert Lance 10s.; James Mortimer 15s.
Dorleston: Thomas Hilliard 4s.; Henry Walker 4s.

The Mermaid Tavern, Monday, 5 March 1733
Justices present: Henry Norris, Alexander Garrett

622. Signed a Warrant of Distress against the several Defaulters who have not paid the poors Rate upon the Oath of M[r] John Davis Churchwarden & Overseer of the poor of the parish of S[t] John at Hackney pursuant to an Order of the last Petty Sessions.

623. Took the Examinacon of Sarah Crew Singlewoman touching her legal Settlem[t] which appeared to be in the Parish of S[t] James Clerkenwell in the County of Middlesex and signed an Order to send her thither. [*See* **641**].

The Mermaid Tavern, Saturday, 10 March 1733
Justices present: Henry Norris, Samuel Tyssen, Alexander Garrett

624. Ordered That M[r]. John Harcourt and M[r] James Huggett Jun[r] the present Survey[rs] of the Highwayes of the Parish of S[t]. John at Hackney have notice to attend at a meeting hereby appointed to be held on Monday the 19th of this Instant March to receive directions for the better repairing and amending the Highwayes belonging to the said parish.

625. Hen: Norris Esq[r] Signed a Warrant to search the House of David Wight in Homerton for 14 Rabbitts Stole out of an Out house adjoyning to the dwelling house of M[r] John Archer and his property on the Oath of the said Archer.

626. Allowed a Certificate owning Francis Woodfield a Lunatick to be an Inhabitant of the Parish of S[t]. John at Hackney in the County of Middlesex.

627. Ordered That a Warrant of Distress be made out against the several persons whose names are hereunder written who have refused or

neglected to pay the poors rate of the said parish of S[t] John at Hackney upon the Oath of John Townesend one of the Overseers of the poor of the said parish.
Church Street: Elizabeth Morris 7s.; Richard Huggins 5s.; Daniel Card 6s.; John Baker 8s.; Christopher Mason 5s.; William Underhill 8s.; Thomas Masling Sen[r] 12s.; Wid[o]. Newcome 4s.; John Singleton 4s.; Eliz[a]. Bruce 8s.; Eliz[a]. Fletcher 4s.; Samuel Bennett 12s.
Mare Street: John Whittle £1; Jacob Crew 8s.; William Shepherd 4s.; Walter Graham 8s.; Richard Stoakes 8s.; Susannah Stallard 10s.; Giles Lomas 5s.; Samuel Summer 5s.; William Brownson 5s.; Robert Bell 4s.
Homerton: Ruth Dennett 4s.; Rob[t] Dumbleton 6s.; James Arnold 6s.; Wm Crotchrode 10s.; John Barker 6s.; Luke Townesend 4s.; John Osman 4s.; John Webb 6s.; W[m]. Pratt £3 15s.; Hez. Walker for Temple Mills £1; Henry Vaughan 8s.; Samuel Stockell 10s.; Joseph Skearing 14s.; Jacob Crew 6s.; W[m]. Eames 10s.; John Archer 8s.; Francis Walker 3s.; Eliz[a]. North 3s.; Thomas Monk 14s.; W[m]. Henderson 10s.; Frances Green 11s.; Eliz[a]. Loroder £1; Henry Godwin £2 3s.; Newman Bourne 6s.; James Simms 5s.; W[m]. Hewitt 4s.; David Taylor 13s.; James Betts 4s.; John [Manshipp] 15s.
Clopton: David Martin £2; John Iles 6s.; John Pettett £1 5s.; John Hanson 15s.; Thomas Archer 4s.; W[m]. Gateley 6s.; Jeremiah Woodley £3 5s.
Grove Street: John Rooke 6s.
Well Street: Thomas Wood £3 5s. 6d.
Newington: Henry Donmer 19s. 6d.; Thomas Barnard 5s.
Shacklewell: Elias Woodfield £1 16s.; Cap[t] Fitzgerald 4s.; James Mortimer £1 10s.
Kingsland: Thomas Bartmaker £1 2s. 6d.; Alexander Spurling 4s.
Dorleston: Thomas Hilliard 8s.
Land Holders: Charles Crane 4s. 6d.; Bootes for Land late Sellmans 8s.

628. Adjorned to Monday next to this place by ten in the forenoon.

The Mermaid Tavern, Monday, 19 March 1733
Justices present: Henry Norris, Samuel Tyssen, Alexander Garrett

629. Henry Norris Esq[r] Signed a warrant to apprehend Sarah Browne Wid[o]. upon the oath of George Freeman her late Serv[t] in Husbandry she refuseing to pay him 7[s] 6[d] for five dayes Labour.

630. Middx:ss Edward Bush and Thomas Cooke of the Parish of S[t] John at Hackney in the County of Middlesex Labourers make oath that yesterday the 18th day of this Instant March they these Deponents together with one John Wheeler Drank five Quarterns of Distilled Liquors called Geneva in the House of David Wight in Homerton in the s[d] parish of S[t] John at Hackney for which [paid *deleted*] they paid Seven Pence halfe penny and they these Deponents further say upon their Oaths that the said David Wight for some time past hath used commonly the selling of Distilled Liquors by retaile to be Drank in his said dwelling house. Edw[d] Bush [*mark*] Tho Cooke [*mark*]. Jurat 19[o] die Martij 1733 coram nobis [*signed*] Henry Norris Samuell Tyssen Alex[a] Garratt.

631. Ordered That Henry Crockford Johnson aged 13 years a poor Child of this Parish be bound apprentice to Thomas Gressingham of the Inner Temple Gent and that M[r] John Davis the Churchwarden do pay him 40[s] with him. NB N[o]. 3 next Aleination Office Kings Bench Walks. [*See* **643**].

The Mermaid Tavern, Saturday, 7 April 1733
Justices present: Henry Norris, Samuel Tyssen

632. The List returned by the Vestry for the Justices to appoint Overseers of the poor of the Parish of Saint John at Hackney in the County of Middlesex for the year ensuing is as follows: 16 years **M[r]. Joseph Sureties; 11 years +M[r]. John Whittle; 16 years +M[r]. John Cox; 17 years +M[r]. John Oswald; 10 years **M[r]. Hezekiah Walker; 11 years +M[r]. Robert Aldwinckle; 20 years +M[r]. Edward Nutt; 7 years +M[r]. John Howard; 7 years +M[r]. William Yelloley; +Mr Gabriel Lopas Dies Piniera; +Mr William Brooks; 11 years +John Jacob Esq[r.]

633. Signed Warrants to appoint M[r] John Davis Churchwarden and M[r] Joseph Suretes and M[r] Hezekiah Walker Overseers of the Poor of the Parish of Saint John at Hackney in the County of Middlesex for the year one thousand seven hundred and thirty three.

634. Middlesex To wit Simon Ireton of the Parish of S[t] John at Hackney in the County of Middlesex Smith and John Woodenton of the same Parish Carpenter make Oath that one Alexander Douglas living at a certain place called the Wick in the parish aforesaid hath for some time past used the selling of ale and Beer [*deletion*] by Retale to be drank in his house in the said parish and particularly on the twenty seventh day of March last he sold to these Deponents two pints of Strong Beer called two penny which [he *deleted*] they drank in his said dwelling house and for which they paid him four pence and they these Deponents further say not. [*signed*] Simon Ireton [and] John Woodington. Sworne before us the Seventh day of Aprill in the year of our Lord one thousand seven hundred and thirty three [*signed*] Henry Norris, Samuell Tyssen. Ordered That a warrant be made out to Levy the sume of twenty shillings upon the said Simon Ireton which he hath forfieted to the use of the poor of the parish of S[t] John at Hackney were [*sic*] the said Offence was committed.

635. Signed the following order upon M[r] John Townesend – Middlesex To wit To M[r]. John Townesend one of the Overseers of the Poor of the Parish of Saint John at Hackney in the County of Middlesex – We whose hands and Seals are hereunto Sett two of his Majesties Justices of the Peace for the County of Middlesex resideing within the Parish of Saint

John at Hackney in the County aforesaid one whereof is of the Quorum having this day appointed Overseers of the Poor of the said parish for the year one thousand seven hundred and thirty three You the said John Townesend one of the Overseers of the poor of the said parish for the year last past are hereby required not to lay out or pay away any more of the money you have Collected and received of the Inhabitants of the said parish in the discharge of that office and also forthwith to make up an account in writing of all moneys by you collected received and paid in the discharge of [that *deleted*] your said Office and being so stated you are to lay the same before us at a Meeting hereby appointed to be held at the Mermaid Tavern in Church Street in the Parish aforesaid on Monday the twenty third day of this Instant Aprill by ten of the clock in the forenoon and in case you faile herein we will proceed against you as the Law directs Given under our hands and Seals the seventh day of Aprill in the year of our Lord one thousand seven hundred and thirty three. Henry Norris, Samuell Tyssen. [*See* **655**, **659**, **665**].

636. Adjourned to Monday the twenty third day of Aprill one thousand seven hundred and thirty three.

The Mermaid Tavern, Monday, 23 April 1733
Justices present: Henry Norris, Samuel Tyssen, Alexander Garrett

637. John Davis of the Parish of Saint John at Hackney undertaker made Oath that Elias Beake lately Deceased was buryed in Sheeps Wool only.

638. Ordered That Susannah Holbrook aged ten years a poor Child of this Parish do go out upon liking to Joseph French of the parish of St Mary Overes in the County of Surry pin maker. [*See* **650**, **654**].

639. Ordered That the Clerk do make out a warrant to convey Elizabeth North to the County Goal on the oath of Mr. John Davis Churchwarden she refuseing to let the parish Officers come into her house to make a Distress for the poors Rate and that the Beadle do give her notice to attend at the next to shew cause why the said warrant should not be signed and Executed against her. [*See* **651**].

640. Ordered That the Clerk do wait upon John Gould and Stephen Ram Esqrs and acquaint them that Complaint hath been made that their Servants do frequently throw weeds and dirt into the Road which hath frequently obstructed the Current of the Waters and been very detrimental to the same and to desire that they will give such directions as may prevent it for the future.

641. Granted a warrant to apprehend Robert Crew and Elizabeth his wife for harbouring and unlawfully entertaining Sarah Crew their daughter now big with Child of a Base Child who hath returned into this parish from the parish of Saint James Clerkenwell whereunto she was legally removed as the place of [his *deleted*] her last Legal Settlement whereby a Burthen and charge is like to be brought upon this parish on the oath of Henry Harrill. [*See* **623**].

642. Ordered That M^{r}. John Davis the Churchwarden do pay Samuel Sadleir his Bill for Business done for the parish from the tenth day of November one thousand seven hundred and thirty two to the twenty third day of Aprill following amounting to the sume of Eleven pounds and Six shillings.

The Mermaid Tavern, Monday, 7 May 1733
Justices present: Henry Norris, Samuel Tyssen

643. Allowed an Indenture of apprenticeship whereby Henry Crockford Johnson aged thirteen years a poor Child of this parish was bound to Thomas Gressingham of the Inner Temple Gentleman. [*See* **631**].

644. Ordered That Mr. John Davis the Churchwarden do pay to John Cawne two shillings & Six pence towards bearing his Expenses into Lincolnshire he being Sick & Weak.

645. John Cawne sworne to Execute the Office of Headborough for Clopton ward & parish of Saint John at Hackney in the room of Benjamin Evans.

646. Robert Barnes Sworne to Execute the Office of Headborough for Church Street ward and parish of Saint John at Hackney.

647. James Martin Sworne to Execute the Office of Headborough for Newington ward and Parish of Saint John at Hackney in the room of Barnard Byfield.

648. Ann Fisher made Oath that Bennet Hougham and Henry Mont [Mary Ross & William Gray *deleted*] lately deceased was buryed in Sheeps Wool only.

649. Elizabeth Blevin made Oath that Mary Ross and William Gray lately Deceased was buryed in Sheep's Wool only.

650. Ordered That Susannah Holbrook aged ten years a poor Child of this parish be forthwith bound apprentice to Joseph French of the parish of Saint Mary Overes in the County of Surry pin maker and that M^{r}. John Davis the Churchwarden do pay forty shillings with her and Six shillings towards provideing some Clothes for her she being almost naked and having had the meazles since she hath been upon likeing with him. [*See* **638**, **654**].

651. Henry Harrill made Oath that he Summoned Elizabeth North to appear before the Justices this morning at this place and told her it was to shew cause why she should not be committed to the County Goal for refuseing to let the Churchwardens and Overseers of the Poor come into her house to make Distress for the Poors Rate and she not appearing pursuant to such notice a warrant was accordingly signed to convey her to Negate [*sic*] and to require him to keep her safely until she pays four shillings and Sixpence which she is rated towards the rielief of the poor of the parish of Saint John at Hackney for the year one thousand seven hundred and thirty two. [*See* **639**].

The Mermaid Tavern, Monday, 4 June 1733
Justices present: Henry Norris, Alexander Garrett

652. Agreed That M^r^. Samuel Bishop be Chosen Headborough for Dorleston and Kingsland [*deletion*] Ward in the parish of S^t^. John at Hackney in the County of Middlesex in the room of Alexander Spurling who was Elected to and served that Office for the said [*deletion*] Ward in the year 1721 and W^m^. Griffith was Sworne to Execute that Office in his room and Stead.

653. Elizabeth Blevin made Oath that Ann Rosewell and Thomas Herrington lately Deceased was buryed in Sheeps Wool only.

654. Allowed an Indenture of apprenticeship whereby Susannah Holbrook aged ten years was bound to Joseph French of the parish of S^t^. Mary Overes of the County of Surry Pin maker. [*See* **638**, **650**].

655. M^r^. John Townesend one of the late Overseers of the Poor of the Parish of St John at Hackney in the County of Middlesex not having laid his accounts in discharge of his said office in writing before us pursuant to several Orders for that purpose Ordered that a warrant be prepared by the Clerk to convey him to his Majesties Goal of Newgate as the Law directs for his contempt and neglect. [*See* **635**, **659**, **665**].

The Mermaid Tavern, Monday, 18 June 1733
Justices present: Henry Norris, Samuel Tyssen, Stephen Ram

656. Ann Fisher made Oath before Stephen Ram Esqr that Richard Batty, Ann Frances and Barbara Rudge late of the parish of Hackney Deceased were buryed in Sheeps Wool only.

657. Elizabeth Blevin made Oath before Samuel Tyssen Esqr that James Wooten and George Small late of the parish of Hackney Deceased were buryed in Sheeps Wool only.

658. Henry Norris Esqr Signed a warrant to apprehend Margaret Hater on the Oath of Thomas Bartrum for assaulting and beating him and breaking his Windows.

659. The above named Justices this day auditted and Examined the accounts of Mr John Townesend one of the late Overseers of the Poor of the Parish of Saint John at Hackney in the County of Middlesex for the year 1732 by which accounts it appears that there is remaining in the said Mr Townesends hands to ballance the said accounts the Sume of thirty three pounds one shilling and one penny which they ordered that he should forthwith pay [the said ballance *deleted*] over to Mr Hezekiah Walker and Mr Joseph Sureties the present Overseers of the poor of the said Parish. [*See* **635**, **655**, **665**].

660. David Bentley applyed to be Licensed in the room of Ludlow Browne at the Kings head at Kingsland, agreed that [*deletion*] it be considered at the General Meeting for Licensing.

The Mermaid Tavern: Monday, 16 July 1733 [The clerk has incorrectly dated this entry Monday 17 July]
Justices present: Henry Norris, Alexander Garrett, Stephen Ram

The Mermaid Tavern, Monday, 3 September 1733
Justices present: Henry Norris, Samuel Tyssen, Alexander Garrett, Stephen Ram

661. Thomas Hilliard of Dorleston Weaver applyed for a License to keep an Ale house at Dorleston But there not being any vacancey agreed that he be not Licensed.[1] [*See* **743**].

1. Hilliard appealed to the Sessions, alleging that his failing eyesight prevented him from earning a living in any other way. He was unsuccessful. MJ/SP/1733/OCT, 78.

662. Ann Fisher made Oath that James Howard and Abraham Hewitt were buryed in Sheeps Wool only.

663. Ordered That Mr John Davis the Churchwarden do pay to Mary Kirby Widow One pound fifteen shillings for nursing and maintaining and necesary Expences for Ann the wife of Thomas Strainer for four weeks the time of her laying Inn she being afflicted with the foul Desease in a Violent manner.

664. Ordered That Mr John Davis the present Churchwarden and Overseer of the Poor of the Parish of Saint John at Hackney do prepare an account in writing of all moneys by him received and paid in the discharge of that Office for the year 1732 and lay the same before Henry Norris, Samuel Tyssen, Stephen Ram, and Alexander Garratt Esq^rs his Majesties Justices of the Peace for the County of Middlesex at a meeting hereby appointed to be held at the Mermaid Tavern on Monday the tenth day of September 1733 in order to be Examined by us.

665. The following order was made upon Mr John Townesend.
Middlesex To Mr John Townesend one of the late Overseers of the Poor of the Parish of S^t. John at Hackney in the County of Middlesex. These are in his majesties name to require you forthwith upon sight hereof to pay to M^r. Hezekiah Walker and M^r. Joseph Sureties the present Over-

seers of the Poor of the said Parish of Saint John at Hackney Thirty three pounds one shilling and one penny being the Ballance due from you to the parish and is remaining in your hands in the discharge of that Office and in case you faile herein we will proceed against you as the Law directs – Given under our hands and Seals the third day of September in the year of our Lord 1733. [*signed*] Henry Norris, Samuell Tyssen, Stephen Ram, Alex[a]. Garrett. [*See* **635**, **655**, **659**].

666. Adjorned to Monday the 10th of this Instant September to this place at nine in the morning.

The Mermaid Tavern, Monday, 10 September 1733
Justices present: Henry Norris, Samuel Tyssen, Stephen Ram

667. Mary Townesend wife of Thomas Townesend made Oath that her said [Late *deleted*] Husband hath frequently used such threatening words to her that she apprehends [her *deleted*] to be in danger of her Life or of some Bodily harm he will do unto her and also that he hath frequently beat and abused her in breach of his [*sic*] peace. Ordered That he be Summoned to attend at the next Meeting to answer the said Complaint.

668. Richard Lawn Serv[t]. to M[r]. W[m]. Thurston Hackney Coachman charged by M[r] Rich[d] Nicholas with defrauding and Cheating him of halfe Guinea. Agreed That it be respited until the next Meeting.

669. Ordered That M[r]. John Davis the Churchwarden do pay to Mary Freeman five shillings for laying Thomas Stringers wife.

The Mermaid Tavern, Saturday, 27 October 1733
Justices present: Henry Norris, Alexander Garrett, Stephen Ram

670. Allowed a Certificate whereby George Kinward and Eliz[a] his wife were owned to be Inhabitants legally Settled in the Parish of S[t]. Mary of Stratford Bow in the County of Middlesex directed to the parish of Dudley in the County of Worcester.

671. Agreed That Richard Stoakes chosen Headborough for Mare Street Ward in the room of Zachariah Thompson removed out of the parish until the next General Court Leet to be held for the Mannor of Hackney and untill an other shall be chosen in his room or be otherwise legally discharged from that office and he was accordingly Sworne to Execute the s[d] Office.

672. Ordered That Susannah Stanley aged 12 years a poor child of this parish be bound apprentice to Robert Roberts of the Parish of S[t] James Clerkenwell in the County of Middlesex Carman and that the Churchwarden M[r] John Davis do pay him forty shillings with her and that she have a Cap two shifts a pair of Shoes and a pair of Stockings out of the worke house. [*See* **675**].

673. Ordered That Sarah George aged ten years a poor Child of this Parish be bound apprentice to Thomas Taylor of the parish of S[t] Andrew Holborn in the County of Middlesex Band Box maker and that M[r] John Davis the Churchwarden do pay him forty shillings with her. [*See* **675**].

674. Adjorned to Monday the 12th of November 1733 to [nine *deleted*] ten of the clock in the forenoon.

The Mermaid Tavern, Monday, 12 November 1733
Justices present: Henry Norris, Samuel Tyssen, Alexander Garrett, Stephen Ram

675. Allowed two Indentures of apprenticeship whereby Sarah George was bound to Tho[s] Taylor of the parish of S[t] Andrew Holborn in the County of Middx Band Box maker & Susannah Stanley to Robert Roberts of the parish of S[t] James Clerkenwell in the same county Carman. [*See* **672**, **673**].

676. Thomas Perry applyed [and *deleted*] for reliefe and acquainted the Justices that he hath Surfeit upon him and desired he might be put into the Hospital for Cure. Ordered That the Clerk do prepare a peticon to get him into S[t] Thomas's Hospital and that M[r]. John Davis the Churchwarden do pay him two shillings towards his present subsistance. [*See* **686**, **767**].

677. Ann Fisher made Oath that Elizabeth King and Mary Elizabeth Bush lately Deceased was buryed in Sheeps Wool only.

678. Signed a Summons [*deletion*] requiring the several Defaulters resideing within Church Street, Mare Street, Well Street Grove Street Homerton and Clopton in this parish that have neglected to perform their Statute worke towards the repairing the s[d] Highwayes of the s[d] parish to appear here on the 26th Instant by nine of the clock in the morning to shew cause why the penalty should not be Levy'd upon each of them as the Law directs.

679. Ordered That M[r]. Joseph Sureties one of the present Overseers of the Poor of this Parish do pay to M[r]. John Townesend one of the late Overseers of the Poor of the s[d] parish the Sum of ten shillings which he had made himselfe Debtor to the parish beyond his receipts in the discharge of that Office.

680. Samuel Tyssen Esq[r] signed a discharge for John Wheeler now in Custody in New Prison.[1] [*See* **9**, **48**, **89**, **119**, **129**, **582**].

1. Wheeler had probably been committed on a charge of wife-beating (**89**).

681. Ordered That the Clerk do prepare a peticon for to get John Raby into S[t] Thomas Hospital. [*See* **570**, **571**].

682. Ordered That John Braceys wife be taken into the workhouse and that her said husband do pay to the Churchwarden M[r] John Davis one shilling pr week towards her subsistance and that in case he failes in paying the same weekly that she be discharged out of the s[d] house. [*See* **381**, **402**].

683. Ordered That M[r] John Davis the Churchwarden do pay eight shillings to get Mary Morris's Clothes out of Pawne also two shillings towards her subsistance and that she be discharged out of the work house.

The Mermaid Tavern, Monday, 26 November 1733
Justices present: Henry Norris, Samuel Tyssen, Alexander Garrett, Stephen Ram

684. It appearing that there is remaining in the hands of Robert Aldwinckle and Edward Nutt Surveyors of the Highwayes of the parish of S[t] John at Hackney in the County of Middlesex for the year 1731 the sum of thirty Seven pounds Six shillings and one Penny to ballance their accounts and that there is due to William Stoakes and James Huggett Jun[r] one of the present Surveyors of the Highwayes of the said parish more than that sum for Ballast by them sold & delivered for the use of the s[d] parish in the said year. Ordered That the said Robert Aldwinckle and Edward Nutt do forthwith pay to the said William Stoakes so much as remains due to him on that account and the residue to James Huggett in part of his Bill for the said year and that the said James Huggett do bring to this years account so much as shall remain due to him over and above what he shall receive of the s[d] Aldwinckle and Nutt and that he do receive the same before any of the Debts contracted in the last year be paid.

685. The several Defaulters resideing within Church Street, Mare Street, Well Street, Grove Street, Homerton and Clopton [*deletion*] in the parish of S[t] John at Hackney who have neglected to perform their Statute worke on the said Highwayes were this day heard pursuant to a Summons under the hands & Seals of the above named Justices Issued out for that purpose.

The Mermaid Tavern, Saturday, 8 December 1733
Justices present: Samuel Tyssen, Stephen Ram, Alexander Garrett

686. Ordered That M[r]. John Davis Churchwarden do pay to Thomas Perry three shillings towards his present Subsistance he being very Infirm. [*See* **676**, **767**].

687. Ordered That Ann Addes do go upon likeing to Thomas Seares of the parish of West ham in the County of Essex Baker. [*See* **704**, **710**].

688. To several Defaulters resideing within Newington, Shacklewell, Kingsland Dorleston and Land Holders in the parish of S[t]. John at Hackney who have neglected to perform their Statute worke on the said Highwayes were this day heard pursuant to a Summons under the hands & Seals of Samuel Tyssen & Alex[a] Garrett two of the above mentioned Justices. Ordered That the Clerk do make out a warrant to Levy the penalty on the several Defaulters within the said parish who have neglected to worke or pay towards the necessary repairs of the said Highwayes according to the several dayes they have made default is particularly specifyed in a List this day settled by us for this present year They having each of them been summoned to attend us to shew cause why they refused or neglected to do the same who either did not attend pursuant thereunto or could not produce any sufficient excuse.

689. Adjorned to Monday the 17th day of December 1733 to this place by ten of the clock in the morning – By order of the Justices.

The Mermaid Tavern: Monday, 17 December 1733
Justices present: Henry Norris, Samuel Tyssen, Alexander Garrett

690. Henry Norris [and *deleted*] Samuel Tyssen [Esq[rs] *deleted*] and Alexander Garrett Esq[rs] Signed a Commandm[t] directed to W[m]. Platt living in Homerton in the Parish of Hackney requiring him not take upon him with out proper License to sell Ale Beer Brandy or other Distilled Liquors by Retail to be Drank in his said house upon pain of being Committed to the County Goal as the Law directs and it was delivered to him in the presence of the said Justices. [*See* **693**].

691. Ordered That M[r]. John Davis the Churchwarden do pay to James Bolton the sume of three pounds for his trouble and attendance for Eight weeks in Executing the Office of Beadle for Henry Harrill who was then Confined in the Marshalsea prison for Debt.

692. Jacob Alvares de Fonseca Gabriel Lopez Pinheiro Jacob Mendez Dacosta and Benjamin Mendez da Costa were heard upon their appeals against the poors Rate pursuant to a refferrence from the Sessions for that purpose they complained [that *deleted*] of there being rated each of them two pounds and ten shillings when other Gentlemen are rated but two pounds that live in as good Houses as they and appear to be in as good or better circumstances which is unequal and therefore prayed to be reduced. Upon Debateing of the matter Ordered That they be each of them reduced to two pounds.

693. William Platt living in Homerton in the Parish of S[t] John at Hackney was served with an order under the hands and Seals of Henry Norris Samuel Tyssen and Alexander Garrett Esq[rs] requiring [not *deleted*] him not sell Ale Beer Brandy or other Distilled Liquors by Retail to be Drank in his said house without a proper License for that purpose upon pain of being committed to the Common Goal for the County of Middlesex as the Law directs. [*See* **690**].

694. Complaint being made against Martha Collins Wid°. at the Sign of the Plow in Homerton for keeping an Ill governed and disorderly ale House. Ordered That she have notice to attend at the next meeting to answer the said Complaint and that M[r] James Bolton the Constable have notice to attend at the same time. [*See* **695**].

The Mermaid Tavern: Monday, 21 January 1734
Justices present: Henry Norris, Samuel Tyssen, Stephen Ram

695. Martha Collins widow living at the Plow in Homerton attended pursuant to her Summons for keeping an [Ale *deleted*] Ill Governed and disorderly ale House and acknowledged her fault and promised to take a great deal of care for the future. Agreed That she be Excused for this time and in case she offend again that her License be Suppressed. [*See* **694**].

696. Thomas Fowles applyed to have a License to sell Ale at the White [Hart *deleted*] Swan on Cambridge Heath in the room of [Philipa *illegible* removed *deleted*] Eliz[a]. Lightwood removed. Agreed That he be Licensed at the next General meeting [for *deleted*] as shall be appointed for that purpose.

697. Richard Tye applyed to be Licensed to sell ale at the Faulcon in Homerton in the room of Philip Dunne removed. The said Richard Tye not being an Inhabitant of this Parish and the Rent of the said House not being Sufficient to make a Settlement, Agreed That further consideration of what is necessary to be done thereupon be respited until the next meeting.[1]

1. Richard Tye obtained a certificate. P79/JN1/398.

698. Ordered That M[r]. John Davis the Churchwarden do pay to Ann Trott afflicted with the foul Desease one shilling for the present and two shillings pr week from this day and until further Orders. [*See* **706**, **726**].

699. Ordered That D°. do pay to Robert Ronsum two shillings and Six Pence towards his present Subsistance he having been very Lame and being very poor and out of Business.

700. Adjorned sine die.

The Mermaid Tavern: Monday, 4 February 1734
Justices present: Henry Norris, Stephen Ram

701. Took the Examinacon of George Barrenger touching his last Settlement which appeared to be in the parish of S[t] John at Hackney.[1]

1. Barrenger, suffering from the 'foul disease' was about to be admitted to St. Thomas' Hospital at parish expense. He was dead within a fortnight of this examination, and was buried at parish expense. P79/JN1/218.

702. Signed an Order to remove Esther Coxon widow of Benjamin Coxon and Mary Esther seven years old and Mary five years old their lawful Issue from the parish of S[t] Mary of Stratford Bow in the County of Middlesex to the parish of Westham in the County of Essex as the place of their last legal Settlement.

703. Ordered That Eliz[a]. Wheeler and Ann Wheeler Children of John and Tomasin Wheeler be received into the work house and entertained there for two weeks. [*See* **707**, **708**].

704. Ordered That Ann Addes a Poor Child of this Parish be bound apprentice to John [*recte* Thomas] Sears of the parish of Westham in the County of Essex Baker and that M[r]. John Davis the Churchwarden do pay him forty shillings with her. [*See* **687**, **710**].

The Mermaid Tavern: Monday, 18 February 1734
Justices present: Stephen Ram, Henry Norris

705. Ordered That Susannah Twitchell aged 13 years a poor Child of the Parish of S[t]. John at Hackney in the County of Middlesex be bound apprentice to Joseph French of the parish of S[t]. Saviour in Southwark Pin Maker and that M[r]. John Davis the Churchwarden do pay forty shillings with her and also twenty shillings towards cureing her of a Scorbutical Humour and that she have the usual Clothing. [*See* **710**].

706. Ordered That M[r]. John Davis the Churchwarden do provide Necessary clothing for Ann Trott. [*See* **698**, **726**].

707. Ordered That Elizabeth and Ann Wheeler be continued in the work house for one Week from this day. [*See* **703**, **708**].

708. Ordered That M[r]. John Davis the Churchwarden do pay to Tomassin Wheeler five shillings towards buying her some Goods to put her into a way to get her living she being very poor. [*See* **703**, **707**].

709. Middlesex Jacob Upham Maketh Oath that this day as he was driving a Coach from the Yard belonging to Henry Davis in Church Street in the parish of S[t] John at Hackney in the said County of Middlesex to the Stand over against the Church as the said Coach came over against the House of M[r] W[m]. Yelloly in Church Street in the s[d] parish the near Wheel Stopped suddenly against a large Stepping Stone in the

Road which the said Mr Yelloly caused to be put against his said dwelling house by which means he was flung from the Coach box into the Road by which fall his Hip is bruised and that the Horses then ran away with the Coach and broke the pole peice. [*signed*] Jacob Upham. Sworn before us the 18th day of February in the year of our Lord 1734 [*signed*] Henry Norris Stephen Ram. Ordered That the said Mr. William Yelloly have notice to attend at the next meeting to answer the said Complaint and that the present Surveyors of the Highwayes of this parish be Summoned to attend at the same time to receive such directions as his Majesties Justices of the peace shall think proper to give relateing to the [*deletion*] said Highwayes. [*See* **713**].

The Mermaid Tavern: Monday, 4 March 1734
Justices present: Henry Norris, Samuel Tyssen, Alexander Garrett

710. Allowed an Indenture of Apprenticeship whereby Susannah Twitchell a poor child of the parish of Hackney was bound to Joseph French of the parish of St. Saviour in Southwark pin maker and also one other Indenture whereby Ann Addes a poor Child of the said parish was bound to Thomas Seares of the parish of Westham in the County of Essex Baker. [*See* **687**, **704**, **705**].

711. Ordered That Sarah Cavennough aged [sixteen *deleted*] fourteen years a Poor Child of the Parish of Hackney be bound apprentice to Randall Burr of Bacon Street in the Hamlet of Bethnal Green in the County of Middlesex Stocking maker and that Mr John Davis the Churchwarden do pay to him forty shillings with her and also twenty shillings to be laid out in necessary Clothing for her. [*See* **735**].

712. John Westrop applyed to be Licensed to keep an ale house at the Bull at [Kingsland *deleted*] Newington in the room of the Widow Ware removed. Agreed That he be Licensed at the next General meeting to be held for that purpose.

713. Ordered That Mr. Wm. Yelloley be Summoned to attend at the next Special Sessions [to *deleted*] for the Highwayes to be held at the Court house in White Chapple to answer what shall be Objected against him for a nusance by him committed in the Common Highway within the parish of St John at Hackney for causing large Stones to be placed in the sd. Road by which meanes several of his Majesties Subjects have sustained Damage and that Jacob Upham have notice to attend at the same time and also the Surveyrs of the Highwayes of this sd parish to receive proper directions for removing the same. [*See* **709**].

714. Henry Harrill made oath that he delivered a Summons to Thomas Mellers requiring him to attend his Majesties Justices of the Peace at this Petty Sessions to give an account of the place of his last legal Settlement – which he neglecting to do Ordered That a Warrant be made out to apprehend him for that purpose he being likely to become burthensome and chargeable to the parish.

The Mermaid Tavern: Monday, 25 March 1734
Justices present: Henry Norris, Samuel Tyssen, Alexander Garrett

715. Allowed an Indenture of apprenticeship whereby Edward Wilson aged Eleven Years a poor Child of this parish [of *deleted*] was bound to Robt. Brown fisherman of the Hamlet of Poplar and Blackwall in the County of Middlesex.

716. Signed Samuel Sadleirs Bill for Business done for the Parish amounting to the sum of nine pounds three shillings & Eight pence from November the 21st 1733 to the 25th of March 1734.

The Mermaid Tavern: Monday, 8 April 1734
Justices present: Henry Norris, Samuel Tyssen, Alexander Garrett

717. Poors Rate appellants: Thomas Pile rated 8s. reduced to 5s.; Robert Iles rated £2, reduced to £1 16s. 0d.; John Copley rated 5s. [*marginal entry*: paid]; John Steward rated 15s., not relieved; Edward Fox rated 8s., to bring a Certificate; William Mills rated 4s., Excused; William Browne rated 12s., Excused; John Sandford rated 7s., to pay; [William Rogers rated 4s. *deleted*]; Thomas Reeves rated 6s., Excused poor; William Rogers rated 4s., Excused poor; Martha Baxter rated 4s., Excused poor; Joseph Moore rated 8s., to pay; William Platt rated 4s., to pay; John Osman rated 4s., Excused poor; Elinor Atchison rated 4s., Excused poor; William Davis rated 8s., to pay 6s. Ordered That a warrant be forthwith made out to Levy the Poors Rate on the several defaulters.

718. Jemima Kirton Singlewoman made Oath that the Place of her last legal Settlement is in the Parish of Hackney by serving Samuel Webb Esqr.[1]

1. Kirton had probably been removed to Hackney. She was previously examined in 1728, apparently also as a result of a removal order and at that time had an illegitimate son aged ten years. H.A.D., P/J/J/P68.

The Mermaid Tavern: Monday, 29 April 1734
Justices present: Henry Norris, Stephen Ram

719. Signed a nominacon warrant whereby Morgan Bynon and Edward Brooksby Churchwardens and Edward Nutt and John Cox Inhabitants of the Parish of Saint John at Hackney in the County of Middlesex were appointed Overseers of the Poor of the said Parish for the year 1734.

720. D^{o}. for Henry Harrill Beadle.

721. Ordered That Mr John Davis Churchwarden do pay to Mary Seager a Poor Traveller whose husband Dyed in a Barn at Dorleston Eight shillings in order to help her and her four Children forward in their Journey.

722. James Odey made Oath that he is legally Settled in the Parish of Hackney. Ordered That the s[d] James Odey have a Certificate directed to the Churchwardens & Overseers of the Poor of the Hamlet of Ratcliffe in the County of Middlesex owning him and Ann his wife [Ann *deleted*] to be Inhabitants Legally Settled in the Parish of S[t] John at Hackney in the said County.

The Mermaid Tavern: Monday, 13 May 1734
Justices present: Alexander Garrett

723. John Jennison made Oath that he is an Inhabitant legally settled in the parish of S[t] John at Hackney in the County of Middlesex.

724. Ordered That Robert Inott aged Eleven years a poor child of this Parish be forthwith bound apprentice to Daniel Loiseauz of the Hamlet of Mile End new Towne in the County of Middlesex Weaver and that M[r] Morgan Bynon the Churchwarden do pay forty shillings with him and also that he lay out twelve shillings in clothing for him he being almost naked.

725. Ordered That Edward Addes aged thirteen years a poor Child of this Parish be forthwith bound apprentice to Edward Poole of the same Parish Brewer and that M[r] Morgan Bynon the Churchwarden do pay forty shillings with him.

726. Ordered That M[r] Morgan Bynon Churchwarden do pay to Ann Trott afflicted with the foul Desease two shillings pr week from this day until further orders. [*See* **698**, **706**].

The Mermaid Tavern: Monday, 27 May 1734
Justices present: Henry Norris, Samuel Tyssen, Alexander Garrett

727. Eliz[a]. Harvey made Oath that John Huntrod father of Lewis Huntrod aged about twelve years was last legally Settled in the Parish of S[t] John at Hackney in the County of Middlesex. [*See* **780**, **782**].

728. Ordered That the warrant Signed by Samuel Tyssen Esq[r] against William Burrell for begetting Elizabeth Robinson Singlewoman with Child of a base Child or Children that when Born are likely to become burthensome and chargeable to the parish of S[t] John at Hackney be

Executed unless he gives Bond with Sureties to Indempnify [*sic*] the parish or [*deletion*] enters into Recognizance to appear at the next Quarter Sessions to answer the same. [*See* **105**, **757**, **786**].

729. Edward Higgs applyed to have a License to Sell ale and Beer at the Sign of the Shipp the Bowling Green house in Clopton. Agreed That he be Licensed at the next General meeting for that purpose upon this Condition that it continues to be a Bowling Green [*deletion*] house.

730. Ordered That Ann Inott aged thirteen years a Poor Child of this Parish be forthwith bound apprentice to Daniel Loiseauz of the Hamlet of Mile End new Towne in the County of Middlesex weaver and that Mr Morgan Bynon the Churchwarden do pay forty shillings with her and also that he lay out twelve shillings in Clothing for her she being almost naked. [*See* **732**].

The Mermaid Tavern: Monday, 10 June 1734
Justices present: Henry Norris, Samuel Tyssen, Stephen Ram, Alexander Garrett

731. William Cumberland apprentice to George Fox a Farrier in Homerton complained against his said Master for beating and misusing him who attended to answer the said Complaint and acquainted the Justices that he Struck him on Thursday last with a small horse-whip [and *deleted*] for not getting up to worke in the morning at four a Clock [in the morning *deleted*] but it appearing to the Justices that the Correction he gave him was immoderate [and *deleted*] advised him not to do so for the time to come and also repremanded the boy and Ordered him to behave himselfe better for the future. [*See* **188**, **233**].

732. Allowed an Indenture whereby Ann Inott aged thirteen years a poor Child of this Parish was bound apprentice to Daniel Loiseauz of the Hamlet of Mile End new Towne weaver. [*See* **730**].

The Mermaid Tavern: Monday, 15th July 1734
Justices present: Henry Norris, Alexander Garrett

733. Jane Ady made oath that Thomas Reynolds lately deceased was buried in Sheeps Wool only.

734. Allowed a Certificate directed to the parish of Mitcham in the County of Surry whereby William Pronton and Mary his wife were owned to be Inhabitants legally settled in the parish of Hackney.

735. Allowed an Indenture of apprenticeship whereby Sarah Cavennough aged fourteen years a poor Child of this parish was bound to Randall Burr of the Hamlet of Bethnal Green Stocking maker. [*See* **711**].

736. Allowed an Indenture of apprenticeship whereby John Inott aged fourteen years a poor child of this parish was bound apprentice to Nicholas Loveman of the Hamlet of Poplar and Blackwall in the County of Middlesex Fisherman.

737. Mary Past peticoned to have a License for one of her houses at Cambridge Heath. The Justices Debateing matter are of Opinion that she ought not to have a License.

738. Ordered That Mr Morgan Bynon Churchwarden do pay to Elizabeth Barnes Widow ten shillings towards her subsistance in going to the place of her Settlem^t^ her husband lately dying here and she having three Children to provide for.

739. Examined and allowed a Bill for Business done by Samuel Sadleir for the parish from Aprill the 6th last past to this day amounting to the sum of ten pounds fourteen shillings and four pence.

740. Ordered That a warrant be made out against George Fowler to answer the Complaint of the Churchwardens and Overseers of the Poor of the Parish of Hackney for neglecting to make provision for his wife and family whereby they are become burthensome and chargeable to the s^d^ parish on the Oath of M^r^. Morgan Bynon one of the Churchwardens. [*See* **805**].

741. Ordered That Warrants be made out against Dorrington Browning Mary Feasant John Blakey and Mary Moreton to answer the Complaint of the Churchwardens and Overseers of the poor of the parish of Hackney for Intruding themselves into the said parish to Inhabit as parishioners contrary to Law they being no legal Inhabitants therein and being likely to become burthensome and chargeable to the said parish and they having refused to attend us to be Examined upon Oath touching the place of their last legal Settlement although duely Summoned for that purpose. [*See* **744**, **774**].

The Mermaid Tavern: Monday, 29 July 1734
Justices present: Samuel Tyssen, Alexander Garrett, Stephen Ram

742. The accounts of Mr Hezekiah Walker one of the Overseers of the poor of the parish of St John at Hackney for the year 1732 not having been audited – Ordered That a Warrant be made out directed to Stamp Brooksbank Esqr M^r^. Matthias King M^r^. John Howard Mr Charles Garrett John Nicholas Esqr Mr Gilbert Page Mr Michael Roan Mr James Lewis Beishers Mr James Huggett the Elder Mr Benjamin De Vinck Mr Robt Aldwinckle Capt Thomas Pangbourne and the present Churchwardens appointing them to be a Committee to audit the said accounts of Mr Hez: Walker and that any five of them be a Quorum and they are desired to make a report in writing under their hands or under the hands of any five of them to his Majesties Justices of the Peace resideing within the said Parish at a meeting hereby appointed to hold at this place this day fortnight at ten in the forenoon how they find the same.

743. Thomas Hilliard applyed to have a License to keep an ale house at Dorleston in the parish of Hackney in the room of Stephen Pattmore who kept the sign of the Two Brewers at Kingsland who lately ran away from the said House – Agreed That he have a License for that purpose at the next General Meeting to be held for Licensing of Victuallers [he *deleted*] his being weak which renders him incapable of following of his Business. [*See* **661**].

744. John Blakey brought by W[m]. Harris one of the Headboroughs of the parish of Hackney by virtue of a Warrant granted by Alex[a]. Garrett Esq[r] to give an account of the place of his last legal Settlement who made Oath that he was legal [*sic*] Settled in the parish of Tottenham in the County of Middlesex in right of his father John Blakey. [*See* **741**].

745. John Hill made Oath that he is a Inhabitant legally settled in the parish of S[t] John at Hackney by serving M[r] John Brewer of the said parish Baker for a year at the wages of ten pounds and desired he might have a Cert directed to the parish of Redbourne in the County of Hertford owning him to be an Inhabitant of the s[d] parish of Hackney. Ordered That he have a Cert according to his said request.

746. Adjorned to this day fortnight to this place at ten in the forenoon.

The Mermaid Tavern: Monday, 12 August 1734
Justices present: Samuel Tyssen, Stephen Ram, Alexander Garrett

747. John Tennant applyed to have a License to keep the Ale house at the Sign of the Six Bells in Church Street in the room of Mary Philpott. Agreed That he be Licensed at the next General meeting to be held for Licensing Victuallers.

748. Ordered That M[r]. Morgan Bynon the Churchwarden do pay towards the support of Elinor Broome wid[o]. a patient in M[r]. Guys Hospital twenty [*deletion*] seven shillings for twenty seven weeks past.

749. Samuel Tyssen and Alexander Garrett Esq[rs]. took the Examinacon of Ann Bull Singlewoman touching the Female Bastard Child she was delivered of in the parish of S[t] Mary Stratford Bow in the County of Middlesex on the nineteenth day of June last which is now living and Chargeable to the said parish [and *deleted*] By which she charged one John Devan late of the Hamlet of Mile End old Towne Velvet Weaver with being the reputed father of the said Female Bastard Child and accordingly signed an adjudication against the said John Devan the reputed father.

750. Signed an [*sic*] allowed the accounts of M[r] John Davis Churchwarden and Overseer of the Poor of the Parish of S^t. John at Hackney in the County of Middlesex for the years one thousand seven hundred and thirty two and one thousand seven hundred and thirty three by which accounts there remains due to the parish the sum of twenty nine pounds seventeen shillings and two pence.

751. Signed and allowed the accounts of M^r. Hezekiah Walker and M^r. Joseph Sureties the late Overseers of the Poor of the parish of St John at Hackney for the year last past by which accounts there remains due to the said Parish the sum of One hundred forty three pounds [ten *deleted*] two shillings and Eleven pence.

752. Ordered That the said Mr John Davis [and *deleted*] Mr Hezekiah Walker and Mr Joseph Sureties do [do forthwith *deleted*] pay over the said several Ballances to M^r. Edward Nutt and Mr John Cox the present Overseers of the Poor of the Parish of St John at Hackney [*deletion*] on Monday next at ten in the forenoon at a meeting hereby appointed to be held at that time at the Mermaid Tavern. [*See* **755**].

753. Adjorned to this day sennight to nine in the morning to this place.

The Mermaid Tavern: Monday, 19 August 1734
Justices present: Samuel Tyssen, Alexander Garrett, Stephen Ram

754. M^r. John Davis late Churchwarden & Overseer of the Poor of the parish of Hackney for the years 1732 and 1733 paid to Mr Morgan Bynon the present Churchwarden & Overseer of the Poor of the said Parish the sum of Eighteen pounds one shilling and Eight pence which with the sum of Eleven pounds fifteen shillings and Six pence being the necessary Expences which he was at with Mr Hez: Walker one of the Overseers of the poor of the said parish in the year 1732 in Erecting the Workhouse and not [allow *deleted*] charged in his account for the said year and this day allowed by us amounts to the sum of twenty nine pounds seventeen shillings and two pence which was Ballance settled at the last meeting and which he was then Ordered to pay over to the said M^r. Bynon.

755. M^r. Hezek Walker and Mr Joseph Sureties Overseers of the Poor of the said parish of Hackney for the year 1733 pursuant to an order made at the last meeting this day paid to Mr John Cox and Mr Edward Nutt the present Overseers of the Poor of the said Parish the sum of One hundred forty three pounds two shillings and Eleven pence being the Ballance of their accounts and due to the parish in the discharge of their said Office. [*See* **752**].

756. The following old Debts were this day discharged, To wit – Paid by M^r. Morgan Bynon Churchwarden: Mr Samuel Stanton apothecary, £17 3s. 0d.; Mr Matthias Woodyard plumber, 11s. Paid by Mr John Cox & Mr Edwd Nutt overseers: M^r. Samuel Stanton apothecary more, £21 11s. 0d.; M^r. Edward Conyears Baker £32 16s. 0d.; M^r. Richard Phelpes Bell founder, £22 15s. 0d.; Mr. Matthias Woodyard plumber more, £40 7s. 0d.; Mr. Markham Spearing Bricklayer, £11. [Total] £146 3s. 0d.

The Mermaid Tavern: Monday, 7 October 1734
Justices present: Henry Norris, Stephen Ram

757. Took the Examinacon of Elizabeth Robinson Singlewoman touching the Female Bastard Child which she was delivered of on the third day of August last in the parish of Hackney in which she hath charged William Burrell a Breeches maker at Newington with being the father thereof. Ordered That an order of adjudication be made out against him and that he pay the sum of Eighteen shillings and Six pence which the parish hath been at and also to pay two shillings pr week so long as it shall continue chargeable to the parish. [*See* **105**, **728**, **786**].

758. Biss Somers made Oath that his last place of last legal Settlement is in the parish of St Michael near Shipton Mallett in Somersetshire. [*See* **992**].

759. Ordered That Mr Morgan Bynon the Churchwarden do forthwith cause the Bridge near the White Horse Ale House in Mare Street to be forthwith effectually repaired.

760. Ordered That Mrs. Sarah Browne have notice to remove the Nusance Occationed by her Cowes laying in the foot path leading from Mare Street and Well Street to Clopton and Homerton and cause the Soyle or filth which they made there forthwith to be taken up and in in [*sic*] Case she refuses or neglects to do it that Saml Sadleir our Clerk do cause a Bill of Indictment to be preferred against her to oblige her at the next Sessions to be held at Hicks=hall.

761. Adjourned to this day fortnight at 10 in the forenoone to this place.

The Mermaid Tavern: Monday, 21 October 1734
Justices present: Henry Norris, Samuel Tyssen

762. Matthew Burgan applyed to have a License at the White Hart at Temple Mills in the Room of Samuel Phillipps. Agreed That he be Licensed at the next General meeting to be held for Granting Licenses.

763. James Bolton on his oath charged Thomas Cooke with assaulting him and kicking him upon his Legg on the 10th day of September last by which it was very much bruised.

764. James Martin of the parish of Saint John at Hackney in the County of Middlesex Gardener and Thomas Cooke of the same Labr make Oath That Elizabeth Horseman keeps a Common ale house or victualling house at the sign of the two Brewers at Kingsland in the said parish and hath used selling of Beer and ale by Retaile to be drank in her said house and did yesterday sell to these deponents three pints of mild Beer [*deletion*] which they drank in the said house and Thomas Cooke one of these deponents paid her four pence halfe penny for the said Beer. [*Signed*] James Martin, Thomas Cook. Sworne before us the 21st day of October in the year of our Lord 1734, [*signed*] Henry Norris Samuell Tyssen. A warrant was signed by the sd Justices to Levy 20s on the said Elizabeth Horseman for her said Offence.

765. Thomas Matthews applyed to have a License at the Bowling house in Clopton in the Room of Edmund Matthews. Agreed That he be Licensed at the next General Meeting to be held for Granting Licenses. [*See* **868**].

766. Elizabeth Lort made Oath that her late husband William Lort was last legally Settled in the parish of St George in Southwark by Renting of a house of Sixteen pounds pr ann in the said parish and paying all parochial Taxes there and signed an Order to remove John her son aged 8 years thither.[1]

1. John was the youngest of Elizabeth Lort's three children; the older ones were 14 and 11. He was probably chargeable to the parish. H.A.D., P/J/P/68.

767. Ordered That Mr. Morgan Bynon the Churchwarden do pay to David Bentley the sum of four pounds and four shillings for Lodging and maintaining Thomas Perry from Aprill the 12th last past to the 21st of September following. [*See* **676**, **686**].

The Mermaid Tavern: Monday, 11 November 1734
Justices present: Henry Norris, Samuel Tyssen, Stephen Ram, Alexander Garrett

768. Mr [*blank*] Hannand applyed for a License for a person to keep an alehouse at the sign of the George in Clopton in the room of Wm. Rowley who is removed to the next Door and is Licensed there – But there not being any Vacancy [and th *deleted*] Agreed that he cannot be Licensed until there is a Vacancy.

769. Mr. Edward Brooksby the Churchwarden having Exhibited his Complaint against John Inott for Insulting him and giving him abusive Language in the Execution of his said Office in the Work house and also refuseing to worke there which appearing notoriously plain by Evidences Examined before his face. Ordered That in Case any Complaint of this Sort shall be made against him for the time to come that he be Committed to the House of Correction.

The Mermaid Tavern: Monday, 9 December 1734
Justices present: Henry Norris, Stephen Ram

770. Examined and allowed Samuel Sadleirs Bill for Business by him done for the Parish from July the 16th last past to the 9th day of

December Instant amounting to the sum of Eight pounds Seventeen shillings and five pence.

771. Took the examination of Mary Edwards Singlewoman touching the Female Bastard Child born of her Body in the parish of St John at Hackney on the sixth day of November last and signed an adjudication against William Goodchild the putative father thereof.

772. Thomas Kirke applyed to be Licensed at the sign of the two Black boys in Well Street in the parish of Hackney in the room of James Matchin. Agreed That he be Licensed at the next General meeting to be held for that purpose.

773. Took the Examination of William Coates passed from Saint Giles in the Fields in the County of Middlesex and it appears by the said Examination that his Settlem^{t} is in this parish by his being a hired [*sic*] by the year wth George Carter Esqr.

774. Took the Examination of Mary Feasant touching the Female Bastard Child born of her Body in this parish wherein she chargeth one Charles Hawes of the parish of St John in Southwark in the County of Surry Oar maker with being the father thereof Ordered that an adjudication be made out against him and that he pay twelve shillings & Six pence charges which the parish hath been at and two shillings pr week for so long time as it shall continue chargeable to the parish.[1] [*See* **741**].

1. There is some error here. The original examination identifies the father as Richard Costin of Southwark. H.A.D., P/J/P/68.

775. Thomas Warner made Oath that he is an Inhabitant legally settled in this parish by being a hired servant by the year with Dinah Wright and serving her Eight years and afterwards with her Executrix Mary Past in her same house for Seven years.

The Mermaid Tavern: Monday, 23 December 1734
Justices present: Henry Norris, Samuel Tyssen, Alexander Garrett, Stephen Ram

776. Ordered That M^{r}. Morgan Bynon the Churchwarden do pay towards the Clothing of Mary the daughter of George Rumsey twelve shillings she being almost naked and Mrs Vandercleus being willing to take her into her service.

777. The Defaulters who have neglected to perform their Statute worke on the Highwayes within the parish of St John at Hackney were this day heard.

778. Ordered That a Warrant of Distress be made out against the several Defaulters who did not appear according to their Summonses and also ag[st] those who did appear but could not assign any reasonable Excuse for their not havinging [*sic*] performed their Statute worke or paid towards the necessary repairation of the said Highwayes to Levy the several Sumes which they have forfeited for their neglect.

The Mermaid Tavern: Monday, 6 January 1735
Justices present: Henry Norris, Samuel Tyssen, Alexander Garrett

779. Henry Harrill having Charged one George Minshall upon oath with going about wandering and begging in the parish of Saint John at Hackney in the County of Middlesex and he not being able to give any good account of himselfe and how he gets his living and [*deletion*] thereby being a [*deletion*] vagrant a mittimus was Signed by the above named Justices to convey him to the House of Correction to hard Labour.

780. Ordered That M[r]. Morgan Bynon the Churchwarden do pay to Samuel Ogle Six shillings to be laid out in Clothing for John [*recte* Lewis] Huntrod a poor child of this parish who is upon likeing with the said Ogle in order to be bound apprentice to him he being almost naked. [*See* **727**, **782**].

781. James Betts [of *deleted*] brought by Thomas Bridgman Headborough by virtue of a warrant granted by Samuel Tyssen Esq[r] for assaulting and beating James Bolton. Discharged both parties being agreed.

The Mermaid Tavern: Monday, 27 January 1735
Justices present: Henry Norris, Samuel Tyssen, Stephen Ram, Alexander Garrett

782. Signed and allowed an Indenture of apprenticeshipp whereby Lewis Huntrod aged fifteen years a poor Child of the parish of Saint John at Hackney was bound to Samuel Ogle of the Hamlet of Ratcliffe within the parish of Saint Ann in the County of Middlesex Painter. [*See* **727**, **780**].

783. Edward Bush living in Homerton acquainted the above named Justices that his wife lies Dead in his house and that [*deletion*] he hath been sick for a considerable time and being in very low Circumstances & thereby incapable of Burying her and therefore humbly desired that his wife might be Buried at the charge of the parish. The Gentlemen Debateing the matter Ordered That M[r] Morgan Bynon the Churchwarden do cause her to be Interred and that the usual sum be laid out for that purpose.

784. Mr Isaac Estwick acquainted the Gentlemen that he is like to agree with M[r]. Morgan Bynon for his Tap house and he appearing to be a Man of Good Character Agreed That in Case they shall agree that he be Licensed at the next General meeting to be held for that purpose.

785. Ordered That M[r]. Morgan Bynon the Churchwarden do pay the necessary Expences in conveying Jere Gregory and William Saunders two notorious Deer Stealers to Newgate being nine shillings and Six Pence.[1]

1. Gregory and Saunders had been committed on 20 November 1734 by Tyssen for assaulting and wounding Robert Iles, a local farmer, and for want of sureties. They were fined 1s. and sentenced to six months labour. For further information see Derek Barlow, *Dick Turpin and the Gregory Gang* (Chichester, 1973).

The Mermaid Tavern: Monday, 10 February 1735
Justices present: Henry Norris, Samuel Tyssen

786. Ordered That Elizabeth Robinson Singlewoman be removed to the place of her Settlement. [*See* **105**, **728**, **757**].

787. Orderd That John Poole aged 14 Years a poor child of this Parish be bound to Thomas Jones of the parish of S[t]. Giles without Cripplegate in the City of London Callender[1] and that M[r]. Morgan Bynon the Churchwarden do pay forty shillings with him. [*See* **790**].

1. Callender (more properly calendrer or calenderer): one who finishes cloth to give it a stiff or glazed finish, *O.E.D*.

788. Ordered That Mr Morgan Bynon the Churchwarden do pay to Elizabeth the wife of John Inott twenty shillings towards putting her into a way of Business and that the Beadle do see that the money is laid out for that purpose.

The Mermaid Tavern: Monday, 3 March 1735
Justices present: Henry Norris, Samuel Tyssen, Stephen Ram

789. Elizabeth Bleven made oath that the bodies of Margaret Brocas, John Starps, Isaac Mitchell and James Underhill late Deceased were buried in Sheeps Wool only.

790. Allowed an Indenture of apprenticeshipp whereby John Poole aged fourteen years a poor Child of this parish was bound to Thomas Jones of the parish of Saint Giles without Cripplegate in the City of London Callender. [*See* **787**].

791. Ordered That M[r] Morgan Bynon the Churchwarden do pay Elinor Oswald her Bill for necessaries for John Barnes a poor man that was almost Drowned in M[rs] Woodfields Cow layer[1] amounting to Six shillings and three pence.

1. Perhaps meaning a large vat for tanning hides, *O.E.D*.

792. Edward Pim applyed for a Lycence to keep [*deletion*] an ale house at the sign of the Red Cow at Dorleston in the room of Richard Brattle Agreed That he be Licensed at the next General meeting to be held [for] that purpose.

793. James Holmes applyed for a Lycense to keep an ale house at the Old Mermaid in Church Street in the room of Joseph Ratcliffe. Agreed That he be Licensed at the next General meeting to be held for that purpose.

794. Ordered That M^r. Morgan Bynon the Churchwarden do pay to Thomas Sheperson fourteen shillings and nine pence for necessaries for Richard Beazely a poor Traveller that Dyed at his house.

795. Ordered That M^r. Bynon the Churchwarden do pay to Bridget the wife of John Jones twenty shillings towards provideing necessaries for her and her three Children. [*See* **854**].

The Mermaid Tavern: Monday, 17 March 1735
Justices present: Henry Norris, Samuel Tyssen, Alexander Garrett

The Mermaid Tavern: Monday, 21 April 1735
Justices present: Henry Norris, Samuel Tyssen, Alexander Garrett

796. Signed and Sealed warrants whereby Lister Selman Churchwarden and Titus Buckingham Churchwarden Elect and William van Leute the Younger Thomas Roades and Thomas Oliver were nominated and appointed Overseers of the poor of the parish of S^t. Mary of Stratford Bow in the County of Middlesex for the year ensuing, being the year 1735.

797. The following Officers were Sworn well and truly to Execute their several Offices, To wit, Constables: James Huggett the Younger, John Davis, James Bolton. Headboroughs: Henry Harrill, Henry Batt, Richard Speed, John Cawne, Thomas Cooper, Thomas Richman, Thomas Fussell, Charles Dean. Ale Conners: Henry Harrill, James Bolton.

798. The Persons whose names are hereunder written were Summoned to attend this day to shew cause why they refused or neglected to pay the poors Rate and why a warrant of Distress should not be Issued out against them.
Church Street: Henry Richard rated 4s., did not attend; William Davis rated 8s., his wife appeared, sum to be paid 5s..
Mare Street: Katherine Ashby rated £1, did not attend; Ann Bell rated £1, did not attend; William Kingsland rated 5s., his wife appeared; Giles Lomas rated 5s., did not attend; Samuel Woodyard rated 8s., D^o; Robert Bell rated 4s., D^o.
Homerton: Mary Vamiulldart rated 5s., D^o; Jonathan Freeman rated £1, appeared, sum to be paid 10s.; John Townesend rated 18s., did not attend; Luke Townesend rated 8s., D^o; Jeremiah Kemp rated 8s., D^o; Thomas Pile rated 5s., D^o; Gamaliel Lewin rated 10s., D^o; John Archer rated 8s., D^o; Thomas Monk rated 15s. 6d., D^o; Henry Godwin rated £1 13s., D^o; William Hewitt rated 4s., D^o.

Clopton: Mary Ashton Widow rated £1, D°; Benjamin Evans rated 10s.[1] appeared, sum to be paid 8s.; Robert Read rated 6s., D°.
Grove Street: Francis Olderherd rated 8s., did not appear.
Newington: Willliam Burrell rated 8s., D°.
Shacklewell: Widow Clarke rated 4s., appeared; George Welland rated £2, did not appear.
Kingsland: Edward Fox rated 8s., wife appeared.
Dorleston: Jacob Hewitt rated 4s., did not appear.
Land Holder: Thomas Boote rated 8s., D°.

1. The original entry has been altered; it may read £1 10s.

799. John Cox Overseer of the Poor made Oath the above mentioned Sumes hath been by him demanded of the said Several Persons & that they have refused or neglected to pay the same so that the said money is now unpaid and in arrear. Ordered That Samuel Sadleir our Clerk do prepare a warrant of Distress to Levy the said several sums of money for the use of the Poor of the parish of Hackney.

The Mermaid Tavern: Saturday, 26 April 1735
Justices present: Henry Norris, Samuel Tyssen

800. Signed and Sealed Warrant whereby Edward Brooksby and William Weston Churchwardens of the Parish of Saint John at Hackney in the County of Middlesex [and *deleted*] were nominated and appointed Overseers of the Poor of the said Parish for the year ensuing being the year one thousand seven hundred and thirty five.

801. Signed and allowed Samuel Sadleirs Bill for Business by him for the said Parish from December the ninth 1734 to the 23^d^ of Aprill 1735 amounting to the Sum of ten pounds seven shillings and two pence.

802. Wm Hayes, John Hague, Headboroughs Sworne.

The Mermaid Tavern: Friday, 2 May 1735
Justices present: Henry Norris, Samuel Tyssen, Alexander Garrett

803. Signed and Sealed a Warrant whereby Gabriel Lopez Pinheiro an Inhabitant of the Parish of Saint John at Hackney in the County of Middlesex was appointed One of the Overseers of the Poor of the said Parish for the year ensuing, being the year 1735.

804. Ordered That Henry Tilcock aged 13 years a Poor Child of this Parish be bound to Bernard Gill of the Parish of St Mary Stoake Newington in the County of Middlesex Peruke maker and that Mr John Cox and Mr Edward Nutt the late Overseers of the Poor do pay forty shillings with him.

The Mermaid Tavern: Monday, 19 May 1735

Justices present: Henry Norris, Stephen Ram, Alexander Garrett

805. Henry Norris Esq Granted a warrant to apprehend George Fowler for refuseing and neglecting to make provision for his wife and children whereby they are become burthensome and chargeable to the parish on the Oath of Mr Edward Brooksby Churchwarden. [*See* **740**].

806. Ordered That Nicholas Cavennough aged 12 years a poor Child of this Parish be forthwith bound apprentice to Thomas Fasbrook of the parish of St Mary Stoake Newington in the County of Middx Inn holder and that Mr Edwd Brooksby the Churchwarden do pay forty shillings with him.

807. Ordered That Mr Morgan Bynon and M^{r}. John Cox and M^{r}. Edwd. Nutt late Churchwarden and Overseers of the Poor of this Parish do Perfect their accounts in Writing of all moneys by them rec^{d} and paid in the discharge of their said Offices and lay them before the above named Justices at a meeting hereby appointed to be held at the Mermaid Tavern on this day fortnight at ten in the forenoon to be then Examined.

The Mermaid Tavern: Monday, 2 June 1735
Justices present: Henry Norris, Stephen Ram, Samuel Tyssen, Alexander Garrett

808. Mr John Cox and Mr Edward Nutt Overseers of the Poor of the Parish of St John at Hackney for the year 1734 pursuant to an order made at the last meeting and laid their accounts before the above named Justices by which their appears to be due from them to the parish to Ballance their accounts in the Discharge of their said Office the sum of twelve pounds five shillings and Eight pence halfe penny. Ordered That the said John Cox & Edward Nutt do forthwith pay to Mr Edward Brooksby the present Churchwarden & Overseer of the Poor the said Sum of twelve pounds five shillings and Eight pence halfe penny.

809. M^{r}. Morgan Bynon the late Churchwarden & Overseer attended likewise pursuant to an Order of the last meeting and produced his accounts but Time being Elapsed – Ordered That the Examinacon thereof be respited till the next meeting. [*See* **822**].

810. Ordered That Samuel Sadleir Collector of the Poors Rate and Turnpike Rate for the year 1734 do forthwith pay to M^{r}. Edwd. Brooksby the present Churchwarden & Overseer of the Poor of the Parish Hackney Seventeen pounds Eighteen shillings and five pence farthing being the ballance remaining in his hands and due to the parish on those Rates.

The Mermaid Tavern: Monday, 7 July 1735
Justices present: Henry Norris, Stephen Ram, Alexander Garrett

811. Took the affadavit of Faith Hassell Widow of John Hassell [which *deleted*] touching the place of her last legal Settlement which appearing to be in the parish of Nantwitch in Cheshire an order was Signed by Henry Norris & Stephen Ram Esq^s^. to remove her from the parish of St Mary of Stratford Bow in the County of Middlesex to the said Parish of Nantwich.

812. Ann [Tipp *deleted*] Trippus Widow and Daniel Middleton [*altered from* Middleson] Applyed to be Licensed at Bow. Agreed That in case their shall be no objection against their Charachters [*sic*] that they be Licensed at the next General meeting to be held for that purpose.

813. Allowed Saml Sadleirs Bill for Business by him done for the Parish from Aprill the 26th 1735 to the 7th day of July following amounting to the sum of Eight pounds fourteen shillings and Six pence.

814. Ordered That a Warrant be forthwith made out to remove Ann Furley widow and her two Children to the parish of Bromley the place of their Settlement.[1]

1. Ann Furley had a third (illegitimate) child, born May 1735, which was chargeable to Hackney. She obtained a certificate during 1735. H.A.D., P/J/P/68; P79/JN1/398.

The Mermaid Tavern: Monday, 21 July 1735
Justices present: Henry Norris, Samuel Tyssen, Alexander Garrett

815. Took the affadavit of Sarah Cooke Singlewoman touching the place of her last legal Settlement and also her Examination touching the Father of her Male Bastard Child and she having on her Oath charged one John Rayner with being the father thereof an order of adjudication was Signed against him accordingly.[1]

1. The child was chargeable to the parish. H.A.D., P/J/P/68.

816. John Batteram made oath of the place of his Legal Settlement which appears to be in the parish of Saint Dunstan in the West in the City of London.

817. Adjorned to this day fortnight to this place by ten of the clock in the forenoon.

The Mermaid Tavern: Monday, 4 August 1735
Justices present: Stephen Ram, Alexander Garrett, Henry Norris

818. Joseph Tribe applyed to have a License at the Sign of the Adam and Eve in Homerton Agreed That the consideration of granting him a License be respited.

819. John Cliffton Coachman to M^r^. Ram and Samuel Howard his Gardener each off them Confessed that on Evening of the preceeding day they profanely Swore two Oaths in the parish of Hackney and also that they were Drunk whereby they each of them forfeited the sum of Seven shillings to the use of the poor of the said parish Ordered that they do forth with pay the said forfeitures into the hands of M[r] Edward Brooksby Churchwarden for the purpose aforesaid which they accordingly did.

820. Esther Cheekley made oath that she is legally settled in the parish of Hackney by virtue of her being bound apprentice to her Grand Mother Ann Cheekley by the Churchwardens and Overseers of the Poor of Allhollows London Wall and serving her in the s[d]. parish of Hackney during her apprenticeshipp.

The Mermaid Tavern: Monday, 1 September 1735
Justices present: Henry Norris, Alexander Garrett

821. Ordered That for the future all persons that are Interred from the Work=house affadavits be made by the Searchers that they were Interred in woolen according to the Act of Parliament made for that purpose and that the Churchwarden do pay them one shilling for each person out of which they are to pay for filling up the affadavit.

822. The accounts of M[r]. Morgan Bynon late Churchwarden and Overseer of the Poor of this Parish were this day Examined and allowed by the above named Justices by which It appears that he rec[d]. on the Turnpike Account One hundred and one pound one shillings and also that he hath paid the same sum on that account and also that he hath Rec[d]. on the Church account Forty nine pounds fourteen shillings and two pence and hath paid on that account One hundred and twenty pounds thirteen shillings and Seven Pence so that there is due to him to Ballance that account Seventy Pounds nineteen shillings and five pence And also that he rec[d]. on the Poors account three hundred forty four pounds Eight shillings and Eight pence and that he hath paid on that account two hundred seventy two pounds fifteen shillings and four pence halfe penny so that there is due to the Parish to Ballance that account Seventy one pounds thirteen shillings and three pence halfe penny upon the whole there remains due from him to the parish the Sum of thirteen shillings and ten pence halfe penny. Ordered That M[r]. Morgan Bynon do forthwith pay over the said sum of thirteen shillings & ten pence halfe penny to the present Churchwarden and Overseer of the Poor M[r] Edward Brooksby for the use of the Parish. [*See* **809**].

823. The several Constables and Headboroughs of this Parish signed the List of Free Holders & Copy Holders resideing in this Parish and Swore to the truth of the said List and a Certificate thereof was Signed by the said Justices.

824. Agreed That Jacob Crew be Licensed at the Naggs head Ale House in Mare Street at the next General renewing of Licenses at the Court house.

825. Randal Beck applyed to be Licensed in the room of his Mother Elinor Oswald Deceased at the sign of the Shoulder of Mutton. Agreed That he be Licensed at the next General Renewing of Licenses. [*See* **930**].

826. It appearing that Mary Tilcock late Servt to Mrs Piller in Brook house is Lunatick Agreed That she be put into Mr Matthew Wrights house for Cure.

The Mermaid Tavern: Monday, 22 September 1735
Justices present: Henry Norris, Alexander Garrett

[**827.** Elizabeth Bleven made oath that the bodies of William Macclary Thomas Bakewell Sarah Harvey Mary Richards John Bennett and Henry Mills lately Deceased were buryed in Sheeps Wool only.

828. Ordered That Henry Harrill the Beadle do endeavour forthwith to procure a Master for Samuel Coleman *entry deleted.*] [*See* **831**, **834**].

829. Ordered That M^r^. Edward Brooksby the Churchwarden do pay towards putting Francis Davis the Beadle and his wife into a way [*deletion*] to get their livings twenty shillings.

830. Ordered That Katherine Parsons and Abigal Ronsum be brought up from the work house at the next meeting to answer the Complaint of Mr Edward Brooksby Churchwarden for [*deletion*] making a Disturbance in the s^d^ house and Insulting & abuseing and assaulting him there.

831. Ordered That Samuel Coleman aged twelve years A poor child of this Parish be bound to Charles Harper of the Hamlet of Bethnal Green Victualler and that M^r^. Edward Brooksby the Churchwarden do pay him forty shillings with him. [*See* **828**, **834**].

The Mermaid Tavern: Monday, 13 October 1735
Justices present: Henry Norris, Samuel Tyssen, Alexander Garrett, Stephen Ram

832. Elizabeth Bleven made oath that William Knight Alice Reeve Ann Bellknapp & Martha Atken late of the Parish of Hackney Deceased were buryed in Sheeps Wool only.

833. Henry Norris Esqr. Signed a warrant to apprehend Thomas Hunt – Sibella his wife having Sworn the peace against him. [*See* **154**].

834. Allowed an Indenture of Apprenticeshipp whereby Samuel Coleman aged twelve years was bound to Charles Harper of the Hamlet of Bethnal Green Victualler. [*See* **828**, **831**].

835. Mary Baker made Oath that her late husband Edward Baker was last legally settled in this parish of St John at Hackney.

836. Ordered That Mary Ann Coleman aged ten years a poor Child of this parish be bound apprentice to Jane Salter of the parish of S^{t}. Sepulcres in the City of London Glover and that M^{r}. Edwd. Brooksby Churchwarden do pay her forty shillings with her. [*See* **841**].

837. M^{r}. Edward Brooksby Churchwarden laid before the above named Justices a Certificate from the Rev^{d}. M^{r}. Peter Newcome Vicar of Hackney setting forth that William Cooke Ann Tatt and Jane Barnard Deceased (but not of the plague) were Buryed in the parish of Hackney To wit W^{m}. Cooke on the 26th day Ann Tatt on the 28th day of September & Jane Barnard on the Second day of October Instant and that no affadavit relateing to their being Interred in Woolen hath been bro^{t} for any of the [persons *deleted*] s^{d} Corps pursuant to the Statute in that case made and provided and the time limited for making such affadavitts being Expired the said M^{r}. Brooksby prayed the s^{d} Justices would Issue out Warrants to Levy the penalty directed to be Levy'd for such neglect. Ordered That the Clerk do prepare proper Warrants for that purpose.

The Mermaid Tavern: Monday, 27 October 1735
Justices present: Henry Norris, Samuel Tyssen, Alexander Garrett

838. John Singleton at the Coffee house applyed for leave to Sell Brandy by Retaile until the next General meeting for Licensing. Agreed That he have leave to Sell 'till that time and that he have a License for that purpose.

839. Thomas Sclater at the Coffee house applyed for leave to Sell Brandy by Retaile until the next General meeting for Licensing. Agreed That he have leave to Sell till that time & that he have a License for that purpose.

840. Ordered That Ann Poole aged twelve years a poor Child of this parish be bound to Thomas Sweatman of the parish of St Mary White Chapple Cord wainer and that M^{r}. Edwd. Brooksby the Churchwarden do pay forty shillings with her. [*See* **857**].

841. Allowed two Indentures of Apprenticeshipp where by Mary Ann Coleman aged ten years was bound to Jane Salter of the parish of S^{t}. Sepulchres London Glover and Richard Ives aged thirteen Years was bound to John Varnham of the parish of Saint Andrew Holborn in the County of Middlesex Cordwainer. [*See* **836**].

842. Took the Examination of Mary Stanley Widow touching the Male

Bastard born of her Body in this parish on the 17th day of September last and signed an adjudication against Edward Bridgfoot the reputed father and also signed a Warrant to apprehend him.[1]

1. The baby was buried 11 November following. P79/JN1/25.

843. Eleanor Bugby made oath that her last Settlem[t] [is] in the parish or Town of Quorn in the County of Leicester.

The Mermaid Tavern: Monday, 10 November 1735
Justices present: Henry Norris, Samuel Tyssen

844. The following person [*sic*] were Summoned to give an account of the places of their last legall settlem[t].
Mare Street: Rich[d]. Maslin; Sarah Aldwinckle; *Thomas Taylor; *John Bridges; *William Battersbey; *James Coldicott; David East; John Clark; Elizabeth Fowles [*later note*: not summoned]; Thomas Ryland; Richard Pratt; *Joseph Bird; Edward Rowstone; *Elizabeth Leaver [*marginal entry*: Ex]; *Edward Oakey.
Well Street: *Thomas Collee [*later note*: to attend next time to make out his Settlem[t] *and marginal entry*: Sworn]; *John Davis [*marginal entry*: Cert: dd]; *Oliver Fitzgerald [*later note*: an Irishman no Settlem[t]: in England]; *Thomas Wilson; *Thomas Turvey; Hannah Baker; *William Nash; Joseph Westwood. [*See* **863**, **864**, **867**].

845. Ordered That the several Persons before mentioned who attended do bring Certificates before this day month and that those who did not attend that warrants be made out to apprehend them for that purpose.

846. Signed an Order to remove Esther Todd and James her Son from the Parish of Saint Mary of Stratford Bow in the County of Middlesex to the Parish of Ware in the County of Hertford.

847. Took the Examinacon of Eliz[a] Noades touching her Base Children. Ordered That an adjudication be made out against the putative father thereof.[1]

1. Elizabeth Noades had two illegitimate children, both chargeable to the parish. She identified their father as George Lever of Walthamstow. H.A.D., P/J/P/68.

The Mermaid Tavern: Monday, 24 November 1735
Justices present: Henry Norris, Samuel Tyssen, Alexander Garrett

848. Agreed That William Uxley of the parish of S[t] Mary of Stratford Bow in the County of Middlesex peruke maker be Headborough for the said parish for the remaining part of this year in the room of John Saunders who is removed out of the said parish and until an other shall be chosen in his room or he legally discharged from that Office. Sworn before the s[d]. Justices faithfully to Execute the said Office.

849. Henry Norris Esq[r] Signed a Warrant to apprehend Henry Bridge on the oath of Mary his wife for assaulting and Beating her.

850. Mary Anderson made Oath that she is legally Settled in this Parish.

851. Agreed That Nicholas Graves of the parish of S[t]. John at Hackney in the County of Middlesex Wheelwright be and he is hereby appointed Constable in the room of M[r] James Huggett the late Constable who is removed out of the parish. Sworn before the said Justices duely to Execute the s[d] Office.

852. Henry Smith made oath that he was born at Worsup in Nottingham shire.

The Mermaid Tavern: Monday, 22 December 1735
Justices present: Henry Norris, Samuel Tyssen, Alexander Garrett

853. Henry Norris Esq Signed a warrant to apprehend Edward Taylor the Younger for unlawfully taking away a Duck the property of William Van Leute of the parish of Saint Mary of Stratford Bow in the County of Middlesex on the 11th Instant on his Oath.

854. Ordered That M[r]. Edward Brooksby Churchwarden do pay to Bridget the wife of John Jones five shillings she having four Children to provide for and her husband being out of Business. [*See* **795**].

855. The above named Justices Signed a Summons upon the Complaint of the Survey[rs]. of the Highwayes requiring [*altered from* required] them to give notice to the several Defaulters whose names are Inserted in the said Summons to attend here this day sennight at nine in the morning to shew cause why the Penalty should not be Levy'd upon each of them as the statutes directs.

856. Adjourned to this day Sennight to this Place to nine of the clock in the morning.

The Mermaid Tavern: Monday, 29 December 1735
Justices present: Henry Norris, Samuel Tyssen, Alexander Garrett

857. The above named Justices allowed two pair of Indentures whereby Ann Poole aged twelve years was bound to Thomas Sweatman of the parish of S[t]. Mary White Chapple Cordwainer and Elizabeth Wheeler aged fourteen years was bound to Mary Allen of the parish of S[t] Sepulchres in the City of London Milk Woman. [*See* **840**].

858. Abel Norwood applyed for leave to Sell ale Beer &c at the Adam & Eve in Homerton until the day for Licensing. Agreed That he have leave accordingly.

859. Richard Bryan [and] William Smith, Headboroughs for the Parish of S[t] Mary Stratford Bow in the County of Middlesex for the year 1735 were Sworn before the above named Justices well & truly to Execute that Office.

860. Ordered That M[r] Edward Brooksby the Churchwarden do pay to James Cushion five shillings he having been Sick & being very poor. [*See* **866**, **867**].

861. Henry Norris Esq[r] Signed a warrant to apprehend Shadrack Husslett upon the Oath of Delme Vanheythryson for assaulting and beating him. Bound wth. Sureties to appear at the next General Quarter Sessions.[1]

1. Husslett was indicted at the January sessions for an assault on Vanheythryson and for another, on the same date, on Matthew Coleman. He was convicted and fined 1s. on each charge. MJ/SR/2649, indts. 6 and 7.

The Mermaid Tavern: Monday, 12 January 1736
Justices present: Henry Norris, Samuel Tyssen

862. William Panter made Oath that he was a hired Serv[t] by the Year with John Palmer of the parish of Rame in the County of Cornwall Farmer and served him under that hiring for one whole Year and hath not gained any legal Settlem[t] elswhere.[1]

1. This was Panter's second examination. He had previously been examined in 1726, when he was given two months to obtain a certificate. H.A.D., P/J/P/68.

863. Thomas [*deletion*] Collee made oath that he is an Inhabitant legally Settled in this parish by serving M[r]. Amplius Reepe.[1] [*See* **844**].

1. Colley was rated to the highways (**366**) and had hitherto been excused from the poor rates in the mistaken belief that he was not settled in the parish. H.A.D., P/J/P/86.

The Mermaid Tavern: Monday, 9 February 1736
Justices present: Henry Norris, Samuel Tyssen, Stephen Ram, Alexander Garrett

864. The persons whose names are hereunder written were Summoned to attend this day to give an acco[t] upon Oath of the place of their last legal Settlement Upon the complaint of the Churchwardens and Overseers. To wit,
Mare Street: Richard Maslin; **Sarah Aldwinckle [*later note*: gone away]; Thomas Taylor; **John Bridges [*later note*: Certificate delivered]; **William Battersby [*later note*: gone away]; **James Coldicott [*later note*: gone away]; David East; John Clarke; **Elizabeth Fowles [*later note*: Examined allowed two weeks for a Cert]; Thomas Ryland; **Richard Pratt [*later note*: gone away]; **Joseph Bird [*later note*: Delivered a Certificate]; **Edward Rowton [*altered from* Rowstone] [*later note*: Examined allowed 1 month for a Cert]; **Edward Oakey [*later note*: Delivered a Cert].
Well Street: ***Oliver Fitzgerald [*later note*: An Irishman and no Settle-

ment in England]; Thomas Wilson; ***Thomas Turvey [*later note*: Exam[d] & allowed 2 weeks to bring a certificate]; **Anne [*altered from Hannah*] Baker [*later note*: Examd & allowed 1 month to bring a certificate]; ***William Nash [*later note*: Exm[d] & allowed to continue]; Joseph Westwood.[1] [*See* **844**, **867**].

1. Taylor (of Mare Street) later delivered a certificate, P79/JN1/398.

865. Henry Harrill Headborough made Oath that he Served the several persons whose names are above written to attend this day to give an account of their Settlem[ts]. they not attending ordered That warrants be made out to apprehend them for that purpose against the next meeting.

866. Ordered That James Cushion and his Son be removed to the parish of Morning Thorp in the County of Norfolk the place of his last legal settlem[t].[1] [*See* **860**, **867**].

1. James Cushion, a mason, was certificated and could therefore be removed only if chargeable to the parish. P79/JN1/398.

867. James Cushion Philip Lynam William Nash & Thomas Turvey made Oath of their last legal Settlements. [*See* **844**, **860**, **864**, **866**].

The Mermaid Tavern: Monday, 1 March 1736
Justices present:

The Mermaid Tavern: Monday, 8 March 1736
Justices present: Samuel Tyssen

The Mermaid Tavern: Monday, 29 March 1736
Justices present: Henry Norris, Stephen Ram, Samuel Tyssen

868. William Harwood applyed to have a License at the Ship in Clopton in the Room of [*deletion*] Edmund Matthews removed. Agreed That he be Licensed at the next General meeting to be held for that purpose. [*See* **765**].

869. William Irwin applyed to have a License [*altered from* licensed] to keep an ale house at Newington in the room of Anthony Hargrove removed. Agreed That he be Licensed at the next General meeting to be held for that purpose.

870. Thomas Cooper applyed for a License at the Sign of the Turnpike on Standford Hill in the room of Thomas Enderbery removed. Agreed That he be Licensed at the next General meeting to be held for that purpose.

The Mermaid Tavern: Saturday, 1 May 1736
Justices present: Henry Norris, Samuel Tyssen

871. The person [*sic*] whose names are hereunder written were Summoned to shew cause why they have not paid the poors Rate for the year 1735

Church Street: William Shepherd; Eben^{z}. Braithwaite; The Rev^{d}. M^{r}. John Bridgen; *Henry Davis [*later note*: Excused for this year]; Henry Richard; *Daniel Milner [*later note*: Excused]; *William Davis [*later note*: paid]; William Underhill; *Capt John Pincock [*later note*: paid]; Robt Aldwinckle; John Singleton; James Thompson [*later note*: abated 2^{s}:6^{d}]; Nicholas Graves; Daniel Card.

Mare Street: James Atkins [*later note*: Excused this Year]; Matthias King Esqr; *William Katherines [*later note*: to pay]; William Kingsland; Giles Lomas; Benjamin Barlow; *Joseph Sherbon [*later note*: paid]; Samuel Woodyard [*later note*: to pay]; *Thomas Smith [*later note*: Excused this year]; *Robert Bell [*later note*: to pay].

Homerton: *Elizabeth Holmes [*later note*: Excused being very antient & poor]; *James Bolton [*later note*: Excused for this year]; *Ruth Bolland [*later note*: Excused not being an Inhabitant]; William Peacock; *Robert Glinton [*later note*: paid]; *George Fox [*later note*: Excused not being an Inhabitant]; *Joseph Goodman [*later note*: paid]; George Lewen Esqr; *Henry Vaughan [*later note*: paid]; Thomas Pile; *Ann Stracey [*later note*: Excused]; Henry Godwin; James Sims; James Betts.

Clopton: Mary Ashton; *Elizabeth Barnett [*later note*: paid]; Elizabeth Fenton [*later note*: gone]; John Field; *Samuel Holdsworth [*later note*: Excused]; *Philip Osborne [*later note*: to pay]; Richard Hedge [*later note*: Excused]; *Ann Betts [*later note*: paid *altered from* to pay]; Jeremiah Woodley.

Grove Street: Richard Coleman.

Well Street: *Mary Streetin [*later note*: Excused]; *Robert Wilson [*later note*: to pay *deleted* to pay].

Newington: Henry Donmer; Henry Haughton [*later note*: paid]; Robert Edwards; *Wid^{o}. Frost [*later note*: Excused being very poor]; John Copley; Thomas Barnard.

Shacklewell: Lambert Lance [*later note*: paid]; *Samuel Jordain [*later note*: Excused]; James Mortimer; John Everett.

Dorleston: *John Rogers [*later note*: to pay]; Jacob Hewett [*later note*: gone].

Land Holders: Thomas Waxham; Ralph Harwood Esqr; Lister Selman; Thomas Boots.

872. Agreed That Margaret White be Licensed at the Bird in hand at Newington now the Yorkshire Gray.

The Mermaid Tavern: Monday, 17 May 1736
Justices present: Henry Norris, Stephen Ram, Alexander Garrett

873. In nomination for Overseers for the Year 1736[1]: 13 Richard Speed [*marginal entry deleted*: Excused by Certificate]; 7 Barnard Byfield [*marginal entry*: attended]; 9 Henry Cock [*marginal entry*: appointed]; 8 William Buck; 4 John Burton [*marginal entry*: attended]; 5 John Titcomb [*marginal entry*: attended]; 21 William Stoakes [*marginal entry*:

Excused by Certificate]; 6 Thomas Rudge [*marginal entry*: appointed]; 5 Richard Peacock; 3 John Rochier [*marginal entry*: attended]; 15 Henry Longbottom [*marginal entry*: attended].

1. The figures probably represent the number of years each individual had been a householder.

874. Edward Roberts was Sworne to Execute the Office of Headborough for the parish of St Mary of Stratford Bow for the year ensuing.

875. The following Officers were this day Sworne faithfully to Execute their Offices, To wit, Constables: Robert Loyd, John Townesend. [Headboroughs:] Henry Harrill for Mr John Heasey, Church Street Ward; Daniel Bromwell, Well Street D°; Henry Riddell for Edward Conyears, Church Ward; John Shaw, Mare Street D°; Joseph Hill, Clopton D°; John Archer, Lower Homerton D°; Edward Fox, Dorleston & Kingsland; William Crow, Newington & Shacklewell. Ale Conners: Henry Harrill, Thomas Masling, Robert Reeves.

The Mermaid Tavern: Saturday, 31 May 1736
Justices present: Henry Norris, Samuel Tyssen, Alexander Garrett

876. Mile End Old Towne: William West appealed against poors Rate for 12 [*illegible*] p^{d} a year amounting to 14^{s} for the year 1735 not relieved.

877. Katherine Griffith Wid°. D°, 15 D°, 8^{s} 9^{d}, not relieved.

878. John Pattison complaind upon oath against John Townesend one of the Constables of the parish of St John at Hackney for refuseing to aid [him *deleted*] and assist [*altered from* assisting] him in secureing one John Smith a Diserter whom he had taken on the 20th day of May 1736. John Townesend of the parish of Hackney Carpenter in £20 To appear at the next General Sessions of the Peace to be held for the County of Middlesex at Hicks=hall in S^{t}. John Street then and there to answer the Complaint of John Pattison for refuseing to aid and assist him in Secureing one John Smith a Deserter he being one of the Constables of the s^{d}. parish &c. [*Marginal entries*: Returned *and* Del]. John Pattison of Hackney Labourer £20 To appear at the next General Sessions to prosecute the s^{d} John Townesend for the sd Offence. [*Marginal entry*: Returned] Taken before the above named Justices the 31st day of May 1736.[1]

1. Townesend's recognizance was respited at the June sessions and discharged the following month. Although described here as a carpenter, Townesend was a prosperous master builder. MJ/SBB/935, recog. 81, MJ/SBB/936, recog. h. H.A.D., H/LD/ 7/2.

879. Ann Archer made Oath that Elizabeth Atwood was buryed in Woolen.

880. Isaac Wintell applyed for leave to sell ale & Beer till the next

General Renewing of Licenses at the Naggs head in Mare Street. Agreed That he have leave to sell 'till that time & that he be then Licensed.

881. Allowed a Certificate directed to the Governours of the Hospital of Bethlahem whereby Marg^{t} Baldrey is owned to be Inhabitant Legally settled in the parish of St John at Hackney.[1]

1. She was buried 24 July 1736 at parish expense. P79/JN1/25.

882. Richard Segood was Sworn to serve the Office of Constable for the parish of Bromley Saint Leonard for the year ensuing.

883. Robert Leesh Sworne to Execute the Office of Headborough for the s^{d} Parish.

The Mermaid Tavern: Monday, 14 June 1736
Justices present: Henry Norris, Alexander Garrett

884. Luke Townesend applyed for leave to draw ale in the house late Mr John Woodwards called Tylers Ferry. Agreed That he have leave to draw drink there till the next General meeting for Licensing.

885. The accounts of M^{r}. Francis Cokayne late Church Warden and Overseer of the Poor of the Hamlet of Mile End Old Towne [*deletion*] were this day [*deletion*] laid before the above named Justices whereby it appeared that he hath rec^{d} the sum of £425=1^{s}=3½^{d} and paid the sum of £393=17^{s}=8½^{d} and that is due to ballance the said account the sum of £31=3^{s}=7^{d} which was allowed & Confirmed by them.

886. Also the accompts of Capt John Redman Overseer of the Poor for the said Hamlet for the said Year were likewise allowed & Confirmed by which he [paid *deleted*] appears to have rec^{d} $^{£}$258=6^{s}=1½^{d} and paid £191=1^{s}=5^{d} and there is due from him to ballance the sum of £67=4^{s}=8½^{d}.

887. Granted a warrant to apprehend John Everton for assaulting Mary Wright on her Oath.

888. Elizabeth Bleven made oath that Mary Barr late Deceased was buryed in Sheeps wool only.

889. Henry Harrill made oath that the body of one Isaac lately Deceased was Buryed in Sheeps Wool only.[1]

1. The burial register indicates that this was an unknown labourer. P79/JN1/25.

890. Signed a Warrant to apprehend Thomas Grissell & Samuel Mallion for Intruding into the Hamlet of Mile End Old Towne to Inhabit as parishioners contrary to Law and refuseing or neglecting to attend upon us to give an account touching their last legal Settlement as oath thereof hath been made before us by Christopher Best one of the Overseers of the poor they being likely to become chargeable to the said Hamlet.

891. Thomas Coleman was Sworn to Execute the Office of Headborough for the parish of S[t] John at Hackney for the year ensuing.

The Mermaid Tavern: Monday, 2 August 1736
Justices present: Henry Norris, Samuel Tyssen, Alexander Garrett

892. Elizabeth Spurling made oath that the Body of Mary Spurling was buryed in Sheeps Wool only.

893. Abigal Harwood applyed for Leave to sell Drink at the Sign of the Ship in Clopton till the time of Licensing. Agreed that she have leave accordingly.

894. Richard Herbert applyed for Leave to sell Drink at the sign of the Plow in Homerton. Agreed that he have leave accordingly.

895. John Masling D[o] at the Sun in Church Street. Agreed That he have leave accordingly.

896. Ordered That M[r] William Weston the Churchwarden do forthwith pay to Richard Moore Seven shillings & Six pence to support him on his Journey towards Ireland he being in great want.

897. Signed an Order to remove Mary Jones widow from the Hamlet of Mile End Old Towne in the County of Middlesex to the precinct of Saint Katherines in the same County.

898. Signed an Order to remove Bennett Burdett from the parish of Hackney to the parish of Saint Peter poor in Broad Street in the City of London.

899. Henry Norris Esq[r] Took the Exam[n] of Mary Frances Singlewoman touching her pregnancy who came Voluntarily before him and Signed a warrant at the request of M[r] John Law one of the overseers of the poor of the parish of Saint Mary of Stratford Bow in the County of Middlesex to apprehend William Mealing the putative father.

900. Thomas Hartley was Sworn before the above named Justices to Execute the Office of Ale Conner for the parish of Saint Mary of Stratford Bow.

The Mermaid Tavern: Monday, 27 September 1736
Justices present: Henry Norris, Alexander Garrett

901. Matthew Clarke applyed for leave to sell ale and Beer at the Dunn Mare on Standford Hill in the room of Thomas Enderbury. Agreed That he have leave accordingly.

902. W^m^. Stevens Convicted on his own Confession of Profanely Cursing one [*entry incomplete*].

903. Richard Scandrett applyed for leave to sell ale and Beer at the Dolphin in Mare Street in the room of Wiliam Wilcox removed. Agreed That he have leave accordingly.

904. James Martin applyed for leave to sell ale and Beer at the Dolphin at Kingsland in the room of John Price removed out of the Parish. Agreed That he have leave accordingly.

The Mermaid Tavern: Saturday, 2 October [altered from September] 1736
Justices present: Henry Norris, Stephen Ram, Alexander Garrett

905. Took the affad^{t}. of Mary Deane touching her Settlement which appeared to be in the Hamlet of Mile End old Towne in the County of Middlesex and Signed an order to remove her thither. Also took her Examination touching her pregnancy.[1]

1. Mary Deane identified the father of her child as John Bullmore. She obtained a certificate from Mile End Old Town during 1736, perhaps as a result of this order. H.A.D., P/J/P/68; P79/JN1/398.

906. Ebenezar Braithwaite made oath that William Riceley was buryed in Sheeps wool only.

The Mermaid Tavern: Monday, 25 October 1736
Justices present: Henry Norris, Samuel Tyssen, Stephen Ram

907. Stephen Ram and Samuel Tyssen Esq^{rs} allowed and Confirmed six months Rate for the parish of S^{t}. Mary of Stratford Bow from Ladyday last to Michaelmass following amounting to the Sum of One hundred and Eighteen pounds Seven shillings and [six *deleted*] three pence.

908. M^{r}. William Weston Churchwarden and Overseer of the Poor of the parish of Saint John at Hackney in the County of Middlesex applyed to the above named Justices for a Warrant to Levy the penalty on the person who caused the Body of Martha Adey to be Buryed no affadavit having been made of its being Interred in woolen. Ordered That proper Enquiry be made and a warrant of Distress made out accordingly.

909. Robert Harding applyed for a License to sell ale & Beer at the Sign of the Black Swan on Cambridge Heath in the room of W^{m}. Browne. Ordered That he have leave to draw Drink 'till the Defaulting day for granting of Licenses and that he be then Licensed.

The Mermaid Tavern: Monday, 22 November 1736
Justices present: Henry Norris, Samuel Tyssen, Alexander Garrett

910. Alexander Garrett Esqr Granted a [*deletion*] Warrant to apprehend

John Curtis for leaving his wife and Children without making any provision for them whereby they are become burthensome and Chargeable to the parish of Hackney on the Oath of M^r^. W^m^. Weston Churchwarden. [*See* **211**, **243**].

911. Agreed That a meeting be held here on Thursday the Second day of December next at nine of the clock in the morning to hear the several Defaulters that have neglected to perform their Statute worke on the Highwayes of this parish for this present year.

912. Agreed That Thomas Enderbury have leave to sell Drink at the sign of the Rose & Crowne at Kingsland late John Prices till the next General Meeting for Licensing.

913. Adjorned to Thursday the 2^d^ day of December next, to this place, to nine in the morning.

The Mermaid Tavern: Tuesday, 2 December 1736[1]
Justices present: Henry Norris, Samuel Tyssen, Alexander Garrett

1. The date is incorrect. The clerk originally wrote Tuesday, 2 November then altered it to 2 December (which was a Thursday).

The Mermaid Tavern: Monday, 31 January 1737
Justices present: Henry Norris, Alexander Garrett, Samuel Tyssen

914. A List of the names of the Farmers summoned to appear here this day: Samuel Keep, rents £85 pr ann, worked 6 days, To pay [*marginal entry*: appeared]; Mary Woodfield, rents £400 pr ann, worked 27 D^o^ [*marginal entry*: Francis – appeared]; Katherine Carter, worked 6 D^o^ [*marginal entry*: appeared]; Henry Cock; John Burton, rents £400 pr ann, paid £6 [*marginal entry*: appeared]; William Finch, done; Thomas Wood, rents £170 pr ann [*marginal entry*: appeared]; Robert Iles, rents £90 pr ann, worked 6 [*marginal entry*: appeared]; James Huggett, rents £80 pr ann, paid 16s, worked 4 [*marginal entry:* appeared]; Thomas Monk; William Pratt; William Stoakes; Henry Mills, rents £65 pr ann, worked 5 [*marginal entry*: appeared]; David Taylor; Thomas Rudge, worked 5, to pay £2=16s=0d [*marginal entry*: appeared]; John Hanson, rents [40 *deleted*:] £33=6s pr ann, worked 2 [*marginal entry*: appeared]; Jeremiah Woodley, rents £300 pr ann [*marginal entry*: appeared]; Humphry Woods, rents £42 10s. pr ann, worked 5 [*marginal entry*: appeared]; Samuel Woodfield, rents £400 pr ann, worked 18 [*marginal entry*: appeared]; Bridgman Browne; Elias Woodfield, rents £80 pr ann, worked 6 [*marginal entry*: M^r^ S: Woodfield appeared]; Edward Nutt, rents £200 pr ann, worked 8 [*marginal entry*: appeared]; Ann Bartmaker; Edmund Bellos; Joseph Sureties, rents £100 pr ann, worked 4 [*marginal entry*: appeared]; Joseph Green, worked 4; Henry Donmer; Ann Burton, rents £200 pr ann [*marginal entry*: Mr Jno Burton appeared]; John Townesend; Thomas Coates; Thomas Mealing, keeps 4 teems £3=12=0 [*marginal entry*: Clerk appeared]; Thomas

Waxham; Samuel Forster, rents £119 pr ann, worked 6 [*marginal entry*: M[r] Huggett appear[d]]. [*See* **916**, **917**, **918**, **920**].

915. Adjourned to Thursday next nine in the morning.

The Mermaid Tavern: Thursday, 3 February 1737
Justices present: Henry Norris, Samuel Tyssen

916. A List of the Farmers Summoned to appear here this day: Henry Cock; Thomas Wood; Thomas Monk; William Pratt; William Stoakes; David Taylor; Bridgman Browne; Ann Bartmaker; Edmund Bellos; Joseph Green; Henry Donmer; John Townesend; Thomas Coates; Thomas Waxham. [*See* **914**, **917**, **918**, **920**].

917. Justices Staid 'till Eleven and neither Surveyors or persons Summoned appeared and then went away. Adjourned to Monday next ten in the forenoon. [*See* **914**, **916**, **918**, **920**].

The Mermaid Tavern: Monday, 7 February 1737
Justices present: Henry Norris, Stephen Ram, Samuel Tyssen

918. A list of the farmers summoned to appear here this day: Henry Cock, rents £74 [*altered from* £75] pr ann [*marginal entry*: appeared]; Thomas Wood; Thomas Monk, rents £28 pr ann, worked 3 days [*marginal entry*: appeared]; William Pratt; William Stoakes; David Taylor; Bridgman Browne; Ann Bartmaker, rents £80 pr ann, worked 6 days [*marginal entry*: appeared]; Edmund Bellos, rents £150 pr ann, worked 7 days [*marginal entry*: appeared]; Joseph Green; Henry Donmer, rents £63 pr ann [*marginal entry*: appeared]; John Townesend, worked 3 days [*marginal entry*: M[r] Monk appeared]; Thomas Coates; Thomas Waxham. [*See* **914**, **916**, **917**, **920**].

919. Henry Norris and Stephen Ram Esq[rs] Signed a Summons requiring the several Defaulters hereunder named of the Parish of Bromley S[t] Leonard in the County of Middlesex to appear before them & others his majesties Justices of the Peace for the said County at a Special Sessions to be held for the consideration of the Highwayes at the Court house in White Chapple on Tuesday the 22[d] of this Instant February at ten in the forenoon then and there to answer the Complaint of Thomas Goodyere and John Keene the present Survey[rs]. of the Highwayes of the said parish for neglecting to perform their respective Statute work on the said Highwayes as they are severally by Law Obliged on the Oaths of the said Survey[rs] – To wit, John [Walcutt], Thomas Carter, [*blank*] Walker, [*blank*] Buckworth, Thomas Fisher, John Piggin, Humphry Morris, Walter Baptist, George Richardson, George Roobe, Thomas Debersen, John Holt, James Glinn, John Walden, Michael Sage, Peter Shouler, [*blank*] Wooley, John Harlin; Land Holders: John Orton, John Warren, James Mayfield.

920. M^{r}. Samuel Keep*, [issued] to work 6 dayes, hath worked 6 dayes, to work anno 1736 6, to work anno 1737 6, Rents £85 pr ann, Teems kept 6* 1; M^{rs}. Mary Woodfield* [issued] to work 27 dayes, hath worked 27 dayes, to work anno 1736 34, to work anno 1737 42, Rents £400 pr ann, Teems kept 48*; M^{rs}. Katherine Carter* [issued] to work 6 dayes, hath worked 6 dayes, to work anno 1736 6, to work anno 1737 6, Rents £25 pr ann, Teems kept 6* 1; *Mr Henry Cock* [issued] to work 12 dayes, hath worked 0 dayes, to work anno 1736 15, to work anno 1737 18, Rents £75 pr ann, Teems kept 24* 4; *Mr John Burton* [issued] to work 15 dayes, hath worked 0 dayes, to work anno 1736 28, to work anno 1737 42, Rents £400 pr ann, Teems kept 48*, paid £6; *M^{r}. Thomas Wood* [issued] to work 6 dayes, hath worked 6 dayes, to work anno 1736 12, to work anno 1737 18, Rents £170 pr ann, Teems kept 18*; *M^{r}. Robert Iles* [issued] to work 6 dayes, hath worked 6 dayes, to work anno 1736 6, to work anno 1737 6, Rents £72 pr ann, Teems kept 6*; *M^{r}. James Huggett* [issued] to work 6 dayes, hath worked 6 dayes, to work anno 1736 9, to work anno 1737 12, Rents £80 pr ann, Teems kept 12* 2; M^{r}. Thomas Monk* [issued] to work 3 dayes, hath worked 3 dayes, to work anno 1736 3, to work anno 1737 6, Teems kept 6* 1; M^{r}. William Pratt* [issued] to work 9 dayes, hath worked 2 dayes, to work anno 1736 6, to work anno 1737 6, Rents £80 pr ann, Teems kept 6* 1; M^{r}. William Stoakes*, [issued] to work 6 dayes, hath worked 5 dayes, to work anno 1736 6, to work anno 1737 6, Rents £80 pr ann, Teems kept 6* 1; M^{r}. Henry Mills* [issued] to work 6 dayes, hath worked 0 dayes, to work anno 1736 6, to work anno 1737 6, Rents £65 pr ann, Teems kept 6* 1; M^{r}. David Taylor* [issued] to work 3 dayes, hath worked 2 dayes, to work anno 1736 6, to work anno 1737 6, Teems kept 6* 1; *M^{r}. Thomas Rudge* [issued] to work 12 dayes, hath worked 5 dayes, to work anno 1736 12, to work anno 1737 12, Rents £140 pr ann, Teems kept 12* 2; *M^{r}. John Hanson* [issued] to work 3 dayes, hath worked 2 dayes, to work anno 1736 4, to work anno 1737 6, Rents £33 pr ann, Teems kept 6* 1; *M^{r}. Jeremiah Woodley* [issued] to work 18 dayes, hath worked 13 dayes, to work anno 1736 24, to work anno 1737 30, Rents £300 pr ann, Teems kept 36*; *M^{r}. Henry Donmer* [issued] to work 6 dayes, hath worked 0 dayes, to work anno 1736 6, to work anno 1737 6, Rents £63 pr ann, Teems kept 6* 1; *M^{r}. Humphry Wood* [issued] to work 6 dayes, hath worked 5 dayes, to work anno 1736 5, to work anno 1737 6, Rents £42 pr ann, Teems kept 6* 1; *Mr Samuel Woodfield* [issued] to work 18 dayes, hath worked 6 dayes, to work anno 1736 27, to work anno 1737 36, Rents £400 pr ann, Teems kept 48* -; M^{r}. Bridgman Browne* [issued] to work 6 dayes, hath worked 0 dayes, to work anno 1736 9, to work anno 1737 12, Rents £112 pr ann, Teems kept 12* -, paid £2 8s; M^{r}. Elias Woodfield* [issued] to work 6 dayes, hath worked 6 dayes, to work anno 1736 6, to work anno 1737 6, Rents £80 pr ann, Teems kept 6* -; *M^{r}. Edward Nutt* [issued] to work 12 dayes, hath worked 8 dayes, to work anno 1736 18, to work anno 1737 24, Rents £200 pr ann, Teems kept 24* 2; M^{rs}. Ann Bartmaker* [issued] to work 6 dayes, hath worked 6 dayes, to work anno 1736 9, to work anno 1737 12, Rents £80 pr ann, Teems kept 12* 2; M^{r}. Edm^{d}.

Bellos* [issued] to work 9 dayes, hath worked 7 dayes, to work anno 1736 13, to work anno 1737 18, Rents £170 pr ann, Teems kept 18* 2; *M^{r}. Joseph Sureties* [issued] to work 6 dayes, hath worked 4 dayes, to work anno 1736 9, to work anno 1737 12, Rents £100 pr ann, Teems kept 12*; M^{r}. Joseph Green* [issued] to work 6 dayes, hath worked 4 dayes, to work anno 1736 6, to work anno 1737 6, Rents £56 pr ann, Teems kept 6* -; *M^{rs}. Ann Burton* [issued] to work 12 dayes, hath worked 0 dayes, to work anno 1736 18, to work anno 1737 24, Rents £200 pr ann, Teems kept 24* -; Mr John Townesend* [issued] to work 6 dayes, hath worked 3 dayes, to work anno 1736 6, to work anno 1737 6, Rents £80 pr ann, Teems kept 6* -; M^{r}. Thos. Coates* [issued] to work 9 dayes, hath worked 0 dayes, to work anno 1736 6, to work anno 1737 6, Rents £86 pr ann, Teems kept 6* -; M^{r}. Thos. Mealing* [issued] to work 9 dayes, hath worked 0 dayes, to work anno 1736 16, to work anno 1737 24, Rents £114 pr ann, Teems kept 24* 4, paid £3 12s; M^{r}. Thos. Waxham [issued] to work 6 dayes, hath worked 0 dayes, to work anno 1736 6, to work anno 1737 6, Rents £75 pr ann, Teems kept 6* -; *Saml. Forster Esqr hath worked 4 dayes, to work anno 1736 9 dayes, to work anno 1737 12, Rents £119 pr ann, Teems kept 12* -. [Totals]: [issued] to work 267 dayes, to work anno 1736 252, to work anno 1737 444, Teems kept 480. [*See* **914**, **916**, **917**, **918**].

The Mermaid Tavern: Monday, 21 February 1737
Justices present: Henry Norris, Samuel Tyssen, Stephen Ram, Alexander Garrett

921. Mr John Collings attended and acquainted the Gentlemen Present that he Intends to leave off selling of ale & Beer and therefore desired that M^{r}. Thos Barnard may have a License in his room. Agreed That the s^{d}. Thomas Barnard have leave to draw till the next General renewing upon Mr. Collings's quiting [*sic*] his Licence.

922. Richard Spurling appeared for Ann Newton and told the Gentlemen that he hath hired her but not for a year and that he doth not know her name. [*See* **923**].

The Mermaid Tavern: Monday, 14 March 1737
Justices present: Henry Norris, Samuel Tyssen, Alexander Garrett, Stephen Ram

923. Complaint being made by M^{r}. W^{m}. Weston Churchwarden of the parish of Hackney against Ann Newton Singlewoman that he hath rec^{d}. Information that the said Ann Newton was about four years agoe delivered of female Bastard Child in the said parish called Hannah [and *deleted*] which is likely to become Chargeable to the said Parish. Ordered That the said Ann Newton be Summoned to attend us at the next meeting to be held here in order to be Examined upon Oath touching the [place *deleted*] putative father of the said Female Bastard Child. [*See* **922**].

The Mermaid Tavern: Saturday, 30 April 1737
Justices present: Henry Norris, Stephen Ram, Samuel Tyssen

924. The above named Justices signed the Reassessment for the Window Tax.

925. Roger Lewis applyed to have leave to draw Drink at the Cock in Church Street in the room of James Thompson until the next Licensing. Agreed That he have leave accordingly.

The Mermaid Tavern: Monday, 27 June 1737
Justices present: Henry Norris, Samuel Tyssen, Alexander Garrett, Stephen Ram

926. John Cawne Sworn to Execute the Office of Headborough in the room of Cap[t]. Thomas Pangbourne [*deletion*].

927. M[r]. Markham Spearing applyed for a License for his house in Mare Street late Collings's. The Gentlemen Debateing the matter and there not being any vacancy Do hereby order that no additional License be granted to any person whatsoever.

928. Bromley Grove applyed for leave to sell Ale & Beer at the Red Cow at Dorleston in the room of Edw[d]. Pim. Agreed That he have leave to draw 'till the next General meeting for Licensing.

929. Hugh Davis applyed for a leave to sell Ale & Beer at the sign of the White Lyon in the Hamlet of Mile End old Towne. Agreed That he have leave according to his said request.

The Mermaid Tavern: Monday, 8 August 1737
Justices present: Henry Norris, Samuel Tyssen, Alexander Garrett

930. Mary Beck wid[o]. of Randolph Beck Deceased applyed for leave to sell ale &c at the Sign of the Catt & Shoulder of Mutton 'till the next General renewing. Agreed That she have leave [of *deleted*] accordingly. [*See* **825**, **943**].

931. Francis Stratton applyed for leave to sell ale &c at the sign of the Yorkshire Gray at Newington until the next General renewing of Victuallers Licenses. Agreed That he have leave accordingly.

932. Frances Browne Widow of Ludlow Browne passed from the parish of S[t]. James Clerkenwell to this parish made Oath that about a year and three Quarters ago she was married to the s[d] Ludlow Browne in the Liberty of the Fleet London according to the usage of the Church of England.

933. Took the affad^{t} of Mary Davis touching her Settlement.[1]

1. Mary Davis had a legitimate daughter aged eight and a newborn illegitimate son by her lodger, William Brewis, cordwainer of Tottenham. H.A.D., P/J/P/68.

934. W^{m}. Hall of Dorleston vict^{r} and Richard [*deletion*] Welfford of Bethnal Green vict^{r} were Licensed to sell made wines.

935. Adjourned to Saturday next nine in the morning.

The Mermaid Tavern: Saturday, 13 August 1737
Justices present: Henry Norris, Samuel Tyssen, Alexander Garrett, Stephen Ram

936. The Examination of Elizabeth Hutton widow of John Hutton was taken on oath touching the putative father of her female Bastard Child Born of her Body in the Hamlet of Bethnal Green on the fourth day of July last past and Signed an adjudication against John Varoon the reputed father thereof by Henry Norris and Samuel Tyssen Esq^{rs}.

The Mermaid Tavern: Friday, 2 September 1737
Justices present: Henry Norris, Samuel Tyssen

937. The above named Justices allowed an Indenture of Apprenticeship whereby James Kelly aged twelve years a poor Child of the Hamlet of Mile End Old Towne was bound to Captain William Bowles of the same Hamlet.

938. An order was Signed to remove Elizabeth March from the parish of St John at Hackney in the County of Middlesex to the parish of North Mim17in the County of Hertford as the place of her last legal Settlement.

939. Elizabeth Rhodes passed from the Parish of Saint Sepulcre in the County of Middlesex was Examined and is Settled here by her being bound apprentice to James North a Gardener and serving him above one year & a halfe.

940. John Cubbidge aged seven years Son of John Cubbidge and Elizabeth his wife [*deletion*] passed from the Liberty of Norton Falgate to this parish – Mary Cubbidge wife of W^{m}. Cubbidge made Oath that the said John Cubbidge Settlem^{t} is here in right of her s^{d} Husband who paid all Parochial Taxes in this Parish. [*See* **942**].

941. Elizabeth Bleven made Oath that the bodies of Elizabeth Bailey Prudence Kirby & George Brownsword lately Deceased were Buried in Sheeps Wool only.

942. Henry Norris Esqr granted a Warrant to apprehend Elizabeth Cubbidge Widow of John Cubbidge Deceased for leaving her son John

Cubbidge an Infant without making any Provision for him whereby he is become burthensome & chargeable to the parish of St John at Hackney on the Oath of Robt Aldwinckle Church Warden of the said Parish. [*See* **940**].

943. James Pryor who hath lately married Mary Beck widow of Randolph Beck applyed for leave to Sell ale & Beer at the sign of the Shoulder of Mutton and Cat 'till the next renewing of Licences for the Tower Division. Agreed That he have leave according to his said request. [*See* **930**].

The Mermaid Tavern: Tuesday, 25 October 1737
Justices present: Henry Norris, Samuel Tyssen, Stephen Ram

944. Henry Norris & Samuel Tyssen Esqrs. Signed an Order to remove Mary Spier to the parish of St. Martin in the fields in the County of Middlesex.

945. Ordered That John Harrison aged ten years a poor Child of this Parish do go upon likeing to James Shears a cordwainer who lives adjoyning to the Work house belonging to the parish of St. Giles in the fields in the County of Middlesex. [*See* **947**].

946. Complaint having been made against John Jones who lives at the watch house on the foot way leading to London for suffering several disorders to be committed in the said house so that it is become a nusance to persons passing and repassing that way Do hereby order that the said Jones do forthwith provide another Lodging for himselfe and family and that the sd. House be shut up and fastened in the securest manner as can be.

The Mermaid Tavern: Monday, 12 December 1737
Justices present: Henry Norris, Alexander Garrett, Samuel Tyssen

947. Henry Norris and Alexa Garrett Esqrs. allowed an Indenture of Apprenticeship whereby John Harrison Aged ten years a poor Child of this Parish was bound to James Shears of the parish of St. Giles in the Fields in the County of Middlesex Cordwainer. [*See* **945**].

948. Zacheus Moyse passed from St Botolph without Aldgate Middx: Examined and his settlemt is in this parish.

949. Sarah Holbrook passed from St. Luke in the County of Middx: Examined and her Settlemt is in this parish.

950. Elizabeth Wheatley passed from the Parish of St. Giles in the Fields in the County of Middlesex Examined and said that her husband Joseph Wheatley told her that he served his time with [Mr Wright a *deleted*] Mr. White a Baker in Church Street in Hackney to be further inquired into,

M^r^. Aldwinckle being of Opinion that the said Mr White never had an Apprentice.[1]

1. Elizabeth Wheatley was a widow; Hackney appealed against the removal order, but no verdict has been traced. MJ/SBB/949, p. 23.

951. Adjourned to Saturday next to this place to ten in the forenoon.

The Mermaid Tavern: Saturday, 17 December 1737
Justices present: Henry Norris, Samuel Tyssen, Alexander Garrett

The Mermaid Tavern: Monday, 27 February 1738
Justices present: Henry Norris, Samuel Tyssen, Alexander Garrett

952. Elizabeth [*recte* Anne] Pasfield was Sworne to Execute the Office of Searcher in the room of Elizabeth Bleven Deceased.

The Mermaid Tavern: Saturday, 22 April 1738
Justices present: Henry Norris, Samuel Tyssen, Alexander Garrett

953. William Webb Coachman to Justice Cooke desired leave to sell Ale and Beer at the sign of the Black Bull at Newington 'till the next Licensing. Agreed That he have leave according to his said request.

The Mermaid Tavern: Saturday, 29 July 1738
Justices present: Henry Norris, Samuel Tyssen, Alexander Garrett, Stephen Ram

954. Appellants against the poors Rate of St John at Hackney for the year 1737: M[r] Philip Higman, Rated £2 10s. 0d., Reduced to £1 17s. 6d.; Richard Stoakes, Rated 10s., Discharged; William Hall, Rated 15s., paid; Sarah Potter, Rated £1 5s., reduced to 18s. 9d.; William [*deletion*] Irwin, Rated 18s., to pay; Edward Poole, Rated 15s., reduced to 7s. 6d.; Elizabeth Wilmot, Rated £1 5s., abated, 6s. 3d.; Ann Stracey, Rated 4s., Discharged; Mary Streetin, Rated 5s., Discharged; Thomas Smith, Rated 10s., to pay 7s. 6d.; Ann Williams, Rated 10s., Discharged; Ann Phillipps, Rated 5s., to pay; Ezekiel Calshott, Rated 10s., abated ½ a year, 5s.; Matthew Booth, Rated 15s., reduced to 10s.; William Kingsland, Rated 5s., to pay; Eleanor Atchison, Rated 7s. 6d., to pay; John Goodwin, Rated 7s. 6d. to pay; Henry Mills, Rated £1 13s. 1½d., to pay; William Fenton, Rated 5s., paid; Anthony Ford, Rated £1 8s. 9d., paid; Amy Weskett, Rated 5s., to pay; Eliz[a]. Cotton, wid[o]. of John, Rated 4s., Discharged; Frances Coshed, Rated 5s., Discharged; William Roome, Rated 5s., Discharged; Griffith Owen, Rated 7s. 6d., Discharged; William Thornton, Rated 5s., Discharged; John Baker, Rated 5s., Discharged; William Browne, Rated 10s., reduced to 6s.; W[m]. Everett, Rated 7s. 6d., [paid *deleted*] to pay; Charles Gosdin, Rated 10s., reduced to 5s.; William Chandler, Rated 5s., to pay; John Howard, Rated 10s., to pay; Daniel Milner, Rated 6s. 3d., Discharged.

The Mermaid Tavern: Saturday, 7 October 1738
Justices present: Henry Norris, Alexander Garrett

955. Mary Scott was brought from the Work house and M[rs]. Fisher the Matron of the work house complained that she frequently misbaved [*sic*] her self and hath been very disorderly in the house and upon her promising to behave well for the future Agreed That she be forgiven for what is past but in case she offends again that [she *deleted*] upon Complaint being made that she shall be punished according to Law. [*See* **970**].

956. Mary the wife of Roger Lewis acquainted the Justices that as her husband was going to White Chapple Court house on Tuesday last to renew his License he was arrested and is now in Custody by which he was prevented from renewing the same and therefore desired leave to sell Drink at their house the Sign of the Cock in Church Street in the parish of Hackney until the next day as shall be appointed for granting Licenses. Agreed That the said Roger Lewis have leave accordingly.

957. Agreed That James Martin have leave to sell ale and Beer at the Dolphin at Kingsland for a fortnight from this day.

The Mermaid Tavern: Saturday, 4 November 1738
Justices present: Henry Norris, Samuel Tyssen, Stephen Ram, Col. Alexander Garrett, Robert Paul

The Mermaid Tavern: Friday, 22 December 1738
Justices present: Henry Norris, Samuel Tyssen

958. Allowed and Confirmed a Rate for the relief of the poor of the Hamlet of Mile End Old Town for Six Callender months from Michaelmass last to Lady day next amounting to the sum of One hundred ninety one pounds fifteen shillings and four pence half penny.

959. The Defaulters that have neglected to perform their Statute work on the Highways of the parish of S[t]. John at Hackney were heard.

The Mermaid Tavern: Thursday, 25 January 1739
Justices present: Henry Norris, Samuel Tyssen

960. Hercules Wright applyed for leave to sell ale and Beer at the House late Roger Lewis's the Cock in Church Street 'till the next day appointed for Licensing. Agreed That he leave [*sic*] accordingly.

961. Edward Pimm applyed for leave to sell ale & Beer at the house late Charles Sympsons at Kingsland 'till the next day appointed for Licensing. Agreed That he have leave accordingly.

The Mermaid Tavern: Tuesday, 20 February 1739
Justices present: Henry Norris, Samuel Tyssen, Stephen Ram

962. Henry Norris and Samuel Tyssen Esq[rs]. Signed a Warrant of Distress against the several Defaulters that have neglected to perform their respective days Labour on the Highways within the parish of S^t^. John at Hackney in the County of Middlesex for the year 1738.[1]

1. A copy of the warrant of distress is preserved at MJ/SP/1739/Feb/1.

963. The Several Farmers whose names are hereunder written were summoned to appear this day to shew cause why they have neglected to perform their Statute work with their Teams on the Highways within the parish of Saint John at Hackney in the County of Middlesex for the year 1738: Samuel Woodfield, To pay £4=16s=0d [*marginal entry*: appeared]; William Pratt, and hath worked 8 Days which is 2 more than he is liable to do, [*marginal entry*: appeared]; Edmund Bellos, upon oath 196£ pr ann hath worked 10 days which is in full [*marginal entry*: appeared]; Anthony Ford, worked 6 Days in full [*marginal entry*: appeared]; Jeremiah Woodley, [*marginal entry*: not summoned]; Thomas Mitchell, acknowledged he kept a Teem and promised to pay [*altered to* paid] £2=8s=0d [*marginal entry*: appeared]; Ann Burton, 91£ pr ann worked Six days which is in full [*marginal entry*: Mr John Burton appeared]; Thomas Coates, to pay £2=8s=0d [*marginal entry*: Summoned]; Edward Nutt, to pay [*altered to* paid] £1=12s=0d [*marginal entry*: appeared]; John Burton, 14 [*altered from* 15] days to pay, £5=12s=0d [*marginal entry*: appeared]; Ann Bartmaker, to pay £1=4s=0d [*marginal entry*: Summoned]; Joseph Sureties, paid £3=4s=0d [*marginal entry*: appeared]; Samuel Forster, [*marginal entry*: not summoned]; Bridgman Browne, to pay £4=16s=0d [*marginal entry*: Summoned]; John Townesend, 8[*illegible*] to pay £2=8s=0d [*marginal entry*: Summoned]; Thomas Malland, to pay [*altered to* paid] £12=0s=0d [*marginal entry*: Mr Brewer his Clerk appeared].

The Mermaid Tavern: Saturday, 17 March 1739
Justices present: Henry Norris, Samuel Tyssen

The Mermaid Tavern: Saturday, 28 April 1739
Justices present: Henry Norris, Samuel Tyssen

The Mermaid Tavern: Saturday, 5 May 1739
Justices present: Henry Norris, Samuel Tyssen

The Mermaid Tavern: Saturday, 16 June 1739
Justices present: Henry Norris, Samuel Tyssen, Robert Paul

964. Giles Searle made Oath that he is an Inhabitant Legally Settled in the parish of West Ham in the County of Essex and allowed a fortnight to bring a Certificate.

The Mermaid Tavern: Saturday, 7th July 1739
Justices present: Stephen Ram, Henry Norris, Samuel Tyssen

965. John Weston made Oath that his settlement is in the Parish of Saint

Luke in the County of Middlesex allowed three weeks to bring a Certificate.

966. Thomas Fouch Hackney Coachman attended being Summoned to answer a Complaint Exhibited against him by M[rs]. Mary Ashton of Clopton in the Parish of Saint John at Hackney in the County of Middlesex for giving her very abusive Language. The said M[rs]. Ashton upon her Oath sayes that on Monday the 24th day of June last the said Thomas Fouch brought her in his Coach from Clopton to the Stand by Hackney Church and then refused to carry her to London unless she would pay him more than the usual Fair[1] and Damned her and gave her very abusive Language and when she was out of his Coach and going into an other Coach the said Fouch went before her and Stood in such manner that should not pass by and Insisted upon it that she should not and assaulted her. Bound to appear at the next Quarter Sessions & in the mean time to be of the good behaviour – Thomas Fouch of Hackney Coachman £20; John Tennant of the same Vict[r], Henry Harrill of the same Butcher, each £10.[2]

1. Coach fares were strictly controlled by law (9 Anne c23): the coachman could not charge more than 1s. for a journey of less than one mile four furlongs; the next band (up to two miles) had a maximum fare of 1s. 6d.
2. Fouch was discharged at the July sessions. MJ/SBB/963, recog. 184.

967. James Roff made oath that his legal Settlement is in the Parish of Newnham near Wallingford in the County of Oxford.

968. Adjourned to this Place to this day seve'night to ten in the forenoon.

The Mermaid Tavern: Saturday, 21 July 1739
Justices present: Henry Norris, Samuel Tyssen, Stephen Ram

969. Millason Matthews Daughter of John Matthews made Oath that the Place of her last legall settlement is in the Parish of Castle Campes in the County of Cambridge. Ordered That she be removed to the Place of her legal Settlement.

970. Mary Scott was brought from the Work=house and M[rs]. Fisher the Matron complained against her upon Oath and sayes that she hath frequently Misbehaved herself and been very disorderly and refused to labour towards her subsistance [*deletion*] and she appearing to be a person of a very bad Charachter a Mittimus was made out and Signed and Sealed by [Henry N *deleted*] the above named Justices and sent to the House of Correction. [*See* **955**].

The Mermaid Tavern: Saturday, 29 September 1739
Justices present: Henry Norris, Samuel Tyssen, Stephen Ram, Robert Paul

971. Thomas Collyer & John Fordham were Examined upon Oath touching their last legal Settlement which appears to be in the Parish of Saint John at Hackney.

972. The above named Justices settled the sums of money to be Collected of the Defaulters by William Weston and Samuel Sadleir Surveyors of the Highways of the parish of S[t] John at Hackney.

973. Stephen Ram and Robert Paul Esq[rs] rec[d]. a Complaint from Peter Mangeder on Oath against Elizabeth Bass otherwise Bath and Edward Kingstone from unlawfully and fraudulently removing and Conveying the goods and Chattels of the said Elizabeth out of a Tenement belonging to the said Peter Mangender late in the occupation of the said Elizabeth in order to defraud the said Complainant of the Rent due to him a summons was signed by the s[d] Justices requiring the said Elizabeth Bass otherwise Bath and Edward Kingstone to appear before them to answer the said Complaint at the Mermaid Tavern in Church Street in Hackney on Monday the 15th day of October next at [ten in the forenoon *deleted*] four in the afternoon.

974. Adjourned to this Place to Monday [next *deleted*] the 15th of October next to [ten in the forenoon *deleted*] four in the afternoon.

The Mermaid Tavern: Monday, 15 October 1739
Justices present: Stephen Ram, Henry Norris, Robert Paul

975. The Complaint of M[r] Peter Mangender was heard and there Appeared to be due to him three pounds for three Quarters Rent [from *deleted*] at Michaelmass last from Elizabeth Bass and it also appeared that the goods that were carryed away by Edward Kingstone were goods that his wife Jane Kingston bought of her and in order to settle the Dispute the said Elizabeth Bass gave the said Peter Mangender her promissory note for three pounds for the s[d]. Rent due as aforesaid and four shillings for two Handkerchiefs she bought of him payable Six Months after date for value received and the said Peter Mangender gave the said Elizabeth Bass a Receipt for the said Promissory Note which when paid is in full of all Demands.

The Mermaid Tavern: Saturday, 27 October 1739
Justices present: Henry Norris, Samuel Tyssen

The Mermaid Tavern: Saturday, 5 January 1740
Justices present: Henry Norris, Ebenezer Mussell

976. John Martin desired leave to sell ale & Beer at the sign of two Brewers at Newington in the room of Anthony Hargrove. Agreed that he have leave according to his said request.

977. I Rebecca Child wife of Anthony Child do upon oath say that I apprehend myself to be in Danger of my life or of some bodily hurt my said husband will do cause or procure to be done unto me and that I desire the peace of him not out of any malice vexation or revenge but for the causes aforesaid. [*signed*] Rebecca Child. Sworn before us the 5th day of January 1740 [*signed*] Ebenez^r^. Mussell, Henry Norris. Anthony Child of the Parish of Saint John at Hackney in the County of Middx: Carpenter £200, W^m^. Griffith of the same parish Gardener, John Bates of the Parish of St Mary White Chappel Carpenter, each £100. Upon condition that the above bound Anthony Child personally appeareth at the next General Sessions of the peace to be held for the County of Middlesex at Hicks hall in Saint John Street then and there to answer the Complaint of Rebecca Child his wife she having Sworn the peace against him and that he shall in the meantime keep the peace towards all his Majesties Subjects especially towards his said wife and not depart the Court without Licence Then this recognisance to be void &c. Taken and acknowledged the day and year first above written. [*See* **317**].

The Mermaid Tavern: Monday, 17 March 1740
Justices present: Henry Norris, Samuel Tyssen

978. George Trussell applyed and desired leave to Draw Drink at the house late Edward Coopers Deceased the sign of the Cock the halfe way house to Newington 'till the next day appointed for granting Licences. Agreed That he have leave according to his said request.

The Mermaid Tavern: Saturday, 26th April 1740
Justices present: Henry Norris, Robert Paul

979. Thomas Wood made Oath that his Settlem^t^ is in the parish of Fassfield in the County of Suffolk.

980. Thomas Dodson Complained against Anthony Ford a Farmer for refuseing to pay him his wages. Ordered That his Master be Summoned to attend here on Wednesday next at four in the afternoon.

981. The Persons whose names are hereunder written were returned by the Vestry to His Majesties Justices of the Peace for them to nominate and appoint Overseers of the Poor for the year 1740. To wit: Barnard Byfield; Joseph Faikney; Nathaniel Geary; James M^c^Gill; William Catling, [*marginal note*: appointed]; John Ellicott; Robert Grubb; Joshua Odams; John Rochier; Henry Baker; Lambert Lance; Lee Steere; Gerrard Vanheythusen; Nathaniel Green.

982. The following Persons were Sworn. Constables: Daniel Bromwell; William Streetin; John Hampson. Headboroughs: Henry Harrill for W^m^. Napton; George Kello for Lee Steere; William Holford for W^m^. Reynolds; Charles Gosdin for Caesar Glusslin; Thomas Cooper for Joshua Odams; John Archer for William Pratt, Isaac Estwick; James

Martin for James Mortimer. Ale Conners: William Newman; John Harbert for Thomas Slater; Henry Harrill for John Beard.

983. Adjourned to this Place to Wednesday next four in the afternoon.

The Mermaid Tavern: Wednesday, 30 April 1740
Justices present: Henry Norris, Samuel Tyssen

984. M^{r}. Robert Grubb a substantial Householder of the Parish of Saint John at Hackney in the County of Middlesex was was [*sic*] by a Warrant under the hands and Seals of the above named Justices nominated and apointed one of the overseers of the poor of the said parish for the year ensuing.

985. Hannah Harrison wife of William Harris gave an accompt upon Oath of the Place of her last legal Settlement.

The Mermaid Tavern: Saturday, 23 August 1740
Justices present: Henry Norris, Samuel Tyssen

986. John Owen applyed for leave to Draw Drink at the three Cups in Mare Street in the Room of Ezekiel Colchett till the General Renewing of Licences. Agreed That he have leave accordingly.

The Mermaid Tavern: Friday, 17 October 1740
Justices present: Henry Norris, Samuel Tyssen

987. Richard Harbert allowed to Draw 'till the next General Renewing.

988. Joseph Wright desired leave to Draw till the next General Meeting. Agreed That he have leave accordingly.

The Mermaid Tavern: Saturday, 8 November 1740
Justices present: Henry Norris, Samuel Tyssen

989. William Cox Complained against William Hohnstead and James House for breaking down the Fence belonging to his Garden Ground. Repremanded and discharged.

The Mermaid Tavern: Friday, 21 November 1740
Justices present: Henry Norris, Samuel Tyssen

990. The several Persons whose names are hereunder Written were Summoned to appear this day to give an accompt upon oath of the places of their last legal Settlements.
Church Street: William Greenwood, Sworn allowed one Month to bring a Certificate; John Moody, Sworn allowed three weeks to D^{o}; John Jebb, appeared, not Sworn allowed one month D^{o}; Thomas Cooke the Younger, Did not appear; William Robertson, Did not appear; Thomas Dawson, Did not appear; Susannah Thompson, Sworn allowed two weeks to bring a Certificate; Joseph Swaby, Gone away; George Bull-

worthy, Sworn allowed one month to get a Cert; Rowland Michael, To be Summoned again.
Mare Street: John Shepherd, Sworn Settlement in this Parish; Elizabeth Best, Did not appear; Mary Ambrose, Sworn allowed two Weeks to bring a Cert; Thomas Uppington, Did not appear, Delivered a Certificate; William Nash, Did not appear;
Thomas Thornton, Did not appear; Henry Currell, Sworn allowed two Weeks to bring a Cert; Eleanor Kettle, Did not appear; George Felton, Did not appear; Andrew Guy, Did not appear.
Homerton: Richard Smith, Sworn allowed two Weeks to bring a Certificate; Elizabeth Samuel, Did not appear; John Sowden, Sworn allowed two Weeks to bring a Cert; Austin Tyer, Sworn allowed two weeks to bring a Cert; Thomas Brignall, Sworn allowed two Weeks to bring a Cert.[1] [*See* **992**, **999**, **1000**, **1129**].

1. John Jebb and Thomas Cooke (both of Church Street) appear as ratepayers at **1030** and **1124** below. Austin Tyer obtained a certificate during the course of the year. P79/JN1/398.

991. Henry Harrill made oath that the several Persons above named that did not appear were duly Summoned. Ordered That warrants be made out to oblige them to give an accompt of their Settlements.

The Mermaid Tavern: Friday, 28 November 1740
Justices present: Henry Norris, Samuel Tyssen

992. The several Persons whose names are hereunder Written were Summoned to give an accompt of their Settlements, To wit,
Homerton: William Naish, Sworn, 1 month allowed to bring Cert; Edward Carns, To be summoned again; John Watson, Did not attend; Richard Grathey, Sworn, allowed 1 week to bring a Cert; John Cresey, Did not attend; William Trepass, Sworn, 1 Month Allowed to bring Cert; Joseph Bodnam, Sworn, 2 Weeks Allowed to bring Cert; John Bull, Sworn, 2 D° Allowed to bring Cert; Biss Somers, Sworn, 1 Month Allowed to bring Cert; Richard Lord, Sworn, Settled here; Isaac Waters, Sworn, 2 Weeks Allowed to bring Cert; Marsh Clarke, Sworn, till the 1st January 1741 Allowed to bring Cert; Thomas Read, Sworn, 1 Month Allowed to bring Cert; Rowland Mitchell, respited. [*The remaining names are separated from the others by an oblique in the original manuscript*] Willam Robertson, Sworn, 2 Weeks Allowed to bring Cert; Thomas Thornton, Sworn; Thomas Cooke Junr, Sworn, 2 Weeks Allowed to bring Cert. [*See* **758**, **990**, **999**, **1000**].

The Mermaid Tavern: Friday, 2 January 1741
Justices present: Henry Norris, Samuel Tyssen

993. The Defaulters that have neglected to perform their Statute work on the Highways within the said Parish for the year 1740 were Summoned to shew cause why the Penalty should not be Levy'd on each of them.

The Mermaid Tavern: Friday, 16 January 1741
Justices present: Henry Norris, Samuel Tyssen

994. The Persons whose names are hereunder Written were Summoned to give an acco^{t} of the Places of their last legal Settlements, To wit – *Clopton*: Robert Tate, Sworn, allowed 2 weeks to bring a Certificate; John Knight, Sworn anno 1731, 2 D^{o}; Thomas Wilson, Sworn, 4 D^{o}; Thomas Lamb, Sworn, 2 D^{o}; Thomas Hodges, Sworn, 8 D^{o}; Thomas Cross, Sworn, 2 D^{o}; Joseph Shaw, Sworn, 3 D^{o}; William Colurn, Sworn, 4 D^{o}; William Unkles, did not attend; John Clemmons, gone away; Sarah Pike, did not attend.
Newington: James Weedon, did not attend; Philip Doucett, did not attend; Thomas Vine, did not attend; Jane Thompson, Sworn, 2 D^{o}; Richard Adams, Sworn, 2 D^{o}; John Cragg, Exciseman, Excused; Mariam Fisher, did not attend; Benjamin Manning, Sworn, 2 Weeks;[1] Joseph Harris, Sworn, 2 Do; James Browne, did not attend; Thomas Rowley, Sworn, 6 Months; Elizabeth Webb, gone away; Susannah Tarry, delivered a Certificate. [*See* **362**, **377**, **384**, **995**].

1. Benjamin Manning delivered a certificate. P79/JN1/398.

995. *Clopton*: William Unkles; Sarah Pike.
Newington: James Weeden; Philip Doucett; Thomas Vine; Marriam Fisher; James Browne.
Henry Harrill made Oath before the above named Justices that the several Persons above named that did not appear were duly Summoned. Ordered That Warrants be made out to oblige them to give an accompt of their respective Settlements. [*See* **994**].

The Mermaid Tavern: Saturday, 14 February 1741
Justices present: Henry Norris, Samuel Tyssen

996. Mr John Cox Church Warden and Overseer of the Poor of the Parish of St John at Hackney in the County of Middlesex made oath that Eleanor the wife of Miles Nuttbrowne very lately applyed to him for relief for her and her child and Complained that her said husband would not make any provision for her and that she was in necessitous Circumstances and that the said John Cox did relieve her accordingly and the said Eleanor also testifyed the same on her oath. The said Justices thereupon Issued out a Warrant at the request of the said John Cox to apprehend the said Miles Nuttbrowne to answer the said Complaint and to be further dealt with according to Law. [*See* **127**, **343**].

997. Elizabeth Burrell applyed and desired leave to draw Drink at the House late Edward Poole's the Sign of the Lamb in Homerton. Agreed That she have accordingly 'till the next General Renewing of Victuallers Licences.

998. Ordered That Mr John Cox do pay to James Arnold Sixteen shillings for nursing and maintaining two Children of William Ingles for one

Month who went away and left them without making any provision for them.

The Mermaid Tavern: Saturday, 21 February 1741
Justices present: Henry Norris; Samuel Tyssen

999. The Persons whose names are hereunder Written Were Summoned to give an accompt upon Oath of the place of their respective last legal settlem^t – To wit
Homerton: Thomas Thornton, did not attend; John Dunkley, Sworn, allowed 3 weeks to bring a Cert;[1] Sarah Jones, Sworn; Thomas Wright, Sworn, 2 Weeks; James Gaskin, Sworn, hath been a Soldier; William Streeton, did not appear.
Clopton: Joseph Smith, To be summoned again being Sick; William Simmonds, did not attend.
Well Street: Margaret Dudrige, Sworn; Arthur Elles, Sworn; Edward Barrow, did not attend.
Kingsland: Henry Stedman, did not attend; William Long, Sworn, Settled here; Thomas Baldwin, Sworn, 4 Weeks; George Tongue, Sworn, 2 weeks; Samuel Kidman, Sworn, 2 Weeks. [*See* **990**, **992**, **1000**, **1003**].

1. John Dunkley obtained a certificate in 1755. P79/JN1/398.

1000. Warrant to be made out against the following Persons on the Oath of Henry Harrill – To wit, Thomas Thornton, William Streetin, William Simmonds, Edward Barrow. [*See* **990**, **992**, **999**].

The Mermaid Tavern: Thursday, 23 April 1741
Justices present: Henry Norris, Stephen Ram, Robert Paul

1001. David Jones allowed [leave *deleted*] to Draw ale & Beer &c at the Shoulder of Mutton & Welch Harp 'till the day for Licensing.

1002. The following Peace Officers were Sworn duly to Execute their respective Offices. To wit, Constables: Samuel Woolmer, Alexander Spurling. Headboroughs: Thomas Cooper for Nathaniel Geary; George Kello for Samuel Trench Esq; Thomas Masling; Henry Harrill for Thomas Rayner; Anthony Ford; Charles Gosdin for Samuel Sumner; Henry Vaughan; John Darnell; James Martin for William Pamplin. Ale Conners: Henry Harrill for Abraham Byde; John Eyles; Robert Edwards.[1]

1. The draft minutes also add to the list of constables: John Holford Sworn at Slaters Coffee House before Mr Norris & Mr Tyssen.

The Mermaid Tavern: Friday, 31 July 1741
Justices present: Henry Norris, Samuel Tyssen

1003. The Persons whose names are hereunder Written were Summoned to give an accompt of their respective settlements, To wit

Church Street: Susannah Joyce, respited; Henry Burtwell, did not appear.
Mare Street: Mary Fenton, did not appear.
Well Street: William Miller, did not appear.
Homerton: John Farrington, did not appear; Isaac Fox, Examined; George Jackson, did not appear.
Shacklewell: Thomas Horton, Examined.
Kingsland: Samuel Colbey, Examined; Richard Harper, did not appear; Simon Compton, Examined; Mark Carter, did not appear; William Long, Examined; Sarah Arnold, did not appear.
Dorleston: William Hampshire, did not appear.[1] [*See* **999**].

1. Simon Compton (of Kingsland) was probably removed. William Long (also of Kingsland) appears as a ratepayer at **1014**, below. H.A.D., P/J/P/68.

1004. Ordered That the several Defaulters above mentioned be brought in by warrant Henry Harrill having made Oath that they were duly Summoned.

1005. Sarah the wife of Thomas Woodward and their two Children were passed from the Hamlet of Mile End Old Town hither and she made Oath that her said Husband Rented a House in Homerton in this parish at the yearly Rent of fourteen pounds and occupyed the same for three years & paid all Taxes. Certificate granted to the said Hamlet.

1006. Ordered That several Officers of this Parish for the years 1737, 1738, 1739, & 1740 be Summoned to appear at a Petty Sessions to be held here on Fryday the fourteenth day of August next at ten in the forenoon and then lay before his Majesty's Justices of the Peace as shall be here present their accompts in writing of all money by them respectively received and paid in discharge of their respective Offices in order that they be Examined according to Law.

1007. Adjourned to this Place to Fryday the 14th day of August next to ten in the forenoon.

The Mermaid Tavern: Friday, 14 August 1741
Justices present: Henry Norris, Samuel Tyssen

1008. The accompts of M^{r}. Robert Aldwinckle Deceased Churchwarden & Overseer of the Poor for the years 1737, 1738, and part of the year 1739 were laid before the s^{d} Justices by which it appeared that he received the sum of One Thousand Eight hundred and Sixty pounds nine shillings and one penny three farthings and that he paid away in the discharge of his said Office the sum of One thousand Eight hundred and fifty four pounds Eleven shillings and four pence farthing so that there is remaining in his Executrix hands and due to the Parish to Ballance the said Accompts the sum of Five pounds seventeen shillings and nine pence half penny.[1]

1. Aldwinckle had continued in office so long because of the vestry dispute over the turnpike (see introduction). By custom he should have been succeeded by Thomas Rudge, the junior church warden, but Rudge was the leader of the opposition to the turnpike and the gentlemen of the vestry therefore refused to appoint him. Litigation ensued and Aldwinckle remained in office until an amicable settlement was reached in 1739. H.A.D., D/F/TYS/12/1.

1009. Samuel Sadleir Overseer of the Poor for the year 1739 laid his acc[t] before the above named Justices by which it appeared that he received the sum of Five hundred forty Six pounds Eleven shillings and Eleven pence and that he paid away in the discharge of his said Office the sum of five hundred and thirty five pounds One shilling & Six pence so that there is remaining in his hands and due to the parish to Ballance his said accompts the sum of Eleven Pounds ten shillings and five pence.

1010. The above accompts were approved of and confirmed by the above named Justices under their hands & Seals and the several Ballances Ordered to be paid to M[r] Edward Nutt the present Church Warden and Overseer of the Poor to the use of the Parish.

1011. M[r]. Robert Grubb and M[r]. William Catlin Overseers of the Poor for the year 1740 attended and acquainted the Justices that they have endeavoured to finish their Collections but that there are a considerable number of persons in arrear whose names are contained in a List by them delivered in and pray'd that the said Justices will be pleased to grant their Warrant for Summoning them to appear before them on such day as they shall think proper to shew cause why they have refused or neglected to pay the sums which they are respectively Rated and assessed and to be proceeded against according to Law. Ordered That they be Summoned to appear at a Petty Sessions to be held here on Fryday the twenty first of this Instant August at nine in the morning.

1012. M[r] John Cox Church Warden and Overseer of the Poor for the year 1740 pray'd further time to prepare his accompts.

1013. Adjourned to this place to Fryday next to nine of the Clock in the morning.

The Mermaid Tavern: Friday, 21 August 1741
Justices present: Henry Norris, Samuel Tyssen

1014. The Persons whose names are hereunder Written were Summoned to appear this day to shew cause why they have refused or neglected to pay the several Sums which they are Rated and Assessed towards the relief of the poor of the parish of Saint John at Hackney in the County of Middlesex for one year ending at Lady day 1741 and why a Warrant of Distress should not be Issued out to Levy the same as the

Law directs. [*Marginal entry*: Mr Robt Grubb, and Mr W^m. Catlin, Overseers.]
Church Street: fo. 2, Samuel Keep rated £2, to pay £1 16s.; fo. 4, Sarah Smith rated 10s., gone; fo. 6, Henry Tysoe rated 5s., gone; Richard Upton rated 10s., paid; fo.7, Thomas Huckfield rated 5s., paid; Richard Spurling rated 6s. 3d., Excused; fo. 8, John Masling rated 10s., Excused; fo. 11, Daniel Milner rated 6s. 3d., Excused; Margaret Jefferies rated 12s. 6d., Dead; fo. 14, Solomon Sanches rated £1 5s., gone; fo. 19, George Harrison rated 7s. 6d., paid; Ebenezer Braithwaite rated 10s., to pay; fo. 20, William Walker rated 7s. 6d., gone; fo. 21, John [James *deleted*] Freeman rated 6s. 3d., to pay; fo. 22, Joseph Ingleton rated 5s., Excused; fo. 23, Robert Gambell rated 10s., paid 7s. 6d.; Mary Kennett rated 12s. 6d., paid; John Brookes rated 7s. 6d., gone; Samuel Bennett rated 10s., to pay; fo. 25, Hercules Wright rated 10s., to pay; William Griffith rated 5s., paid.
Mare Street: fo. 29, Mary Lee rated 12s. 6d., paid; fo. 30, Elizabeth Perkins rated 6s. 3d., paid; fo. 35, John Owen rated 10s., paid 5s.; fo. 37, Matthew Eaglesoe rated 7s. 6d., to pay; Robert Wilson rated 5s., Excused; fo. 39, Thomas Shepperson rated 4s., Excused; Angelo Ancona rated £1 17s. 6d., to pay; fo. 42, James Pryor rated 12s. 6d., gone; fo. 43, Catherine Carter rated 12s. 6d., gone; fo. 45, Ann Phillipps rated 5s., to pay; William Browne rated 10s., paid; fo. 50, Martha Cams rated 10s., Paid; fo. 52, Barnard Merest Byfield rated 18s. 9d., paid 9s. 4½d.; Leonard Browne rated 5s., to pay; fo. 53, John Titcomb rated 10s., Dead; fo. 54, William Fating rated 12s. 6d., to pay.
Homerton: fo. 59, John Fletcher rated 6s. 3d., to pay; fo. 60, The Revd George Kenwrick rated 12s. 6d., gone; fo. 62, Edward Ireson rated 10s., Dead; fo. 63, Katherine Davey rated 7s. 6d., to pay; fo. 64, Edward Poole rated 7s. 6d., gone; Robert Dumbleton rated 7s. 6d., Excused; John Dawson rated £2 10s., to pay; fo. 65, John Harcourt rated £1, paid ¼, 5s.; John Lane rated £1 5s., gone; fo. 66, Richard Griffin rated £1 5s., gone; Silas Hooper rated £1 11s. 3d., to pay; fo. 67, John Hancock rated 7s. 6d., paid 3s. 9d.; fo. 68, Hugh Lake rated 10s., to pay; fo. 69, John Coxall rated 7s. 6d., Excused; Thomas Hyde rated £1 6s. 10½d., to pay; fo.72, Richard Worthley rated 10s., gone; Jane Stoakes rated £2 8s. 9d., to pay; fo. 73, John Townesend rated £2 2s. 6d., In Goal; fo. 75, Ann White rated 5s., to pay; James Kemp rated 5s., Excused; Ann Williams rated 10s., Excused; Philip Barnes rated 15s., paid 7s. 6d.; fo. 78, John Giles rated £1 5s., to pay; Henry Hedger rated 5s., gone; fo. 80, Thomas Soper rated 12s. 6d., to pay 4s. 4½d.; Abraham Felstead rated 15s., to pay; fo. 81, Joseph Wright rated 10s., paid; Thomas Wight rated 15s., to pay; fo. 85, John Streetin rated 10s., to pay.
Clopton: fo. 87, Abraham Lurie rated 15s., to pay; fo. 88, Moses Jesseron rated 6s. 3d., paid; fo. 89, Pain Maples rated 12s. 6d., gone; fo. 90, Mary Ashton rated 15s., gone; Henry Boon rated £1 5s., Dead; fo. 93, William Cawne rated 7s. 6d., to pay; Margaret Gelding rated 7s. 6d., to pay; fo. 95, Thomas Underwood rated 15s., to pay 10s.; fo. 98, James Matthews rated 6s. 3d., Excused; fo. 100, Elizabeth Rotherford

rated 6s. 3d., Excused; James Conniers rated 10s., to pay; fo. 103, Mary Townesend rated 5s., Excused; Nicholas Bartmaker rated £2 3s. 9d., to pay; Humphry Woods rated £2 2s. 4½d., to pay; fo. 104, Richard Slater rated £1 5s., gone.
Grove Street: fo. 106, John Coombes rated 5s., paid.
Well Street: fo. 109, Mary Streetin rated 5s., gone; Charles Gosdin rated 5s., Excused; fo. 112, Christopher Harris rated 7s. 6d., gone; Robert Day rated 12s., gone; Henry Hyde rated 5s., Excused.
Newington: fo. 116, Francis Stratton rated 10s., gone; fo. 117, Robert Edwards rated 7s. 6d., paid; William Everett rated 7s. 6d., gone; John Martin rated 7s. 6d., gone; fo. 119, John Copley rated 6s. 3d., Excused; Thomas Barnard rated 6s. 3d., Excused; fo. 121, Samuel Cross rated 10s., gone; Benjamin Cokayne rated £1 5s., gone.
Shacklewell: fo. 124, James Mortimer rated £1 10s., paid 15s.; William Roome rated 5s., Excused; fo. 125, Ann Holloway rated 5s., Dead.
Kingsland: fo. 126, James Martin rated 5s., to pay; Edward Pim rated 10s., Dead; John Knott rated 10s., gone; William Newton rated 5s., to pay; William Long rated 10s., to pay; John Chivers rated 10s., paid 6s. 3d.; James Kroger rated 10s., gone; fo. 127, Ann Bartmaker rated £1 17s. 6d., to pay; William Pegsworth rated 6s. 3d., paid; fo. 128, Mary Cuthburt rated 7s. 6d., gone; Mary Askew rated 7s. 6d., to pay.
Dorleston: fo. 131, Charles Bishop rated 5s., Excused.
Land Holders: fo. 133, Benjamin Coker Junr rated £2 13s. 9d., to pay; Ralph Harwood Esqr rated £1, to pay; fo. 136, Widow Chavalier rated 1s. 3d., to pay.

The Mermaid Tavern: Saturday, 24 October 1741
Justices present: Henry Norris, Ebenezer Mussell

1015. The above named Justices settled the sumes to be paid by the Inhabitants of the parish of S^t. John at Hackney that have made default to perform their Statute work for this present year.

1016. Allowed an Indenture of apprenticeship whereby Sarah Collyer was bound to Ann Browne of St Leonard Shoreditch Widow.

1017. John Parr was Examined upon oath touching the Place of his last Legal Settlem^t which is in the parish of St John at Hackney by being a hired Servt by the year to M^rs. Bates and serving her for three or four years.

The Mermaid Tavern: Thursday, 28 January 1742
Justices present:

The Mermaid Tavern: Thursday, 11 February 1742
Justices present: Henry Norris, Ebenezer Mussell

1018. The following persons that have made default to perform their Statute work for the year 1741 were Summoned to appear this day to shew cause why they made default & have refused to pay in lieu thereof & why a Warrant of Distress should not be Issued out to Levy the same as the Law directs. [*No list of names follows*].

1019. Agreed That John Davidson at the Riseing Sun in Church Street have leave to draw Drink 'till the next General Meeting for Licensing Victuallers.

The Mermaid Tavern: Saturday, 15 May 1742
Justices present: Henry Norris, Samuel Tyssen

1020. The Persons whose names are hereunder Written were by the vestry belonging to the parish of Saint John at Hackney in the County of Middlesex returned to the said Justices of the Peace for them to nominate and appoint Overseers of the Poor of the said parish for the year 1742, To wit: John Southern, hath been a housekeeper 19 yrs; Edward Conyers, hath been a housekeeper 18 yrs, appointed; Daniel Bromwell, hath been a housekeeper 16 yrs; Thomas Masling, hath been a housekeeper 14 yrs, appointed; Joseph Parsons, hath been a housekeeper 14 yrs; Edmond Bellis, hath been a housekeeper 11 yrs; William Reeves, hath been a housekeeper 11 yrs; Samuel Brasier, hath been a housekeeper 10 yrs; Thomas Slater, hath been a housekeeper 10 yrs; Jacob Marson, hath been a housekeeper 13 yrs; Gerrard Vanheythussen, hath been a housekeeper 19 yrs; Edward Dixon, hath been a housekeeper 8 yrs; John Collett, hath been a housekeeper 8 yrs; Joshua Odams, hath been a housekeeper 12 yrs [*marginal entry*: Dead]; James Holmes, hath been a housekeeper 7 yrs; Joseph Faikney, hath been a housekeeper 6 yrs; Thomas Warren, hath been a housekeeper 12 yrs; John Tennant, hath been a housekeeper 7 yrs; William Napton, hath been a housekeeper 9 yrs. [Total] 19.

1021. Warrants were Signed and Sealed by the above named Justices whereby Joseph Sureties & Henry Cocks Church Wardens of the said parish of St John at Hackney and Edward Conyers Thomas Masling and Samuel Sadleir were appointed Overseers of the Poor of the said parish for the year 1742.

1022. The Persons whose names are hereunder set down were Elected at the Court Leet to Execute the following Offices for the year 1742.
Kings Hold: Constable, John Shaw. Headboroughs: Thomas Russell, Church Street Ward, Sworn; Joseph Moore, Well Street Do, Sworn. Ale Conner: George Hawksford Sworn [for] Jonathan Newton.
Lords Hold: Constables: Jonathan Collyer Esqr; Mr James Lewis Berchers. Headboroughs: Thomas Cooper [for] Henry Swell, Church Street Ward; W^m^. Katherines [for] George Collins, Mare Street; William Cawne [for] Thomas Warren, Clopton; Henry Harrill [for] Stamp Brooksbank Esqr, Upper Homerton; John Coombes, Grove Street, Sworn; Robert Reynolds, Dorleston and Kingsland, Sworn in Court; John Daniel, Newington & Shacklewell, Sworn; Thomas Pile, Lower

Homerton, Sworn. Ale Conners: William Wood, Sworn; Robert Merriton, Sworn.

1023. Samuel Sadleir's Bill for Business done for the Parish from the twenty third day of Aprill 1741 to the fourteenth day of May 1742 amounting to the sum of thirty two Pounds Sixteen shillings and two pence was Examined.

The Mermaid Tavern: Friday, 6 August 1742
Justices present:

The Mermaid Tavern: Friday, 19 November 1742
Justices present: Henry Norris, Samuel Tyssen

1024. Agreed That John Doe at the Black Bull at Newington and Samuel Meager at the Red Cow at Dorleston have leave to Draw Drink at their respective Houses 'till the next meeting for Licensing.

The Mermaid Tavern: Tuesday, 22 February 1743
Justices present: Henry Norris, Samuel Tyssen

1025. Agreed That John Southern and Thomas Blemeney be appointed Survey[rs] of the Highways of this parish for the year ensuing.

The Mermaid Tavern: Saturday, 30 April 1743
Justices present: Henry Norris, Samuel Tyssen

1026. The following persons are in nomination to be Overseers of the poor for the year 1743, To wit, Daniel Bromwell, John Tennant, Richard Parsons, William Napton, Edmund Bellis, James Holmes, Thomas Slater, Jacob Marsom, Robert Reeves, Edward Dixon appointed, John Southern, Samuel Brazier appointed, John Collett.

1027. W[m]. Smith to be bound to M[r]. John Woolveridge Plaisterer Church Warden to pay him forty shillings with him and Seventeen shillings which he must pay for his Bedding he being a freeman of the City of London.

1028. The Persons whose names are hereunder set down were Elected at the Court Leet to Execute the following Offices, To wit,
Lords Hold: Constables: John Cox; Thomas Bridgman. Headboroughs: Benjamin Cooper, [Mare *deleted*] Church Street Ward; William Katharines, Mare Street Ward; Matthew Booth, Clopton, Sworn; Thomas Rudge, Upper Homerton; Matthew Burgoin, Lower Homerton, Sworn; Henry Harrill Sworn [for] John Clarke, Grove Street; William Pegsworth, Dorleston and Kingsland, Sworn; Robert Edwards, Newington & Shacklewell, Sworn. Ale Conners: William Fenton, Sworn; William Lacy, Sworn.
Kings Hold: Constable: William Yelloly. [Headboroughs:] William

Plant, Church Street Ward, Sworn; Thomas Kirke, Well Street Ward, Sworn. Ale Conner: Nathaniel Green.

The Mermaid Tavern: Tuesday, 10 May 1743
Justices present: Henry Norris, Samuel Tyssen

1029. James Boulton was Sworn to Execute the Office of Headborough in the Room and Stead of M^r^. Thomas Rudge.

1030. The Persons whose names are underwritten were Summoned to appear here this day to shew cause why they have refused or neglected to pay the several sums of money set down against each of their names which they are Rated towards the relief of the Poor of the parish of Saint John at Hackney in the County of Middlesex and were due at Lady day last past.
Church Street: fo. 2, Samuel Keep rated £1 5s., no Distress; fo. 3, Joseph Faikney rated £1 17s. 6d., Empty a year; fo. 5, John Perkins rated £1 5s., Empty ¼, 18s. 9d. paid; fo. 6, William Pain rated £1 17s. 6d., paid; fo. 7, Mary Wall rated £1 5s., Empty ¼, 18s. 9d. paid; *Richard Spurling rated 10s., to pay; *fo. 8, John Davidson rated £1, to pay; fo. 9, William Yelloly rated £3 2s. 6d. [*altered from* £3 2s. 2d.], Empty ¼, £2 6s. 10½d. paid; *John Jebb rated 15s., to pay; *fo. 10, William Peters rated 15s., paid; Edward Dudson rated £1, 10s. paid; John Howard rated £1, to pay; fo. 11, Daniel Milner rated 6s. 3d., Excused; fo. 12, Mary Scott rated 15s., Excused; Benjamin Evans rated £1, 10s. paid; *fo. 13, Robert Hull rated £2, to pay; *fo. 14, Thomas William Fussell rated £2, to pay; *fo. 15, George Jenckes rated £1 5s., to pay; John Farquaharson rated £4, No Distress to be had; fo. 16, John Rogers rated 10s., paid; William Fenton rated 7s. 6d., paid; *fo. 18, John Davis rated 15s., to pay; *fo. 19, Mary Woodyard rated 10s., to pay; Benjamin Cooper rated 15s., no Distress to be had; *fo. 20, William Griffith rated 17s. 6d., to pay; *fo. 21, Frances Pitts rated £2 10s., to pay £1 5s. for ½ a year; fo. 23, Benjamin Johnson rated £1, 15s. paid; *Mary Wright rated 12s. 6d., to pay 10s.; *Samuel Bennett rated £1, to pay; fo. 25, John Hancock rated £1, No Distress to be had.
Mare Street: *fo. 29, Hannah Wright rated £2 10s., to pay £1 5s. for ½ a year; *fo. 32, John Whittle rated £3 15s., to pay; *fo. 33, William Groom rated £1, to pay; fo. 35, William Knight rated £2 10s., paid; *Hannah Sandford rated 10s., to pay; fo. 37, Walter Graham rated 10s., paid; Matthew Eaglesoe rated 15s., Excused; *Robert Wilson rated 10s., to pay; fo. 38, Elizabeth Melton rated 15s., no distress to be had; *John Gibbs rated £1 7s., to pay 2 y^s^; *Thomas Blemeney rated £2 3s. 9d., to pay; fo. 40, Angelo Ancona rated £6 15s., No Distress to be had, 2 y^s^; fo. 41, Sarah Miller rated 15s., paid; fo. 42, Henry Wheatley rated 10s., Excused; *Aron Gomez Da Costa rated £1 8s. 9d., to pay; *fo. 43, Thomas Rayner rated 9s. 4½d., to pay; fo. 44, Henry Cock rated £7 6s. 3d., pa, paid; *fo. 45, Ann Phillipps rated 10s., to pay; fo. 46, John Burton rated £28, paid; Rachael Tyssen rated £5, paid; fo. 47, William Browne rated 10s., Dead no Distress to be had; fo. 52, John Owen rated

15s., no Distress to be had; John Clowdes rated 10s., ½ a year 5s., Paid; fo. 53, Robert Ward rated £1, to pay, paid; fo. 55, Robert Hawkins rated £1 5s., paid.

Homerton: fo. 57, Gerard Vanheythuyssen rated £5, no Distress to be had; *fo. 59, The Rev[d]. Thomas Newcomb rated £1 10s., to pay; *fo. 62, Elizabeth Powell rated 12s. 6d., to pay; *fo. 63, Katherine Davey rated 15s., to pay; John Streetin rated £1, paid; fo. 64, Elizabeth Burrell rated £1, 10s., paid; Robert Dumbleton rated 10s., Dead & no Distress to be had; fo. 65, William Austin rated £2, paid; *fo. 66, Samuel Butler rated £2 10s., to pay; Abraham Dias Fernandus rated £3 15s., £2 2s. paid; *Sarah Frisby rated 10s., to pay; fo. 67, Edward Bayley rated £1 5s., 10s. paid; fo. 69, James Shewell rated £3 2s. 6d., £2 6s. 10½d., paid; Joshua Coxall rated 15s., Excused; *William Lucas rated £1 6s. 3d., to pay; fo. 71, Mary Gillshigh rated £1 10s., ¾ a y[r], £1 2s. 6d. paid; *fo. 72, Richard Wright rated £1, to pay; *William Stoakes rated £4 17s. 6d., to pay; *fo. 73, Sarah Townesend rated 10s., to pay; *fo. 75, Robert Wood £1 5s., to pay; fo. 76, Eleanor Cooke rated £1 10s., ¼ Empty, £1 2s. 6d., paid; *fo. 76, John Dean rated 10s., to pay; fo.78, William Taylor rated 15s., no Distress to be had; fo. 79, Newman Bourne rated 15s., no Distress to be had; fo. 80, Thomas Soper rated 10s., Excused; *fo. 81, David Taylor rated £2 5s., to pay; *Joseph Wright rated £1, to pay; Thomas White rated £1 10s., paid; fo. 82, Peter Stringer rated 10s., paid; fo. 83, Samuel Sadleir rated £1 11s. 3d., paid; fo. 84, Samuel Sumner rated £2 10s., £2 2s. paid; fo. 85, Jane Harris rated £1 5s., no Distress to be had; John Cox rated £1, paid.

Clopton: fo. 87, William Thurston rated £1 5s., no Distress to be had; Christopher Wyville Esq rated £5, Empty a year; *fo. 88, Richard Smith rated £2 10s., to pay; *fo. 90, Abraham Masiaes rated £2 10s., to pay; *Isaac Viana rated £2 10s., to pay; fo. 93, William Cawne rated 10s., no Distress to be had; fo. 94, Margaret Gelding rated 10s., Excused; fo. 95, Thomas Pangbourne rated £8 5s., £7 17s. 6d. paid; Jane Walker rated 10s, Excused; *fo. 96, James Milner rated £1 17s. 6d., to pay, 17s. 6d.; *fo. 98, Sarah Field rated 15s., to pay; *John Hampson rated £2, to pay; *Thomas Mitchell rated £6 5s., to pay; *James Matthews rated £1 2s. 6d., to pay; *fo. 99, George Stanton rated 12s. 6d., to pay; fo. 100, Elizabeth Rotherford rated 12s. 6d., Excused; *Burdett Marville rated 10s., to pay; fo. 101, James Conniers rated £1, no Distress to be had; fo. 102, Soloman Moses rated £1 5s., no Distress to be had; fo. 103, Mary Townesend rated 10s., Excused.

Grove Street: fo. 107, John Coombes rated 10s., Excused.

Well Street: *fo. 110, William Wint rated 10s., to pay; Mary Gosdin rated 10s., Excused; fo. 115, Thomas Collee rated 15s., 10s., paid.

Newington: fo. 117, Matthew Clarke rated £1, no Distress to be had; Bartholomew Buckee rated £1, not to be found; *fo. 119, John Daniel rated £1, to pay; fo. 120, John Mason rated 15s., Excused; Thomas Fowler rated £1, 15s., paid; *fo. 121, Sarah Potter rated £1 17s. 6d., to pay; *fo. 122, Ann Freeman rated £1 5s. to pay 10s.; Samuel Cross rated £1 10s., £1, paid; Barnard Merest Byfield rated £1, paid.

Shacklewell: fo. 124, William Harvey rated £2 10s., Empty a year; *Elias

Woodfield rated £3 15s., to pay; *fo. 125, Samuel Jordain rated 10s., to pay; *John Everett rated £5 10s., to pay;
*fo. 126, Henry Arnold rated £1, to pay.
Kingsland: fo. 127, James Martin rated 10s., no Distress to be had; *William Newton rated 10s., to pay; fo. 128, Christopher Chivers rated 12s. 6d., 5s., paid; John White rated £1, No Distress to be had; *Ann Bartmaker rated £3 15s., to pay; fo. 129, Alice Fox, rated £2 17s. 6d., £1 17s. 6d., paid.
Dorleston: *fo. 131, Joseph Sureties rated £11 8s. 9d., to pay; *Benjamin Torrey rated 15s., to pay; fo. 132, Joseph Faickney rated £1 10s., paid; fo. 133, Ann Gam rated £1 10s., paid; *Bate Prissick rated £1 10s., to pay, £1; Charles Bishop rated 10s., Excused.
Land Holders: *fo. 134, William Hill rated £2 12s. 6d., to pay; Benjamin Coker rated 10s., no Distress to be had; fo. 135, Thomas Fasbrook rated £1 16s. 3d., £1 5s., paid; *fo. 136, Ralph Harwood rated £2, to pay; *William Shell rated 10s., to pay; *John Archer Shish Esqr rated £6 5s., to pay; fo. 137, Jacob Nortzale rated 3s. 9d., no Distress to be had; *Nicholas Bartmaker rated £3 15s., to pay; fo. 138, Dianah Cock rated £2 5s., paid.

1031. Warrant Distress Ordered on the Oaths of Mr Thomas Masling and Edward Conyear the late Overseers and Samuel Sadleir the late and present Overseer of the Poor and Henry Harrill Beadle.

The Mermaid Tavern: Monday, 20 June 1743
Justices present: Henry Norris, Samuel Tyssen

1032. Several Persons that have Neglected to pay the Poors Rate for 1742 were heard.

The Mermaid Tavern: Saturday, 4 February 1744
Justices present: Henry Norris, Samuel Tyssen

1033. Defaulters heard of highways: 155 Dianah Cox . . .[1]

1. Entry added from draft minutes.

The Mermaid Tavern: Thursday, 8 March 1744
Justices present: Henry Norris, Samuel Tyssen

1034. John Cox Thomas Bridgman and Daniel Brumwell were sworn before the above named Justices well & truly to Execute the Office of Constables for the parish of St John at Hackney.[1]

1. Entry added from draft minutes.

The Blue Posts Tavern: Tuesday, 30 April 1751
Justices present: Henry Norris, John Dekewer

1035. The Persons whose Names are hereunder written were by the

Vestry belonging to the Parish of Saint John at Hackney in the County of Middlesex returned to the said Justices of the Peace for them to nominate and appoint Overseers of the Poor of the said Parish for the year 1751. To wit: John Southern, 27 years a housekeeper; Joseph Parsons, 23 years a housekeeper; Edmund Bellis, 20 years a housekeeper; William Pratt, 19 years a housekeeper; John Darnell, 13 years a housekeeper; John Woodfield, 12 years a housekeeper; Joseph Hawkins, 10 years a housekeeper; Robert Stebbing, 10 years a housekeeper; William Hazard, 10 years a housekeeper; John Killingworth, 12 years a housekeeper; John Chavalier, 9 years a housekeeper; John Bynon, 8 years a housekeeper; John Lambert, 7 years a housekeeper; Daniel Cotier, 9 years a housekeeper, appointed; Daniel Flores, 7 years a housekeeper, appointed. [Total:] 15.

1036. The Persons whose Names are hereunder written were sumoned to give an Accompt upon Oath of the Place of their respective last legall Settlement. To witt,
Kingsland: *Richard Dodson, Sworn, allowed 3 weeks to bring a Cert; *David Boswell, Sworn, 3 weeks; *William Howard, Sworn, 3 weeks; John Grimes, Irish; Patrick Larkin, D°. Roman; *Joseph Hawkins, Sworn, 3 weeks; *Edward Lawney, Sworn, 3 weeks; William Doughty, did not appear; *Ruth Neal, Sworn; *William Rotherford, Sworn; *Joseph Farrington, Sworn, 3 weeks; *John Wilkinson, Sworn, 1 week; Samuel Wade, rented £10 a year in Hackney, Setled [*sic*] here; *William Haynes, Sworn, 1 week.[1] [*See* **1043**].

1. Edward Lawney was in receipt of a regular allowance from his parish of settlement, which was Waltham Abbey, Essex. Ruth Neal was pregnant and had been deserted by her husband. H.A.D., P/J/P/68.

1037. The Persons whose Names are hereunder Set down were Elected at the Court Leet to Execute the following Offices for the year 1751.
Kings Hold: Constable: Mathew Eagelsoe, Sworn [for] Jonathan Newton. Headboroughs: James Atkins, Sworn [for] John Arrundall, Church Street Division; Andrew Grinley, Sworn [for] Joseph Hawkins, Well Street D°. Aleconner: John Howard, Sworn.
Lords Hold: Constables: Abell White Sworn [for] William Pratt; George Collins, Sworn. Headboroughs: John Cowling Sworn [for] John Bride, Church Street Division; Henry Currill, Kingsland & Dalston D°, Sworn; James Bolton Sworn [for] Israel Brandon, Clapton D°; William Cawne Sworn [for] William Shepperd, Upper Hummerton D°; John Doe, Newington & Shacklewell D°, Sworn; Thomas Tayler Sworn [for] Benjamin Ball, Mare Street D°; John Dunks, Grove Street D°, Sworn; Samuel Holland, Lower Hummerton D°., appeared, but was not Sworn. Ale Conners: John Flatman, Sworn; James Atkins Sworn [for] Joseph Pases.

1038. The above named Samuel Holland appeared, and the Justices [declared *deleted*] told him they were ready to Swear him into his said

Office which he refused alledging That he is not a Housekeeper in this Parish, having let his House in Hummerton.

1039. John Darnell and Daniel Bellnap appeared and paid the Sum of Four Pounds One Shilling and Seven pence halfpenny being the Ballance of their Accompts already [passe *deleted*] given in & allowed for the year 1748 to John Woodfeild their Successor in the said Office.

1040. John Woodfield appeared and paid the sum of Ten Pounds Ten Shillings and five Pence halfpenny being the Ballance of the Accompts of the said John Woodfield and Joseph Faikney the Surveyors of the Highways for the year 1750 to William Hazard the present Surveyor of the Parish of Saint John at Hackney.

1041. Adjourned to this Place to Teusday the 21st of May instant at Nine of the Clock in the Forenoon.

The Blue Posts Tavern: Tuesday, 21 May 1751
Justices present: Henry Norris, John Dekewer

1042. The Persons whose names are underwritten were Sumoned to appear here this Day to shew Cause why they have refused or neglected to pay the several sums of Money set down against each of their Names which they are rated towards the Releif of the Poor of the Parish of Saint John at Hackney in the County of Middlesex and were due at Ladyday last past.
Clapton: fol. 90, Abraham Lurie rated 12s.; fol. 98, Robert Meriton rated 6s., to pay; fol. 103, Anthony Ford rated 19s. 6d., Excused; fol. 104, Thomas Reeves rated 6s., 6s. paid; Mary Phythian rated 18s., not to be found; fol. 108, William Pickett rated 6s., to pay [*possibly altered to* paid]; fol. 109, Nicholas Bartmaker rated £2 5s.; fol. 111, Willliam Bells Exor rated 6s., 6s. paid; fol. 97, Margaret Gilding rated 6s., Excused; fol. 106, Henry White rated 6s., 6s. paid; fol. 99, Jane Brasier's Exor rated 7s. 6d., 7s. 6d. paid.
Hummerton: fol. 63, Frances Wright rated 6s., to pay; fol. 65, George Fowler rated 6s., Excused; fol. 67, Garrison Harcourt rated 15s., 15s. Paid; fol. 70, Samuel Palmer rated 6s.; fol. 73, Deborah Vanderclus rated 12s., to pay 6s. paid; Thomas Cooper rated 6s., Excused; fol. 74, Lyonell Batsford rated 6s., 6s. paid; fol. 77, Grace Allen rated 12s., to pay 9s. paid; Nathaniel Howard rated 14s. 3d., 14s. 3d. paid; fol. 78, Samuel Holland rated 15s., 15s. paid; fol. 79, John Hampson rated 6s., Excused; fol. 80, Thomas Middleton rated 12s., 12s. paid; fol. 83, Philippa Maria Bates rated 6s., to pay; fol. 86, Samuel Sadler rated 15s., Excused; fol. 87, William Dakin rated 15s.; fol. 88, John Cox rated 19s. 6d.
Church Street: fol. 2, Isaac Silver rated 15s., to pay; fol. 3, Joseph Faikney rated £3; fol. 4, Martha Brooks rated 6s., to pay; fol. 11, Nathan Marsom rated 6s., to pay 6s. paid; fol. 12, Daniel Milner rated 6s., Excused; Joseph Davison rated 10s., 10s paid; Ann Foxall rated

£3; fol. 19, Clare Gordon rated 18s., 18s. paid; fol. 17, James Morison rated 9s., to pay 9s. paid; fol. 18, Ann Effingstow rated 9s., Excused; fol. 19, William Hazard Junr. rated 6s., to pay 6s. paid; fol. 21, John Cowling rated 6s., Excused; Elizabeth Spurling rated 6s., Excused; fol. 22, James Hodges rated 18s., 18s. paid; fol. 27, Mathew Perks rated 12s.
Mare Street: fol. 32, William Collins, rated 6s., 6s. paid; James Corkett rated 6s., Excused; fol. 36, William Groom rated 12s., 12s. paid; fol. 40, [James Gordon *deleted*] Samuel Jordan rated 12s., 12s. paid; fol. 45, Aaron Da Costa rated 18s., to pay 18s. paid; fol. 47, John Lambert rated 16s. 6d.; fol. 48, Joseph Swaby rated 12s., 12s. paid; John Thompson rated 6s., 6s. paid; fol. 49, Thomas Pritchard rated 3s., 3s. paid; fol. 52, Nathaniel Potts rated 6s., 6s. paid; fol. 55, Stanhope Dickson rated 12s., Excused; fol. 56, Thomas Caddock rated 15s., to pay ¾ 11s. 3d.; fol. 57, Edward Dudson rated 3s., 3s. paid; Edmund Colnett rated 6s.
Well Street: fol. 116, Philip Holmes rated 12s., 12s. paid; fol. 117, Elizabeth Sadleir rated 6s., Excused.
Grove Street: fol. 113, Joseph Harris rated 12s., 12s. paid.
Kingsland: fol. 136, Thomas Fox rated 12s.
Dalston: fol. 139, Joseph Daniel rated 9s., to pay.
Newington: fol. 127, Ann Freeman rated 9s.; Ann Umfreville rated £1 10s., Dead.
Shacklewell: fol. 129, [Elizabeth *deleted*] Elianor Clarke rated 6s., Excused; fol. 130, William Panther rated 3s., 3s. paid; fol. 131, William Pamplin rated 9s., 9s. paid; fol. 132, Robert Ward rated 12s.
Land Holders: fol. 141, John Bradley rated 17s. 3d., 17s. 3d. paid; John Clark rated £1 7s., £1 7s. paid; fol. 143, Humphrey Haden rated 2s. 3d., 2s. 3d. paid; fol. 144, Jerry Cotterell rated 5s. 3d., 5s. 3d. paid; fol. 146, Simon Bolton rated £1 10s., Excused; Edward Jones rated 4s. 6d., 4s. 6d. paid; Amos Wenman rated 4s. 6d., 4s. 6d. paid; fol. 147, Samuel Scott rated £3 0s. 9d., £3 0s. 9d. paid; James Huggett rated 2s. 3d.; William Bond rated £1 10s., £1 10s. paid; Thomas Webb rated 15s., 15s. paid.

1043. William Doughty was Examined upon Oath touching the Place of his last legall Settlement which is in the Parish of Saint Leonard Shoreditch in the County of Middlesex by serving One John Batts a Gardiner at Hogsdon in the said Parish for Two years and upwards by the Leave and Consent of Thomas Long Citizen and Merchant Taylor of London to whom he was bound Apprentice for Seven Years during the continuance of his said apprenticeship. [*See* **1036**].

1044. Adjourned to this Place of Teusday the 4th. Day of June next at Nine of the Clock in the Forenoon.

The Blue Posts Tavern: Tuesday, 4 June 1751
Justices present: Henry Norris, John Dekewer

1045. Charles Edwards complains against Bridgeman Brown the

Younger for unlawfully taking two Chickens his Property at Stoke Newington in the County of Middlesex on the first Day of June instant. Bridgeman Brown, the Younger of the Parish of [Saint Mary *deleted*] Stoke Newington [and] Bridgeman Brown of the same Parish, Farmer, each £5 Upon Condition That the above bound Bridgeman Brown the Younger do personally appear at the next General Quarter Sessions of the Peace to be held for the County of Middlesex at Hicks Hall in Saint Johns Street then & there to answer the Complaint of Charles Edwards for unlawfully taking two Chickens his Property at Stoke Newington aforesaid on the first Day of June instant and in the mean time to be of good behaviour and not to depart the Court without Licence Then this Recognisance to be void &c. Taken and Acknowledged the Day and Year first above written.

1046. William MacAndrew was Examined upon Oath touching the Place of his last legall Settlement.[1]

1. William MacAndrew obtained a certificate from St. James, Westminster that year. This was his second examination; he was first examined in 1748. P79/JN1/398; H.A.D., P/J/P/68.

1047. Adjourned to this place on Friday the 14th: Day of June instant at Nine of the Clock in the Forenoon.

The Blue Posts Tavern: Friday, 14 June 1751
Justices present: Henry Norris, John Dekewer

1048. The Persons whose Names are hereunder written were sumoned to give an Account upon Oath of the Place of their respective last legall settlements. To witt,
Church Street: Henry Howship, sworn, allowed 1 week to bring a Certificate; George Granger, sworn, till Michas next; Thomas Lane, sworn, 1 Month; John Marshall, has a Certificate from Trumpington in Cambridgeshire; Thomas Miller; William Houtton; William Thorp; William Griffin, sworn, 1 Month.
Mare Street: William Wilson; Richard Capper; Thomas Pells, sworn, 1 Month; Robert [Dickenson *deleted*] Diggins, will bring a Certificate to Justice Norris 17 June which he said he had [by *deleted*] at Home; Robert Royston; Richard Capper, sworn, 1 Week.
Cambridge Heath: John Beavis; William Cleaver, Sworn, 4 Months; Richard Leeds, Sworn, 1 Month; John Muncey; Henry Baker; Benjamin Thompson, Sworn, 4 Months; William Ivory; John Barrans, Sworn, 1 Month; William Allen; Edward Flack.[1] [*See* **1050**, **1051**, **1052**, **1054**, **1057**, **1061**].

1. Howship (of Church Street) did not obtain a certificate until 1754. Robert Diggen (of Mare Street) delivered a certificate which had been issued in 1749. P79/JN1/398.

1049. Ordered That Mary May Daughter of William May deced be Removed from this Parish (being Chargeable to the same) to the Parish of S[t]. Mary Stoke Newington in the County of Middlesex and that an Order be made out for that Purpose. [*See* **1064**].

The Blue Posts Tavern: Friday, 26 July 1751
Justices present: Henry Norris, John Dekewer

1050. The Persons whose Names are hereunder written were Sumoned to give an Account upon Oath of the Place of their Respective last legal Settlements, To witt,
Church Street: *William Houton not Sumoned; *William Thorp not Sumoned; John Keymer did not appear; Richard Morgan Sworn, allowed 2 weeks to bring a Certificate.
Mare Street: William Wilson, Sworn, D°. imediately D°; Robert Diggins did not appear; Robert Royston refused to be Sworn.
Homerton: Pheebe Hams did not appear; Joseph Jones did not appear.
Clapton: *James Green not Sumoned.
Cambridge Heath: John Beavis, Sworn, D° forthwith D°; John Munsey, Sworn, D°. 2 weeks, D°; *Henry Baker not Sumoned; William Ivory, Sworn, D°. till Michaelmas next, D°; William Allen did not appear; Edward Flack did not appear; Elizabeth Barrans Wife of John.[1] [*See* **1048**, **1051**, **1052**, **1054**, **1057**, **1058**, **1060**, **1061**, **1063**, **1066**, **1099**].

1. Elizabeth Barrans (or Heath) was not examined until June 1752. At that time her two children by John Barrans, aged 10 years and four months, were chargeable to the parish. John Barrans had been examined 14 June previously (**1048**) but the parish officers may already have discovered that the couple were not legally married and that the children were therefore illegitimate. H.A.D., P/J/P/68.

1051. Robert Royston Appeared and gave an Account of his Settlement, To witt, That he was born in the Parish of Eccleston in the County of Chester and could not make appear that he had gained any legal settlement elsewhere and being required to make Oath of his said Settlement he refused [and *deleted*] to be sworn and being asked by the Justices if he was one of the People called Quakers and offered by the said Justices his affirmation in case he was a Quaker The said Robert Royston declared he is not a Quaker.[1] [*See* **1048**, **1050**, **1054**].

1. The draft minutes include the following marginal entries: 16 Jan[ry] 1741, 21 Feb[y] 1741, 31 July 1741, perhaps indicating that Royston had been summoned on those dates.

1052. Ordered That a Warrant be made out to oblige the following Persons to give an Accompt of their respective Settlements on the Oath of James Atkins that they were duly sumoned To witt, John Keymer, Robert Diggins, Phebe Hams, Joseph Jones, William Allen, Edward Flack. [*See* **1048**, **1050**, **1054**, **1057**, **1058**, **1063**, **1099**].

1053. Adjourned to this Day four Weeks, and Ordered That the Accompts of the several Church Wardens and Overseers which have not yet been Signed by the Justices be brought to the next Petty Sessions for that Purpose. And that those which have not yet been passed be gott ready by that time.

The Blue Posts Tavern: Thursday, 5 September 1751
Justices present: Henry Norris, John Dekewer

1054. The Persons whose Names are hereunder written were summoned to give an Account upon Oath of the Places of their Respective last legal Settlements. To witt,
Church Street: Robert Abbott, Sworn, allowed One Month; John Thorne, sworn, One Month.
Well Street: Samuel Beasor, did not appear; Thomas Spring, Sworn, [allowed *deleted*] imediately to bring a Cert; Thomas Redford, not Sworn; Francis Spencer, Sworn, imediately; Robert Smith, did not appear; Thomas Punt, Sworn, allowed One Month; Edward Thornby, did not appear; James Cornwall, Sworn, One Month; Mathew Dixon, Sworn, One Month; Robert Harrison, Sworn.
Mare Street: Robert Royston, Sworn; John Thorn, Sworn, One Month; Robbert Abbott, Sworn, One Month; William Allen, Sworn, Six Weeks. [*See* **1048**, **1050**, **1051**, **1056**, **1057**, **1060**, **1062**, **1066**].

1055. Ordered That M^{r}: Thomas Slater, Church Warden do pay to James Bolton the sum of Ten Shillings for Assisting James Atkins the Beadle in the Execution of his said Office while the said James Atkins was sick being about fourteen Days.

1056. Complaint being made by Richard Dann Overseer of the Poor of the Parish of Saint John at Hackney [That *deleted*] against Elizabeth Riddle Singlewoman That he hath received information That the said Elizabeth Riddle was about Ten Weeks agoe delivered of a Male Bastard Child in the said Parish called Henry which is now living and likely to become chargeable to the said Parish. Ordered That the said Elizabeth Riddle be sumoned to attend us at the next Meeting to be held here to be Examined upon Oath touching the putative Father of the said male Bastard Child. [*See* **1062**, **1107**].

1057. William Allen brought in Custody of Mathew Eagelsoe Constable on a Warrant granted against him to Oblige him to give an Account of his Settlement was Examined upon Oath touching the Place of his last legall Settlement which is in the Parish of Saint Peters in the East in the City of Oxford by being a yearly servant to one John Rawlins a Scowerer there at Two Pounds & Ten Shillings a year and serving him in the said Parish One year & Six Months. [*See* **1048**, **1050**, **1052**, **1054**].

1058. Ja^{s}. Bolton Inf. Pheebe Hams threatned to leave her Children to the Parish.[1] [*See* **1050**, **1052**, **1063**].

1. Entry inserted from draft minutes.

1059. Adj[d]. this day fortnight.[1]

1. Entry inserted from draft minutes.

The Blue Posts Tavern: Friday, 20 September 1751
Justices present: Henry Norris, John Dekewer

1060. The Persons whose Names are hereunder written were sumoned to given an account upon Oath of the Places of their respective last legall Settlements. To witt,
Clapton: Margarett Macomb, did not appear; Abigail Nugent, did not appear; John Dennis, Sworn, allowed; Richard Roney, Sworn; James Green, not Summoned; Elianor Kane, Sworn.
Church Street: Mary Nicholls, Sworn.
Homerton: Richard Birchall, Sworn, One Month; Charles Dennett, Sworn, forthwith.
Well Street: Thomas Redford, Sworn, Christmas next; Edward Thornby, did not appear; Robert Smith, Sworn; Richard Cowdrey, Sworn, two Weeks; William Tibbing, Sworn. [*See* **1050**, **1054**, **1066**].

1061. Edward Flack was brought in Custody of Mathew Eagelsoe Constable on a Warrant to be Examined upon Oath touching his last legall settlement and was Examined and Sworn thereto which is at Barkway in Hertfordshire having lived a Yearly Servant with one William Stallabrass a Farmer there for two years at £5:5[s]: a year and was allowed One Month to bring a Certificate. [*See* **1048**, **1050**, **1052**].

1062. Elizabeth Riddle Singlewoman was brought in Custody of Taylor Headborough to be Examined on Oath touching a Bastard Child born of her Body in the Parish of S[t]. John at Hackney which is now living and likely to be chargeable to the said Parish and Signed an Adjudication against Mathew Dixon of the same Parish as the reputed father thereof. [*See* **1054**, **1056**, **1107**].

1063. Pheebe Hams Widow of Richard Hams deced was brought in Custody of James Bolton Headborough to give an Account of her settlement She declared she is marryed since the Death of the said Richard Hams and that her s[d] Second Husband is now alive but refused to tell his Name, who he is, or where he lives but said That She hath been marryed about 3 years and that her now Husband is the Father of her last Child born since the Death of the said Richard Hams. James Bolton made Oath That about 10 or 12 Days agoe the said Pheebe Hams told him That if the Justices insisted That she should declare the Father of her last Child She would go away and leave her 3 Children to the Parish Whereupon a Warrant was Ordered to committ her to the House of Correction as an Idle and disorderly Person.[1] [*See* **1050**, **1052**, **1058**].

1. Phoebe Hams was finally examined in April 1756, at which time she had a two year old illegitimate daughter (not actually chargeable to the parish). She was removed to Bethnal Green. H.A.D., P/J/P/68.

1064. Mary Etheridge wife of — Etheridge made Oath That [*entry incomplete*].[1]

1. This entry almost certainly relates to the birth of Mary May, who appears to have been a child of about eight or nine years of age (see **1049**). Mary Etheridge gave a sworn statement as to the child's birth in the following December. On this date James Atkins, the Beadle, swore to the effect that the child was chargeable to the parish. H.A.D., P/J/P/68.

1065. Granted a Search Warr^t^.[1]

1. Entry inserted from draft minutes.

The Blue Posts Tavern: Friday, 8 November 1751
Justices present: Henry Norris, John Dekewer

1066. The Persons whose Names are hereunder Written were summoned to give an Account upon Oath of the Places of their respective last legal Settlements. To witt,
Clapton: Margaret Macomb, Sworn, allowed One Month to bring Certif; Abigail Nugent, did not appear; James Green, Sworn, Six Weeks D^o^.
Newington: Elizabeth Wright, Sworn, Signed an Order to Remove; William Bass, Sworn, two Weeks to bring Certif; Samuel Bass, Sworn, two Weeks D^o^; John Bowman, Sworn, two Weeks D^o^.
Homerton: John Doughtee, brought a Certificate from Ewelm in Oxfordshire; John Seagood, Sworn, [one *deleted*] Three Months; Fortune Waters, brought a Certificate from St Andrew Undershaft; John Seal, Sworn; John Stacy, Sworn, One Month.
Well Street: Joseph Ellis, Sworn, One Month; Edward Thornby, Sworn, three Months. [*See* **1050**, **1054**, **1060**, **1111**, **1113**, **1129**, **1133**].

The Blue Posts Tavern: Friday, 20 December 1751
Justices present: Henry Norris, John Dekewer

1067. The Persons whose Names are hereunder written were summoned to give an Account upon Oath of the places of their respective last legall settlements. To witt,
Homerton: John Archer, did not Appear; Henry Shepherd, Sworn, 1 M^o^; Richard Bull, Sworn, 2 Weeks; Thomas Willmot, Hannah his Wife Sworn (he not living wth Her); Thomas Simpson, Sworn, Settlem^t^. in this Parish.
Cambridge Heath: John Dennett, Sworn, 1 M^o^; Mathew Thornton, did not appear; Thomas Chapman, Sworn, brot a Cert from South Mims Middx.
Clapton: William Suert, Sworn, 2 M^os^:
Church Street: George Whybourn, did not Appear. [*See* **1071**, **1074**].

1068. George Neadham Attended and desired leave to draw Drink at the Yorkshire Grey in Homerton in the room of Abel White till the next

General renewing of the Licences of Victuallers. Agreed That he have Leave accordingly.

1069. M[r] Daniel Deflores attended on a Sumons to Shew Cause why he refuses to take upon himself the Office of one of the Overseers of the Poor of the Parish of Saint John at Hackney in the County of Middlesex for the present year (to which he hath been appointed) on the Complaint of M[r] Daniel de Votier one other of the Overseers of the Poor of the said Parish and the said M[r] Daniel de Votier also attended And It was agreed between them That [*entry incomplete; the remainder is taken from the draft minutes*] Mr. Flores alledged That M[r] Votier the other Ov. proposed & offered to do the Duty for him and told him to take no Care about it only you give me what you would give another And that he is ready to pay M[r]. Votier £10 to do the whole Duty & will pay it [Teusday *deleted*] next week.[1]

1. An unsigned receipt for £10 paid by de Flores to de Votier in return for discharging his duties as overseer is amongst the loose enclosures in the volume.

1070. John Blackwell attended and made Information on his Oath That on the nineteenth Day of this Instant December he did hear Robert Abbott of the Parish of Saint John at Hackney in the County of Middlesex Saylor swear Six prophane Oaths saying each time By God And Curse Six prophane Curses saying each time Damn Your Blood in the said Parish of Saint John at Hackney. Granted A Sumons for the said Robert Abbott to appear at a Petty Sessions to be held at this Place on Monday the [Thirty fir *deleted*] thirtyeth day of this Instant December. [*See* **1075**].

1071. Thomas Chapman produced and delivered a Certificate dated the 19th of April 1727 whereby he and [*blank*] his Wife are owned to be Inhabitants of South Mims in this County And he was Sworn that he hath not gained any Legal Settlem[t]. since. [*See* **1067**].

1072. Signed an Order for G Clear Ch. W. &c 1749 to pay the Ballance of his Accompts as such to M[r] Slater the prsent Ch. W.[1]

1. Entry inserted from draft minutes.

1073. Adj[d]. to Monday 30th Instant.[1]

1. Entry inserted from draft minutes.

The Blue Posts Tavern: Monday, 30 December 1751
Justices present: Henry Norris, John Dekewer

1074. The Persons whose names are hereunder written were summoned to give an Account upon Oath of the Places of their respective last legall settlements. To witt,
Homerton: John Archer, Sworn, till Ladyday; [*blank*] Mackintosh.

Clapton: William Caton, not Sworn; William Symonds, Sworn, One Month; John Jones, Sworn, One Month; Richard Barton, Sworn, One Month.
Church Street: Thomas Wood, Sworn, Six Weeks; George Whybourn, Sworn.
Cambridge Heath: Mathew Thornton, Sworn, One Month.
Kingsland: Samuel Geary, Sworn, bro^t^ Certificate from the parish of S^t^. Peter in S^t^. Albans, Hertf.[1] [*See* **1067**, **1077**].

1. Richard Barton (of Clapton) obtained a certificate in 1755. P79/JN1/398.

1075. Robert Abbott appeared on his Sumons to answer to an laid [*sic*] before Henry Norris Esq against him for Swearing Six prophane Oaths saying each time By God and cursing six prophane Curses saying each time Damn your Blood on the Nineteenth Instant in the Parish of Hackney Of which John Blackwell now made Oath Whereupon the said Robert Abbot was convicted of the said Offences and (being the second Conviction) he was fined and paid down the Sum of two Shillings for each of the said Oaths and the further Sum of two Shillings for each of the said Curses making in the whole the Sum of One Pound and four Shillings.[1] [*See* **1070**].

1. The draft minutes continue with the following deletion: & 1^s^. for the Conviction.

The Blue Posts Tavern: Friday, 17 April 1752
Justices present: Henry Norris, John Dekewer

1076. The Persons whose Names are hereunder written having been elected at the Court Leet to Execute the following Offices for the year 1752 appeared to take upon them the same,
Kingshold: Constable: James Bolton sworn [for] William Plant. Headborough: Samuel Stanroyd, Church Street Division sworn. Aleconner: James Atkins Sworn [for] Benjamin Wensley.
Lordshold: Constable: Andrew Grinley Sworn [for] Walter Graham. Headboroughs: James Atkins Sworn [for] William Branson, Mare Street Division; John Rogers, [Mare Street] Division, Sworn;
John Cowley Sworn [for] Alexander Sheafe, Upper Homerton Division; William Cawne Sworn [for] Benjamin Shervill, Clopton Division; John Johnson Sworn [for] John Clarke, Grove Street Division; Robert Ward, [Grove Street] Division, Sworn.[1]

1. The draft minutes add to the list for the Lordshold: Headboroughs Josiah Wallis did not appear; Paul Bishop, refused but afterw^ds^. offered to nominate a Person in his Stead ag^t^. next Petty Sess. [and] Aleconner Thomas Corbett.

1077. The Persons whose Names are underwritten were Sumoned to give an account of their respective last settlements. To witt
Clapton: William Caton, Sworn.
Mare Street: Samuel Webb, Sworn.
Dorleston: Richard Dale, Sworn, One Month.

Well Street: William Johnson, Sworn, One Month; William Room, Sworn.

1. William Caton and Samuel Webb obtained certificates in 1754 and 1753, respectively. William Johnson's widow obtained a certificate in 1753. P79/JN1/398.

1078. Mr S. Woolmer desired an Order to Mr Slater to pay him the Ball. of his Acc^t^. as Ch. W. [*Marginal entry*: to bring his Ac^ot^. next P. Sess.][1]

1. Entry inserted from draft minutes.

1079. Adj^d^. to [Fryday *deleted*] Teusday next 11 o'Clock.[1]

1. Entry inserted from draft minutes.

The Blue Posts Tavern: Tuesday, 21 April 1752
Justices present: Henry Norris, John Dekewer, George Garrett

1080. Nathaniel Roberts who lately kept an Alehouse at the Sign of the Cock and Red Cap on Stanford Hill Attended and complained That he is turned out of the said House by his Landlord And therefore desired That he may have his Licence continued to him in some other House which he shall take for that Purpose. Ordered That Jacob Green who hath now taken the said House have Notice given him and be Sumoned to appear at the next Petty Sessions to Shew cause why he takes upon him obstinately and upon his own Authority to keep a Comon Alehouse or Victualling House within this Parish And uses Commonly the Selling of Ale Beer &c to be drank in his said House he not having a Lawfull Licence for that Purpose And why he should not be proscecuted according to Law for the Same. [*See* **1086**].

1081. Paul Bishop, who was Elected at the Court Leet for the Lords Hold to Execute the Office of Headborough for Dolston and Kingsland Division for the Year 1752. Appeared and desired that Thomas Taylor might be sworn into the said Office in his Stead which the Justices agreed to and he was Sworn accordingly to Execute the said Office.

1082. Benjamin Wright appeared and complained That one John Davy did on the [*blank*] cheat & defraud him of Two Shillings and Six Pence under pretence That he was Sumoning Bailiff and that he was come to sumon the said Benjamin Wright to serve on A Jury And that for the s^d^ Two Shillings & Six Pence he would Excuse him therefrom And [*blank*] Chase the Summoning Bailiff attended and declared That the said Benjamin Wright is not Sumoning Bailiff Therefore on the Oath of the said Benjamin Wright as aforesaid and that he did give credit to the said pretence of the s^d^. John Davy and accordingly did give him the said Two Shillings and Six Pence for the Purpose aforesaid A Warrant was granted to apprehend the s^d^. John Davy.

1083. Warrants were Signed and Sealed by Henry Norris and John Dekewer Esqs whereby Nehemiah Ring and Edward Barnard Church-

Wardens of the Parish of Saint John at Hackney were appointed Overseers of the Poor of the said Parish for the Year 1752.

1084. Ord[d]. Notice to Jerry Bowne & W[m] Perkins to appear.[1] [*See* **1088**].

1. Entry inserted from draft minutes.

1085. Adjourned to this Place to Fryday next at Eleven of the Clock in the Forenoon.

The Blue Posts Tavern: Friday, 24 April 1752
Justices present: Henry Norris, John Dekewer, George Garrett

1086. Jacob Green Attended being Sumoned to Shew Cause why he takes upon him obstinately and upon his own authority to keep an Ale House or Victualling House within this Parish and uses commonly the selling of ale Beer &c to be Drank in his said House he not having a lawfull Licence for that purpose And why he should not be prosecuted according to Law for the same and confessed that he does so and begged Pardon of the Justices for the said Offence. And the said Justices Signed a Licence authorizing and allowing him to draw and sell Beer and Ale [& Beer *deleted*] untill the next General renewing of the Licences of Victuallers. [*See* **1080**].

1087. M[r] Nehemiah Ring, Church Warden and Overseer of the Poor of the Parish of Saint John at Hackney in the County of Middlesex made Oath that Mary Denby Wife of Thomas Denby very lately applyed to him for releif for her and her Child and complained That her said Husband is run away from her without making any Provision for her And that She is in necessitous circumstances And he did releive her accordingly And the said Mary also testyfyed the same on her Oath The said Justices thereupon Issued a Warrant at the request of the said Nehemiah Ring to apprehend the said Thomas Denby to answer the said Complaint And to be further dealt with according to Law.

1088. Signed Warr[t] appointing Jerry Bowne an Overseer.[1] [*See* **1084**].

1. Entry inserted from draft minutes.

1089. Ord[d]. Notice to Dan[ll]: Stacy.[1]

1. Entry inserted from draft minutes.

1090. Signed a Pass to Remove Ann Leaking (the wife James Leaking who &c) & her [2 Children *deleted*] Sons to wit [Dan *deleted*] James aged ab[t]. 2 Y[rs] & Daniel aged ab[t]. 8 Mo[s]. to the Parish of Ridge in the County of Hertford in their Way to the Kingdom of Ireland the Place of [his & *deleted*] their last legal Settlement as a Vagrant Wandring abroad & Lodgeing in the open air and not giving a good acc[t]. of herself.[1]

1. Entry inserted from draft minutes.

The Blue Posts Tavern: Thursday, 7 May 1752
Justices present: Henry Norris, John Dekewer, George Garrett

1091. The following Persons were sumoned to appear this Day to answer a Complaint Exhibited against them for having exercised their Trades or Ordinary Callings in the Parish of S^t: John at Hackney in the County of Middlesex on Sunday the 3^d Day of May instant and to Shew Cause why they should not be convicted and the Penalty levyed on them as the Law directs. Viz:
Ann Kemp, at the Catt and Shoulder of Mutton, in Mare Street On the Oaths of Nehemiah Ring and Edward Barnard Church Wardens 8 Persons drinking, others drinking in other rooms, Mrs Kemp making Liquors Cakes made ready for baking, which she confessed, and was therefore Convicted and ordered to pay 5^s. [*Marginal entry*: Convicted & paid 5^s.]
Philip Holmes, at the Green Dragon, in Well Street Vict. On the Oaths of Nehemiah Ring and Edward Barnard & his own Confession – Convicted & Ordered to pay 5^s. [*Marginal entry*: Convicted & paid 5^s.]
Ann Williams, at the Spread Eagle, Homerton Vict. Only one came out of the House Drunk, which she alledged came in drunk & was turned out by her. [*Marginal entry*: Excused.]
Michael Walton, at the Flying Horse, in Mare Street, Vict. The Evidence not being Clear, he was not convicted. [*See* **1103**].

1092. Ordered That the $appell^{ts}$ [for *deleted*] against the Poors Rate be heard on Fryday the 29th: Instant.

The Blue Posts Tavern: Saturday, 16 May 1752
Justices present: Henry Norris, John Dekewer

1093. The Persons whose names are hereunder written were by a Warrant under the hand & seal of Henry Norris Esq sumoned to appear here this Day to shew cause why they should not be convicted and the Penalty levyed on them as the Law directs for severally exercising their Trades or Ordinary Callings on Sunday the Tenth Instant in this Parish, viz
James Vaughan, at the Mermaid Tavern in Church Street On the Oath of Nehemiah Ring, Church Warden Company drinking had Wine on the Table before them, which he Confessed and was therefore Convicted and Ordered to pay 5^s. [*Marginal entry*: Convicted & paid 5^s.]
Robert Gardiner, at the two Black Boys in Well Street Victualler On the Oath of Nehemiah Ring Several Persons sat on benches in the Yard with Drink before them and others in the Garden but it appearing not to be quite three o'th Clock And promising not to offend was Excused. [*Marginal entry*: Excused.]
Thomas Wood, at the Falcon in Homerton Victualler. On the Oath

of Nehemiah Ring several Persons sitting on Benches in the Yard drinking with drink before them about half an hour after three therefore Convicted and Ordered to pay 5ˢ. [*Marginal entry*: Convicted and pᵈ. 5ˢ.] Joseph Souter, at the Greyhound in Homerton Victualler On the Oath of Nehemiah Ring four or five Persons drinking in an Arbour in the Garden and [more *deleted*] several Company's drinking and Smoaking in other Parts of his premises therefore Convicted he having Confessed the same and Ordered to pay 5ˢ. [*Marginal entry*: Convicted & paid 5ˢ.] Henry James Holloway, at the Adam & Eve in Homerton Victualler. On the Oath of Nehemiah Ring Company Drinking in his House abᵗ. half an hour after three o'th Clock Which he Confessed Therefore was convicted and Ordered to pay 5ˢ. [*Marginal entry*: Convicted & pᵈ. 5ˢ.] Sarah Hattersley, at the Mermaid & Bird in Hand, in Church Street Vict. On the Oath of Nehemiah Ring Several Companys drinking and Beer bringing out of the Cellar about half an hour after three o'th Clock Which She Confessed therefore Convicted and Ordered to pay 5ˢ. [*Marginal entry*: Convicted and paid 5ˢ.]
Elizabeth Hurdle, in Mare Street, Chandler. On the Oath of James Atkins That he delivered her a Sumons to her Signed by Mathew Eagelsoe Constable to appear here this Day for that Purpose. She Did not appear. [*Marginal entry*: Summoned, did not appear.] Nehemiah Ring, One of the Church Wardens of the Parish of Sᵗ. John at Hackney in the County of Middlesex gave an Information upon Oath against Elizabeth Hurdle aforesaid for Exercising her Trade or Ordinary Calling in the said Parish on Sunday the Tenth Day of May instant To wit Serving Customers with Chandlery Wares. The said Justices signed a Sumons requiring her to appear at the House of Henry Norris Esq in Well [*recte Grove*] Street, in this Parish on [Fryday *deleted*] Tuesday next at five of the Clock in the afternoon to answer the said Information. [*See* **1102**, **1108**, **1127**].

The Blue Posts Tavern: Friday, 29 May 1752
Justices present: Henry Norris, John Dekewer, George Garrett

1094. The Persons whose Names are underwritten were sumoned to appear here this Day to shew cause why they have refused or Neglected to pay the several Sums of Money set down against each of their Names which they are rated towards the relief of the Poor of the Parish of Saint John at Hackney in the County of Middlesex and were due at Ladyday last past.
Church Street: fol. 2, Isaac Silver rated £1 10s., to pay, £1 [*marginal entry*: pᵈ]; Joseph Faikney rated £3, Empty; fol. 5, Martha Walker rated 6s., Excused; fol. 13, Daniel Milner rated 6s., Excused; fol. 23, William Margerum rated £1 2s. 6d., to pay, £1 2s. 6d., Paid; James Hodges rated £1 4s., to pay, 18s., Paid; fol. 26, Nathaniel Irlam rated 6s., Excused; fol. 28, Mathew Perks rated 12s., Gone; fol. 30, Thomas Bishop rated 4s., Excused.
Mare Street: fol. 34, Thomas Davis rated 6s., [To pay ¾. *deleted*] Excused [4s. *deleted*]; fol. 44, William Flaxmore rated 6s., to pay, 6s., Paid; fol.

45, Henry Godfrey rated 6s., Paid ½ a year, 3s., p^d; fol. 49, John Rust rated 12s., Paid 12s., pd; fol. 51, Aaron Gomez da Costa rated £1 4s., to pay, 12s. [*marginal entry*: p^d]; fol. 53, [Joseph *deleted*] Edward Parsons rated 6s., [*marginal entry*: Ex]; fol.55, *James Bowine, rated 16s. 6d.; fol.56, Elizabeth Thompson rated 6s., Paid, 6s., p^d; William Archer rated 10s. 6d., Paid, 10s. 6d. pd; fol. 61, Deborah Olderhead rated 6s., Excused; fol. 62, Ann Potts rated 6s., Paid, 6s., pd.

Well Street: fol. 69, Elizabeth Sadler rated 6s., Excused; fol. 70, William Morris rated 12s., Excused; fol. 72, Peter Mangender rated 6s., Excused.

Homerton: fol. 81, Andrew Ram rated £1 2s. 6d., Paid, £1 2s. 6d., pd; fol. 86, James Todd rated 6s., Paid, 6s. pd; Elizabeth Lloyd rated £1 2s. 6d., Paid, £1 2s. 6d., pd; fol. 87, James Rolph rated 9s., Excused this year; fol. 88, Edward Brooksby rated £1 17s. 6d., to pay, £1 17s. 6d., Paid; fol. 93, Deborah Vandercluse rated 6s., Paid, 6s., pd; fol. 96, Thomas Cooper rated 6s., Excused; fol. 97, Charles Wale rated £1 10s., Paid, £1 10s., pd [*marginal entry*: John Mathews]; fol. 98, Abel White [and] George Needham rated 12s., Paid 1 Qu^t, 3s., pd [*marginal entry*: Ex]; fol. 99, Robert Singfield rated 10s. 6d., Gone; Margaret Jones rated £1 2s. 6d., Gone; fol. 100, Ann Williams rated 12s., Excused; fol. 101, John Hampson rated 6s., Excused; Elizabeth Morgan rated 12s., to pay 12s., Paid; fol. 106, Philippa Maria Bates rated 6s., Paid, 6s., pd; fol. 109, Margaret Sadleir rated 6s., Excused; fol. 110, Daniel Stacy rated £4 11s. 6d., to pay £4 2s. 6d. [*marginal entry*: pd]; fol. 112, John Cox rated 19s. 6d. [*marginal entry*: pd].

Clopton: fol. 116, Elizabeth Trevor rated 12s., Not to be found; Nathaniel Simpson rated 15s., Paid, 15s., pd; fol. 118, Robert Reeves rated £1 10s. 9d., Excused; fol. 121, Margaret Gilding rated 6s., Excused; Mary Dixon rated 9s., Paid, 9s., pd; James Oliver rated 9s., Excused; fol. 122, Daniel Thomas rated 6s., Paid, 6s., pd; fol. 124, John Watson rated 6s., Gone; fol. 128, Abraham Judah rated £3 6s., to pay £3 1s. 6d. [*marginal entry*: Spial Warr^t]; fol. 131, Thomas Reeves rated 6s. [*marginal entry*: Ex]; fol. 133, Henry White rated 6s., Paid, 6s., pd; John Pickett rated 6s., Paid, 6s., pd; fol. 134, Richard Hedge rated 6s., Excused; fol. 136, John Wolf rated 6s., to pay ½ Year, 3s., Paid; fol. 137, Nicholas Bartmaker rated £2 12s. 6d., to pay £2 5s., Paid.

Newington: fol. 142, Ann Crow rated 12s., Paid, 12s., pd; Stephen Humphries rated 7s. 6d., Paid, 7s. 6d., pd; fol. 147, William Lacey rated 6s. [*marginal entry*: Ex]; fol. 149, John Hughes rated 12s. [*marginal entry*: Ex]; fol. 150, John Brooksby rated £1 10s., to pay, £1 10s., Paid; John Stonard rated 12s., to pay, 9s., Paid.

Shacklewell: fol. 151, Henry Simson rated 12s., Excused this Year.

Kingsland: fol. 161, Elizabeth Chace rated 9s., Excused.

Dorleston: fol. 163, George Henderson rated 9s., Gone; fol. 164, Michael Metcalfe rated 6s., Excused; Paul Bishop rated 6s., Paid, 6s., pd.

Landholders: fol. 166, Thomas Johnson rated 3s., to pay, 1s. 6d., Paid; Dinah Cox rated £1 17s. 6d., Paid, £1 17s. 6d., pd; Simon Boulton rated £1 10s., Excused; fol. 168, John Taylor rated 12s., to pay, 12s. [*marginal entry*: pd]; Samuel Holland rated 3s., Excused.

1095. John Dekewer Esq Signed a Warrant to apprehend John Keymer on the Oath of John Moore for threatning to do him a Mischeif and fire his House And for that he is afraid of some bodily harm to be done to him by the said John Keymer.

1096. Abraham Judah, appeared being sumoned to appear here this Day in order to shew Cause why he did refuse or neglect to pay the Sum of Three Pounds and Six Shilllings which he is rated and assessed towards the releif of the Poor of this Parish and was due at Ladyday last, and why a Warrant of Distress should not be Issued out to levy the same as the Law directs And he now refused to pay the said Sum so rated and Assessed upon him as aforesaid Although the said Justices offered to abate the Sum of four shillings and Six Pence part thereof and to accept the sum of Three pounds One Shilling and Six pence in [full *deleted*] stead thereof.[1] [*See* **1100**].

1. The draft minutes add that a special warrant of distress was issued.

1097. William Smethergill applyed for leave to draw Drink at the Six Bells in Church Street in the room of Hester Tennant removed Which the Justices will consider off and he was directed to produce an Attestation of his good behaviour under the hand of Col. Willoughby; who he had declared would give him such a one.

The Blue Posts Tavern: Tuesday, 2 June 1752
Justices present: Henry Norris, John Dekewer

Forenoon, from ¼ before 10, to 12.
Afternoon, from ¼ before 3, to ¼ before 5.

1098. The Persons whose Names are hereunder written were by a Warrant under the hand and Seal of Henry Norris Esq sumoned to appear here this Day to shew Cause why they should not be convicted and the Penalty levyed on them as the Law directs for severally exercising their Worldly Trades or ordinary callings on Sunday the Twenty fourth day of May last in this Parish, viz:
Robert Nutkins at the Kings Arms at Kingsland Victualler On the Oath of Edward Barnard Church Warden Entertaining Company in his House which he confessed Convicted and Ordered to pay 5^{s}. [*Marginal entry*: Convicted and p^{d}. 5^{s}.]
William Bunch, at the Red Lyon at Dorleston Victualler On the Oath of Nehemiah Ring Church Warden Several Persons drinking in his House and two men drinking in his Yard Convicted and Ordered to pay 5^{s}. [*Marginal entry*: Convicted & p^{d}: 5^{s}.]
John Lavinder, at the Black Bull, at Kings land Victualler On the Oath of Edward Barnard Church Warden Two Persons drinking in a Room with Liquor before them which he Confessed Convicted

and Ordered to pay 5s. [*Marginal entry*: Convicted & pd. 5s]
Samuel Wade, at Kingsland, Pastry Cook Charged by Nehemiah Ring Church Warden with making Cakes and heating his Oven to bake them all which he Confessed and justifyed. Convicted and Ordered to pay 5s. [*Marginal entry*: Convicted and pd. 5s.]
Robert Ward, at the Cock at Shacklewell Victualler On the Oath of Nehemiah Ring Church Warden Several Persons drinking in his House and Yard Which he Confessed Convicted and Ordered to pay 5s. [*Marginal entry*: Convicted and pd. 5s.]
John Hughes, at the Coach and Horses at Newington, Victualler Charged by Nehemiah Ring Church Warden with Entertaining Company the Doors open To witt 3 Persons drinking up one pair of stairs He Confessed That Two Persons (and not more) were drinking up Stairs But alledged in his Excuse That they were relations Viz one of them his Brother and the other his Brothers Wifes Brother and that they dined with him and were there as Freinds and not Guests and did not pay for any thing they eat or drank therefore was Excused, and promised not to entertain Company on the Lords Day. [*Marginal entry*: Excused]
Henry Field, at the Jolly Butchers at Newington Victualler Charged by Edward Barnard Church Warden with Several Persons drinking in his House to which he Confessed. Convicted and Ordered to pay 5s. [*Marginal entry*: Convicted and pd. 5s]
Joseph Goodwin, at the Weavers Arms, at Newington, Victualler On the Oath of Edward Barnard Church Warden Several Persons drinking at the Door of his House and in the back-Yard belonging to and behind his House and drinks before them all, The Doors all open backwards and forwards Which he confessed. Convicted and Ordered to pay 5s. [*Marginal entry*: Convicted & pd. 5s]
Elizabeth Ward, at the Bird Cage, Stanford Hill, Victualler On the Oath of Edward Barnard Church Warden Several Persons drinking in [the *deleted*] her House Convicted and Ordered to pay 5s. [*Marginal entry*: Convicted & pd. 5s]
Isaac Garrett, at the Sign of the Turnpike, Stanford Hill, Victualler Charged by Edward Barnard Church Warden with Several Persons drinking in the fore Room of his House which he confessed Convicted and Ordered to pay 5s. [*Marginal entry*: Convicted & pd. 5]
Samuel Woolmer, at the White Hart, at Clopton, Victualler. Confessed entertaining Company and that Several Persons were Drinking in his House Convicted and Ordered to pay 5s. [*Marginal entry*: Convicted & pd. 5s] [*See* **1108**].

1099. Ordered That John Keymer have Notice That he bring a Certificate from the Place where he was last legally Settled, in fourteen Days. [*See* **1050**, **1052**].

1100. Qu[ery] Abraham Judah, q if Rate lawfully demanded of him haveing been dem: only by the last Overseer (then out of Office).[1] [*See* **1096**].

1. Entry inserted from draft minutes.

1101. Allowed R[ichard] D[ann]'s Bill for Business done for the Parish on the account of M^{r}. Thos. Slater the late Churchwarden from 14 Oct^{r}:1751 to 21 April following amounting to [*blank*]. R[ichard D[ann]'s Bill for Business &c was Examined & allowed.[1]

1. Entry inserted from draft minutes.

The Blue Posts Tavern: Wednesday, 17 June 1752
Justices present: George Garrett, John Dekewer

1102. The Persons are [*sic*] hereunder written were by a Warrant under the Hand and Seall of George Garrett Esqr Sumoned to appear here this Day to answer a Complaint Exhibited against them by Nehemiah Ring and Edward Barnard Church Wardens on the fifteenth Day of June instant for having Exercised their several & respective Trades or Ordinary callings in the Parish of S^{t}. John at Hackney in the County of Middlesex on Sunday the Seventh [and on Sunday the fourteenth *deleted*] Day of this Instant June and to shew cause why they should not be Convicted And the Penalty levyed on them as the Law directs. Viz:
Mary Gibbs, at the Sign of the Tower, in Church Street in Hackney Victualler Convicted on her Confession for Entertaining Company on Sunday the 7th. Instant in her House and Ordered to pay 5^{s}. [*Marginal entry*: Convicted and paid 5^{s}.]
Hugh Kennedy at the White Horse & Cock in Church Street in Hackney, Victualler On the Oath of Nehemiah Ring Church Warden – Company drinking in his House Convicted and Ordered to pay 5^{s}. [*Marginal entry*: Convicted & p^{d}. 5^{s}.]
John Farnell, at the Six Bells, in Church Street, Victualler On his own Confession two Persons Drinking in his House. Convicted and Ordered to pay 5^{s}. [*Marginal entry*: Convicted & p^{d}. 5^{s}.]
Joseph Swaby, at the Rose & Crown, Cambridge Heath, Victualler On the Oath of Edward Barnard Church Warden several Persons drinking and Smoaking in his House Convicted and Ordered to pay 5^{s}. – NB. He did not appear but sent his Wife (who was heard what she could say). [*Marginal entry*: Convicted & p^{d}.]
Michael Walton, at the Flying Horse, in Mare Street, Victualler Some favourable Circumstances appearing in his behalfe he was for this Time Excused. [*Marginal entry*: Excused.]
Sarah Hattersley, at the Mermaid & Bird in Hand in Church Street, Victualler Convicted on the Confession of John Bourn whom she sent in her Stead 4 Persons drinking in one Room in her House and one Man & one Woman in another Room in her House and Ordered to pay 5^{s}. [*Marginal entry*: Convicted & p^{d}: 5^{s}.]
Martha Herbert, at the Plow in Hommerton Victualler On Confession of J Guy her Son in Law (whom She sent in her Stead) One Person drinking Convicted and Ordered to pay 5^{s}. [*Marginal entry*: Convicted and p^{d}. 5^{s}.]

Joseph Souter, at the Greyhound in Hommerton, Victualler Convicted on his own Confession Entertaining Company – Several Persons drinking in his House & Gardens and Ordered to pay 5^{s}. [*Marginal entry*: Convicted & p^{d}. 5^{s}.]
Thomas Wood, at the Falcon, in Homerton, Victualler. Charged with two or three Persons Drinking in his House which he confessed and alledged they were relations of his Wife who came to see him on a Visit and as Visitors & not as Guests and did not pay for anythink [*sic*] they did eat or Drink Wherefore he is Excused for this time. [*Marginal entry*: Excused.] [*See* **1093**, **1108**, **1127**].

1103. The following persons were also sumoned to appear here this Day by a Warrant under the hands & seals of George Garrett Esqr for having Exercised their Several Trades or Ordinary Callings on Sunday the fourteenth day of June instant in the said Parish To witt,
Gabriel Carter, at the Wick, Millman His Wife attended and declared That he is 100 Miles Distant and confessed That his Servants did Exercise the Trade on that Day But that it was a Case of Necessity and therefore on her Promise not to work any more on a Sunday he was Excused. [*Marginal entry*: Excused]
John Goaler, at the White Hart, at Temple Mills, Victualler Convicted on his own Confession several Persons Drinking in his House and Yard and Ordered to pay 5^{s}. [*Marginal entry*: Convicted & p^{d}. 5^{s}.]
Lyonell Batsford, at the Ferry in the Marsh, Victualler Confessed a Great Many Persons drinking in his House and Yard but in Consideration of his having a large Family and that he promised not to offend again was Excused for this time. [*Marginal entry*: Excused]
John Crosley, at the Ferry in Clopton Victualler Confessed Several Persons drinking But promising to behave better for the future was Excused for this Time. [*Marginal entry*: Excused]
William Coleburn, at the Kings Head, in Clopton, Victualler. Confessed five or Six persons drinking at the Door of his House Convicted & Ordered to pay 5^{s}. [*Marginal entry*: Convicted & p^{d}. 5^{s}.]
Mary Hill, at the Crooked Billet, in Clopton, Victualler Confessed Several Persons drinking in the Yard belonging to her House but in Consideration of her great Age (78 Years) and bad Circumstances she was Excused for this time on her Promise not to offend again. [*Marginal entry*: Excused]
James Brasier, at the Ferry, in Clopton Victualler Confessed Entertaining Company but promising to do so no more on a Sunday Excused for this time. [*Marginal entry*: Excused]
Jacob Green, at the Swan, Stanford Hill Victualler Convicted on his own Confession Several Persons drinking in his Yard belonging to his House and Ordered to pay 5^{s}. [*Marginal entry*: Convicted & p^{d}. 5^{s}.]
Ann Kemp, at the Shoulder of Mutton & Catt in Mare Street, Victualler On the Oath of Nehemiah Ring making and Baking Tarts which was also confessed by a Person whom She sent to Excuse her not attending And also That she was Sumoned therefore the said Ann Kemp is Convicted and Ordered to pay 5^{s}. [*Marginal entry*: Convicted] [*See* **1091**].

The Blue Posts Tavern: Monday, 3 August 1752
Justices present: Henry Norris, George Garrett

1104. Mary Lucy applyed for Leave to draw Drink at the Yorkshire Grey in Homerton late the House of George Needham removed till the next General Licensing which the Justices granted and Signed a Permissive Licence for that Purpose.

1105. The Person underwritten was by a Warrant under the Hand and Seal of Henry Norris Esqr sumoned to appear here this Day to answer a Complaint Exhibited against him by Nehemiah Ring and Edward Barnard Church Wardens for having exercised his Trade or Ordinary calling on Sunday the Second day of August instant in the Parish of Saint John at Hackney in the County of Middlesex and to shew Cause why he should not be convicted and the Penalty levyed on him as the Law directs
John Cowling of Mare Street, in Hackney, Butcher On consideration of the Circumstances (which are but very indifferent) of the said John Cowling he is Excused on his Promise not to offend again in like Manner. [*Marginal entry*: Excused]

The Blue Posts Tavern: Saturday, 15 August 1752
Justices present:

The Blue Posts Tavern: Friday, 28 August 1752
Justices present: Henry Norris, John Dekewer

1106. Stoke Drayton brought in Custody of [*blank*] on a Warr^{t}. Signed by Henry Norris and John Dekewer Esqrs for begetting Mary Atkinson Singlewoman with Child of a Female Bastard Child born of her Body in the Parish of S^{t}. John at Hackney in the County of Middlesex And the said Justices Signed an Adjudication of the said Stoke Drayton to be the reputed Father thereof [a *deleted*] One Copy of which was then Served on the said Stoke Drayton and another on the said Mary Atkinson. Stoke Drayton of Newington, Hackney, Labourer, George Watson of the same Wheelwright, bound each in £20, for the Appearance of Stoke Drayton at the next General Sessions of the Peace to abide such Order as the Justices shall then make concerning the s^{d}. Female Bastard Child Whereof he is adjudged the reputed Father (if they shall make any) or else to abide the said Order made by the said Henry Norris and John Dekewer Esqs.[1]

1. The draft minutes indicate the following costs to the parish: Lying in, £1 10s.; Midwife, 5s.; Examination, 12s. 6d; maintenance for two weeks 5s. Total: £2 12s. 6d. The draft minutes show that Drayton lived in Newington and contain marginal notes (apparently relating to Drayton's settlement) indicating that he originated from Barkway, Hertfordshire, where he had been in service as a ploughman with William Harrill, and that he was already married.

1107. Mathew Dixon was committed to the House of Correction for want of Sureties [to indempnify *deleted*] and not indempnifying the Parish ags[t]. a Bastard Child born of the Body of Elizabeth Riddle Singlewoman in the Parish of S[t]. John at Hackney in the County of Middlesex. [*See* **1054**, **1056**, **1062**].

The Blue Posts Tavern: Tuesday, 12 December 1752
Justices present: Henry Norris, John Dekewer [justices' names supplied from draft minutes]

1108. The Persons whose Names are hereunder written were by a Warrant under the hand and seal of [*blank*] Esq sumoned to appear here this Day to Shew cause why they should not be convicted and the Penalty levyed on them as the Law directs for severally Exercising their Trades or ordinary Callings on Sunday the Third Day of December instant in this Parish. Viz:
Joseph Sowter, at the Greyhound in Hommerton, Victualler On Oath of Edward Barnard That several Persons were drinking in the Garden belonging to the said Joseph Sowter's said Dwelling House which he also confessed he was convicted and paid the Penalty being 5[s]. [*Marginal entry*: Conv. & paid 5[s].][1]
Jeremiah Bowne at the Coach & Horses, Homerton Victualler Confessed that Company were drinking in his House [*draft minutes add*: but alledged the Gents had lodged at his House Saturday night] therefore convicted & paid 5[s]. [*Marginal entry*: Convicted & p[d]. 5[s]]
Daniel Bellnapp of Homerton Butcher. Confessed That a Peice of a Breast of Mutton was Sold by his Servant [*draft minutes add*: to John Price] (but said it was without his knowledge) declared he hath not, and promised he will not, sell Meat on Sundays Therefore was, for this time, Excused. [*Marginal entry*: Excused]
John Rust, of Church Street, Poulterer Charged with selling a Leg of Pork He alledged that it was sold on the Saturday before but owned That it was sent home to the Customer on the Sunday And was Convicted & paid 5[s]. [*Marginal entry*: Conv. & p[d]. 5[s]]
Mathew Booth, at the Blackmores Head, Clopton Victualler On Oath of Edward Barnard That a Soldier and two or three other Persons were drinking in his House which he confessed and that they were not part of his Family but alledged That they came to him about business and that he asked them to eat & drink but took no Money for it, was Convicted & p[d]. 5[s]. [*Marginal entry*: Conv. & p[d]. 5[s].]
Robert Anderson, at the three Rabbitts, Clopton Victualler his wife appeared And confessed That her Maid Servant let in M[r]: Samuel Woodfields Cowkeeper without her knowledge (She the s[d]. M[rs]. Anderson being then at Church and promised not to offend therefore Excused. [*Marginal entry*: Excused]
Samuel Woolmer, at the White Hart, Clopton, Victualler Confessed that five Persons came to see him from London as Old acquaintance (they being [born *deleted*] natives of Clopton) and dined at his House and staid, but had nothing to drink during divine service, was Convicted

& paid 5[s]. [*Marginal entry*: Conv. & p[d]. 5[s]][2] [*See* **1093**, **1098**, **1102**, **1127**, **1130**].

1. Draft minutes cross refer to 17 June (**1102**).
2. Draft minutes cross refer to 2 June (**1098**).

The Blue Posts Tavern: Monday, 29 January 1753
Justices present: Henry Norris, John Dekewer

1109. Stephen Cook gave an Information upon Oath against Thomas Smith of Kingsland in the Parish of S[t]. John at Hackney in the County of Middlesex Baker for Exercising his Worldly Business and Employment of a Baker on Sunday the Twenty Seventh Day of January instant in the said Parish of S[t]. John at Hackney And Henry Norris Esq signed a [Notice *deleted*] Sumons requiring the s[d]. Thomas Smith to appear before him at his House in Grove Street, Hackney on Thursday the first Day of February next at four of the Clock in the afternoon. [*See* **1128**].

1110. The several Defaulters who have neglected to perform their Statute Work on the Highways within the Parish of S[t]. John at Hackney in the County of Middlesex for the Year 1752 were sumoned to appear here this Day to shew Cause why the Penalty should not be levyed on each of them And those of them who appeared were heard.

1111. Ordered That Samuel Bass and his Wife be removed from this Parish to that of Stoke Newington being the Place of their Settlement And that an Order be made out for that Purpose. [*See* **1066**, **1113**].

1112. Ordered That Thomas Rumbald be Sumoned to give an account of the Place of his Settlement. [*See* **1136**].

The Blue Posts Tavern: Wednesday, 31 January 1753
Justices present: Henry Norris, John Dekewer

1113. Henry Norris and John Dekewer Esqs Signed an Order to remove Samuel Bass and [*blank*] his Wife from the Parish of S[t]: John at Hackney to the Parish of Stoke Newington as the Place of their legal Settlement. [*See* **1066**, **1111**].

1114. The said Justices also Signed a Warrant of Distress against the several Defaulters who have neglected to perform their respective Days Labour on the Highways within the Parish of S[t]: John at Hackney in the County of Middlesex.[1]

1. The draft minutes add: returnable Sat. 17: Feb[ry] 5 Afternoon at the House of Justice Norris in Grove Street.

1115. Ord. That Notice be given to John Rust, John Everett That they are fixed upon for Surveyors of the Highways for [to appear here on *deleted*] the Year ensueing.[1]

1. Entry inserted from draft minutes.

The Blue Posts Tavern: Thursday, 10 May 1753
Justices present: Henry Norris, John Dekewer

1116. The said Justice Norris convicted Hesekiah Kestor on the Oath of Nehemiah Ring for Riding on his Cart in Edmonton Road contrary to the Statute And he paid the Penalty being Ten Shillings.[1]

1. Kestor was convicted under 24 Geo II c43, which made it illegal to ride on a cart in London or within ten miles of London, unless there was someone on foot to guide it. Had Kestor been the owner of the cart the fine could have been increased to 20s.

1117. The Persons whose Names are hereunder written were Elected at the Court Leet to Execute the following Offices for the Year 1753. To Witt,
Kingshold: Constable: Mathew Eagelsoe Sworn [for] John Tyssen. Headboroughs: John Cowling Sworn in Court [for] John Howard, Church Street Division; John Johnson Sworn [for] William Hazard, Well Street Division. Aleconner: Thomas Cooper Sworn [for] Thomas Wade.
Lordshold: Constables: Mathew Booth, John Trot. Headboroughs: Roger Humphreys, Church Street Division, Sworn; William Flaxmore, Mare Street Division, Sworn; Thomas Taylor, Sworn [for] Robert Grosvenor, Grove Street Division; John Shooburt Sworn [for] Jacob Albert, Upper Homerton Division; Thomas Cooper Sworn [for] Francis Roberts, Lower Homerton Division; William Cawne Sworn [for] Moses Lamego, Clapton Division; William Lacey, Sworn [for] John Hughes, Newington & Shacklewell D°; Samuel Smith, Sworn, Dorleston & Kingsland D°. Aleconners: Oxton Chapman, Sworn; Adam Dewer, Sworn.

1118. Adjourned to this Place to Monday next at four of the Clock in the Afternoon.

The Blue Posts Tavern: Monday, 14 May 1753
Justices present: Henry Norris, John Dekewer, William Caslon

1119. James Bolton was Sworn to Execute the Office of Constable in the room and Stead of Mathew Booth.

1120. Adjourned to this Place to Wednesday next at four of the Clock in the Afternoon.

The Blue Posts Tavern: Wednesday, 16 May 1753
Justices present: Henry Norris, John Dekewer, William Caslon

1121. The Justices Signed Warrants appointing Edward Barnard and John Bride the Church Wardens Elect and Richard Dann Overseers of the Poor of this Parish for the year 1753.

1122. Adjourned to this Place to Saturday next at four of the Clock in the Afternoon.

The Blue Posts Tavern: Saturday, 19 May 1753
Justices present: Henry Norris, John Dekewer

1123. The Justices Signed Warrants appointing John Killingworth and John Woodfield Overseers of the Poor of this Parish for the Year 1753.

The Blue Posts Tavern: Tuesday, 19 June 1753
Justices present: Henry Norris, John Dekewer, George Garrett, William Caslon

1124. The Persons whose names are under written sumoned to appear here this Day to shew Cause why they have Refused or Neglected to pay the Severall sums of Money set down against each of their Names which they are Rated towards the Releif of the Poor of the Parish of S^t^. John at Hackney in the County of Middlesex.
Church Street: fol. 2, Ralph Cock rated 6s., to pay ½ a year, 3s.; fol. 11, Daniel Milner rated 6s., Excused; fol. 12, Thomas Cook rated 6s., Excused; fol. 14, Elizabeth Reep rated 6s.; Roger Humphries rated £2 18s. 6d.; fol. 15, Phillip White rated 9s., Excused; fol. 18, William Hazard Junr rated 6s., to pay, 6s.; [*blank*] Farnis rated £1, taken off; Elizabeth Reep late Bruce rated 12s., to pay, 12s.; fol. 20, William Margerum rated £1 2s. 6d., paid; fol. 24, Ann Bennett rated 12s., to pay, 12s., paid; fol. 26, Thomas Rudd rated 11s. 3d.
Mare Street: fol. 37, Richard Speed rated 2s. 3d., Overcharged; fol. 38, William Flaxmore rated 6s., Excused this Year; fol. 39, Elizabeth Evorodd rated 12s., reduced for ½ a year to 4s. 6d., Paid; fol. 44, John Woodfeild rated £11 5s., £11 5s., paid; fol. 45, Aaron Gomez da Costa rated 12s., 12s., paid; fol. 49, William Archer rated 10s. 6d., 10s. 6d., paid; fol. 51, Thomas Davis rated 12s., Abated to 6s., Paid; fol. 53, Deborah Olderhead rated 6s., Excused; fol. 56, Thomas Smith rated 6s., to pay, 6s., Paid.
Well Street: fol. 60, William Webb rated £1 14s. 6d., to pay, £1 11s. 6d., Paid; Elizabeth Sadler rated 8s. 3d., Excused; fol. 61, Andrew Grinley rated 12s.; fol. 63, Peter Mangender rated 6s.; fol. 64, John Meeks rated 6s., to pay ½ a Year, 3s., Paid.
Grove Street: fol. 66, Thomas Richmans rated £1 11s. 6d., to pay, £1 2s. 6d., £1 2s. 6d., Paid.
Hommerton: fol. 71, Elizabeth Lucas rated £1 2s. 6d., Empty; fol. 73, Edward Buck rated £1 5s. 6d., to pay (abated), £1 1s., Paid; fol. 74, Joseph Cotterell rated 6s., Excused; fol. 78, John Myles rated £1 12s. 3d., to pay, £1 12s. 3d.; fol. 79, William Turnbull rated 6s., Excused this year; Margaret Walton rated 15s., Taken off by the Just; fol. 80, Giles Clement rated 6s.; fol. 81, Elizabeth Mintern rated £1 1s. 9d., Excused; Deborah Vandecleuse, rated 6s., Excused; fol. 84, Lyonel Batsford rated 6s., to pay, 6s., paid; fol. 86, William Sumpter rated 12s., Gone & can't be found; fol.87, Heneage Robinson rated £3, £3, paid; John Grove rated £1 2s. 6d.; fol. 88, Ann Williams rated 12s., to pay, 12s.; John Hampson rated 6s.; fol. 89, Thomas Middleton rated 12s., [to

pay *deleted*] Excused this year; fol. 93, Phillippa Maria Bates rated 6s., 6s., paid; fol. 94, Jeremiah Bownes rated £1 7s., abated to 19s. 6d., Paid; fol. 98, John Cox rated 19s. 6d., Excused.
Clopton: fol. 100, Samuel Harris rated 6s., Excused; fol. 101, Moses Jessurun rated 7s. 6d.; Dinah Cox for late Mosman rated 7s. 6d., 7s. 6d., paid; fol. 102, Mathew Simpson rated 15s., to pay, 7s. 6d., Paid; Benjamin Rosswell rated £2 5s., reduced this year to £1 15s.; fol. 104, [*blank*] Ozier rated £2 5s.; Henry Baker rated £1 17s. 6d., to pay, £1 10s., paid; fol. 106, Margaret Gelding rated 6s.; fol. 107, Thomas Archer rated 6s., Excused this year; Daniel Thomas rated 6s., Excused; fol. 111, John Ellwood rated 15s.; fol. 112, Jacob Grant rated £1 7s. 9d., to pay, 19s. [*altered from* 19s. 6d.], Paid ; fol. 113, William Bond rated £3 18s., to pay, £3 16s. 6d., paid; fol. 114, George Hyam rated £1 4s.; fol. 115, Thomas Reeves rated 6s., Excused; fol. 117, Henry White rated 6s., 6s., paid; John Pickett rated 6s.; fol. 118, Thomas Edwards rated 18s., to pay, 18s., Paid; fol. 119, William Streetin rated 6s., Excused; fol. 120, Isaac Polock rated 6s., not found; fol. 121, Nicholas Bartmaker rated £2 12s. 6d., to pay, £2 5s., p.
Newington: fol. 127, Stephen Humphries rated 7s. 6d., Gone & can't be found; fol. 133, Edward Nutt rated £1 10s. [to pay, overcharged, paid *all deleted*] taken off mistake.
Shacklewell: fol. 136, Henry Simpson rated 12s., to pay, 12s.; Elias Woodfeild rated £2 12s. 6d., £2 12s. 6d., paid; Charles Sheppard rated £2 14s. 9d., to pay, £2 4s. 9d.; fol. 137, Robert Godlingtone rated 18s., to pay, 6s.
Kingsland: fol. 146, Thomas Fox rated 18s., to pay, 18s.; fol. 147, Elizabeth Chave rated 9s., to pay, 9s.
Dorleston: fol. 148, Joseph Surities rated £7 13s. 9d., to pay, £7 3s. 3d.; fol. 149, Joseph Daniel rated 9s., to pay, 6s.; John Arnett Boad rated 9s.; fol. 150, Ann Poussett rated 12s., to pay, 12s., paid; Paul Bishop rated 6s., to pay, 6s.; William Atkinson rated 12s., Abated this year, 12s.; [*blank*] Price rated 15s.
Land Holders: fol. 151, John Bradby rated 17s. 3d.; Humphrey Haydon rated 2s. 3d.; fol. 153, Dinah Cox rated £1 17s. 6d., to pay, £1 10s. 9d., paid; fol. 154, John Taylor rated 12s.; Samuel Holland rated 3s., Excused.

1125. Thomas Wood at the Falcon, Marsh Gate Vict. On Oath of Edwd. Barnard for having on 10 June last 20 aft 4 12 Persons [drinking *deleted*] having company Viz^{t} 12 Persons drinking & [*illegible*] in his House Convicted. [*Marginal entry*: Conv. & pd 5].[1]

1. Entry inserted from draft minutes.

1126. James Betts of the Parish of S[aint] J[ohn] at H[ackney] in ye C[ounty] of M[iddlesex] Master Coachman. On Oath of Edward Barnard Convicted of swearing One prophane Oath saying By God & paid the Penalty 1^{s}.[1]

1. Entry inserted from draft minutes.

1127. Joseph Souter of Greyhound Homerton Vict. On the Oath of Edwd. Barnard.[1] [*See* **1093**, **1102**, **1108**].

1. Entry incomplete and apparently deleted; inserted from draft minutes.

1128. Thomas Smith of Kingsland Pastry Cooke & Baker. On Oath of Edwd Barnard Sunday 10 June [kneading *deleted*] Rolling Dough and had just been baking [*deletion*] Puffs, did not appear Convicted & Ord^{d}. Warr^{t}. of Distress.[1] [*See* **1109**].

1. Entry inserted from draft minutes.

The Blue Posts Tavern: Thursday, 16 August 1753
Justices present: Henry Norris, William Caslon

1129. The Persons whose Names are hereunder written were summoned to give an Account upon Oath of the Places of their respective last legal Settlements, To witt
Church Street: Daniel Worster, Sworn, [14 days *deleted*] One Month.
Grove Street: Richard Freeman, Sworn.
Cambridge Heath: Edward Marshall.
Well Street: Thomas Upchurch, Sworn, One Month.
Homerton: John Seal; James Summerson, Sworn, One Month; Francis Nash; Richard Smith, Sworn, One Month.
Clopton: William Kidder [*marginal note*: Kinner], Sworn, 14 days; John Dawson.
Newington: Roger Cranaway; Samuel Jennery.[1] [*See* **990**, **1066**, **1133**, **1136**, **1138**].

1. Daniel Worster of Church Street obtained a certificate during 1753. P79/JN1/398.

1130. John Rust, of Church Street, Poulterer Charged with Picking a Fowl or Duck on Sunday the 29th. of July last confessed Picking 2 Ducks but on his promise of not offending therein for the future was Excused for this time. [*See* **1108**].

1131. James Brasier, at the Ferry, Clopton, Victualler did not attend but sent his Wife who was heard and Thomas Taylor made Oath That the s^{d}. James Brasier [*deletion*] on Sunday 29th of July had several Company's and many Persons drinking in & about his House Which his Wife confessed and would not promise amendment but persisted that her s^{d}. Husband must do it and could not live without it He [was *deleted*] is convicted and Ordered to pay 5^{s}. which She paid. [*Marginal entry*: Convicted & p^{d}. 5^{s}.]

1132. Thomas Stacy brought in Custody of Mathew Eagelsoe, Constable on a Warrant under the Hand & seal of Henry Norris Esq to find Sureties to answer to an Indictment found against him for wilfully malitiously unlawfully & injuriously breaking open the Gate of the Turnpike erected for repairing the road from Shoreditch Church through Hackney &c ag[t]. the form of the Statute and for want of sureties was Committed by the above Justices to Bridewell. [*See* **320**, **1140**].

1133. Ordered That a Warr[t]. be made out to oblige the following Persons to give an Accompt upon Oath of the Places of their last legal Settlements on the Oath of John Cowling That they were Sumoned To witt, Francis Nash, John Dawson, Edward Marshall, Roger Crannaway.[1] [*See* **1129**, **1138**].

1. The draft minutes also include the names of John Seal (see **1066**) and Samuel Jennery (see **1136**), both deleted.

1134. Ann Price als Rowley of Church Street Hackney Shopkeeper Convicted of Cursing two profane Curses on Oath of John Cheetham.

1135. Adjourned to this Place to Thursday the 30th. of August instant at Nine of the Clock in the Forenoon.

The Blue Posts Tavern: Thursday, 30 August 1753
Justices present: Henry Norris, William Caslon [names supplied from draft minutes]

1136. The Persons whose Names are under mentioned were sumoned to give an Account upon Oath of the Places of their respective last legal Settlements To witt
Church Street: John Smith.
Mare Street: Daniel Taverner, Sworn, 1 M[o].
Homerton: John Searle, Sworn, 1 M[o]; [Richard Bull *deleted*]; John Brooks, Sworn, 1 M[o].
Shacklewell: Mortimore Chappell.
Kingsland: Thomas Rumbald, Sworn, 1 M[o]; William Cooper, Sworn, 1 M[o].
Newington: Samuel Jennery. [*See* **1112**, **1129**, **1133**].

1137. Elizabeth Brace brot in Custody of John Cowling Headborough on a Warr[t]. under the Hands & seals of Henry Norris & W[m] Caslon Esqs. to be Examined touching a Female Bastard Child born of her Body in the Parish of S[aint] J[ohn] at H[ackney] in the County of M[iddlesex] was Examined before the s[d]. Justices. Ord[d]: a Warr[t].[1]

1. Entry inserted from draft minutes. Elizabeth Brace told the justices that she had had so many partners that she was incapable of identifying the father of her child. H.A.D., P/J/P/68.

1138. John Dawson by Warr[t]. Cert 1 M[o].[1] [*See* **1129**, **1133**].

1. Entry inserted from draft minutes.

1139. Eliz. Cooper.[1]

1. Entry incomplete; inserted from draft minutes.

1140. Q[uery] Indictment ag[t]. Stacy to be tryed Fryday [next *deleted*] Sennight.[1] [*See* **320**, **1132**].

1. Entry inserted from draft minutes.

1141. Constables & Headboroughs for the year 1733. Constables: Jur. M[r]. W[m]. Weston; James Bolton Jur. [for] M[r]. John Cotton; Jur. M[r]. Robert Dumbleton. [Headboroughs:] Henry Batt Jur. [for] M[r]. Daniel Cowper, Well Street; Jur. M[r]. Rob[t]. Barnes, Church Street; Jur. M[r]. Zach. Thompson, Mare Street, removed [*marginal entry*: Jur. Richard Stoakes chosen in his room]; John Cawne Jur. [for] M[r]. Benj[a]. Evans, Clopton; Henry Harrill Jur. [for] M[r]. Samuel Woodfield, Upper Homerton; William Platt Jur. [for] M[r]. Samuel Phillipps, Lower Homerton; Jur. M[r]. W[m]. Browne, Grove Street; W[m]. Griffith Jur for Sam[l] Bishop chose [for] M[r]. Alex[a]. Spurling, Dorleston & Kingsland; James Martin Jur [for] M[r]. Barnard Byfield, Newington & Shacklewell. Ale conners: Jur. M[r]. W[m]. Griffith; Jur. M[r]. Thomas Townesend; Jur M[r]. John Sandford.

1142. Aprill 29th 1734, Jurat coram Hen Norris and Step Ram – Constables: Sworn – William Peters, John Harcourt, Thomas Hilliard. [Headboroughs:] W[m]. Harris [for] Capt William Stone, Church Street; Sworn, William Katherines, Well Street; Henry Harrill [for] George Harrison, Church Street; Henry Riddell [for] Walter Graham, Mare Street; John Cawne [for] George Wildey, Clopton; Sworne, Thomas Bridgman, Upper Homerton; Thomas Cooper [for] William Crotchrode, Lower Homerton; Sworne, Francis Olderhead, Grove Street; D[o], James Martin, Dorleston and Kingsland; D[o], Robert Piggott, Newington & Shacklewell. Ale conners: Jur in Cor, John Hague; Sworne, Matthew Walter; Jur in Cor, William Austin.

1143. Constables and Headboroughs for the year 1735. Constables: Sworn, James Huggett Jun[r]; John Davis; James Bolton [for] Richard Morris. Nich[o] Graves Constable in the room of James Huggett removed out of the parish. Headboroughs: Henry Harrill [for] Nich[o]. Bosquett, Church Street; Henry Batt [for] Benj[a]. Devinck, Well Street; William Hayes, Church Street; Richard Speed, Mare Street; John Cawne [for] Tho[s]. Rotherford, Clopton; John Hague [for] Marmad[k]. Emersone, Upper Homerton; Thomas Cooper [for] William Austin, Lower Homerton; Thomas Richman, Grove Street; Th[o]. Fussell, Dorleston & Kingsland; Cha[s]. Dean, Newington & Shacklewell. Ale conners: William Bell; Henry Harrill [for] William Cox; James Bolton.

1144. [*Undated entry from draft minutes*] [*blank*] applyed for leave to draw Drink at the Y. G. in Homerton in the Room of A W. till the next Gen: Ren. of y[e] Lic of Vict. Agreed that he have Leave accordingly.

1145. [*Undated entry from draft minutes*] J C Ch W. & Ov. of &c made Oath that E the W of M N [*entry incomplete*].

1146. [*Undated entry from draft minutes*] Mr Slater Ch. W. & Overseer made Oath That Susannah Eldridge Wife of Francis Eldridge hath [often *deleted*] and doth not applyed to her [*sic*] for Releif for her and 4 children and that her Husband will not work [or do anything towards *deleted*] make [*altered from* making] any Provision for her or her Children And that she is in Necessitous Circumstances and that She [*sic*] hath often Releived her accordingly and s^{d}. Susannah testyfied the same upon her Oath.

1147. [*Undated entry from draft minutes*] George Lenth, in Windmill Street near Haymarket a Butcher his Wife wants Eliz Shearne upon likeing to learn Huswifry (Parish S^{t}: James Westm^{r}:).

INDEX

References in small roman numerals are to pages of the introduction. The full forms of names abbreviated in the text have been supplied where possible from the Hackney Burial Register (G.L.R.O., P79/JN1/25). Information from the same source on occupations has also been added, in parentheses. Historic counties have been used in the indexation of places, using the following abbreviations:

Cambs., Cambridgeshire
Ches., Cheshire
Corn., Cornwall
Herts., Hertfordshire
Leics., Leicestershire
Hunts., Huntingdonshire
Mx., Middlesex
Notts., Nottinghamshire
Oxon., Oxfordshire
Salop., Shropshire
Som., Somerset
Suff., Suffolk
Wilts., Wiltshire
Worcs., Worcestershire

LONDON RECORD SOCIETY

The London Record Society was founded in December 1964 to publish transcripts, abstracts and lists of the primary sources for the history of London, and generally to stimulate interest in archives relating to London. Membership is open to any individual or institution; the annual subscription is £12 ($22) for individuals and £18 ($35) for institutions. Prospective members should apply to the Hon. Secretary, Miss Heather Creaton, c/o Institute of Historical Research, Senate House, London, WC1E 7HU.

The following volumes have already been published:

1. *London Possessory Assizes: a calendar*, edited by Helena M. Chew (1965)
2. *London Inhabitants within the Walls, 1695*, with an introduction by D. V. Glass (1966)
3. *London Consistory Court Wills, 1492–1547*, edited by Ida Darlington (1967)
4. *Scriveners' Company Common Paper, 1357–1628, with a continuation to 1678*, edited by Francis W. Steer (1968)
5. *London Radicalism, 1830–1843; a selection from the papers of Francis Place*, edited by D. J. Rowe (1670)
6. *The London Eyre of 1244*, edited by Helena M. Chew and Martin Weinbaum (1970)
7. *The Cartulary of Holy Trinity Aldgate*, edited by Gerald A. J. Hodgett (1971)
8. *The Port and Trade of Early Elizabethan London: documents*, edited by Brian Dietz (1972)
9. *The Spanish Company*, edited by Pauline Croft (1973)
10. *London Assize of Nuisance, 1301–1431: a calendar*, edited by Helena M. Chew and William Kellaway (1973)
11. *Two Calvinistic Methodist Chapels, 1743–1811: the London Tabernacle and Spa Fields Chapel*. edited by Edwin Welch (1975)
12. *The London Eyre of 1276*, edited by Martin Weinbaum (1976)
13. *The Church in London, 1375–1392*, edited by A. K. McHardy (1977)
14. *Committees for Repeal of the Test and Corporation Acts: Minutes, 1786–90 and 1827–8*, edited by Thomas W. Davis (1978)
15. *Joshua Johnson's Letterbook, 1771–4: letters from a merchant in London to his partners in Maryland*, edited by Jacob M. Price (1979)
16. *London and Middlesex Chantry Certificate, 1548*, edited by C. J. Kitching (1980)

17. *London Politics, 1713–1717: Minutes of a Whig Club, 1714–17*, edited by H. Horwitz; *London Pollbooks, 1713*, edited by W. A. Speck and W. A. Gray (1981)
18. *Parish Fraternity Register: fraternity of the Holy Trinity and SS. Fabian and Sebastian in the parish of St Botolph without Aldersgate*, edited by Patricia Basing (1982)
19. *Trinity House of Deptford: Transactions, 1609–35*, edited by G. G. Harris (1983)
20. *Chamber Accounts of the sixteenth century*, edited by Betty R. Masters (1984)
21. *The Letters of John Paige, London merchant, 1648–58*, edited by George F. Steckley (1984)
22. *A Survey of Documentary Sources for Property Holding in London before the Great Fire*, by Derek Keene and Vanessa Harding (1985)
23. *The Commissions for Building Fifty New Churches*, edited by M. H. Port (1986)
24. *Richard Hutton's Complaints Book*, edited by Timothy V. Hitchcock (1987)
25. *Westminster Abbey Charters, 1966–c.1214*, edited by Emma Mason (1988).
26. *London Viewers and their Certificates, 1508–1558*, edited by Janet S. Loengard (1989)
27. *The Overseas Trade of London: Exchequer Customs Accounts, 1480–1*, edited by H. S. Cobb (1990)
28. *Justice in Eighteenth-century Hackney: the Justicing Notebook of Henry Norris and the Hackney Petty Sessions Book*, edited by Ruth Paley (1991)

Most volumes are still in print; apply to Clifton Books, 34 Hamlet Court, Westcliff-on-Sea, Essex SS0 7LX. Price to individual members £12 ($22) each, to non-members £20 ($38) each.